The Eth

Asylum has become a highly charged political issue across developed countries, raising a host of difficult ethical and political questions. What responsibilities do the world's richest countries have to refugees arriving at their borders? Are states justified in implementing measures to prevent the arrival of economic migrants if they also block entry for refugees? Is it legitimate to curtail the rights of asylum seekers to maximise the number of refugees receiving protection overall? This book draws upon political and ethical theory and an examination of the experiences of the United States, Germany, the United Kingdom and Australia to consider how to respond to the challenges of asylum. In addition to explaining why asylum has emerged as such a key political issue in recent years, it provides a compelling account of how states could move towards implenting morally defensible responses to refugees.

MATTHEW J. GIBNEY is Elizabeth Colson Lecturer in Forced Migration at the Refugee Studies Centre, Queen Elizabeth House, University of Oxford, and Official Fellow of Linacre College, Oxford. He has published many articles on asylum and immigration and is the editor of *Globalizing Rights: The Oxford Amnesty Lectures* (2003). He is currently editing (with Randall Hansen) a three-volume encyclopedia *Global Migration in the Twentieth Century* (forthcoming).

The Ethics and Politics of Asylum

Liberal Democracy and the Response to Refugees

Matthew J. Gibney

PUBLISHED BY THE PRESS SYNDICATE OF THE UNIVERSITY OF CAMBRIDGE
The Pitt Building, Trumpington Street, Cambridge, United Kingdom

CAMBRIDGE UNIVERSITY PRESS
The Edinburgh Building, Cambridge, CB2 2RU, UK
40 West 20th Street, New York, NY 10011–4211, USA
477 Williamstown Road, Port Melbourne, VIC 3207, Australia
Ruiz de Alarcón 13, 28014 Madrid, Spain
Dock House, The Waterfront, Cape Town 8001, South Africa

http://www.cambridge.org

© Matthew J. Gibney, 2004

This book is in copyright. Subject to statutory exception
and to the provisions of relevant collective licensing agreements,
no reproduction of any part may take place without
the written permission of Cambridge University Press.

First published 2004

Printed in the United Kingdom at the University Press, Cambridge

Typeface Plantin 10/12 pt. *System* LaTeX 2ε [TB]

A catalogue record for this book is available from the British Library

Library of Congress cataloguing in publication data
Gibney, Matthew J.
The ethics and politics of asylum: liberal democracy and the response to refugees / Matthew J. Gibney.
p. cm.
Includes bibliographical references and index.
ISBN 0 521 80417 5 (hb.) – ISBN 0 521 00937 5 (pb.)
1. Asylum, Right of. 2. Refugees – Government policy. 3. Refugees – Legal status, laws, etc. I. Title.
HV8652.G52 2004
172′.2 – dc22 2003060533

ISBN 0 521 80417 5 hardback
ISBN 0 521 00937 5 paperback

The publisher has used its best endeavours to ensure that URLs for external websites referred to in this book are correct and active at the time of going to press. However, the publisher has no responsibility for the websites and can make no guarantee that a site will remain live or that the content is or will remain appropriate.

For Chimène

Contents

Acknowledgements

This work began life in the 1990s at Cambridge University. At King's College, I had the good fortune of being supervised by John Dunn. Not only was he an enthusiastic supporter of the idea of bringing political theory to bear on the (then far less controversial) topic of asylum, but he encouraged me to approach the topic in a way that confronted directly the challenges it posed for normative theorising about politics. His way of thinking about politics has remained with me over the last decade and I want to record my deep thanks to him here.

I also had the pleasure of drawing upon the advice, friendship and general intellectual ambience provided by a wonderful group of Cambridge graduate students in social and political sciences and philosophy. I would like to thank, in particular, Jacky Cox, Sam Glover, Rob Hopkins, Don Hubert, David Kahane and Melissa Lane. My long and enduring friendship with Jeremy Goldman, formed in my first days at Cambridge, began with a debate on Michael Walzer. In the years since this conversation, he has taught me a great deal about what it is to think systematically about political theory.

My period at Cambridge was made possible by a generous scholarship by the Commonwealth Scholars and Fellowship Plan, and near the end of the thesis by the financial support of King's College and the Holland Rose Trust.

In the years since the thesis was submitted, I changed the text both to update the empirical chapters and to take into account intellectual encounters with colleagues in New Haven, Connecticut; Cambridge, Massachusetts; and Oxford. A number of scholars in the UK, the US and Canada commented on the thesis or drafts of early chapters in many different shapes and forms. Joe Carens, Gil Loescher, Brian Barry, Richard Tuck, Howard Adelman, Andrew Linklater, Matthew Price, Andrew Shacknove and Phil Triadafilopoulos, all provided useful comments. I owe a particular debt to Rogers Smith, formerly of Yale University and now at the University of Pennsylvania. My early period living in the US (after following my wife to Yale) could have been an isolating experience. But demonstrating the kind of generosity with his time and intellectual energy that will be familiar to any student who has crossed his path, Rogers showed a real interest in my work and made himself freely available to discuss it.

The ideas expressed in this work changed even more in the light of my experiences at Oxford, which began in 1997. My colleagues at the Refugee Studies Centre deepened my understanding of refugee issues and the legal and international framework within which they are located. Michael Barutciski, Stephen Castles, Agnes Hurwitz, Maryanne Loughry and Nick Van Hear, may not have shared my approach to refugee issues, but they helped shape it nonetheless. Other colleagues at Oxford, including Dawn Chatty, Andy Hurrell, Des King, Adam Roberts, Andrew Shacknove, Paul Slack and Frances Stewart have proven great sources of encouragement and intellectual support. Guy Goodwin-Gill and Neil MacFarlane have been valued sources of guidance, and exceedingly generous in sharing their knowledge on international law and international relations respectively. Randall Hansen, who shares my interest in the politics of migration and asylum, has collaborated with me on a number of articles and works. I have not always shared his sceptical and forthright approach to the issue of asylum, but his views have been a blast of fresh air. Working with him has been one of the great pleasures of my time at Oxford.

From the moment I set foot on St Giles', David Turton, the (now former) Director of the Refugee Studies Centre, made me feel at home. In the years since, I have come to admire his rigorous scholarship and intellectual generosity. His practical commitment to the ideal of scholarship as a mutual and ongoing conversation amongst equals has made him an exemplary academic role model.

At Oxford I have also drawn upon the help of two assistants, Heidi Becker, who helped me to update some of the empirical chapters and Kate Prudden, who performed a vast array of activities, not least proofing some of the chapters. I would like to acknowledge the support of Queen Elizabeth House's Oppenheimer Fund for financial assistance with travel and research support. The staff of the Refugee Studies Centre Library, ably led by Sarah Rhodes, have also greatly assisted this research.

Beyond my circle of colleagues in Oxford, I have learnt a great deal about asylum or received encouraging feedback from a range of people. I would like to mention in particular Chaloka Beyani, B. S. Chimni, Jeff Crisp, Jim Hathaway, John Scratch, Gerry Van Kessel, Joanne Van Selm, Monette Zard and Aristide Zolberg.

John Haslam at CUP has been an extremely patient and helpful editor.

Earlier versions of some parts of this book were published in the *American Political Science Review* as 'Liberal Democratic States and Responsibilities to Refugees' (March 1999, 1: 169–81) and in *Government and Opposition* as 'Crisis of Constraint: The Federal Republic of Germany's Refugee Imbroglio' (Summer 1993: 372–93). I would like to thank the editors of these journals for permission to use sections from these articles.

While this book was written in the United Kingdom and the US, some of its deepest debts lie on the other side of the world. As an undergraduate at Monash University in Melbourne, Australia, I was encouraged to pursue graduate studies in political theory at Cambridge by two remarkable teachers, Ray Nichols and Andrew Linklater. Ray Nichols, my honours year supervisor, exhibited a faith in my abilities that I still find hard to fathom. Andrew Linklater exhibited a similar faith and showed me how impressive the results of bringing political theory and international relations into mutual engagement could be. His innovative approach to politics had a strong influence on my choice of asylum as a thesis topic while at Cambridge, and thus on my subsequent career.

In addition, I owe many debts to my family, some of them financial. My parents, in particular, have waited a long time for this book, and I hope they consider the wait worthwhile. I realise this book is no substitute for a grandchild. But they can hope that it has a long and happy life.

My thanks to all of these leads inexorably to my dear Chimène. This is a book about the state as a refuge. There are, however, many different types of refuge. Chimène Bateman has been a personal one: an inexhaustible source of love, support and advice during the long years through which this book has been in process. I dedicate this book to her with all my love and appreciation.

Introduction

> Not the loss of specific rights, then, but the loss of a community willing and able to guarantee any rights whatsoever, has been the calamity that has befallen ever-increasing numbers of people. Man, it turns out, can lose all so-called Rights of Man without losing his essential quality as man, his human dignity. Only the loss of a polity itself expels him from humanity.
>
> Hannah Arendt 1986 [1951]

> The dwellers in refugee camps can best be compared to America's African slaves. And as we look on helplessly at the ever-growing numbers of human refuse heaps, we might perhaps listen to the voice of conscience. At the very least we might re-examine anew the claims that are made for and against the call of conscience in the face of group loyalty.
>
> Judith N. Shklar 1993

Over the last twenty years, asylum has become one of the central issues in the politics of liberal democratic states. In 1993 the German Parliament embarked upon the politically onerous task of amending the country's constitution, the Basic Law, in order to slow the arrival of asylum seekers on to state territory. One year later, the Clinton Administration in the US, faced with criticism over its policy of summarily interdicting asylum seekers on boats heading for Florida, launched a military intervention into the island nation of Haiti, largely to restore a regime less likely to produce refugees. In 2001, the Australian government embroiled itself in a heated international controversy by forbidding asylum seekers picked up by a Norwegian freighter, the *Tampa*, to land on its territory; this tough new line virtually guaranteed the government reelection for a second term. And less than two years after the *Tampa* incident, in 2003, the British government announced that annual asylum figures had reached unprecedented levels, even though Prime Minister Tony Blair had, some months earlier, assumed personal control of asylum policy. Liberal democratic states, it would seem, have fallen like dominoes to the so-called problem of asylum. Despite the best efforts of governments, a diverse and somewhat unruly collection of foreigners have found themselves at the front of the political stage.

This is a work that aims to subject this central political issue of our time to ethical scrutiny. Asylum brings into relief a conflict between the claims of refugees and those escaping desperate economic situations to a secure place of residence and the claims of citizens to act together to limit access to the territory and resources of their community. It is a conflict on which the governments of the world's richest states have recently expended a great deal of human and financial resources. All Western states have implemented over the last three decades a remarkable array of restrictive measures. Practices to prevent or deter asylum seekers have ranged from external measures such as visa regimes, carrier sanctions and airport liaison officers to internal measures like detention, dispersal regimes and restrictions on access to welfare and housing. Yet, paradoxically, all of these measures have been operated in a context in which states continue publicly to acknowledge legal responsibilities to refugees and others in need of protection (as defined by the 1951 UN Convention Relating to the Status of Refugees and the 1967 Protocol and a range of other human rights instruments) and trumpet the moral importance of the principle of asylum. A kind of schizophrenia seems to pervade Western responses to asylum seekers and refugees; great importance is attached to the principle of asylum but enormous efforts are made to ensure that refugees (and others with less pressing claims) never reach the territory of the state where they could receive its protection.

The last two decades may have captured public, media and government attention, but they are not, of course, the first time in living memory that refugees have been a focus of international concern. In 1951 the *émigrée* political philosopher Hannah Arendt described refugees as 'the most symptomatic group in contemporary politics' (Arendt [1951] 1986: 277). For Arendt, the emergence of refugees across Europe since the turn of the century symbolised the triumph of the nation-state. The use of national or ethnic criteria by states to determine who did and did not belong in a particular political community led to groups of people who were not only forced to flee their traditional homeland but simultaneously deprived of any reasonable prospect of attaining a new one (Arendt 1986: 293–4). In spite of the lofty rhetoric of human rights (of rights accruing to human beings as human beings), the implications of a lack of citizenship in a world carved up amongst sovereign nation-states were, as Arendt realised, absolutely devastating. Those who lost the protection of the state were denied not only specific rights but the protection 'of a community willing and able to guarantee any rights whatsoever' (Arendt 1986: 297). In a world where responsibilities and duties were determined by citizenship, no state accepted responsibility for the refugee. In an international system where sovereign states each claimed the right to fashion their entry and citizenship policies according to their own national or ethnic criteria, refugees were outcasts. They were, in Arendt's words, 'the scum of the earth' (Arendt 1986: 269).

In the years since Arendt wrote, practical concern with the responsibilities of states to refugees has waxed and waned. Between 1950 and 1970 there was reason to feel slightly optimistic about the plight of European refugees. The post-war economic expansion across Western Europe and the growing labour and population requirements of nation-building states such as Australia, Canada, New Zealand and, to some extent, the US eased the dilemma of huge numbers of post-war refugees by creating a range of resettlement opportunities. Moreover, from the late 1940s, the Cold War gave some states added incentive to accept refugees from communist states; as the Western response to refugees from Hungary in 1956 and Czechoslovakia in 1968 showed, liberal democratic states could be highly responsive to the claims of necessitous outsiders when responding to their needs also served to demonstrate the moral bankruptcy of communism. By the end of the 1970s, however, international economic recession and changes in the international economy had severely reduced the demand for external supplies of labour across the West. The restrictive force of this development and changes in the patterns of refugee movement were simply reinforced by the end of the Cold War in 1989, which deprived Western states of an obvious security rationale for resettling refugees. In the face of tough and indiscriminate new entry restrictions coming into force to combat rising numbers of asylum seekers and illicit migrants, the absence of a coherent response to the question, who is responsible for the refugee?, once again became starkly apparent.

Since the early 1980s a sharp rise in asylum claims has occurred across Western countries. Whereas the total number of applications across Western Europe averaged no more than 13,000 annually in the 1970s, the annual totals had grown to 170,000 by 1985, and to 690,000 in 1992. Between 1985 and 1995, more than 5 million claims for asylum were lodged in Western states. By the beginning of 2000 the number of claims had dropped off somewhat to 412,700 for the states of Western Europe, still, however, far in excess of the levels of the 1970s and 1980s, even without accounting for unauthorised entrants.[1] The rising trend in applications has also been evident outside Europe. Out of twenty-one Western countries, only three received fewer asylum applications in the three-year

[1] UNHCR, *State of the World's Refugees 1997–1998* (Oxford: Oxford University Press, 1997), pp. 145–185; UNHCR, *State of the World's Refugees 2000* (Oxford: Oxford University Press, 2000), p. 325.

period between 1998 and 2000 than they received between 1995 and 1997. In the vast majority of countries the numbers rose dramatically (Gibney and Hansen 2003).

The growth in numbers reflects an expansion in the number of the world's refugees in recent decades, mostly as a result of civil conflicts in the former Yugoslavia, Sri Lanka, Somalia, Central America and the Great Lakes region of Africa. In 1975 there was estimated to be almost 3 million refugees in the world; by 1980 the number had grown to around 9 million, and to 18.3 million by 1992. By the beginning of 2000, the number had dropped off slightly to around 11.7 million (UNHCR 2000: 310). These totals, moreover, exclude another 10 million people either displaced within their own country, or who while not satisfying the UN definition of a refugee are considered to be 'of concern' to the UNHCR (UNHCR 2000: 309). The plight of these last two groups is often as desperate as that of official refugees (Cohen and Deng 1998). But rising numbers of asylum seekers in the West are also related to developments in transportation and communication that have lessened the distance between the world's richest and poorest countries.

In recent years, a kind of globalisation of asylum seeking has occurred whereby many victims of conflict and persecution, as well as individuals in pursuit of better economic opportunities, have been able to move intercontinentally in pursuit of asylum. This has fed fears that growing pressures are merely the thin edge of a wedge of much vaster numbers of people, refugees and non-refugees alike, who would move to the world's richest states if the opportunity presented itself. Certainly, the impact upon the West of this extraordinary movement of people has until now been softened by the actions of the poorest states. While Germany has had to deal with hundreds of thousands of refugees, Pakistan has been home to well over 3 million. Even the desperately impoverished African states of Malawi, Burundi, Congo and Sudan share over a million refugees among them, many more than most liberal democratic states.

The circumstances that confronted Europe with refugees between 1930 and 1950 had their source in what have turned out to be relatively transient forces (war, totalitarian regimes) that emanated from *within* Europe. The current refugee crisis primarily has its driving forces *outside* Europe (though not exclusively, as recent events in the Balkans testify), and is linked to the prevalence of violent civil and international wars and ethnic conflicts, to the increasing involvement of citizens in military conflict, and, most fundamentally of all, to the grave difficulties involved in maintaining durable and humane state structures in conditions of economic underdevelopment and poverty. The present refugee context thus differs significantly from that which moved Arendt to write in the aftermath of World War II. The many refugees currently fleeing civil war, ethnic conflict and political instability are only the extreme end of a rising number of the world's denizens who respond to the uneven distribution of security and welfare across states by migrating.[2]

Controversy over asylum in liberal democratic states must therefore be understood as a part of a much broader international problem in which refugees and asylum seekers are merely the vanguard of a world where life chances and economic opportunities are distributed with great inequality. This reality, made daily more obvious by the forces associated with globalisation, throws up a number of tough challenges for asylum policy: for example, in the midst of scarcity of entrance places and different categories of people in need, which claimants for entry deserve priority in immigration admissions? To what extent, if at all, is it legitimate to curtail the rights of asylum seekers and refugees in order to maximise the number of refugees receiving asylum overall? Is it possible to construct generous asylum policies that are not overwhelmed by applicants seeking to migrate for economic reasons? Every Western government is presently engaged, through legislation and public pronouncements, in answering these questions. Their answers are in need of close scrutiny. My aim in this work is to provide some reflections on just what a morally acceptable response to refugees and asylum seekers would look like. I will use the resources of political theory – in combination with the actual experiences of Western states – to construct a critical statement of the responsibilities of states to refugees. But before I commence this task, it is important to consider just who a refugee is and how his/her claim to enter differs from those of other immigrants.

Defining refugees and other claimants for entrance

In recent years, the spectrum of foreign settlers in Western states has been dominated by four major groups of entrants: refugees, asylum seekers, economic migrants and family migrants. I will now take some time to define each of these immigrant groups and examine the nature of their different claims.

Refugees

What is a refugee? The most influential answer to this question is given by the 1951 UN Convention Relating to the Status of Refugees (and extended in the 1967 Protocol), to which all liberal democratic states are signatories. According to this document, refugees are individuals who

[2] According to the UN Population Division, in 1990 there were some 120 million migrants (individuals who had spent over a year in foreign countries), fewer than 3 per cent of the world's entire population (Martin 2001).

owing to a 'well founded fear of persecution' for reasons of political opinion, race, religion, nationality or membership in a particular social group are outside their country of nationality and are unable or, as a result of such fear, unwilling to return to it.[3] It is evident that this definition, the one used by most of the world's states, emphasises three primary features as central to the attribution of refugee status. First, a refugee is someone who is *outside* his or her country of nationality. In terms of the UN definition, people displaced within their own country are not considered refugees, and thus technically do not fall under the ambit of those requiring protection and assistance. Second, the reason the refugee has fled and cannot return home is because he or she faces the reality or the risk of persecution. Third, the persecution that an individual faces or risks facing is due to reasons of political opinion, race, religion, nationality or membership in a particular social group.

The emphasis on refugees as persecuted people reflects the Convention's origins in the early Cold War period. The Western states responsible for its creation viewed refugees – not least for ideological reasons – as a product of oppressive, totalitarian regimes, like that which existed in Nazi Germany and those forming in the communist states of Eastern and Central Europe, that preyed on certain sections of their citizenry. Refugees were seen thus as a product of a certain kind of political rule in which the normal responsibilities of a state to its citizens were deliberately and directly violated. Even Arendt, prescient as she was about the modern impact of refugees, could be said to have viewed refugees primarily in state-centric terms as individuals for whom the normal bond of trust, loyalty, protection and assistance between a person and his or her government has been broken or does not exist (Shacknove 1985: 275).

In recent times, the adequacy of defining a refugee in terms of these three features has come into question. The term 'refugee' has been extended in common parlance and, more fitfully, in the practices of the UNHCR and liberal democratic states, to include all people forced to flee their homes even if they have not crossed international boundaries. The assistance Western states gave to Kurdish refugees in Iraq in 1991 and the UNHCR's efforts to evacuate people during the war in Bosnia indicate how international assistance is sometimes made available to threatened individuals whilst still in their country of normal residence.[4] These individuals, refugees within their own country, are commonly referred

[3] Goodwin-Gill (1996) offers a superior guide to the Convention's history, as well as international law pertaining to refugees more generally.

[4] Though UNHCR's involvement with internally displaced persons has been extremely controversial and the subject of criticism. See, for example, Goodwin-Gill (1999) and Barutciski (1998).

to as 'internally displaced persons' (see Cohen and Deng 1998). They are a group of growing concern to the international community, not least because their numbers are rising (partly due to restrictive asylum policies) and their vulnerability is often great. Intellectual support for assistance to these men and women has come from Andrew Shacknove, amongst others, who has argued that refugeehood is 'conceptually . . . unrelated to migration' (1985: 283). For Shacknove, one does not need to cross international boundaries to be a refugee. Rather, a refugee is simply someone 'whose basic needs are unprotected by their country of origin, who have no remaining recourse other than to seek international restitution of their needs, and who are so situated that international assistance is possible' (quoted in 1985: 277).

The UN definition has also come under fire because its conception of 'persecution' can be used to exclude many people brutally forced out of their country of origin. Under the somewhat dubious interpretation of the Refugee Convention recently used by France and Germany, women who have fled the oppressive strictures of the Taliban, Iraqis displaced by the US and British war to disarm Saddam Hussein, in addition to Zairians escaping the deadly Ebola virus, may not be considered refugees. For these groups are not on the move because they have been *persecuted*, in the sense that their state has deliberately targeted them for ill-treatment. Under the 1951 Refugee Convention, there is no necessary link between refugee status and life-threatening states of affairs, such as situations of generalised violence, like war, or natural disasters or plagues. In Africa, the Organization of African Unity (OAU) has filled this void by offering an alternative to the UN definition. As well as covering those fleeing persecution, the OAU has, since 1968, attributed refugee status to 'every person who, owing to external aggression, occupation, foreign domination or events seriously disturbing public order in either part or the whole of his country of origin or nationality, is compelled to leave his place of habitual residence in order to seek refuge in another place outside his country of nationality' (quoted in Shacknove 1985: 275–6).

Throughout this work I will use the term 'refugee' (except where explicitly stated otherwise) to denote those people in need of a new state of residence, either temporarily or permanently, because if forced to return home or remain where they are they would – as a result of either the brutality or inadequacy of their state – be persecuted *or* seriously jeopardise their physical security or vital subsistence needs. This definition is broader than the UN's (and virtually identical to the OAU's) in that it includes victims of generalised states of violence and events seriously disturbing the public order, such as famine and natural disasters, as well as individual persecution. But it does not take us as far from the current practices of most liberal democratic states as might be supposed. Many Western countries use forms of humanitarian status to provide protection to individuals who do not meet the standards of the Refugee Convention but who would risk life or limb by returning home.[5] At the same time, this definition is narrower than Shacknove's as it does not include everyone who is in a position to receive international assistance whose basic needs are not met. In my account, refugeehood *is*, in one vital respect, conceptually related to migration; what distinguishes the refugee from other foreigners in need is that he or she is in need of the protection afforded by short or long-term asylum (i.e., residence in a new state) because there is no reasonable prospect of that person finding protection any other way. The central claim of the refugee is therefore, 'grant me asylum for, if you do not, I will be persecuted or face life-threatening danger'.

It follows from my definition that whether someone should be considered a refugee or not has as much to do with how they can be protected as the nature of the threat they face. For threatened people already *outside* their country of origin, the question of whether or not they should be considered refugees is for the most part clear cut. The only way of protecting such people in the short term is by granting them asylum where they are or helping them to move on to another safe country; no other form of assistance is likely to be able to be marshalled as quickly or effectively. For individuals still *within* their country of origin, however, the issues are more complex. Often, as in the case of victims of famine or natural disasters, it is easier for outside parties to deal with the threats people face by exporting assistance or protection (food, building supplies, clean water) to people where they are than to arrange access to asylum. Even internally displaced persons, escaping war or hostile state activity, may in many cases best be helped *in situ*, through diplomatic pressure exerted by outside actors or even, subject to considerations of proportionality, military intervention. All this is to say that whether suffering peoples still inside their country of origin can be considered as requiring asylum should be determined by taking into account the options available in each case. We should, however, resist the temptation to define all threatened peoples as 'refugees'. There are other ways of drawing attention to the plight of people in need of protection and assistance than lumping them into a single amorphous category.

[5] Indeed, some of these protections are a part not simply of national but of international law, for example the *non-refoulement* provisions of the European Convention on Human Rights and the Convention Against Torture. For a fuller discussion of the legal implications of these treaties, see Goodwin-Gill (1996) and Lambert (1999). For a discussion of their broader political implications, see Gibney (2003).

To define refugees is not, of course, to suggest that liberal democratic states have a moral responsibility to assist them. In this work I will furnish some grounds – the principle of responsibility for harm and, in more depth, the humanitarian principle – for determining the responsibilities of states to refugees. But one implication for conceptualising these responsibilities does flow directly from my definition – if states do indeed have a responsibility to meet the needs of these desperate men and women, their primary responsibility must be to ensure that they receive asylum. Asylum is not the only responsibility of states. Liberal democracies may have a key role to play in assisting in refugee repatriation and in addressing the economic, military and political causes of refugee generation. However, what the refugee needs in the first instance *qua* refugee is the security of a new state within which to reside. For that reason I will be concerned in this work primarily with the entrance duties of liberal democratic states.

Asylum seekers

When we ask whether a state – take Britain, for the sake of example – has a responsibility to aid refugees, we could be enquiring about its responsibilities to one of three groups of people: refugees, such as those in Bosnia in the early 1990s, who were in danger within their own country and therefore required assistance in fleeing to a safer country; refugees in temporary border camps, like Kosovar Albanians in Macedonia and Albania in 1999, who were eligible for resettlement; and those foreign individuals at the borders of or within British territory claiming to be refugees, such as the numerous Iraqis who have claimed asylum at Heathrow in recent years. While the first two groups fit neatly under the refugee definition I have just outlined, the last group, commonly referred to as asylum seekers, constitute a second distinct category of entrant to liberal democratic states.

The asylum applicant makes exactly the same moral claim for entrance as the refugee: allow me to enter for if you do not I will be persecuted or placed in life-threatening danger. Despite the similarity of the claim, however, asylum seekers raise a unique set of practical and moral issues. The category of the asylum seeker is in one respect *narrower* than that of the refugee. For any particular state, asylum seekers include only those refugees who actually arrive at its own borders. Indeed, it is the growth in asylum seekers that has, over the last thirty years, made refugees such a burning political issue in Western states. For while these states could once ignore refugees confined far from their borders, within the continental bounds of Africa and Asia, frequent and relatively inexpensive travel and communications have made possible intercontinental transportation and greatly increased the number of denizens from refugee-producing countries travelling to the West to claim admittance.

The appearance of the asylum seeker at the border immediately raises an important ethical question. Do states have a special responsibility to refugees in their own territory that justifies them giving priority to these men and women over others in danger who are further away? To answer 'yes' appears to commit one to the contentious position that physical proximity should make a difference to a state's moral responsibilities. Yet to answer 'no' seems to commit one to rejecting the one international norm pertaining to refugees that states generally acknowledge: the principle of *non-refoulement*. This norm, enshrined in Article 33 of the Refugee Convention, demands that states not refuse entrance to an asylum seeker if doing so would force that person back to a country where he or she would be likely to be persecuted on one or more of the grounds specified in the UN definition. Recent writers on morality and refugees have been divided on the issue of asylum seekers. Peter Singer and Renata Singer, for instance, have condemned the existence of a special responsibility to asylum seekers based on proximity (1988: 119–20). They argue that need should be the primary determinant of whom a state should admit for entrance. Michael Walzer, on the other hand, argues for a special responsibility to asylum seekers grounded in part in the fact that to turn them away would involve using force against 'helpless and desperate people' (1983: 22–3). The conflict between these perspectives raises important issues and I shall return to them later.

Even if we agree on a moral basis for assisting asylum seekers, immense practical difficulties still face liberal democracies in dealing with their claims. For the category of the asylum seeker is at the same time a more *expansive* one than that of the refugee; unlike refugees in camps and those who gain entry through resettlement programmes (most of whom have received the UN's imprimatur or are obviously escaping life-threatening situations like war), the status of an asylum seeker as an endangered person is typically undetermined. To be an asylum seeker an individual merely has to *claim* to be a refugee. It is perhaps unsurprising, then, that the politics of asylum in Western countries is dominated by concerns that bogus asylum seekers are exploiting the generosity of the host country.[6] If systems for determining asylum claims might be expected to dampen these controversies, they often fail. The quasi-judicial processes used to evaluate applications tend to be expensive and time-consuming, providing a large and slow-moving target for

[6] Such concerns about asylum seekers are far from new. Caron (1999) shows that Jewish refugees from Nazi Germany attempting to enter France in the 1930s were commonly viewed as economic migrants.

those politicians whose electoral fortunes might be improved by generating hostility to new entrants (Gibney 2004).

As we shall see, liberal democratic states have generally responded to the rise of asylum seeking as a political issue by using a range of indiscriminate deterrent and preventative measures to reduce the flow of applicants to their frontiers where they could claim asylum. One consequence of the widespread use of these measures has been the emergence of huge disparities in the asylum seeker burdens of individual states; those countries which have not been able to use deterrent and preventative measures effectively because they border refugee outflow states have ended up drastically reducing asylum opportunities or attracting a wildly disproportionate number of claimants. The current international response to asylum thus suffers from the dual handicap of being unfair to those states that bear a disproportionate burden of refugees as well as inadequate for the needs of the many legitimate asylum seekers who are prevented from reaching liberal democratic states.

Economic migrants

If states are justified in distinguishing legitimate asylum seekers from illegitimate ones, then it makes sense to identify a third category of claimants for entrance – those commonly referred to as economic migrants. Whereas a refugee claims to enter because he or she is being persecuted or faces a situation of life-threatening danger, economic migrants are driven to seek entrance by (often only slightly) less pressing considerations, such as the desire to improve a low standard of living. Individual economic migrants might be located at various points on a continuum according to their reason for entrance, with those seeking to improve an appallingly low quality of life marked by serious economic deprivation (like many immigrants from Africa and Asia) at one end and those migrating between first world countries in order to take up more lucrative employment opportunities (such as academics and business people) at the other. Clearly, some, though not all, economic migrants have a strong claim to enter based upon need.

The traditional way of distinguishing between economic migrants and refugees has been by reference to the 'push' and 'pull' factors that motivate international migration. Put simply, 'push' factors are generally conceived of as negative influences that encourage people to emigrate from a country, such as political instability, a low standard of living, civil war, etc. 'Pull' factors, on the other hand, are positive influences that draw immigrants to a particular state such as a high standard of living, democratic political institutions, excess demand for labour, etc. Another way of expressing this distinction is to say that economic migrants, pulled towards countries that offer better opportunities, have a choice whether or not to move, but refugees, pushed out of their traditional country, do not. The distinction between push and pull factors fails to capture much of the complexities involved in why people move between particular countries, when and where they do.[7] However, it does provide a rudimentary framework for understanding why economic migration between the Southern and Northern countries – between, that is, the world's richer and poorer states – is likely to remain a pressing international issue in the years ahead.

Can a legitimate moral distinction be drawn between the responsibilities states have to refugees and those they have to economic migrants? Economic migrants, as I have suggested, are often in great need. At the extreme, their claim to entrance is: 'Take me in or I and my family shall be condemned to a life of great poverty.' The lifestyle they seek to leave behind is often far below the standards of living commonly on offer in Western liberal democracies. Clearly, if the rectification of severe economic inequalities is a moral goal, their claims to enter liberal democratic states are anything but trivial. That said, I shall be concerned primarily with the claims of refugees in this work because, I believe, a distinction *can* be drawn between the moral force of the refugee's claim and that of the economic migrant's. The difference is rooted in the fact that the needs of refugees, involving as they do persecution and life-threatening states of affairs, are more urgent than those of migrants attempting to escape poverty. If economic migrants are refused entry, they are forced to remain in a situation of poverty; if refugees are turned away, their very lives may well be on the line. In a world characterised by great scarcity of entrance places, it makes sense to prioritise claimants for entrance; and in a conflict between the needs of refugees and those of economic migrants, refugees have the strongest claim to our attention.[8]

As with asylum seekers, grave difficulties confront states in the practical task of identifying economic migrants. While the distinction between push and pull factors captures a conceptual difference between the refugee and the economic migrant, in practice it is often very difficult to determine

[7] More sophisticated and newer accounts tend to stress, *inter alia*, the important role of migration networks in explaining the why, where and when people migrate; see, for example, Massey *et al.* (1993) and Van Hear (1998).

[8] It is worthwhile noting that to prioritise the claims of refugees in this fashion in no way entails accepting that liberal democracies have no responsibilities to economic migrants. They might still be morally required to assist these men and women *where they are* – in the countries where they are located – through, perhaps, some kind of redistribution of wealth, technology or resources. Indeed, many would argue that this is the most effective way of responding to their very real needs in the long term. See, for example, Barry (1992).

whether a migrant has been pushed or pulled (or both) towards a particular state, as recent controversies in Western states over who is a refugee testify. These difficulties are compounded by the limited usefulness of the term 'economic migrant'. The attempt to escape situations of famine and below subsistence poverty are obviously economic reasons for migration. Yet they are every bit as violent and life threatening as political or military causes of departure and thus can be constitutive of refugee status under the definition I have offered above.[9] Moreover, in many states political instability and civil war are often inextricably associated with – if not the direct result of – economic underdevelopment. As one observer has noted of the pre-1994 Haitian state: it 'serves as a vehicle for the enrichment of a small elite at the expense of the majority of the population. The Haitians who have fled in the tens of thousands for the past several decades have escaped extreme poverty *caused* by political exploitation' (Loescher 1993: 16; my emphasis). Many individuals who have strong economic reasons for seeking life in a country other than their own often have strong political and basic security reasons for doing so as well.

As will become evident in the case studies I consider, the importance of distinguishing asylum seekers from economic migrants has grown dramatically since the early 1970s when the countries of Western Europe (and to a lesser extent Australasia and North America) wound down economic and guestworker migration programmes. One unintentional result of this increasing restrictiveness was to increase the incentives for economic migrants to apply for entrance on the grounds of asylum. This subsequent increase in demand for asylum has, as we shall see, made it difficult to maintain the credibility of policies which aim at assisting genuine refugees. While the usefulness of having a clear idea of who is a refugee and who is not is undeniable, the real difficulties and costs that states face in drawing these distinctions in practice are a matter of extreme importance when constructing prescriptions for state action.

Family reunion

There is one final group of claimants for entrance we will come across that should be noted here: family migrants. These entrants claim to be admitted on the grounds that they should be allowed to join – to be reunited – with their family members, their spouses, children, siblings,

[9] The problem for Western states is lessened in practice by the fact that victims of famine rarely have the resources to make it to liberal democratic states. Moreover, as I suggested in my attempt to define refugees, victims of famine are usually best helped where they are. There is no doubt, though, that these men and women can, under certain circumstances, satisfy the criteria for a refugee I have outlined.

etc. While refugees and other economic migrants often base their claim for entrance on need alone,[10] the situation of the family entrant is more complicated. In their case, the state is faced with a claim on two fronts: not only does the foreigner concerned have a claim for entry based on *universal* considerations – 'Take me in because families should be together.' But the state's members, many of whom are former immigrants, also have a claim of a more *particular* sort: you owe it to me as a citizen to allow my cousin, daughter or spouse to enter.

It is no doubt a tribute to these dual pressures upon the state that the importance of family migration in the current entrance policies of liberal democracies is enormous. Family migration constitutes the bulk of all new settlement in many Western countries, including the US (Martin 2001: 5–6). In the US, about half a million people a year were allowed entrance under family schemes by the mid 1990s. Even states that deny that they are countries of immigration allow substantial numbers of immigrants to enter each year to join the families of those who entered as guest workers before the mid 1970s. As I will indicate in the course of this work, this migration has played an important role in unwittingly changing the ethnic composition of Australia, the US and Germany.

It is not hard to understand the moral force that underlies the claims of family migrants to be admitted. Few things are more important to individuals than their family and, in particular, their spouse and dependent children. Without the opportunity to have these people around us, we would be deprived of those who give meaning to our lives. Under most circumstances, to demand that family members remain apart is to ask them to bear an enormous emotional burden. To draw upon terminology I will use in the course of this work, the claims of families to be together represent the partial view at its strongest.

In what follows I shall, for the most part, consider the issue of family migrants only in passing. That said, it is difficult to ignore the enormous bias liberal democratic states show in favour of their claims compared to those of refugees in current entrance practices. If residence in liberal democratic states is a scarce good, the distribution of which raises questions of justice, we can't ignore the question of how states should rank the claims of family entrants against those of refugees. In the final chapter of this work, I shall turn explicitly to this question by arguing that the entrance practices of liberal democratic states would be morally superior if the claims of refugees were considered as important as those of family entrants. This conclusion gains added force if we distinguish between

[10] Though, as I have shown, not always – the asylum seekers' claim comes from a conjunction of need and proximity (i.e., being at the borders of the state in question.)

two types of family entrants commonly allowed to enter Western states – immediate (spouses, dependent children, etc.) and extended (siblings, non-dependent children, etc.) family members.

The requirements of a political theory

Now that we have a clearer view of what a refugee is, and how their claims are related to those of other aspiring entrants, it is easy to see why a critical standard for assessing the responses of states to refugee claims is so urgent: competition for entrance is fierce and admission decisions can, in some cases, determine whether an individual will live or die, and almost invariably whether his or her basic rights will be respected. But what would a convincing account of how states should respond to these men, women and children look like? What should the criteria for an adequate standard for assessing the responses of states to refugees and asylum seekers be?

Adequate prescriptions for the responses of states must, I believe, possess ethical force (be informed by a convincing value or furnish a credible moral ideal) and practical relevance (take account of the character and the capabilities of the agents at whom it is directed, and of the probable consequences of their actions). Recent writers on national and international responses to refugees (and on immigration in general) have paid little attention to the importance of bringing together considerations of value with those of agency in this way. Those from legal, sociological and international relations perspectives, whose primary focus has been empirical, have often been quick to criticise the ethical shortcomings of current state responses to refugees and asylum seekers. But they have done little to shed light on what morality might actually demand in terms of the treatment of these entrants. The possibility, for example, that the requirements of morality might be the subject of different interpretations or the site of conflicting values has usually been ignored.[11]

Moral and political theorists, by contrast, have considered more closely the ethical issues raised by entrance practices. But their focus has usually been on what account of responsibilities to refugees people have good reason to accept as morally ideal. They have searched, for instance, for those acts or policies that would maximise total utility or would be chosen by individuals in a global contract situation. In doing so, these theorists

[11] Gil Loescher, for example, criticises the international community for failing to meet its 'ethical obligations to aid and protect refugees' in Loescher (1993). He makes no attempt to explain why Western states have these duties or to outline, within a coherent moral theory, just what these duties might be. He is far from the only writer on refugee issues to use the language of morality without pausing to examine its implications.

have typically abstracted from the character of existing states – by assuming, for instance, that their current schedule of responsibilities can be replaced – and, particularly in the case of global liberalism, from many of the features of the practical environment which currently shapes and constrains the responses of states to refugees, including the constraints that emerge from politics. The result has been somewhat otherworldly prescriptions enjoining open borders or policies that maximise the total utility of all those affected by entrance policies. The question of how the ethical ideals resulting from their analyses might be made relevant to real states is usually postponed with the injunction that agents operating in non-ideal circumstances have a 'natural duty' to do what they can to 'further just arrangements not yet established' (Rawls quoted in Beitz 1988: 48).

I believe, however, that the central question posed by the current crisis straddles the concerns of value and the challenges of agency: how should states act if they are to promote morally defensible responses to the claims of refugees?[12] To undertake a form of analysis that combines empirical and theoretical elements in an attempt to bring considerations of values and agency together is likely to make some normative theorists uncomfortable. For normative theory, it will be claimed, is about what should be, not about what can be practically achieved; it is about what is ultimately desirable, right or valuable. There is an important truth in this objection. Some degree of abstraction from what is currently politically possible is essential if widely supported – and deeply entrenched – practices, such as entrance policy, are to be thoroughly scrutinised. However, by choosing to address the current crisis from a theoretical perspective so disengaged from the actual capabilities of states, normative theorists have deflected attention from the question of what responsibilities we have good reason to demand that actually existing states accept here and now. They have left unresolved the pressing and intensely political question of how liberal democracies should act if they are to fulfil their duty to further the establishment of practices and institutions that treat refugees justly.

There are, moreover, real risks in failing to bring values and agency together. The distinct social and political hazards involved in asylum policy mean that one likely consequence of a government implementing a political agenda far in advance of what is acceptable to its citizens is a backlash that sets back the whole attempt to implement morally defensible

[12] I have been strongly influenced here by John Dunn's view that the major role of political theory is the very practical one of trying 'to tell us how to act given where we now are' (1990a: 196). See, more generally, Dunn (1990a).

practices. No Western state has matched Germany's liberality with asylum seekers in recent times; throughout the 1990s, the Federal Republic bore almost two-thirds of the European Community's entire asylum burden. Yet, as we shall see, this burden resulted in a huge social and political backlash that led to the creation of some of the most restrictive asylum policies of any European country. It is less than fruitful – and sometimes downright hazardous – to ignore the way in which limited abilities can corrupt the best of intentions in politics. When one is dealing with an issue as politically controversial and morally important as asylum, there are compelling reasons for paying close attention to the interconnections between values and agency.

It is more likely, however, that in concentrating exclusively on what is ethically desirable, and ignoring the question of what is politically possible, theorists will simply talk past rather than engage with the claims, interests and agendas of governments. It is hard to believe, for example, that the current British government, facing a political environment in which 'softness' (read: inclusiveness) in asylum policy is interpreted by the Conservative opposition, the tabloid newspapers and large sections of the electorate as a fatal flaw, is well positioned to do much to respond to ideal theory's findings. The failure to address the legitimate difficulties and dilemmas that confront political leaders in constructing entrance policy will condemn the viewpoint of political theory – and, of course, its account of responsibilities to refugees – to practical irrelevance. Whether this will matter greatly is hard to determine in advance. It depends upon which alternative views and values on the treatment of refugees best capture the public and the government mood at a particular point in time, which in turn depends upon many other considerations. But recent events across Europe and Australia – in particular, the rise of far-right leaders such as Jorg Haider (Austria), Jean-Marie Le Pen (France) and Pauline Hanson (Australia) – offer little assurance that the most influential perspectives will be ones that are sensitive to the desperate needs of refugees.

Needless to say, I don't believe the choice we face is confined simply to endorsing current (very restrictive) practices or constructing unrealisable ideals. In the course of this work, I will try to illustrate the features of an approach to the responses of states that avoids both of these extremes. The task of bringing together values and agency is, however, a formidable one. Taking these two requirements for a political theory seriously not only bluntly reveals the limitations of the dominant theoretical accounts of state duty, but also sets stringent terms for a more satisfactory alternative.

Beginning with the requirement of *ethical force*, any standard needs primarily to navigate the real and intractable clash between the claims of states (to self-determination, to cultural autonomy) and the claims of outsiders (to basic security, to greater economic prospects) – claims to be examined in detail in this work. The current asylum controversy throws forth a number of ethical questions, many of which are essential for the formulation of an adequate ideal for state action: Is the modern state a morally defensible form of political organisation? Are states justified in privileging the claims of their own citizens over the claims of refugees, asylum seekers or other immigrants in need? Do states have an obligation to admit for entry any outsiders at all and, if so, from what does this obligation derive? What is the correct criterion by which to decide where anyone is entitled to reside in the contemporary world (birth? need? citizenship? preference? contribution to the maximisation of total global utility?)? At what point might states be said to have fulfilled their obligations to those seeking to enter their territory (when more entrants would increase unemployment? threaten the welfare state? cause a racist backlash?)? What gives any group of people organised into a state the right to exclusive control of a territory? There is no shortage of theories purporting to answer these questions: rights-based approaches appeal to a human right of free movement; utilitarians argue for entry policies which maximise total global utility; and communitarians and nationalists would defend the state's right to construct policies that preserve a society's national culture. Each of these approaches possesses some ethical force and captures an aspect of human value. But, as I will suggest, none has a convincing claim to be the single authoritative standard of value for considerations on entry.

Ensuring that normative prescriptions meet the test of *practical relevance* poses a set of challenges no less daunting. Fundamentally, if we intend to provide guidance for government action, we need to begin by attempting to understand the kind of agent the modern state is, as well as the range of factors that will influence its capacity for morally informed action to assist refugees. In addition, issues of resettlement raise two other special difficulties for a political theory. The first is the necessity of accounting for wide variations in the absorptive abilities of states. A diverse range of factors including a state's integration history, economic strength, and population size, simply have to be reckoned with if one is accurately to assess a state's ability to provide asylum. In our hurry to give a general account of state duties it is easy to overlook the fact that the term 'state' refers solely to the status under international law of independent, territorially based political systems (Krasner 1993: 301). The term indicates nothing at all about the practical ability of the entity in question. The point is particularly pertinent in a world where a substantial number of 'states' (Burundi, Somalia, Liberia) lack the ability to provide for the security of even their own citizens. However, even amongst the world's richer states, with whom I shall concern myself in this work, the practical ability to settle outsiders can vary widely and will be shaped by different factors (and in ways that are not simply reducible to differences in financial resources).

A second difficulty is posed by the immense problem of accurately predicting the economic, political and social consequences of asylum for a state. This difficulty emerges because of the tendency of movements of migrants and refugees to 'snowball', thus confounding all expectations of the number of entrants likely under a particular policy or standard. But it also grows out of the hazards of predicting the trajectory of the various factors that will determine the consequences of reception. Future terrorist attacks by foreigners, for instance, are likely to affect the scope that even the best intentioned of US political leaders have to expand commitments to refugees and asylum seekers in the years ahead, but who could confidently predict the likelihood of such attacks? If we wish our political theory to guide action over time this presents a serious problem. For how can we demand that states follow a particular course when the consequences of doing so are unforeseeable and potentially very serious?

In this work, I demonstrate the importance of facing the challenge of deriving prescriptions for the actions of states in a way that takes into account the practical environment in which they must act. My aim is to derive prescriptions for state action that emerge from a process of reasoning in which the results of ethical theorising are modified by an empirical account of the possibilities actually available to states. In the last chapter of this work, I suggest one, modest way to begin the process of thinking through the responsibilities of liberal democratic states: the principle of humanitarianism. True to my emphasis on practical implications, I suggest some ways that liberal democratic states could reform their current practices to bring them closer to living up to the demands of this principle.

Conclusion

This work is divided into three sections. In the first I consider the two dominant ethical perspectives on the responsibilities of states in entrance. (Chapter 1), 'Partiality' argues that states are morally entitled to privilege the interests of their own citizens in entrance. The approach, championed by communitarians, conservatives and nationalists (amongst others) justifies the right of states to decide admissions according to their own criteria by appealing to the importance of political and cultural autonomy for communities. While I argue that partialism has a degree of ethical force, its viewpoint is weakened by its unjustifiable assumption of the legitimacy of the current territorial holdings of states, its elision of the claims of states and those of nations or distinct cultures, and its failure to account for the harm that states do. I proceed next to an examination of what is often described as the distinctly 'moral' view: impartiality (Chapter 2). This view, which characterises global liberal and utilitarian approaches, argues that states are obliged to take into account the interests or rights of the human community in its entirety in decisions on entry. The impartial view, too, is a powerful ethical perspective. However, I argue that impartialism is greatly weakened as a standard for entrance by its limited ability to account for the claims and interests of citizens. By way of illustration, I show that one of the likely costs of impartially justifiable entrance policies could be the demise of the welfare state, those public policies that lessen some of the impact of economic inequalities. Employing the work of Thomas Nagel, I then proceed to show why an adequate ideal for entrance policy needs to find a way to integrate both partial and impartial moral perspectives.

I then turn to practical realities of entrance policy by examining the factors that have shaped receptivity to refugees in the post-war period in four states: Germany (Chapter 3), Britain (Chapter 4), the United States (Chapter 5) and Australia (Chapter 6). These states have been selected because they offer contrasting approaches to asylum policy and practice. The responses of Germany to refugees and asylum seekers, for example, have been greatly influenced by the fact that the country has, since 1949, recognised a constitutional right of asylum. In the UK, by contrast, political leaders, in the absence of a written constitution and constraints on the system of parliamentary democracy, have had a freer hand to implement policies reflecting popular prejudices towards immigrants and refugees. The inclusion of the United States in this work is essential, not simply because it offers perhaps the best example of a country in which responses to asylum have been informed by considerations of national security and foreign policy, but also because it has been the largest receiving country for refugees in the West. Australia constitutes an important country because of the way it has pioneered new forms of restrictive policies (territorial redefinition, mandatory detention) towards asylum seekers over the last decade or so, all the while continuing to operate relatively inclusive resettlement schemes. In all, the diverse histories, political structures and attitudes towards asylum of these liberal democracies offer essential insights into the challenges and dilemmas likely to confront efforts to create more effective and just responses to refugees.

In the final section of the work, I bring together the ethical and practical lessons of the previous chapters in order to derive some critical standards for states. In the penultimate chapter (Chapter 7), I argue that the process of translating the results of ideal theory into practical responsibilities for governments must be informed by the fact that states are particularistic moral agents, that their integrative abilities are politically constructed, and that there are real difficulties in predicting the consequences of particular asylum (or entrance) policies in advance. In the final chapter (Chapter 8), I propose the principle of humanitarianism as the best available common standard for states. Differentiating my version of this principle from the one articulated some twenty years ago by Michael Walzer, I argue that humanitarianism is a modest, sober and painstakingly realistic criterion. I show how this principle might have practical implications for the current policies of liberal democratic states. I conclude this work by considering the justifiability of, first, practices that propose to trade off the rights of asylum seekers and refugees to maximise the availability of asylum, and, second, measures to restrict the entrance of asylum seekers and refugees on the grounds of national security.

Before I begin it is important that I defend this work from one objection that might be raised about the analysis that follows. Given the huge numbers of refugees in existence in the contemporary world, one might well ask whether it would not be better to concentrate on the duties of states to refugees where they are rather than focus on admitting them for entry. In recent years, international bodies, like the United Nations High Commissioner for Refugees (UNHCR), the European Union and individual states, have suggested that increasing emphasis needs to be given to repatriating refugees and tackling the 'root-causes' of forced migrations. Notwithstanding this new focus, there is, I believe, still a great need for an account of the entrance responsibilities of states. This is not least because the current popularity of repatriation and root-causes approaches indicates as much about the constrained options that international organisations face, given the reluctance of states to resettle refugees, as it does about what is in the best interests of refugees themselves (see, for instance, Harrell-Bond 1996; Turton and Marsden 2002). An ethical examination of entrance responsibilities is important, then, precisely because of the role that the availability of entrance places play in influencing which options will be used to respond to refugees. Analysing entrance is made pressing also by the huge practical difficulties involved in dealing with root causes. The goals of ending ethnic violence, rebuilding devastated economies and establishing durable democratic structures are much easier to profess than accomplish. Even if we make the questionable assumption that states and international organisations have the knowledge and ability to achieve these goals, these tasks would take many years to achieve. There is, then, little danger that the relevance of an account of the resettlement or entrance duties of states will diminish in the foreseeable future.

1 Partiality: community, citizenship and the defence of closure

> Do we want people to be virtuous? Let us then start by making them love their fatherland. But how are they to love it if the fatherland is nothing more for them than for foreigners, and accords to them only what it cannot refuse to anyone?
>
> Jean-Jacques Rousseau 1755

> The right to choose an admissions policy . . . is not merely a matter of acting in the world, exercising sovereignty, and pursuing national interests. At stake is the shape of the community that acts in the world, exercises sovereignty, and so on. Admission and exclusion are at the core of communal independence. They suggest the deepest meaning of self-determination.
>
> Michael Walzer 1983

How would liberal democratic states respond to refugees if their actions were motivated solely by moral considerations? Would these states be justified in restricting the entrance of refugees, or, for that matter, other needy entrants, in order to protect the social, political and economic interests of their citizens? On what criteria would a morally defensible admissions policy for states rest? At least two sharply opposed responses to these questions can be gleaned from the major strands of contemporary political theory. One view, partialism, works with an ideal of states as distinct cultural communities possessing a right to self-determinination which justifies priority for the interests of citizens over those of refugees in entrance decisions. Another view, impartialism, works with an ideal of states as cosmopolitan moral agents, and argues that the only legitimate admissions policy is one that takes into equal account the interests (or rights) of refugees and citizens. In this chapter and the next I will consider each of these viewpoints. I will begin with the partial view.

In the partial view, the claim that states, in their role as representatives of communities of citizens, are morally justified in enacting entrance policies that privilege the interests of their members is defended. This view is characteristic of the communitarian, conservative and constitutionalist realist strands of political theory.[1] Writers in each of these strands have mostly ignored the issue of the responsibilities of states to refugees and foreigners more generally, concentrating their attention primarily on the reciprocal duties of citizens, those, in other words, already sharing a state. In doing so, they have, like many other political theorists, implicitly assumed that the question of who is and should be a member of the political community is basically unproblematical.

Notwithstanding their failure to spell out a full defence of the priority of citizen interests in entrance decisions, partialists generally adhere to the view that the exclusive rights of states are derived from the moral claims of distinct peoples or nations to self-determination. They argue that members of nations are entitled to the 'widest possible degree of autonomy' (Tamir 1993: 74) in order to shape together their collective life. The relevant degree of autonomy is that afforded by the modern sovereign state which exercises control over entry on behalf of its citizens.

What, then, is the nature of the partialist argument? On what grounds does the right to self-determination confer on states the right to judge for themselves whom they shall admit to their territory? For partialists, the right of states to self-determination grows out of a claim about the entitlements of men and women to give public expression to their shared culture.[2] However, a number of different arguments for this entitlement have been put forward by political theorists in recent times. One argument with a distinctly liberal flavour claims that participation in a living culture is essential for individual autonomy. In order for individuals to be free, Will Kymlicka (1995) argues, they must be able to make choices between different ways of living their lives. Cultures are essential because they provide individuals with a range of options from which to make such choices. Moreover, it is only against a particular cultural backdrop that these options available to men and women can take on meaning and significance. Culture orients individuals in the world: it provides them with a language, vocabulary, through which to make meaningful choices about

[1] Contemporary partialist defences of the state can be found in the work of communitarians such as MacIntyre (1984), Sandel (1982), and with some qualification Walzer (1983) and Miller (1995), conservatives such as Scruton (1990) and realists such as Hendrickson (1992). While not all of these writers discuss the question of entrance policies directly, their views on the moral priority of citizens lend strong support to the views on entrance discussed in this chapter.

[2] There are a number of other ways that one might defend the exclusive claims of communities. One might, for instance, argue that cooperative relations amongst the members of a state justify privileging responsibilities to compatriots over those to outsiders. (For a discussion of these approaches, see Black (1991) and Miller (1988).) These arguments, however, are often weakened by their ability to establish why such cooperation should make a moral difference and by the fact that many cooperative practices found in the state often extend beyond its borders as well.

what is and what is not of value (Kymlicka 1995: ch. 5). In addition, cultural membership provides men and women with a form of identity that is particularly secure and reliable across time and historical circumstance. For cultural identification is based on belonging and not accomplishment (Raz 1994: 117). It is thus particularly well suited, as Margalit and Raz comment, to serve as 'an anchor for self-identification' in the modern world (quoted in Kymlicka 1995: 89).[3]

A more conventional line of argument is offered by more communitarian writers such as Michael Walzer (1983, 1995), Michael Sandel (1982), David Miller (1995) and Charles Taylor (1993). They emphasise that the identities of men and women are constituted largely by their membership in cultural and national communities. The culture into which we are born and live shapes our goals, our relationships, our very sense of self. While liberal theories of justice require that we abstract ourselves from our identity when reflecting upon how we ought to act, communitarians emphasise the role that our cultural circumstances play in making us moral agents in the first place. Men and women are, according to partialists, fundamentally cultural beings. Indeed, many of the responsibilities and attachments we incur through our membership in a culture, these theorists argue, are so integral to our individual personality that to 'divest ourselves of such commitments would be, in an important sense, to change one's identity' (Miller 1988: 650).[4]

A key consequence of the link between culture and individual identity is that people's self-regard is usually 'bound up with the esteem in which their national group is held' (Kymlicka 1995: 89). Whether a culture is doing well or badly – is prospering or is under threat – ultimately influences the well-being of its constituent members, and the prospects for a morally desirable political order. The relationship between individual well-being and prospering of cultural groups characteristically leads partialists to argue that national communities have a moral right to protect their 'integrity'; communities, in other words, have a right to reproduce their culture free from the interference of outsiders. This right, argues Michael Walzer, 'derives its moral and political force from the rights of contemporary men and women to live as members of a historic community and to express their inherited culture through political forms worked out amongst themselves' (1983).

It is characteristic of partialism that a right of nations to self-determination, derived from the cultural entitlements of members, slides

[3] Joseph Raz writes, 'familiarity with a culture determines the boundaries of the imaginable. Sharing in a culture, being part of it, determines the limits of the feasible' (Raz 1994: 119).

[4] Compare Richard Rorty's discussion of moral obligations to close relatives in Rorty (1999).

into a claim about a right of states to self-determination, derived from the claims of their citizens. According to Charles Taylor, national communities have the right to be sovereign states because people 'have the right to demand that others respect whatever is indispensable to . . . [their] being full human subjects' (1993: 53). Typically, modern state boundaries are assumed to demarcate unique and largely autonomous cultural communities composed of men and women sharing a set of common practices and understandings – a way of life – that binds them together into a distinct group of people with a special commitment to each other. The particular way of life shared by citizens differs, of course, between states, according to their national mores, customs and traditions. But where the bonds of citizenship are mutually recognised and valued, they always indicate that members share something more substantive than the same legal status and residence in a territorial entity recognised under international law. What citizens share is membership in a rich cultural community constituted by common social practices, cultural traditions and shared ethical understandings. This kind of political community, moreover, provides the necessary context for collective political projects in pursuit of the common good of the nation. It offers the largest feasible site for a politics of the common good – a politics that transcends the diverse and idiosyncratic conceptions of the good that characterise liberal politics and looks to the good of the citizen community as a whole.

The community of citizenship that partialists see as forming the basis of the modern state owes its existence to members sharing and identifying with a common national history. For partialists, the current citizens of a state are the living embodiment – the inheritors – of a historic community whose identity has been transmitted by members across generations. For Roger Scruton, the modern nation-state is best seen as the site of a '*moral* unity between people, based in territory, language, association, history and culture' (Scruton 1990: 320; my emphasis). For Michael Walzer, sovereign states demarcate and make possible the survival of distinct '*communities of character*, historically stable, ongoing associations of men and women with some special commitment to one another and some special sense of their common life' (Walzer 1983: 62). On most issues in contemporary politics the left-communitarian, Michael Walzer, and the conservative, Roger Scruton, disagree profoundly. But they are in harmony with each other – and, moreover, with Edmund Burke – in viewing the modern state as a kind of intergenerational cultural project: a contract between the living and the dead and those who are yet to be born (Burke 1969: 194–5).

Partialism thus makes a virtue of the contemporary international system in which states have a sovereign right to decide who they will admit for entrance. Sovereignty is seen as the guarantee of the survival and prospering of the many and varied national communities of people sharing special duties that shape individual identities. Attempts to move beyond the state as a political community with the sole right to distribute membership are ethically undesirable (because they ignore the moral importance of culture) and politically dangerous (because undemocratic forms of government are required to repress particularistic identities). The community of citizens is, as Michael Walzer has suggested, 'the ideal political order' (1981: 101).

The political community and foreigners

Where do foreigners fit into the partialist picture of the state? Partialist writers, with some notable exceptions, are strangely silent on the question of what responsibilities states have to outsiders. Yet as one writer has put it, the 'privileging of community members logically implies a comparatively diminished concern for the welfare of outsiders' (Seidman 1995: 139). Moreover, if one accepts the partialist view of the state as a warm and intimate association, what separates citizens from foreigners is clearly a great deal more than legal status; they are separated also by the mass of shared understandings, practices and common history which make the political community a site of special importance. Foreigners are not a part of the bond that unites members. What is more, they are, according to Walzer, not even in a position to question the reality and meaningfulness of the bond, since, as outsiders, they can have had no experience of what membership of the political community means (Booth 1997). This stark opposition between foreigners and members does not necessarily confine outsiders to being permanently alien to the political community in question. Partialists are not ignorant of the fact that all states have been shaped over the course of their history by immigrants and refugees; new members are not only changed by the cultural community they enter, but change the community in turn through their presence and contribution to society. But if one views the modern state as an intimate association, the maintenance of which is often of fundamental moral significance because of its indispensability for human fulfilment, what is on the line in membership decisions is clearly of great significance. For it is always possible that the entry of foreigners may disturb the distinct way of life and bonds of attachment that citizens currently share and which currently make the political community the object of their allegiance.

How might the admittance of foreigners to membership disturb the state's current way of life and the special commitment citizens share? One answer is that large flows of entrants would lead to racial violence and tension, place extreme pressure on the state's infrastructure, undermine liberal democratic institutions and jeopardise law and order in the state. New settlers might threaten, in other words, what Habermas refers to as the 'functional' requirements (1992: 16) of liberal democratic societies: the ability of these states to fulfil their fundamental responsibility to meet the basic needs and security requirements of their citizens. There are, as one observer has noted, 'instances in human history when the migration of peoples seems indistinguishable in its effects from the conquest of an invading army' (Hendrickson 1992: 217).

This, however, is a pretty extreme scenario. It is highly plausible that liberal democratic states could accept large numbers of entrants without jeopardising their existence as functioning entities. The existence of countries of mass migration, such as Australia, Canada and the US, suggests that under the right circumstances modern states can integrate huge numbers without the breakdown of social order. Thus, while protecting the functional requirements of the state might provide grounds for setting outer limits on the responsibilities of a state to admit foreigners, this rationale clearly falls short of justifying a broad-ranging prerogative on behalf of members to decide the number of foreigners they will admit.

Unsurprisingly, then, the force of the partialist case rests on some more subtle consequences of foreigner entrance. In particular, partialists are sensitive to the way the refugees and immigrants might change the cultural environment of the political community, even if they do not actually threaten the existence of the community *per se*. The thrust of the partialist claims is nicely captured by Myron Weiner:

> If 35 million hardworking Chinese were allowed to settle in Burma, the Burmese economy might very well prosper, and the Burmese themselves might be economically better off. But for the Burmese their country would no longer be Burma. The Burmese would no longer be able to control the central cultural symbols of their national life; and, of course, the Burmese would have lost political control over their own state. (Weiner 1985: 443)

Michael Dummett makes a similar point when he suggests that allowing immigration to 'swell to a size that threatens the indigenous population with being [culturally] submerged' would be an injustice (2001: 20).[5] The right to control over membership and entrance is grounded in the entitlement of political communities to give public expression to their collective identity.

[5] As Michael Dummett considers this argument for controlling entry to be applicable only to a very small number of vulnerable communities and only in extreme circumstances, he is, I believe, rightly characterised as an impartialist in matters of entrance. I consider some of his arguments in Chapter 2.

There are numerous ways in which large flows of new entrants might change a state's cultural environment. For example, refugees and immigrants can influence the levels of political support for certain public goods which a particular community considers integral to its particular way of life, such as higher education, the fine arts, cultural events and memorials, etc. through the democratic process. New settlers in the state with different values and tastes from members of the host community may be reluctant to support the distribution of these goods on a free or subsidised basis (Black 1991: 361–2). If the number of new settlers is large enough, the traditional preferences of more established members risk being drowned out.

Changes in membership can also affect a state's cultural environment in less directly political ways. Even without wielding political power, the culmulative effects of new settlers in a state often result in changes in the language, mores and the forms of religion that predominate in the political communities they enter (Black 1991: 360). While Germany has in recent years generally restricted the political rights and access to citizenship of former guestworker migrants resident in the country, its efforts have not prevented these migrants from transforming Germany into a multicultural society, diversifying religious practices, customs and the languages spoken.

Many of these concerns about the effects of foreigners are far from new. Two hundred years ago, Thomas Jefferson also worried about the consequences of new entrants for the American polity. In the face of new immigrants to the American republic from monarchical states, he argued:

> They will bring with them the principles of the governments they leave, imbibed in their early youth . . . These principles, with their language, they will transmit to their children. In proportion to their numbers, they will share with us the legislation. They will infuse into it their spirit, warp and bias its direction, and render it a heterogeneous, incoherent, distracted mass. (Quoted in Whelan 1988: 18)

While such concerns may not be new, the huge pool of refugees and immigrants in the contemporary world provides uniquely strong grounds for believing that cultural features valued by citizens would be threatened by far less restrictive entrance policies.

Now if one agrees that communities have a right to preserve the integrity of their cultural forms, then these possible effects of foreigner admission would seem to provide strong reasons for giving states broad-ranging prerogatives in entrance. The entitlement of citizens to guarantee the cultural outcomes of their political system lends support to the idea that they should have a great deal of freedom in entrance decisions. For while it might be possible objectively to decide the point at which states are justified in restricting entry in the interests of preserving their *functional requirements* (e.g., states are entitled to restrict the entry of those who would threaten law and order), determining when a *culture* is endangered seems a considerably more hazardous enterprise. Who is in the best position to judge when a 'culture' is under threat? Partialists rely implicitly on the belief that this decision is best made from the *inside*: that the members of a culture are best placed to be the judges since they can be expected to know their own culture more intimately than anyone else. Who would be more aware, for instance, than the French when the entry of foreigners onto their territory is undermining the key elements of their culture? Once one argues that communities have the right to protect their distinctive cultural form, it is hard to deny that members are in the best position to judge what is a threat to their culture. Attachment to the value of cultural self-determination thus creates a strong presumption in favour of giving citizens the discretion to decide who shall be allowed to enter.

But the partialist concern with the cultural implications of immigration is not motivated only by a belief in the intrinsic value of cultural recognition. Partialists are also sensitive to the effects that changes in the composition of membership can have on the state as a political agent. The tendency of partialists to see the modern state as a *community* is indicative of a particular view of the conditions that must hold in modern states for distributive justice, citizen impartiality and meaningful democracy to be realised and maintained. According to partialists, all of these achievements depend on the 'partiality of membership' (Booth 1997), on citizens seeing themselves as sharing a *common life* with their compatriots. What a community *is*, in this view, is a group of people who, in the course of time, have come to trust and identify with each other in a special and exclusive way. The impartiality of modern citizen relations and the attempt to create more just, egalitarian and democratic states is often dependent upon the strength of the partial attachments that citizens have for each other.[6] The route to better societies, partialists believe, lies in making stronger the bonds of trust and solidarity that hold between members and thereby increasing the sense that citizens share a common life. 'A citizen democracy', argues Charles Taylor, 'can only work if most of its members are convinced that their political society is a common venture of considerable moment' and for citizens to hold this conviction there must be 'a special sense of the bonding amongst the people working together' (1996: 120).

[6] Note David Miller's point that members of a nation can 'appeal to the their historic identity, to sacrifices made in the past by one section of the community on behalf of others, to back up the claims they make on one another now' (1995: 42).

Partialists disagree amongst themselves on what actions or policies are required to strengthen the bonds of citizenship in liberal democracies. But they do not doubt the importance that commonalities of language, religion, ethnicity and historical residence play in creating a spirit of cooperation and mutuality. This minimal point of agreement has important implications for how partialists view the prerogatives of states in entrance. For one consequence of admitting foreigners to a political community is the dilution of the commonalities that members currently share. In the face of this change, some key questions naturally emerge: Can feelings of trust amongst citizens that have emerged over many generations survive large numbers of new entrants? Will citizens made worse off by more open borders (for example, those in low wage occupations) continue to see their political community as a 'common venture' if it fails to put their interests before those of foreigners? Will current members become alienated from a polity that no longer reflects their shared culture? One would clearly need to know something about the size and composition of the entrance flows as well as the particular state under consideration in order to answer these questions satisfactorily. But they serve well enough to focus attention on the varied ways in which new entrants may influence a state's capacity for effective political action in the pursuit of social justice. Moreover, these concerns provide support for the view that members should have some discretion to decide questions of entrance and membership, at least if one values the fruits of collective political action. For whether any particular group of entrants is likely to undermine – or bolster – citizen solidarity is going to depend in large part upon the subjective attitudes of current members and these attitudes will differ across communities.

There are, then, two complementary but ultimately distinct arguments that communitarians, conservatives and nationalists move between to defend a broad right of states to discretion in entrance policy. The first and primary one defines what I call partialism. This argument points to the fundamental importance of identity for human beings. States have the right to distribute membership as they please because without this right people could not protect and reproduce their cultural identity, and therefore would be unable to express an aspect of themselves that is essential to their sense of who they are. In this argument, the existence and reproduction of sovereign states within which citizens are especially attentive to the needs of their compatriots (those with whom they reproduce their culture) is a legitimate and powerful ideal.

The second argument is more contingent, and runs like this: even if one is sceptical of the moral legitimacy of special attachments based on nationality, one may still have good reason to give citizens broad discretionary control of entrance. For one cannot deny the *practical role* that ties of culture and nationality play in facilitating collective political action in the pursuit of justice. To ignore the force of these attachments (and the way the entry of foreigners might jeopardise them) could lead one to advocate entrance policies that actually undermine just and egalitarian political regimes where they exist. That is to say, it might well be in the interests of humanity as a whole to tolerate – at least in the short term – entrance policies that accommodate the cultural aspirations of political communities and thus privilege the interests of citizens over those of foreigners.

Partiality and refugees

So far I have shown why partialists defend the view that the interests of citizens should be given priority in entrance decisions. Now I want to turn to the issue of refugees. To say that the citizens should take priority does not mean that partialists give no weight to the interests of foreigners or believe that moral considerations are irrelevant in considering how a state should respond to their needs. Notwithstanding its emphasis on the prerogatives of states, partialism is not equivalent to political realism: the view that moral considerations are irrelevant to questions of how states should treat foreigners.[7] On the contrary, partialism claims to be an ethically defensible account of the legitimate entitlements of political communities. Once we begin to examine the bases on which partialists decide how much weight the claims of refugees should be given, some differences between the various strands of this viewpoint become apparent.

What partialists share is the belief that in order to be legitimate a refugee policy must reflect the values and interests of the state's members. Partialists differ, however, on how these values and interests are to be interpreted. In one view, the question of what constitutes a legitimate response to the claims of refugees is answered simply through the results of democratic politics. What the *demos* of a particular state chooses through fair and democratic processes that respect civil and political equality is the legitimate response for the government to pursue. Conversely, those policies which the electorate rejects or would reject are illegitimate. Kay Hailbronner appears to defend this view when he argues:

> 'Moral' claims to citizenship . . . are generally inappropriate. There are no moral and therefore generally applicable criteria in judging a nation's citizenship policy apart from the principle forbidding a state to deprive a citizen arbitrarily of his

[7] See Hendrickson (1992) for an exceedingly tame defence of the realist position in relation to entrance policy.

citizenship. Naturalization policy, like immigration policy, cannot be determined by questions of what is good or bad, moral or immoral. It has to be determined by balancing divergent political interests. (Hailbronner 1989: 74–5)

A similar position is found in James Clad's view that decisions on entrance should be constrained by little more than the play of politics: 'The US has the sovereign right, *if it constitutionally reflects the majority view*, to exclude others from coming here. It is that simple; it is that awkward. The essence of sovereignty remains the power to exclude' (Clad 1994: 150). The most obvious implication of relying on democracy as a standard is that it may confer moral legitimacy on the actions of states that completely disregard the claims of refugees. Indeed, if we make the plausible assumption that most citizens view electoral politics as the most appropriate (and fair) way of determining the state's policies to refugees, then this approach has very little critical force in face of the current restrictive measures. Interpreting the views and values of citizens in this way seems only to vindicate very broad-ranging prerogatives to exclude.

Perhaps this is how issues of entrance control should rightly be viewed. But many partialists have been reluctant to endorse this way of approaching the issue of entrance. Instead, they have argued that it is necessary to go beyond current public opinion and election results and examine the 'shared understandings' of members in order to derive a critical standard for admissions (Walzer 1983). In this second view, the task of identifying the responsibilities of states requires an act of cultural interpretation, an examination of the characteristic practices and institutions of the political community in question. For it is only by interpreting the beliefs that underlie these practices and instititutions that we can determine how citizens understand what membership in their community means.

The key question, then, is whether this approach can yield an argument for states giving more weight to the claims of refugees than they currently do. In order for this to be the case, partialists must show, first, that citizens share certain values and, then, that these values are more inclusive than the principles on which their governments currently act. Many criticisms have been made of the shared understandings approach (Barry 1995; Smith 1996). But the strongest reason for doubting its adequacy with respect to entrance is that the existence of an underlying consensus in liberal democracies on what membership means and therefore on how refugees should be treated is highly dubious. As Rogers Smith has recently shown, the citizenship policies of even the US – historically the most inclusive of liberal democracies – have been shaped by at least three distinct understandings of the national community, each of which results in conflicting standards for foreigner admission (Smith 1988). An even stronger case for a tension between different understandings is evident in the case of Germany, which had, until very recently, simultaneously supported an inclusive liberal democratic constitution *and* a very exclusive, ethnic conception of citizenship (Carens 1995: 24–8). It is a key defect of the shared understandings approach that the beliefs, practices and institutions of modern states and their constituent members often reflect and are consistent with conflicting views of how the state should respond to refugees. The attempt to articulate a substantive set of shared values is thus likely to become, as Brian Barry has argued, an exercise in tendentious theorising (Barry 1995: ch. 1).

The existence of diverse views and complex practices regarding refugees does not, I believe, completely preclude the possibility of a consensus on entry in liberal democracies. But it does mean that the nature of any consensus is more likely to involve agreement only on the *procedures* by which the entry of refugees should be decided. More than likely, the consensus would involve agreement on the principle that the number and variety of refugees entering a state should reflect the democratic will of the state's citizens. However, if a consensus of this sort does exist, then the results of the shared understandings approach seem virtually indistinguishable from the democratic/electoral approach I outlined previously. For both support the view that the amount of weight a state should give to the claims of refugees at any given time should be decided politically; and, moreover, both approaches are plagued by the problem that their reliance solely on the interests and values of citizens to judge states leads them to lend legitimacy to policies that disregard the urgent needs of refugees. It may be the desire to avoid a conclusion of this sort that leads Michael Walzer, the only political theorist systematically to apply the shared understandings approach to entrance decisions, to move beyond the particularities of communal understandings when considering responsibilities to refugees. In *Spheres of Justice*, Walzer argues that while immigrants can rightfully be admitted according to a community's particular understanding of membership, states are constrained by the universal demands of the principle of mutual aid in their dealings with refugees (1983: 48–51). Notwithstanding the seeming inconsistency of this position, Walzer provides no clear rationale for departing from communal understandings in this case.

We can conclude, then, that partialism's reliance on basing the responsibilities of states on the views and values of citizens tends to vindicate the current actions of states in giving a low weighting to the claims of refugees. Of course, there is nothing inevitable about this outcome. The attitudes of citizens can change and bring about reasons for a more inclusive and generous response to refugees. Democracy can work for the admission of refugees as well as against their admission, as the public pressure for admitting the refugees from the Kosovo crisis of 1999 showed (Gibney 1999b). But it is crucial to note that in the current international environment, where there is a great deal of hostility in liberal democratic states to refugees and other foreigners, partialism possesses very little critical power for standing firm against this citizen hostility or the restrictive entrance policies that have flowed from it.

The state: territory, identity, agency

Because partialism tends to vindicate the current policies of liberal democracies, there is good reason to subject its central claim – that the right of citizens to preserve their collective identity entitles them to distribute membership according to their own criteria – to critical scrutiny. There is no doubt that in its concern for the continued viability and cultural integrity of communities, partialism captures an important dimension of human value; nor can one deny that it presents a fundamental challenge to the attempt to construct an expansive account of the responsibilities of states to refugees and other necessitous strangers. What is less clear is how sturdy a defence it offers of letting states decide who will enter and reside in their territory. The need for such a defence grows as the consequences for outsiders of not being allowed to enter become more serious. For instance, it is one thing for partialists to defend the moral legitimacy of the state's control over regular immigration. The costs for outsiders of not entering a particular state in this situation are confined, perhaps, to a denial of the opportunity to live in a sunny climate, to take up a promotion or to improve their economic prospects. Many people, perhaps even amongst those excluded, would accept this as a legitimate area of discretion because the state may have relatively important interests of its own to protect. But, as we have seen, the partialist reliance on the interests and values of members would allow the state legitimately to bar the entry of people for whom a great deal more is on the line. For refugees and asylum seekers, the costs of not entering can be the loss of their life or condemnation to a life barely worth living.

Any ethical theory that allows states to disregard the needs of those who might be refugees requires a watertight case for investing members with the right to decide who will be admitted. I think the partialist case for allowing states the right to distribute membership according to their own criteria is less than compelling. The root of the problem lies in the inadequate picture of the modern state appealed to by partialists. This picture, which underpins their argument for why citizens have the right to control entrance, fails to do justice to the complexity of modern states in two different ways. First, partialists simplify matters with the implicit assumption that the only ethically relevant feature of states with respect to admissions is that states are *cultures*. Real states, however, are a lot more: they are also *territory* – they divide between them the earth's habitable surface – and they are *agents* – actors in an increasingly interconnected global environment. Both of these features of states, I believe, raise ethical questions about entrance that problematise the claims of political communities to control admissions based on their nationhood. Second, and perhaps most obviously, the partialist assumption that states possess a distinctive and singular national identity which they are entitled to protect from foreigners conveniently glosses over the very apparent ethnic and cultural diversity of contemporary liberal democracies.

The significance of partialism's simplifying assumptions becomes clearer if we consider the following three questions: (i) *What gives any particular state the right to exclusive use of the territory it occupies?* This reveals partialism's unspoken and unjustifiable assumption of the legitimacy of the current territorial holdings of states. (ii) *What is shared by citizens that distinguishes them from outsiders?* This illustrates the elision of the claims of states and those of nations that plagues the partialist account of the state as a human community. (iii) *Are states responsible for the harm they cause?* This makes clear the failure of partialists to deal with the full implications of states as *agents*, as actors in the world. Only the second of these questions is considered in any depth by partialists, and there are good reasons for being dissatisfied with the answer they give to it.

In the remainder of this chapter I will explore these questions in depth and consider the problems they pose for the claim that states have a moral right to control entry. Partialism's failure to answer these questions adequately does not completely undermine the ethical force of states giving priority to the interests of their citizens. As I will suggest in concluding this chapter, partialism highlights some crucial moral issues relevant to entrance policy. But these questions do bring to light the reasons why partialism falls short of providing a definitive answer to the question of how it would be ideal for states to respond to refugees.

What gives the state the right to exclusive use of the territory it occupies?

The first problem with the partialist defence of the right of states to decide questions of entrance lies in the fact that modern states are territorial entities. One could be forgiven for thinking that partialists see modern states solely as human communities, as groups of men and women sharing a common life together. But modern states do not simply rule over and act as the agents for separate communities of citizens. Each of the world's states also rules over a portion of the earth's surface and claims for itself the natural resources within that portion. Thus residence in a particular state entails not simply membership in a particular community, but also the legal right to reside on a particular piece of the earth's surface. States control the distribution of membership in political communities and the distribution of territorial rights.

This territorial dimension makes the state fundamentally different from other entities often considered analogous in their right to determine membership and exclude outsiders. Notwithstanding the existence of some similarities, the entry prerogatives enjoyed by club members and by the owners of private property are not the same as those exercised by territorial states.[8] For the force of both of these popular analogies, which equate the international realm with aspects of domestic society, hinges on the implication that being in a club or on a person's private property is a matter of choice and that there exist viable alternatives (for instance, not being a member of a club, or entering a public space upon leaving someone's private property). But just this feature of choice is lacking in an international realm where sovereign territorial states occupy virtually all of the world's inhabitable land and where, save for parts of the high seas (which hardly constitute a serious residential option), there exists no equivalent of public (non-state) spaces. In the modern world, people have no alternative but to live in the territory of some particular state.

The territoriality of the state has important implications for the legitimacy of entrance restrictions. For once we acknowledge that entry controls exclude foreigners from membership in national communities *and* from residence in territory, it is no longer obvious that partialists can defend the claims of states solely by appealing to the rights of cultural communities. Partialists now need to provide a normative defence of the territorial appropriations of states. Partialists must show why the current territorial holdings of states are morally justifiable, if they are to offer a robust account of the entitlements of states to exclude.

Perhaps the most credible way of defending the state's territorial claims is by arguing that a commitment to the security and survival of cultural communities effectively *entails* support for exclusive control of territory. Partialists can argue, for instance, that without a right of territorial exclusion, it would be impossible for a community to maintain its collective identity over time. This claim seems plausible. Historically, national identity and geographical coexistence have been closely linked; the fact that

[8] For the club analogy see Walzer (1983) and for the private property analogy see Cranston (1973).

members have shared residence in the same clearly defined territory has been crucial to the formation and concretisation of particular attachments. Moreover, as Walzer has argued, 'because so many critical issues (including issues of distributive justice, such as welfare, education and so on) can best be resolved within geographical units, the focus of political life can never be established elsewhere' (1983: 44). If communities have the right to live and develop in accordance with the shared culture of their members, then something like territorially divided states seems inevitable.

Credible as this argument may be, it falls a long way short of providing an adequate defence for the territory states *currently* possess. In the face of the claims of refugees (people who, by definition, lack a secure territory), the key question is not whether the American, Australian and Canadian people, for example, need territory in order to survive culturally, but whether they need as much territory as they currently have.

Natural law writers of the seventeenth and eighteenth centuries such as Grotius, Locke and Vattel, who were often as keen as modern partialists to defend the exclusive rights of states, believed that control over territory opened states up to the claim of necessity, particularly when the state in question possessed more territory than its members needed. These theorists worked from the Christian assumption of a world given by God to humankind radically in common (Dunn 1992b: 282–3). This assumption did not rule out the establishment and legitimation of private property (as owned by individuals or by states) if the existence of such property could be shown to be fair and in the interests of all. But this starting point did mean that if the consequences of exercising one's exclusive right to property were death or serious injury to a person who needed the protection that property afforded, the right of exclusive ownership lapsed. As Grotius argued: 'it is justified that in direst need the primitive right of man revives, as if common ownership had remained, since in respect to all human laws – the law of ownership included – supreme necessity seems to have been excluded' (Grotius 1925: ch. 2, sec. 6). Vattel argued similarly almost two centuries later:

> Banishment and exile do not take away from a man his human personality, nor consequently his right to live somewhere or other. He holds this right from nature, or rather from the Author of nature, who has intended the earth to be man's dwelling place. The introduction of private ownership of land cannot be in derogation of this right to the means of obtaining the necessities of life, a right which belongs to every man by birth. (Vattel 1916: ch. XIX, sec. 229)

In articulating this principle, the natural law theorists of the sixteenth and seventeenth centuries could not have envisaged the volume of entrants that Western states now face (nor the kind of lifestyles most citizens in

Western states now enjoy). But their attempt to grapple with the ethical issues raised by communal control of territory is informed by a deep appreciation of the normative issues at stake in disputes over entrance.

It might be suggested, however, that the argument for territory based on communal autonomy rather misses the point. A nation's territory is important not just because it allows the community freedom from the influence of foreigners; rather, the territory is in *itself* 'a crucial feature of national identity' (Walzer 1983: 44). Anthony Smith, for instance, has stated that the 'solidarity that a nationalist desires is based on the possession of land: *not any land, but the historic land; the land of past generations, the land that saw the flowering of the nation's genius*' (1979: 3; my emphasis). Nations do not have territory so much as they have *homelands*: a part of the globe to which they have formed a special attachment. To sever the connection between a cultural community and its homeland, partialists might argue, is to deprive a people of a key element of their national identity. In order to respect the integrity of nations, we must acknowlege the right of cultural communities to that territory that they see as their own.

Once again, this is an important observation. It shows why a national community might have a good claim to territory larger than that which the nation needs to survive as a distinct entity. But the right of nations to their homelands still raises as many questions as it answers. For instance, what should be done if there is more than one nation laying claim to a particular piece of territory? In a world of finite territory, what should the status of newly formed or mobilised cultural communities to territory be? To answer these questions it is necessary to provide an account of how it is that cultures can come *legitimately* to acquire homelands.

Partialists offer no explicit account of what makes territorial appropriations legitimate. However, because they are committed to defending the exclusive powers of existing states, partialists are backed into justifying the results of a historical process of carving up the world's territory between states that primarily has been achieved through the force of arms, and has (accordingly) resulted in a gross mismatch between human needs and natural resources. Indeed, to the extent that partialists accept the legitimacy of sovereign states as recognised by international law, they must be sobered by the thought that current international law 'cannot help but recognise as valid a nation's right to its *de facto* territorial holdings – however it has come by them – at least if it has controlled those holdings long enough for the world to get used to it' (Reiman 1989: 168). Contemporary international law adjusts itself to the realities of power relations. In implicitly defending the current appropriations of states partialists risk sacralising these relations.

There are good reasons for investing current borders with at least some legitimacy. Redrawing the world's borders in line with a universal blueprint of the just claims of cultural communities would be enormously costly in terms of human suffering and social and political disruption. Moreover, if all cultural communities have territorial rights, no matter when they were formed, the boundaries between states could never be stable. As soon as a new culture emerged, claiming its share of land space, the boundaries of all other states would have to be redrawn (Brilmayer 1989). It is well to recognise that whoever else has a good moral claim to live on the island of Australia or on that portion of the earth's surface known as Germany, no one outside these territories has *more* of a right to live there than the current inhabitants. The current residents have already made their lives there. Given that the passing of time in a particular territory is intimately linked to the formation and concretisation of bonds, associations and friendships, denying people's claim to continue to live where they have been for an extended period of time is cruel and inhumane.[9]

But recognising the ethical dubiousness of the way territory is currently distributed does highlight a critical gap in the partialist account of why states are entitled to control entrance. For the fact that some people are in a position to control entrance to a particular piece of territory is more often a tribute to their (or their predecessors') good luck in seizing control of a particular piece of territory before anyone else, or their use of the force of arms to push aside the land's original occupants, than to the justice of their claim. Neither of these features of real-world territorial appropriation could form the basis of a very forceful ethical response to a needy foreigner who asks: What gives you the right to exclude me from residence in your territory?[10]

This rather pessimistic conclusion begs an important question: What could be done to rectify the contingency of the current territorial holdings of states? One way that states could act to lessen some of the cruellest consequences of maldistribution of territory is for them to allow admission to refugees. The argument for doing so seems especially strong in the

[9] This raises the morally vexed and politically important question as to whether the consequences of resettlement that result from occupation should be vindicated. Do the current Israeli inhabitants of the West Bank or Indonesians relocated into the once occupied territory of East Timor have any moral claim to stay living where they are? I do not have the space to consider this question here.

[10] Consider, for instance, the huge numbers of people who annually break US law by surreptitiously crossing from Mexico into territory that was once claimed by the Mexican state (see Lichtenburg (1983: 22)). I discuss the relationship between the legitimate acquisition of territory and entrance policy in the case of Australia in Chapter 6.

case of those states whose territorial appropriations are far in excess of their needs and where their historical claim is particularly problematical (as in the case of new world countries, such as Australia, New Zealand and the US). Addressing the ethical issues raised by territory in this manner has the very obvious and important benefit of reducing some of the great hardships caused by border divisions for people in need without completely undermining the legitimacy of borders or, for that matter, the cultural communities that these borders supposedly protect.

What is shared by citizens that distinguishes them from outsiders?

As I have shown, the partialist case for the sovereignty of states in entry is dependent upon a particular view of the modern state as a cultural unity: as the site of a shared history, practices, understandings and, often, ethnicity. This view of the state gives rise to a fundamental distinction between members and strangers where those inside the state share a way of life which sharply distinguishes them from those outside it. The entrance prerogatives of states are legitimate, argue partialists, because states, through their protection of cultures, make real the right of people to have their cultural identities respected. I want to consider now the adequacy of this view of the modern state as an autonomous cultural unit. In doing so, we will get a clearer picture of whether the cultural claims of citizens can do the job of legitimating the exclusive powers of the modern state. However, it is worth noting at the outset that the cultural argument used by partialists is underdetermined as an ethical justification for states excluding refugees. For even if one concedes that national cultures should be valued, it is unclear why cultural claims should be put to work defending collective rights of exclusion rather than collective rights of inclusion. Refugees are often members of persecuted cultural groups and restrictive entrance policies often jeopardise their cultural survival as well as their physical survival. If preserving cultural diversity is important, then surely the cultures of all peoples matter. Partialism offers no clear answer as to why the claims to exclusion of cultural groups currently residing in a secure state should trump the claims of those cultural groups currently unprotected by any state whatsoever.

But what of the partialist view of the state as a cultural community? A common feature of partialism is, as I have mentioned, the tendency to slide from a claim about the right of members of nations to autonomy to a claim about the right of citizens to self-determination. Is this move justifiable? If a 'people's' right to a cultural or a national identity is to serve as grounds for legitimating the discretionary claims of the *state*, it is necessary that the boundaries of nations or cultures and those of states be contiguous. If they are not, then the existence of a cultural community or distinct cultural identities cannot provide a justification for states – as opposed to some other entity (such as more local communities or trans-state associations) – possessing an exclusive entitlement to decide who enters.

As a consequence, many partialists argue that it is at the level of the political community that the way of life of the nation – the key identity to be preserved – comes together. Walzer, for instance, argues that the political community is the 'closest we can come to a world of common meanings. Language, history and culture come together (come more closely together here than anywhere else) to produce a collective consciousness' (Walzer 1983: 28).

This assumption of a neat fit between the state boundaries and cultural and national communities is not a completely irrelevant claim in the contemporary world. But its relevance is currently confined to about four or five of the world's almost 200 existent states. As several critics have noted, most modern states are culturally heterogeneous, containing within their borders two or more distinct nations. As Will Kymlicka has noted, 'the world's 184 independent states contain over 600 living language groups, and 5,000 ethnic groups' (quoted in Carens 2000: 52). The Aboriginals of Australia, the Quebecois and the indigenous peoples of Canada, and the Native Americans in the United States, are all examples of separate minority nations embodying different 'ways of life' within modern liberal democratic states. Indeed, it is sensitivity to the claims for cultural or national autonomy of these groups (linked as these claims are to issues of cultural *survival*) that has led one observer to criticise the partialist claim that it should be the political community in these states that has the sole prerogative to control entry. Will Kymlicka (1989: ch. 11) argues that rather than the entry prerogatives of states being a way of ensuring the flourishing of distinct ways of life, they can seriously undermine the cultural claims of minority nations within the state, especially if the majority of the political community favour relatively open entry policies. Kymlicka's argument involves taking seriously the claim that the right to cultural autonomy should involve a right to control entry. If one upholds the right of national self-determination it is most unclear why the state – at least in multinational societies – should be the privileged site for making decisions on entry.[11]

[11] In many countries, including Canada and Australia, indigenous groups do have certain rights to control entry to the reservations and territories on which they live; see Kymlicka (1989).

The political account of membership

Now it could be argued that the plight of minority nations simply indicates that the dominant political community and the minority nations *both* should enjoy a prerogative to control entry in order to protect their ways of life. For instance, in the case of Australia, not only should minority Aboriginal groups which claim title to certain territories be able to exclude, so too should the (predominantly) European community that currently controls the state, and whose practices are dominant in Australian society. However, it is argued by some, call them adherents to the *political account of membership*, that a closer examination of the dominant 'community' in most Western states illustrates the contingent relationship between cultural forms and state boundaries. If the idea of citizenship in a democratic state means anything as a way of life, it involves a general commitment by citizens to liberal or social democratic institutions and to rights that accrue to individuals *independent* of membership. To be sure, each Western state possesses a distinct narrative of founding, or a history which tells how these values and commitments came to be embodied in the state. But the resulting political practices and institutions are remarkable for their similarity. What the citizens of large and diverse liberal democratic states primarily share, then, is not membership in a single cultural or ethnic community, but a commitment to a political culture – that is, to a framework of institutions and rights that enables individuals to pursue different and diverse ways of life.[12]

The political account of membership draws strength from the fact that most Western states are highly integrative, at least in principle. The process of attaining membership (becoming naturalised) in Western states normally requires only that participants acknowledge their faith in certain liberal and democratic principles and possess the language skills necessary to understand and join in political practices, and not that they possess ties of religion or blood to the dominant community.[13] Nowhere is the

[12] As Habermas argues with reference to the modern state, the 'concept of popular sovereignty does not refer to some substantive collective will which would owe its identity to a prior homogeneity of descent or form of life. The consensus achieved in the course of argument in an association of free and equal citizens stems in the final instance from an identically applied procedure recognised by all. This procedure for political will formation assumes a differentiated form in the constitution of a democratic state' (Habermas 1992: 4).

[13] Western states do differ in the degree to which their laws encourage or allow the naturalisation of foreigners. Germany has traditionally been more reluctant to turn foreigners into citizens than almost any other Western state. The Federal Republic has only recently begun to abandon the exclusive conception of citizenship which sees membership in the dominant ethnic community as a prerequisite for membership in the state. (For an historical explanation of the prevalence of this exclusive conception of citizenship,

existence of this type of a political culture more in evidence than in the United States. In reference to this example, Kent and Scanlan argue:

> [While] it makes good sense to speak of intersubjective values that are attributable to the nation as a whole, and in terms of which people identify themselves with as citizens . . . the unity that these values provide the nation cannot plausibly be considered to imply basic agreement about what ethnically or ideologically constitutes 'our own way of life'. On the contrary, it more likely reflects an implicit moral agreement about how the nation's social and political institutions ought to be governed, *given the fact that individuals disagree* fundamentally over what that way of life is or ought to be. (Scanlan and Kent 1988: 86)

Now while adherents to the political account cannot appeal to cultural or ethnic factors as a basis for excluding outsiders, they still have some grounds for controlling entrance. It is consistent with this view, for instance, that new residents share the political values of the community in which they wish to reside. Nonetheless, viewing states as a site of agreement only on political values does reduce the degree of discretion that states might legitimately claim to construct entrance policy.

One reason why this is so is that to the extent that the citizens of any particular modern Western state constitute a human community of people sharing common values, they most clearly are not a community that ends at the borders of the state. If one accepts that a political culture is the limit of what is shared amongst the members of modern multicultural societies, then it is clear that this way of life is not unique to any single state. The shared Western beliefs in the importance of democracy and of certain minimal rights are examples of these kinds of cross-state understandings. Indeed, the political philosopher, Charles Taylor, has argued that the conception of the individual rights-bearing subject that dominates liberal societies is dependent upon an entire 'civilisation' to support it (Taylor 1985: 206). Yet if what is shared by those inside the state cannot differentiate them from those outside the state, the key distinction between members and strangers on which the partialist defence of the entry prerogatives of states is based is seriously weakened.

But even if one were to accept contiguity between political culture and state boundaries, arguments based on an appeal to political or civic values provide a far weaker justification for state discretion in entry than general cultural arguments. What lent credibility to the partialist argument for extensive discretionary rights, it will be remembered, was the belief that the threat new entrants could pose to a particular culture was best judged

see Brubaker (1990).) This kind of exclusive conception stands in stark contrast to the policies of nation-building states like Australia and the US which actively encourage immigrants to become naturalised.

by the *members* of that culture. However, if what is being protected is a political culture, it is far less obvious why such discretion on behalf of current members is justified. The preservation of the political culture of any Western state appears entirely compatible with large increases in the number of entrants as long as they are committed to democratic values. Refugees, for instance, are often the most committed of immigrants to the political practices of their new country of residence, simply because they realise that there is no realistic option for them to return to their original homeland.[14] One might still want to grant the current members of the state the right to close their borders in situations where there were clear threats to the state's political culture or something else of great value. But there is little reason to believe that the interests of citizens should, as some partialists would have it, be the *sole* basis on which to determine whether or not certain groups of outsiders should be accepted for entry.

The modified partialist account of membership

The political account of membership offers, I believe, an important corrective to the view that what distinguishes citizens from strangers is the sharing of a common culture. But one could be forgiven for thinking that adherents of the political view see the modern state as no kind of community whatsoever – as an arbitrary collection of people sharing similar political values. Yet this picture does not seem accurate. As Will Kymlicka has suggested, 'it does not explain why the world is divided into almost two hundred separate countries. If principles of freedom and equality are the basis of political legitimacy, why don't all democratic countries become amalgamated into one unified country?' (1993: 376).

How can we explain the special attachment that citizens of large, culturally heterogeneous liberal democracies feel for their compatriots? The partialist claim that citizens share something more than simply political values seems to have some force here. For modern political communities are characterised by relations of solidarity amongst members; in important respects, citizens view their own fate as especially entwined with that of their compatriots. Just how this citizen solidarity is formed is not easy to explain, not least because the factors that bond citizens together can vary across states. Nonetheless, time invariably plays a key role: the simple fact that groups of diverse people share the same territory and political structures over a long period creates habits of cooperation, a sense of

[14] Judith Shklar has argued powerfully for the unique loyalty of refugees and other exiles in Shklar (1993).

common implication, and feelings of trust that cement the bonds of community. In many instances, the kinds of cultural and ethnic similarities emphasised by partialists – the sharing of historical experiences, a common language, the development of shared practices and understandings – also assist in the creation of bonds amongst a large swathe (if not all) of the membership of modern states. It's hard to deny, moreover, that the bonds resulting from these commonalities are often crucial to the success of the redistributive programmes associated with social democracy. If national welfare programmes, disaster assistance, regional subsidies and the like are to find support at the national level, members must believe that they have obligations not only to those in their region, class or ethnic group but to their fellow citizens *qua* citizens. It should not surprise us that the US, widely seen as the exemplar of a state whose members share only political values, is arguably also the least social democratic of Western states. In the course of the twentieth century, immigrant societies have often proven less successful than ethnically homogeneous ones, such as the Scandanavian countries, in forging ties between citizens that ground public support for redistributive measures (Walzer 1995: 248).[15]

The view of the state as community presented above shares affinities with the partialist view: both, for instance, recognise the importance of solidarity in maintaining liberal egalitarian politics. Yet the former view of membership – let us call it the modified partialist account – need not vindicate the glamorised picture of the modern state, along with its implausibly intimate and homogeneous way of life, that partialists present. For while it is important to recognise that the citizens of liberal democracies share a common identity – they view themselves as Swedes, Americans or Australians, for instance – it is misleading to exaggerate the commonalities that underlie this identity. In large and culturally complex modern societies the content of the identity shared by citizens (the *state's* identity) typically changes over time and is, at any particular point in time, a matter of great dispute. This is true even of states that tightly control entrance to their territory. According to Bhiku Parekh, for instance, the content of British identity 'has changed considerably over the centuries and it is not defined in the same way today as it was before the Second World War. The Scots define it quite differently from the way the English and the Welsh do. Moreover, within each group, the definition tends to vary with class and gender' (1994: 102). Needless to say, these competing conceptions of the state's identity provide one reason why citizens often

[15] This argument is probably overstated and not simply because many factors have probably played a role in the scant provision of national welfare in the US. Other immigrant countries, such as Canada and Australia, offer contrary evidence on the compatibility of social welfare programmes and mass migration (Bader 1995: 250).

disagree on whether the state has responsibilities to particular groups of refugees or immigrants. While most citizens of modern liberal democracies have come to feel themselves associated with their state (and their fellow compatriots) in a special way, just what kind of entity citizens see themselves attached to stems from different interpretations of the state's identity and history.

The modified partialist account I have just outlined also seems better placed to account for the key role the state plays in creating and shaping the identity that citizens share. While communitarians often assume that the state is the 'expression of a pre-existing cultural community' (Parekh 1994: 104), it is historically more accurate to recognise the active role that states have played in making their members a community or a nation; the state's historical efforts, in other words, in forging a common citizen identity out of individuals with diverse cultural and ethnic backgrounds. It is, as Parekh argues, 'the state that self-consciously sets about unifying its otherwise diverse members by educational, industrial, cultural, symbolic and other means . . . Most nation states are really state-nations, nations created by states in the dubious pursuit of cultural and moral homogeneity' (1994: 104). Rather than accommodating humankind's cultural diversity, political elites have typically engaged in processes of nation-building, creating a common citizen identity that overrides, undermines or eliminates the cultural attachments of their subjects (see, for example, Smith 2001).

Certain implications for entrance entitlements follow once we recognise the complex ways in which the modern state is a cultural community. Suppose, for the sake of argument, we grant the partialist claim that states have a right to protect their cultural integrity. When we acknowledge that the identity of the state is contested in practice, it is unclear *whose* view of the state's identity ought to inform entrance decisions. While we may believe that the views of the dominant cultural community have the strongest claim, this simply begs the question of how much ethical force the claims of those with alternative interpretations of the state's identity should have. The cultural integrity argument looks even shakier once we recognise that the identity of citizens has itself been constructed by the state. For if the state's ethical legitimacy cannot be derived from its claim to represent an antecedent cultural community, then cultural communities themselves cannot provide any independent support for the exclusive entitlements of states. Furthermore, those cultural affinities that currently do exist might be seen more as a reflection of the exercise of state power in eliminating difference than as the state's accommodation to and respect for the cultural entitlements of its citizens. Given that common citizenship often has been built through the elimination or repression of minority cultures, the state seems a dubious vehicle through which to defend cultural claims.

Where does modifying the partialist view leave the claim that citizens have a right to distribute membership and the availability of asylum according to their own criteria? Once we concede that the meaning of citizen identity is contested, and that states play a large role in the construction of any such identity, we need to change our account of how new entrants might affect the political community. While refugees in large enough numbers might influence the political values of a state, it's hard to see how they could threaten any *objective* cultural unity because national boundaries do not demarcate unified, homogeneous or distinct cultures. Modern states are probably best conceived as *federations* of different cultures (Parekh 2000). The grounds for granting states the discretion to refuse entry to outsiders on the basis of cultural or ethnic criteria thus seem weak. Nonetheless, there are reasons for giving states some discretion. As I have suggested, states are usually the site of a *subjective* cultural unity; the passage of time under the same political institutions – and the actions of states themselves – usually leads to the development of some degree of special attachment amongst citizens. Now if one believes that this solidarity – the sense of sharing in a common social project – is important for redistributive and social democratic programmes, there may well be grounds for allowing states some control of entrance. For while states are rightly seen as vehicles for the construction of a common citizen identity, the task of dealing with large and rapid changes in membership could place enormous strains on citizen solidarity, and, in great enough volume, might even undermine the social importance people attach to citizenship. It seems plausible, then, to join with partialists in allowing states some discretion in controlling the volume and rate of entrance of outsiders, but rejecting partialism's additional claim that states should be free to decide upon the cultural (or ethnic) character of new entrants.

Are states responsible for the harm they cause?

The partialist case for discretion in entrance is built upon the right of citizens to have their culture protected by a sovereign state. The state is seen as a human community whose members are responsible for each other because they interact and cooperate together to reproduce the conditions of their common life. In the previous section I showed that this argument is weakened by the complex relationship between modern states and cultural communities. This line of criticism leaves open one of the central claims of partialism: the assumption that people are responsible primarily to those with whom they share a common life. Would states have any entrance duties to outsiders if the world *were* reorganised such that states and cultures were made contiguous, and territory was divided between states according to a fair procedure? This question, in turn, begs the issue of whether states have any obligations to human beings *qua* human beings – obligations which do not derive from shared membership in a national or cultural community. While I will take up the broader aspects of this issue in more depth in Chapter 2, I want now to consider whether the ability of states greatly to affect the lives of men and women beyond their territory is a matter of ethical significance.

One powerful view is that states have an obligation to refrain from engaging in actions which would 'harm' outsiders, at least where this is clearly avoidable. 'Harming' could be defined here as acting in such a way as to make another party seriously worse off than they otherwise would have been. This standard, often referred to as the 'harm principle', shifts attention in the consideration of the responsibilities of political communities from the state as a 'human community' to the state as an 'agent'; from the state as a relatively static entity which protects the way of life of its members from external threats, to the state as an active shaper of events in the world beyond its territory. The idea of responsibility for harm has long been considered a fundamental moral principle. Writing in the seventeenth century, the natural law theorist, Samuel Pufendorf, could confidently claim that:

> First among the absolute duties is the duty not to harm others. This is at once the most far-reaching of duties, extending as it does to all men as men, and the easiest, since it consists in the mere omission of action, except in so far as passions in conflict with reason must sometimes be restrained. It is also the most essential duty, since without it human social life would be utterly impossible. (Pufendorf 1991: 56)

More recently, the principle has been applied to relations between countries by Brian Barry:[16]

> If one country builds tall smokestacks and pumps sulphur into the atmosphere, which descends on another country downwind in the form of acid rain, then it has injured another and, as a matter of justice, should either clean up its industry or compensate the other country. There need be no reciprocal advantage or even any other form of relationship between the two. (Barry 1991: 170–1)

What creates a duty of justice or a relation of responsibility towards the members of the neighbouring state in this case is that the emission of

[16] The duty not to harm others has been an integral part of liberal thought since at least Mill's *On Liberty* (1989). It is put to use in thinking about the duties of Western states to outsiders in the production of hazardous materials in the work of Henry Shue (1981) and in relation to refugees by Mark Gibney (1986).

sulphur by one state damages the interests of the residents of the other state. The duty not to harm non-citizens imposes a moral constraint on the productive decisions of the first state, regardless of whether the members of the first state consented (even unanimously) to the production process or not. It is easy to see why one would not attach priority to the state's right to discretion in production in this case: the claim of the first state to autonomy is seriously weakened by the fact that the effects of its decisions are not confined to the members of the first state. In this situation it is not enough that the members of the state from which the miasma has emanated give their consent.

It is unlikely that most partialists would explicitly reject the argument derived from the above case that 'harms' visited upon outsiders provide a moral constraint on the right of states independently to determine questions of production. But acknowledging the relevance of harms raises real questions about the adequacy of the partialist account of responsibility. For accepting a principle of responsibility for harm means that the scope of state duties is going to be set not by the borders of the state or the boundaries of the nation, but by the causal reach of the state – the scope of its ability to do harm to individuals.

Is there a case for seeing states as having a duty under the harm principle to accept outsiders for entry? In considering these questions here I will not attempt to present a full account of the duties of states derivable from such a principle. I intend only to call into question the partialist view that states have a right to fashion entrance policy on the basis of their own criteria by showing a *prima facie* case for the existence of such duties.

For the harm principle to be applicable in the realm of entry two things need to be shown: first, that the outsiders seeking entry have actually been harmed (or risk being harmed); second, that the states of attempted entry can be said to be responsible for that harm. There seems no doubt that real harm can be done by the entry policies of states. While many issues of entry and residence involve concerns that are relatively trivial, what is on the line in the case of the refugee or asylum seeker is a matter of strict necessity. The refusal of entrance to a refugee may force that person back to the country from which they fled and into a situation where they risk losing life or limb or being unjustly deprived of their freedom.

The question of whether the states which refugees wish to enter are responsible for the harm done to them is more complex. While there is no doubt that real harm can result from strict entry policies, in what sense can this harm be said to be *inflicted* by the state that refuses to allow the refugee(s) to enter? It is at this point that the force of the harm principle as grounds for expanding the current responsibilities recognised by states begins to waver. For surely the party responsible for the infliction of harm upon the refugee or asylum seeker is their *own* state? It is, after all, that state that has forced them to flee or failed in its duties to protect them.

This is an important argument and one that is echoed in public attitudes towards refugees and asylum seekers. Most people accept that states are responsible (to at least some degree) for the harm they do and that refugees are the victims of harm. They simply deny that *their* (Western) state is responsible. This denial of responsibility is premised upon two dubious assumptions which I shall now challenge. The first is the empirical claim that the harms that generate refugees are caused solely by the states that they have fled; the second is a moral claim that states are responsible only for those refugees whose plight they have directly brought about. In challenging these assumptions, I will distinguish between two kinds of responsibilities incurred under the principle of harm which correspond in turn to two distinct types of harm: *primary responsibilities* are duties to refrain from the harmful actions which serve to create refugees and to compensate those whom one has harmed in this fashion; *secondary responsibilities* are duties to prevent, at least when the costs are low, serious harm coming to those who have already been made refugees by the actions of others.

Assumption I: the West and the creation of refugees

Because they are rarely a source of refugee movements, it is sometimes assumed that liberal democratic states have few or no duties to the world's refugees. The international refugee predicament is commonly seen as the product of tyrannical governments across the globe whose violations of their citizens' rights force people to flee. Indeed, the United Nations' definition of a refugee encourages this perspective: the definition highlights the relationship between citizen and state by defining a refugee as someone who has a well-founded fear of persecution based on discrimination against them on the basis of their race, religion, ethnic origin or political opinions (Zolberg *et al.* 1989: 260). But this view, which sees the emergence of refugees as the result simply of a few bad states, and the solution to the sources of the current crisis as lying thus in respect for human rights by the states of refugee outflow, is inadequate. It sees first-world states as innocent bystanders to harm done by others, and thus systematically denies the role that Western states play in producing the conditions from which refugees are forced to flee. What it ignores is that, in many situations, Western states *cause* or *contribute to* the harm that leads to refugee movements. I will distinguish here between some of the different ways that Western states as external actors can cause harms which lead to the emergence of refugees.

Most obvious of all are situations in which a state is a *major* or *primary cause* of harm. The case of direct foreign military intervention is perhaps the most common example of this kind of primary and externally caused harm. The US and Australian involvement in Indo-China in the 1960s and 1970s was a case where at least some responsibility for the creation of refugees could hardly be denied, not least because in fighting in the Vietnam war, these countries had deeply implicated themselves in the plight of the fleeing men and women. Responsibility to Kurdish refugees at the end of the Gulf War was similarly difficult to gainsay because the US had encouraged Kurds to rise up against Saddam Hussein's regime. More controversially, the NATO bombing campaign might not have been the most direct cause of the expulsion of Kosovan Albanians from the disputed territory in 1999. But the furious response it unleashed linked the NATO countries to the plight of the refugees in a powerful way.

More commonly, a state can harm others by *contributing* to a refugee crisis. In these situations, while the actions of a state are not on their own sufficient to generate a refugee movement, they are still important (or, indeed, crucial) in bringing one about. A further distinction might be made within this category between *negligent* and *non-negligent* actions. *Black's Law Dictionary* (1968) defines a 'negligent' act as one which shows 'a flagrant disregard for the safety of others, or wilful indifference to an injury likely to follow so as to convert an otherwise lawful act into a crime when it results in personal injury or death' (Black 1968: 193). Drawing on this term's moral rather than legal sense, an array of actions by a state might accurately be characterised in this way, for example, the sale and supply of military equipment, such as the sale of chemical weapons by German and British governments to Iraq during the late 1980s and South Africa's provision of arms, including land-mines, to the ruling Hutu majority in Rwanda, arms which were subsequently used in the act of genocide in that state; and the provision of economic and political support for regimes that cause refugee outflows, as in the US's support for dictatorial governments that sponsored or ignored the activities of death squads in Central America during the 1980s.

States can also contribute to the making of refugees through actions that are not usually seen as negligent because they involve consequences that are both unintended and difficult to foresee. Aristide Zolberg, for instance, has pointed to the way refugee-causing regimes can be supported or propped up by external actors:

> external parties by action or inaction can significantly influence the processes that generate refugees. Refugees do not simply appear because they are persecuted by government X or victimised by brutalising rulers in weak states; such governments exist within a necessary structure of international support. (Zolberg *et al.* 1989: 264)

It is at least arguable that the participation of states in the international economic system might also be said to belong to this broad conception of what it is to cause harm. One of the most obvious consequences of the activities of Western states since the end of World War II in pursuing the material conditions necessary for sustaining their way of life has been the development of ever more intimate and systematically interconnected relations between states and outsiders.[17] These relations have increased the capacity of states to affect drastically what happens beyond their borders. The emergence over the last half century of a global economy has not only led to a 'widening economic and demographic rift' between first and third-world countries, but has simultaneously resulted in an '*eclipse of distance* between the two through the mutually reinforcing links of transportation, communication and migration' (Brubaker 1990: 384, my emphasis). The unintended consequences of this increasing intimacy are readily apparent in the role that international economic factors play in creating refugee movements. The conditions of state breakdown and political instability usually associated with the widespread human rights violations that give rise to refugees are often inextricably linked to the position of a state in the world economy.[18] For example, many observers have recently argued that some violent conflicts have emerged because of the destabilising effects of neo-liberal economic policies and structural adjustment forced on countries by Western funded international organisations, such as the IMF and the World Bank.[19] Even ignoring the role of these organisations, the world's poorest, least stable and most insecure states, for instance, have economies that, because they trade in few commodities, are heavily dependent upon international trade, and hence more vulnerable to the capriciousness of international markets than their Western counterparts (Krasner 1993: 314–15).

In order to allocate blame, if blame is the right word, for the creation of many of the world's refugees, it would often seem fairer to turn attention

[17] Partialists rarely mention that the ways of life they see states as justified in protecting are dependent for their survival on certain economic preconditions. The goods that Western citizens associate with social citizenship and modern liberty cannot be provided solely out of the internal resources of a liberal democratic state. To be sure, for the survival of these goods certain conditions need to hold within the state: a certain degree of solidarity amongst the citizens is necessary and the state probably needs to have sufficient resources. But where the defining ingredients of the Western way of life exist they have been attained and ensured through action by the state (and other economic entities protected by it) in the pursuit of economic, military and political goals in the broader international environment.

[18] The complex role that economic factors play in creating dangerous political conditions presents a powerful reason for treating sceptically attempts by Western states to draw a simple distinction between 'economic' and 'political' refugees. See Castles and Miller (1993) and Loescher (1993).

[19] For relevant considerations on this theme, see Chimni (2002), George (2003) and Shiva (2003).

to the workings of the world economy, rather than to the source state, itself often a victim of forces that it can neither shape nor stem.[20] There are grounds, then, for seeing all states that participate in the world economy as responsible to some extent for its undesirable consequences. It is, however, hard to see how the harm done by any individual participant could be sufficiently direct to make it responsible for any particular group of refugees.

This last example demonstrates how broadly the principle of 'harm' can be used in arguments concerning the attribution of responsibility. There are real difficulties in deciding when a state has caused enough harm to a particular group of outsiders to warrant it being obliged to resettle them. Yet these complexities concerning the allocation of duties to assist and resettle should not obscure the fact that once we recognise that states are agents whose actions can dramatically affect the lives of those beyond their borders, the moral immunity often claimed by non-refugee-producing states becomes questionable.

Assumption II: inflicting harm and failing to aid

The arguments of those who deny that Western states have responsibilities to refugees also hinge upon a second assumption: that the distinction between inflicting harm and failing to aid is of moral significance. Western states do not inflict harm on refugees, it is argued, that is done by their own state, they (merely) refrain from preventing harm occurring. Given that it is the act of inflicting harm that creates a duty, Western states have no obligations to asylum seekers under this principle. The distinction between harming and failing to aid has a long pedigree. Pufendorf (quoted above) appeals to it implicitly when he argues that the duty not to harm others is the 'easiest' of absolute duties because 'it consists in the mere *omission* of action' (emphasis added). For Pufendorf, the duty of individuals not to harm is confined to a responsibility to refrain from injuring others.

In more recent times, considerable intellectual energy has been expended on the attempt to limit the duties under the principle of harm to the requirement of refraining from certain actions.[21] All of these attempts, however, find great difficulty in dealing with a range of cases where the

[20] The links between the international economy and refugees are also evident in the case of asylum seekers. It is no coincidence that a substantial percentage of the applicants for asylum in European countries emanate from states that have either strong political or economic links with the country in which they wish to reside.

[21] See Feinberg (1984: ch. 4) for an impressive rebuttal of a range of different attempts to deny that failures to render assistance breach the principle of harm.

costs of aiding are relatively minor and the negative consequences of withholding aid to individuals are both dire and imminent. In these situations, it is virtually impossible to draw a convincing moral distinction between acting and failing to act.[22] Consider, for example, the case of the asylum seeker. Can a state deny that it is inflicting harm when it forcibly turns an individual back at its borders, driving them home and into a situation of grave danger? In this situation, the state becomes responsible for the asylum seeker simply because the direct consequences of repudiating such responsibility are so dire and so clearly apparent. Again, it is important that few partialists who directly consider this issue deny the existence of secondary responsibilities to those at risk.[23] Michael Walzer, for instance, sees the claim for asylum as 'virtually undeniable' at the extreme. He argues that states are bound to grant asylum for two reasons: first, 'because its denial would require us to use force against helpless and desperate people' and, second, 'because the numbers involved, except in unusual cases, are likely to be small and easily absorbed' (Walzer 1981: 51).

It must be said that the difficulty of denying (secondary) responsibilities for asylum seekers raises as many questions as it answers: if it is immoral to deny the entry of necessitous people at the border, what are we to make of the way states use deterrent and preventative measures (such as detaining or imprisoning asylum seekers and fining airlines for accepting passengers without the required visa) which aim to reduce the number of needy people who arrive at their borders? What duties do states have today where for some the number of people claiming asylum in any one year can amount to hundreds of thousands? But the plight of those seeking asylum does show that no bright line between inflicting harm and failing to aid is available to furnish Western states with moral immunity, especially when the costs of assisting are low.

If one accepts that states have at least some responsibilities to asylum seekers, then they may also have a range of derivative responsibilities to other states. It is apparent in the contemporary world that states are not equally effective at sealing their borders from claims to asylum. While some are able to insulate themselves from refugee flows, many face huge

[22] The distinction between harming and failing to aid is an example of a wider ethical debate over the differences between acts and omissions. The work of Peter Singer has presented a sustained, though not always convincing, attack on this distinction. For a discussion of its applicability with regard to the actions of Western states *vis-à-vis* refugees, see Singer and Singer (1988) and Carens (1992b).

[23] It is significant also that *non-refoulement* (the principle that a state should not force a non-citizen to return to a territory where his or her life would be threatened) is the primary customary international law rule that limits the sovereignty of states in entry. In practice, this principle has often amounted to a virtual duty of asylum. See Martin (1991).

burdens in entry because of their proximity to the source of refugee movements, the fact that they have long land borders, and/or the fact that they have previously settled large numbers of refugees from the source country of the refugee flow. Is it right that the number of asylum seekers that Australia took in 1993 amounted to a few thousand, while Germany was obliged to process the claims of hundreds of thousands? Should the duties of states depend upon the caprice of geography? Once one acknowledges that states have a duty to accept asylum seekers, the issue of justly distributing the asylum burden between states emerges. The state's acceptance of a duty to grant asylum may thus prove hard to separate from its acknowledgement of obligations to other states (Gibney 2000b).

What, then, are the implications of the principle of harm for the partialist argument? First, if one accepts that this principle constitutes an important standard of right, then it is hard to deny that Western states have some primary responsibilities, at least to those refugees whom they have been crucial in generating. Indeed, one partialist, Michael Walzer, acknowledges that in the cases where the harm is sufficiently direct, states may be obliged to accept the refugees for entry:

> Towards some refugees, we may well have obligations of the same sort we have towards fellow nationals. This is obviously the case with regard to any group of people whom we have helped turn into refugees. The injury we have done to them makes for an affinity between us: thus Vietnamese refugees had, in a moral sense, been effectively Americanized before they arrived on these shores. (Walzer 1983: 49)

Any argument against giving at least some weight to the claims of outsiders is clearly undermined once one accepts the existence of such responsibilities. But what of duties a state has to those refugees it has only contributed to generating? There is, I think, room for legitimate debate in allocating responsibility in this case. At the least, however, states should cease or modify their actions so that they minimise any harm to foreigners. Beyond this, a recognition of the many and varied ways – intentional and unintentional – in which external actors contribute to refugee creation adds to the moral case for the participation of Western states in schemes to share the refugee burden. Second, the case of secondary responsibilities illustrates the intimate connection between accepting a duty not to harm and giving positive assistance to those in need when the costs are low when the danger to the outsider is severe and imminent. If partialists accept a role for the principle of harm, they can hardly deny that states have responsibilities, within reason, to those seeking asylum at their borders. Taken together, the existence of primary and secondary responsibilities for harm provides strong moral reasons for rejecting the view that states should be free to make entrance decisions according to their own criteria. In a world where global forces bring the interests of citizens and the needs of outsiders increasingly into conflict, acknowledging these responsibilities would have profound implications for the entrance policies of states.

Conclusion

Partialists raise a number of ethical concerns that cannot be ignored in the search for a morally defensible criterion for the response of states to refugees. Foremost amongst these is the way that membership in a modern state involves the sharing of a common identity. While they tend to overstate the sense in which the modern state is a community, partialists rightly stress that states are something more than a set of legal institutions or collection of individuals sharing similar political values. Those who see the world of states simply as a 'giant supermarket . . . where [one's] place of residence is to be decided by the particular basket of goods (jobs, amenities, climate, etc.) available there' are, as David Miller has observed, missing something (Miller 1995: 14). In their emphasis on identity, partialists speak to very powerful sentiments in the modern world. Many of the world's denizens are deeply attached to their country of citizenship and to their compatriots; many others, like the Kosovans, the Palestinians and the East Timorese seek protection for their cultural or ethnic identity by gaining their own state. These people seek a state for the same reason that those with states believe they have the right to control entrance: they feel entitled to reproduce their identity over time through political institutions run by their fellow nationals. If people have the right to preserve their citizen identity – or to construct one – it is difficult to deny the moral force of this claim.

But even if we do not see identities based on citizenship as ideal from an ethical point of view, we may still have reasons for allowing states some degree of control over entrance. For the solidarities which spring from collective identities often play a key role in grounding cooperative ventures to improve the plight of the weakest members of modern societies (and in responding to the needy outside the state). In other words, for many people, shared citizenship itself offers a reason for assisting those in need. Can we be confident that taking admission decisions from those who currently share an identity – and have used that identity to create a relatively just society – would improve the situation of the world's most vulnerable? This is a question I will examine in greater depth in Chapter 2.

What I hope to have shown here, however, is that, in spite of its appeal, the partialist claim that states should be free to decide admissions according to their own criteria faces significant problems which weaken its claim to be the authoritative standard of value for entrance. The ethical force of any community's claim to control entrance cannot ultimately be separated from the moral legitimacy of the modern state. In its defence of wide-ranging entrance rights, partialism sidelines many features of modern states that make them dubious claimants for moral immunity from the interests of outsiders. When the state's right to its own territory, the elision of state boundaries and cultural communities, and the state's claim to choose freely for itself alone are all brought into question, the moral case for allowing states (and their citizens) to be judges in their own cases on entrance decisions is less than compelling.

Partialism upholds the claims to justice of people as members of political communities. It emphasises the entitlement of citizens to preserve their shared way of life and, along with it, the social and economic goods associated with this way of life. In so doing, it sharpens our awareness of the potential hazards of more inclusive policies towards outsiders. Partialism's claim for the priority of citizen interests is hardly an unfamiliar moral claim, located as it is at the centre of contemporary debates about the entrance of immigrants and refugees. But this claim ultimately relies on the legitimacy of privileging the claims of citizens over those of strangers. While partialism sheds light on the historical advantages of citizen priority, the costs have included the brutal fate that has awaited those who claim membership in extremely unpleasant or dangerous states or, like the refugee, claim effective membership in none at all. In Chapter 2, we will see how the claims of refugees fare in ethical approaches that refuse to privilege the claims of citizens over those of outsiders.

2 Impartiality: freedom, equality and open borders

> If it be said that so broadly marked a distinction between what is due to a fellow countryman and what is due merely to a human creature is more worthy of savages than of civilized beings, and ought, with the utmost energy to be contended against, no one holds that opinion more strongly than myself.
>
> John Stuart Mill 1993 [1861]

> Citizenship in the modern world is a lot like feudal status in the medieval world. It is assigned at birth; for the most part it is not subject to change by the individual's will and efforts; and it has a major impact upon a person's life chances . . . Liberals objected to the way feudalism restricted freedom, including the freedom to move from one place to another in search of a better life. But the modern practices of citizenship and state control over borders tie people to the land of their birth almost as effectively.
>
> Joseph H. Carens 1992a

In Chapter 1 we saw both the force and the limitations of the partial viewpoint as an ethical guide for states in responding to refugees. Let us now turn to the dominant theoretical alternative to this perspective, the impartial view. Partialists, it will be remembered, worked with an ideal of states as cultural communities, claiming a right of self-determination on behalf of their citizens which justified exclusive privileges in entrance. Impartialism, in contrast, works with an ideal of states as cosmopolitan moral agents, and sees states as morally required to take into equal account the interests or rights of citizens and foreigners in entrance decisions. It requires, in other words, that states consider impartially the claims of members and strangers alike. The best-known perspectives expounding this view are global liberalism and utilitarianism. In a world where states generally claim the prerogative to include and exclude foreigners as they please, impartialism represents a radical challenge not only to the partial view, but also to well-entrenched state practices.

Notwithstanding its radical implications, impartialism is often seen as the traditional moral point of view. The impartial view is linked as an ideal to the idea of universalisability – the belief that if a particular action or policy is genuinely impartial it must be the morally appropriate choice for anyone to make who faces the same set of circumstances (Friedman 1992: 933). The consequences of applying the criterion of impartiality to entry policy for Western states, as relatively attractive places of residence in a world marked by dramatic inequalities, seem enormous. As Michael Walzer has noted, 'affluent and free countries are, like elite universities, besieged by applicants' (1983: 32).

Liberals and utilitarians

The consequences of applying the principle of impartiality to entrance decisions have been illustrated in recent writings by global liberals and utilitarians.[1] While most writers in the major impartialist strands of political theory have ignored questions of entrance, concentrating – in spite of the univeralist languages of these theories – on the reciprocal duties of citizens (Black 1991; Booth 1997), those few who have considered these issues almost invariably argue for radical changes in the policies of current states. For global liberals operating within a rights-based framework, such as Joseph Carens (1992a), Ann Dummett (1992) and Michael Dummett (2001), current entrance restrictions on immigrants and refugees are a gross violation of human liberty. Taking seriously the universalistic implications of liberalism, they argue that the right of a community to fashion its own entrance policy is circumscribed morally by the right of all individuals to reside wherever they wish.

Liberal writers use different bases to ground this right. Carens, for instance, argues that support for a right of individuals to move and settle freely in different countries can be derived from the work of John Rawls. In *A Theory of Justice* (1971) Rawls argues that the basic structure of a society is just if it is consistent with principles that would be chosen by individuals in a hypothetical 'original position' in which the participants are deprived of the kind of knowledge (e.g., their race, gender, talents etc.) that would enable them to tailor principles to their personal advantage. Individuals in the original position are thus under what Rawls describes as a 'veil of ignorance', a hypothetical set of knowledge constraints designed to ensure that the social principles consented to are impartial, fair and just. According to Rawls, people bound by these conditions of fairness would agree to two principles. First, they would consent to the priority of liberty, what Rawls calls the 'Basic Liberties Principle' (1971: 60–4); the right of

[1] In addition to the writers discussed in this chapter, the principle of impartiality is applied to entrance policy by Ackerman (1980: 89–95) and Hudson (1986: 51–62).

individuals to certain basic civil and political liberties (such as rights to a fair trial, freedom of speech, freedom of movement). Second, participants would agree to distribute the fruits of social and economic cooperation in a way that maximised the benefits accruing the least well-off members of society. This Rawls describes as the 'Difference Principle' (1971: 60–4).

While Rawls' principles focus on a single, closed society, Carens extends the logic of original position globally – to humankind as a whole – in order to examine the justice of entrance restrictions imposed by states. According to Carens, people in a global original position would choose a right of free movement *between* states for exactly the same reasons that individuals in Rawls' contract would support free movement *within* states – both are usually essential to individuals' life plans and to the realisation of other liberties (Carens 1987: 258; 1992a: 26–8). In Carens' view:

> [e]very reason why one might want to move within a state might also be a reason for moving between states. One might want a job; one might fall in love with someone from another country; one might belong to a religion that has few adherents in one's native state and many in another. (1992a: 27–8)

The liberty to move freely would, Carens argues, form a crucial part of the life plans of individuals even in a world where political and economic security was evenly distributed across states. However, in the current global context, characterised by great inequalities between countries, the case for a right of free movement is even stronger. For membership in a state does a great deal more than simply allocate living space; it largely determines the standard of living, public goods and the amount of political security an individual will enjoy over the course of his or her lifetime. By virtue of its powerful consequences, citizenship in the modern world is, Carens argues, 'a lot like feudal status in the medieval world. It is assigned at birth; for the most part it is not subject to change by the individual's will and efforts; and it has a major impact upon that person's life chances' (1992a: 26). Just as liberals first banded together to attack the restrictions and inherited inequalities of feudalism, so liberals must now challenge 'modern practices of citizenship and state control over borders that tie people to the land of their birth almost as effectively' (1992a: 26–7).

The belief that entrance restrictions violate freedom has been echoed by other liberals. In *On Immigration and Refugees* (2001) the philosopher Michael Dummett takes as his starting point the claim that respect for human freedom places the onus on states to provide legitimate grounds for the exclusion of foreigners. Believing that virtually all such grounds are morally unsound or practically inapplicable to Western states, Dummett concludes that 'the idea that national frontiers should everywhere be open should become far more than a remote aspiration: it should become a principle recognised by all as the norm' (2001: 72–3).

Other writers attempt to derive an open borders position from current state practices. Ann Dummett, for instance, argues that support for a right of free movement can be derived from the deep commitment that liberals have for the right of individuals to emigrate, a right that has come to be embodied in international law. 'Logically', Dummett argues,

> it is an absurdity to assert [a right to emigrate] . . . without a complementary right of immigration unless there exists in fact . . . a number of states which allow free entry. At present, no such state exists and the right of emigration is not, and cannot be in these circumstances, a general human right exercisable in practice. (1992: 173)

Liberal states that support the right to exit are thus bound on pain of contradiction to open their borders to those who wish to enter. Robert Goodin points to another contradiction when he suggests that there is something hypocritical in the way liberal states support free international movement of goods and services while restricting the free movement of people (1992: 12–13).

Most of these liberal writers weld together deontological claims about the importance of individual liberty with more consequentialist (and thus empirically contingent) claims about the role of borders in reproducing poverty in their arguments in support of free international movement (Bader 1997: 28). Utilitarians, such as Peter Singer and Renata Singer, on the other hand, concentrate exclusively on the consequences of restrictive entrance practices. In their article, 'The Ethics of Refugee Policy' (1988), Singer and Singer examine the legitimacy of the current entrance policies of liberal states through a utilitarian lens. Arguing that the universal demands of morality require adherence to the principle of the equal consideration of all interests, they lambast current immigration policies which privilege the economic, political and social concerns of citizens. The equal consideration principle which, the Singers suggest, simply encapsulates widespread views on human equality, requires that

> immigration policy should be based on the interests of all those affected, either directly or indirectly, whether as an immediate result of policy or in the long run. Where the different parties conflict, we would attempt to give equal consideration to all interests, which would mean that the more pressing, more fundamental interests take precedence over the less pressing, less fundamental. (1988: 121–2)

Liberal democratic states are obliged to increase their intake of new entrants, taking into account both the benefit to them and the costs to residents, until the costs to current residents outweigh the benefits accruing to new entrants.

Singer and Singer's starting point of equal consideration of all interests biases the composition of any morally sound entrance policy in favour of refugees. For the claim of refugees for entrance is often based on interests as fundamental as the interest in life itself (1988: 128). But not only would the *composition* of entrants be changed by adherence to the utilitarian calculus; the *volume* of immigrants accepted by states would also increase dramatically. Indeed Singer and Singer argue that the requirement of equal consideration might oblige states to accept refugees up to the point that

> the resident community had eliminated all luxuries that imperilled the environment, and yet the basic needs of an expanding population were putting such pressure on fragile ecological systems that a further expansion would do irreparable harm . . . Or . . . [when] tolerance in a multicultural society was breaking down because of resentment among the resident community . . . and this loss of tolerance might reach a point where it was a serious danger to the peace and security of all previously accepted refugees and immigrants from other cultures. (1988: 127–8)

In spite of their methodological differences, global liberals and utilitarians are at one in demanding far more open borders. For all these theorists the requirements of morality are *universal*, owed to human beings *qua* human beings. Global liberals and utilitarians acknowledge no prima facie reason for respecting the 'special obligations' that grow out of membership in a political community or a nation. Our fellow citizens or nationals have no greater or lesser claim to our ethical concern than anyone else.

This does not mean that impartialists recognise an unlimited obligation on states to admit foreigners. Utilitarians, as we have seen, view constraints on entry as legitimate when the costs to the state of admitting one more individual would be greater than the benefit to the individual concerned. Rights-based impartialists concede to the state a range of narrowly defined moral grounds for entrance restrictions. Global liberals, for example, typically see states as justified in introducing restrictions if additional entrants would jeopardise public order, national security or the maintenance of liberal institutions. Ann Dummett, for instance, contends that

> if and only if, the exercise by great numbers of people of their right to move threatened the fundamental human rights of other individuals, the right to move could properly be limited and this limitation could be imposed by state authorities which have a duty to preserve human rights within their jurisdictions. On this view, the collective interest of a receiving society could not be weighed against the individual's right to move, in the sense that the interests of an economy, a culture or a theory of the nation could not be advanced against the right. (1992: 177)

Some, however, would allow other grounds for closure. Carens argues that culturally homogeneous states, like Japan, might have legitimate reasons for limiting entry based on the preservation of their collective culture (Carens 1992a).[2] Michael Dummett asserts that a national group has the right to exclude when it is 'in genuine danger of being [culturally] submerged' by foreigners or when more migration would result in 'serious overpopulation' (2001: 73). These are, according to the writers concerned, very limited concessions, and, in any respect, not applicable to culturally diverse and relatively underpopulated Western states.

In the impartial view, the current entry practices of Western states seem to fall a long way short of what is morally required. While the demand for entrance to Western states is probably large enough to justify the limits in global liberal or utilitarian terms,[3] no Western state (including, as we shall see, Germany, which has accepted vast numbers of asylum seekers in recent years) comes close to allowing entry in this fashion. What we need, according to Michael Dummett, is 'a complete transformation of current Western attitudes to immigration' (2001: 74).

The force of impartiality

The strength of the impartialist account of the entry responsibilities of modern states lies in its inclusiveness. The *only* good reasons for restricting the entry of outsiders into a particular state are reasons that could be justified to *all* members and non-members alike. While partialism attached great importance to the cultural and political particularity of human existence, impartialism's force derives from its attempt to capture human commonality. All individuals, regardless of their membership, share in common the ability to suffer or to be deprived of liberty. Why should nationality or citizenship make any difference to the obligations we have to our fellow human beings? In a world where technology thrusts human beings of different cultures and nationalities into ever closer proximity, impartiality pits itself against the potential for capricious judgement by states on an issue as important to human aspirations and life-chances as where one lives.

The roots of the modern idea of universal justification derive from the Christian idea that human beings are all members of a single human community. As I showed in Chapter 1, the original commonality of the world placed the onus, as all of the great natural law theorists of property were aware, on those who wished to depart from this principle by

[2] Carens' most recent reflections on open borders can be found in Carens (1999).

[3] Though, interestingly, impartial theorists often attempt to evade the full demands of their principles by denying that immigration would occur in much greater volume in a world of open borders; see, for instance, Carens (1987: 249–250).

justifying the existence of exclusive or private property. For believers, the natural constituency of ethical justification was the human community in its entirety. As contemporary references to human rights testify, scepticism over the existence of God has not completely undermined the belief that something is owed to human beings *qua* human beings.

As a theory of the legitimate conditions under which states could claim rightful control of territory and thus justify the prerogative to exclude outsiders, the principle of impartiality still retains great cogency and simplicity. It is difficult to gainsay the ethical force of the claim that Joseph Carens says has been central to all his writings on immigration control: 'Exclusion has to be justified' (1999: 1083). Furthermore, it does not take much to see that the current territorial claims of states, in conjunction with their restrictive entry policies, are incapable of impartial justification. Impartialists are aware of the fact that state boundaries do not simply demarcate different cultural forms. National borders mark off a world carved up amongst states in a vastly uneven manner – a world of the most blatant inequalities in population density, natural resources and wealth. Restrictions on entry stand as a barrier to a more equal world by helping to protect the privileges of those who live in the richest, least-crowded states. Given that immigration and refugee movements are driven primarily by inequality – inequality in the provision of welfare and security between states – impartialism would seem to provide a principled justification for the redistribution of large numbers of people from poorer to richer countries.

The huge break that impartialism seems to require with current practices provides a good reason for subjecting its central claims to critical scrutiny. In what remains of this chapter, I will consider the adequacy of impartialist argument for open borders. I will begin by considering the claim that open borders are the logical outcome of other liberal commitments, such as the right to leave a state. I will then consider the implications of open borders for social and economic inequalities by considering the likely impact of free movement for the welfare state. My discussion will conclude by considering whether the impartial view offers an exhaustive account of the obligations of individuals and, derivatively, those of states. By highlighting some of the deficiencies in the impartialist position, we will be in a better position to derive an ideal account of the responsibilities of states to refugees.

Liberal inconsistencies?

Impartialists, as we have seen, commonly point to a range of inconsistencies in the current commitments of liberals to support the case for open borders. Let us consider these putative inconsistencies in turn. The first is the way liberals support the free movement of people *within* states – their right to 'change membership in subnational communities at will' (Carens 1992a: 27) – as an important value, while refusing to support free movement *across* states. Carens persuasively argues that the reasons why an individual might want to move internationally are no less compelling than his or her reasons for moving domestically. Do liberals have a response to this apparent double standard? They can start by noting that the inconsistency at issue here is not quite as stark as it may first appear. All sorts of restrictions apply on the movement of people within the liberal state (Perry 1995: 108–9). As Carens himself acknowledges, restrictions exist to protect private property (one can't simply take up residence on someone else's front lawn), national interests (states usually reserve large areas for military purposes, etc.) and certain vulnerable collectivities (such as indigenous groups claiming traditional lands).

Furthermore, it is unclear why such inconsistencies as do exist between internal and external migration should be addressed by opening national borders rather than imposing greater restrictions on internal movement. This is the position, for example, of Brian Barry (1992). He argues that there are often compelling reasons why governments should restrict movement inside a state. Barry points, in particular, to the importance of protecting culturally unique and highly valued areas, such as Wales or the Lake District, endangered by mass migration. He also suggests that restrictions can sometimes be justified to lessen the inegalitarian and socially disruptive effects of migration. To this end, he cites the negative consequences of the post-World War II movement of southern blacks to Chicago and New York (1992: 284–5). The pressure for migration in this case, he argues, would have best been dealt with by moving jobs, resources and opportunities to the southern US states rather than by allowing migration north.

Barry's examples demonstrate that there may be important reasons for limiting free movement within the state when doing so serves social ends valued by liberals or promotes equality. Of course, the existence and defensibility of such restrictions does not completely nullify the cry of double standards. However, it's plausible that the case for limiting movement *between* states would be much stronger than the case for restrictions within them. For the volume of potential mass movement (due to the degree of international inequality and the numbers of people involved), and thus the potential adverse consequences, are much greater. Therefore, we might indeed concede that a double standard between domestic and international practices exists, and that rectifying this disparity requires more inclusive entrance policies. But this concession is a long way from accepting that free movement – which is neither a reality nor morally uncontestable at the domestic level – is required for eliminating the double standard.

A second argument marshalled for open borders is the moral inconsistency between a globalised world where the free movement of capital, goods, services and information is encouraged, but where the international migration of labour is largely restricted. If investors can search for the best return on their money, why shouldn't workers be able to seek out the best return on their labour? This question has moral force largely because of the appalling conditions and pay to which the majority of the world's labouring people are subject, but does the analogy support the case for open borders? Only, I think, if one believes that the movement of people raises the same issues as the movement of capital, goods and investment. And there are strong reasons for seeing the issues related to the movement of people as unique. Inward flows of immigrants change 'the shape of the community that acts in the world' (1983: 61–2), as Michael Walzer has argued. To be sure, foreign investment and trade may also reshape the character of a state. But the consequences of mass migration are qualitatively different. Immigration can influence a public culture directly by changing things as profound as the dominant language. More importantly, immigrants in a liberal polity must eventually become part of the *demos*. They are therefore given a direct say in the character, priorities, and decisions of governments, and thus in how the community evolves over time.

Yet people and money do not only differ in the way they impact upon a society. They are also different in how they may be treated. We see this clearly when we flip the question of entry around and consider the circumstances under which foreign investment or immigrants can be *removed* from a state. Closing a state to international trade or foreign investment always remains within the legitimate power of a political community. During the 1970s, parts of the Australian Labour party and many unions in Australia advocated 'buying back the farm'. They wanted to purchase land, property and enterprises in foreign (typically US and Japanese) ownership to place them in domestic hands. This may have been an unwise policy option, but few would deny that it was one that the Australian voters had the right to choose if they so wished. Foreign investors could not plausibly claim a moral entitlement to keep investing in Australia (though they had a legitimate claim to compensation for losses occurring as a result of this policy). By contrast, the expulsion of long-term legal (and, more controversially, illegal) immigrants would be immoral, regardless of the wishes of the Australian electorate. Once people have put down roots in a place for an extended period of time, they have a moral right to remain living where they are based on the attachments they have made and the hardships uprooting them would exact.[4] There is no analogous moral claim for the removal of property, goods or money. This difference is justifiably reflected in entrance policy as well. Because immigration gives rise to unique moral responsibilities, it is understandable that states use different criteria to govern the entrance of people than trade and investment.

The liberal inconsistency most commonly pointed to by impartialists is between widespread support for emigration rights and the rejection of a corresponding right to enter. Once again, this claim has intuitive implausibility. Surely if a state that refuses to allow its citizens to exit (as, for instance, the Soviet Union did up to 1989) is violating a basic human liberty, so too are states that refuse to allow entrance to that state's citizens? Presented in this form, the argument for open borders seems strong. However, a closer consideration of the nature of the right of emigration that is widely supported by liberal democratic states muddies the water considerably.

One problem with this argument is that it rests upon the false assumption that the (current international law) right of emigration is equivalent to a right of individuals to *leave their state*. What the international law right of emigration actually is – and what the widespread liberal understanding of this right is – is a *negative* right; it is a right for an individual not to be held back from exiting his or her state. Two things follow from this understanding of the right at stake: first, the right concerned is not a right to leave or emigrate as such, it is only a right not to be *prevented* from leaving. Second, the duty that corresponds to this right rests unambiguously and completely upon the state that the individual wishes to leave. Only the state concerned is under an obligation not to impede exit.

It is significant and totally in keeping with the confined and negative nature of this right that international law does not see states as having any positive duties to ensure the efficacy of this right by, for instance, providing transport to the border for citizens who cannot afford to leave. The requirements are actually far more minimal, requiring only that states do not actively impede exit. Returning to Dummett's argument, we can make the following observation: if we do not hold the agent with the immediate duty – that is, the state being exited – responsible for the circumstances which make the exercise of this right possible, it hardly seems credible (or logical) to hold another, different state – let alone *all* other states – responsible through the provision of open borders for the existence of an environment favourable for its exercise. This is not to say that that one could not have a more expansive understanding of emigration rights, one

[4] Significantly, Joseph Carens asserts an analogous principle in Carens (1998).

that might entail duties of entrance on behalf of other agents. But it is to say that liberals need not have such an understanding of emigration rights, so their current commitment to rights of exit without rights of entrance is not necessarily contradictory.

Open borders and the welfare state

Most impartialists believe that individuals, in addition to possessing a range of civil and political rights, also possess a range of social rights. To this end, they argue that any liberal state worthy of the name should to some degree be a *welfare state*: the provider of a range of public measures (such as health care, unemployment benefits, etc.) that temper the worst aspects of societal inequality. Moreover, for Singer and Singer, states have no right to restrict the benefits of the welfare state only to citizens. They argue that

> whereas all developed nations safeguard the welfare of their residents in many ways – protecting their legal rights, educating their children, and providing social security payments and access to medical care . . . refugees receive none of these benefits unless they are accepted into a country. Since the overwhelming majority are not accepted, the overwhelming majority will not receive these benefits on the grounds that they are not residents of the countries that provide them to residents. But is this distinction in the way we treat residents and non-residents compatible with our professed belief in the equality of all human beings? (1988: 116)

The question, for the Singers at least, is rhetorical. We need to ask, though, how would relatively open borders affect the kinds of social rights, such as subsidised health care, old age pensions, unemployment benefits, etc., that the Singers feel states have no right to withhold from others, and which liberal egalitarians, like Carens, typically see as required by justice?

No one can be sure of the outcome for Western states of an extended regime of open borders. The contemporary world is characterised by enormous amounts of poverty. According to the World Bank, half of the world's people live on less than US$2 a day. It seems reasonable to conclude that, under conditions of free movement, many people would seek to improve their living standards by migrating. However, we know from recent migration scholarship that poverty alone rarely leads to immigration. For international movement to take place, other factors, such as inequalities in economic opportunities, the ability to gain entrance, the existence of social networks and information about conditions in the destination country are necessary. Many of these precipitating factors do indeed link large numbers of the world's population to liberal democratic countries. Decades of migration in countries such as the US, France, Germany and Australia have created strong ethnic communities in each of these countries (North Africans in France; Chinese in the US; Nigerians in the UK) that act as a magnet to further migration. Moreover, huge and growing inequalities currently exist between the richest liberal democratic countries and the rest of the world's states. According to statistics cited by Susan George, the overall differential between 'Northern and Southern countries was about 2 to 1 in the eighteenth century and 30 to 1 in 1965. By the late 1990s it was over 70 to 1 and rising' (George 2003). These inequalities are, moreover, widely known and increasingly well advertised through the global media and entertainment industries. Finally, there seems little doubt that demand for migration to Western countries currently far outstrips the supply of entrance places. The excess demand is reflected in the many migrants who use the services of traffickers and endure awful conditions to gain (illicit) entrance into liberal democratic countries (Morrison and Crosland 2001; Gibney 2000c). Many more people seem likely to join them if the barriers to entry to these states were lowered.[5]

Let us assume, for the sake of argument, that Western states, under current economic and political conditions, would have to allow their populations to increase significantly, perhaps even to double, before an impartialist theory would recognise the legitimacy of curtailing entry. Could the goods of social democracy be provided in Western states that were twice as populous as they are now? The answer depends on how the new entrants affect two things that underpin the provision of these

[5] Some argue that the European Union's experience with open borders demonstrates that the amount of migration in a world without immigration control would be small. But the EU is, I believe, an improper analogy for an international regime of free movement. Consider some of the commonalities amongst participant states that underpin the EU's free movement provisions: first, the maintenance of the right to settle anywhere in the Union is seen by all states as in their medium and long-term interests, largely because it is an important corollary to the free flow of goods, services and capital. Second, member states, at least so far, share at least some basic cultural, religious and political similarities. All have predominantly white populations, are historically Christian and have democratic political systems and institutional protections for human rights. Third, all are industrialised and relatively economically affluent. These three commonalities work in different ways – the third and (part of) the second act to deter the emigration of large numbers of the residents of Union states (people do not tend to stream out of stable, democratic, political regimes that enjoy a moderate standard of living) and the first two militate against residents of any particular state becoming hostile towards an inward flow of Union citizens if a relatively large movement does occur (because the flow is considered as at least potentially reciprocal, and cultural similarities reduce the likelihood of a racist backlash). All of these features would be lacking if an end to border restrictions were to be implemented on a global scale. It is no coincidence that the EU's current movement provisions have as their flip-side extraordinarily tough entrance restrictions for citizens from outside the Union.

public goods: the economic well-being of the state and the maintenance of favourable citizen attitudes towards the provision of public goods. Let us consider each of these in turn.

Would a situation of open borders bring more economic benefits (in terms of tax revenue, etc.) to the welfare state than it took away (in terms of health care, unemployment benefits, etc.)? While it is beyond the scope of this chapter to engage in a detailed accounting of the economic implications of immigration, some observations are in order. Many economists believe that migration is generally beneficial for national economies. The post-war history of advanced capitalist states suggests, for instance, that the countries with high net immigration in the period between 1945 and 1973 (West Germany, Switzerland, France and Australia) had higher economic growth rates than those countries (such as the US and the UK) with relatively lower levels of immigration (Castles and Miller 1993: 76). This should not be surprising. As classical liberal economists have traditionally argued, free movement of labour as well as other factors of production are essential to maximising the efficiency of production through labour market competition (see Simon 1989). Immigration can also bring other benefits. New entrants can offer a fast way of solving skill shortages in particular industries and non-skilled entrants often take on jobs that domestic labourers will not (or at wage levels that citizens will not accept). Furthermore, immigrants can expand the demand for goods and services in a state by increasing the size of domestic markets, as well as increasing the size of the tax base, with important implications for state service provision.[6] There seems little doubt that, under the right conditions, particularly in situations of low unemployment and high demand for labour, immigration can be economically advantageous.

But no one denies that mass migration can also exact costs. At least in the short term, new immigrants may be disproportionately reliant on public services, such as language training, subsidised housing, education, health services (Leiner 1998). Low-skilled indigenous workers may be adversely affected by labour market competition and the availability of cheap labour sources may discourage the development of new labour-saving and more productive technologies. While these costs are only likely outcomes under conditions of controlled entrance, many of them would become compelling certainties in a regime of free movement. When entrance is restricted, the costs of immigration can be reduced or

[6] A UN Population Division Report (2000) has argued that European countries will need mass migration to compensate for the effect of ageing indigenous workforces. The retirement of increasing proportions of the workforce and low birth rates will, without an injection of new workers, undermine the tax base necessary to fund pensions and other state services.

eliminated by active government intervention. In countries where immigration was (economically) beneficial in the post-war period, who entered and how many entered were decided and controlled by the state, often acting in conjunction with employer groups, unions and, sometimes, community organisations (this was most notably the case in Canada and Australia). Under these circumstances, government intervention ensured at least a rough correlation between the number and types of entrants (often including their language and employment skills) and the labour needs and settlement capacities (in terms of housing, educational facilities, etc.) of the state concerned.[7]

In a regime of open borders, however, who and how many will enter is left either entirely up to the individual immigrant (as in global liberalism) or decided by the interplay between the interests of outsiders and those of residents (utilitarianism). Given that entry decisions would not be determined (or will only be determined in part) by a state's integrative abilities or economic needs, open borders would be likely to result in huge mismatches between the location and number of entrants and the availability of jobs, housing and other features of the public infrastructure, such as schools. One result of these mismatches would be extreme pressures on the resources of the welfare state, notably unemployment benefits, at least during an initial period of adjustment. Would migration soon slow down in recognition of the lack of employment prospects and undesirable living conditions? This would depend not only on accurate information about the circumstances inside the state reaching potential new immigrants in a timely manner. It would also require that potential new entrants did not find the offerings of the welfare state an attraction in themselves. Given that state benefits in liberal democratic states in many cases would offer a higher standard of living than the countries from which some of the entrants would be coming, this is hardly an assumption one could feel confident in making.

Of course, it is possible that the welfare state could survive under these new circumstances. A huge injection of resources could expand its ability to deal with the increasing pressure caused by new migration. However, the expansion of the welfare state is not simply an economic matter.[8] For public goods to be provided, it is also necessary that there exists a

[7] Often the nature of this control was highly illiberal. Guestworker programmes, for instance, involved restrictions on the type of labour that immigrants were allowed to do and where they could live. Even the Australian government, which allowed immigration for permanent settlement, placed tight restrictions on the location and occupations of new immigrants. See Chapter 6.

[8] Interestingly, Gary Freeman has commented that 'it is no accident that state-sponsored social protection schemes first emerged in countries pursuing essentially mercantilist economic policies. The same impulses that lay behind tariffs . . . and other protectionist

wide consensus amongst members that each citizen is owed something *qua* citizen of that particular community – for instance, free health care and, if out of work, unemployment benefits. This was an issue that, as we saw, exercised the minds of partialists. Political scientists writing on the welfare state have also noted that a certain degree of solidarity based on 'fellow feeling' (Freeman 1986: 52) and 'mutual trust' (Whelan 1988: 29) is essential if people are to recognise a responsibility to assist each other and contribute to communal welfare in this way. In the case of many liberal democracies, where admission to membership is based primarily on a public commitment to certain civic principles, it's easy to overlook the subjective element in membership. Yet if what members share is to be extended to new entrants, or if membership is to continue to call forth a strong sense of communal responsibility, this collective solidarity needs to be maintained.

To return to a question we began discussing in Chapter 1, could the solidarity or common identification necessary for the welfare state be maintained in a situation where the composition of membership was changing rapidly? The empirical evidence is inconclusive. The post-1945 experiences of Canada and Australia indicate that a wide-ranging welfare state can prosper in the midst of large-scale migration. On the other hand, some scholars have argued that the recent decline in social provision in Scandanavian countries is partly a result of the growing multiculturalism of societies once characterised by an unusual degree of ethnic homogeneity (Wolfe 1989: 247–8). Others have looked to the experience of the US. The country's immigrant history, scholars have argued, is one reason why a full-fledged welfare state, let alone an effective socialist tradition, has never taken root there (Walzer 1995, Woodward 1992; but compare Bader 1995).

It seems likely that, while racial and other differences do not preclude acceptance of immigrants into membership, national understandings of membership are never infinitely flexible in the short term. Large gaps, which are corrosive to public provision, can open up between legal and public understandings of who is a member where a state admits a very large number of new entrants very quickly. Impartialism's requirement that liberal democracies open their borders would likely result in far more prodigious gaps than have hitherto been evident. Because the volume of new entrants would be so large over the short term (at least in comparison to current levels), collective solidarity would not be able to keep pace

measures designed to preserve and enhance national wealth drive the effort to insulate national populations from the disruption to their livelihoods caused by world business cycles. In this sense, the welfare state may be seen as the pursuit of protectionism by other means' (1986: 53–4).

with changes in the composition of the state's members. The result would be a general backlash against the welfare state, as indigeneous members refuse to fund public goods for new arrivals that they perceive as depleting rather than contributing to public resources.[9] The effect of immigration on the existence of social solidarity should not be overstated. Large, modern, industrial societies are highly absorptive and can often integrate large numbers of new entrants from diverse backgrounds over short periods of time with little problem.[10] But it is unlikely that such states could substantially increase their population size over a short time period without affecting the consensus within them required for distributing public goods.

We may conclude, then, that the possible economic and political effects of free movement imply a practical tension between the principle of impartiality in entry and the maintenance of the kinds of goods that we, in Western states, associate with the welfare state. But does this threat to the social democratic agenda mean that rights-based impartialists should rethink the ethical desirability of free movement? According to Joseph Carens, the answer is no. Global liberals, Carens argues, should concede that if the effect of free movement on public goods does not constitute a good reason for controlling people's right to move *within* states (for instance, from one province to another), then it should not serve as a ground for restricting movement *between* states.

> Should Wisconsin have the right to keep out people from Illinois . . .? Or should Canada be obliged to admit people from the United States? If these two cases are different how and why are they different? . . . Despite my attachment to Canada's social welfare policies, I do not think that they justify restrictions on movement. (Carens 1992a: 42)

Consistently respecting the freedom and equality of all human beings requires recognising that nation-state boundaries are as morally arbitrary as provincial or regional ones.

Few global liberals would be as ready as Carens to trade social democracy for open borders. Many, no doubt, would want to safeguard the welfare state where it exists by restricting entry to only the neediest of entry claimants, such as refugees. While this response seems wise, one

[9] See Wolfe (1989) for a brief discussion of the deleterious effect of recent immigration on the traditionally generous social welfare policies of the Nordic countries. Gary Freeman argues that from the perspective of the welfare state 'there can be no doubt that . . . [large scale migration to Western Europe] has been little short of a disaster' (1986: 61).

[10] Conservative theorists often assume an extremely fragile view of states and citizen solidarity in their attempt to criticise current entrance levels, though the more sophisticated amongst them avoid any lengthy discussion whatsoever of the implications of their views on the nation for entry policy. See, for instance, Scruton (1990): ch. 28).

should note that pruning back the entrance entitlements to the neediest in this manner – giving priority to refugees, for instance – is inconsistent with the claim that there exists a general moral right of free movement. As James Woodward has observed, liberals who suggest that free movement is a basic human right and then proceed to give priority in entry to the needy are not taking the idea of a human right seriously. For in the case of other basic human rights, such as the right to free speech, liberals would not think it 'justifiable to adopt policies which differentially respect (or give priority to the satisfaction of) rights held by needy people over the rights of non-needy people' (Woodward 1992: 61).

Utilitarians, who eschew a rights-based approach, appear better placed to justify priority for refugees. The different claims of individuals can be weighed in the utilitarian calculus on the basis of whose marginal utility would increase most by entering. However, while this approach would probably justify priority for refugees because of their desperate need, the utilitarian calculus has not finished its work once the interests of refugees have been taken into account. There are huge numbers of people in the world, including those whose subsistence needs are only barely met, whose marginal utility would also be dramatically increased by resettlement. Indeed, in the midst of breathtaking international inequality, huge numbers of people in poor countries would seem to have a stronger reason for entering Western states than the residents of Western states would have for keeping them out. Even if welfare state systems collapsed under the weight of this new migration, it might still be consistent with the goal of maximising global total utility to allow new entrants to continue to enter, at least as long as conditions in Western states remained superior to those in the countries from which the people concerned were emigrating. While Singer and Singer (1988) argued that the principle of equal consideration of all interests provided a moral rationale for extending social democratic goods to increasing numbers of the world's denizens, it seems that adhering consistently to the utilitarian calculus would undermine the conditions necessary for the reproduction of these goods.

Unsurprisingly, given the tension between social democracy and open borders, not all impartialists accept that Western states are required to adopt more inclusive entrance practices. While both Brian Barry (1992) and Kai Neilson (1988) support the impartial principle that ethically defensible policies must take into account the interests of all, they reject the view that open borders are the best way of respecting this principle. After providing an account of the costs of more liberal entrance policies, including the deleterious effects such policies would have on world population pressures and remittance payments, Barry argues for the superiority of international wealth and resource redistribution as a response to global inequalities of security and welfare. Policies by Western states that promote the economic development of poor countries represent, he claims, a far more effective response to international poverty than free movement (1992: 280–5). Kai Neilson, on the other hand, acknowledges that the poor of crowded, resource-depleted countries like Bangladesh have a just claim to enter richer and more sparsely populated states like New Zealand in order to improve their security. He adds, however, that by redistributing global resources more equitably, richer states could avoid the practical conflict that this kind of redistribution of people would inevitably generate by sapping the world's poor of any reason to move (1988: 272–3).

Does this alternative account of impartiality's demands save social democracy? Barry and Neilson are, I believe, right to suggest that open borders are not the only – or necessarily the most effective – way of respecting the equality of all human beings. Free movement may indeed have negative overall consequences for attempts to combat the causes of global impoverishment. Nonetheless, the plansibility of these writers' claims depends on what role one's moral argument for free movement allots to consequences. If one views free movement as a fundamental moral *right*, as Carens and Dummett do, then this right cannot easily be trumped by consequential considerations of the type that Barry and Neilson present.

Significantly, even if one accepts the consequentialist approach, in-country solutions, of the type Barry and Neilson support, are hardly the appropriate response for *all* outsiders in need. Refugees are those who, by definition, cannot be helped (at least in the short term) within their state of normal residence. For, as Michael Walzer, has suggested:

> The liberty that makes certain countries possible homes for men and women whose politics and religion is not tolerated where they live is . . . not exportable; at least we have found no way of exporting it. These goods can be shared only within the protected space of a particular state. (Walzer 1983: 43)

The consequentialist impartialism of Barry and Neilson may well provide strong grounds for assisting needy *immigrants* where they are. However, unless it is to justify ignoring the needs of people fleeing their country of normal residence – some task in an approach that claims to consider the interests or rights of all equally – it must demand that states accept refugees and asylum seekers for entrance. And in the current global context, in which there are well over 10 million official refugees and many more unofficial ones, this obligation would prove very onerous. Indeed, in the face of such great need, consistent adherence to impartial principles might still be inconsistent with the existence of social democracy.

Impartiality versus partiality

I have considered so far the claim that liberals who do not accept open borders are being inconsistent. I have also shown that one likely implication of free international movement would be the demise of the welfare state. Both of these discussions give reasons for being sceptical of the impartialist case for moving towards a world of free international movement. However, in an important sense, the discussion so far has merely snipped at the heels of impartiality as an ethical perspective. It is, for example, one thing to say that adhering consistently to impartiality would undermine the viability of the welfare state, and another thing altogether to say that this makes it an erroneous ethical position. Acting morally often involves making sacrifices; it might well be that the demise of the welfare state is one of them.

I now want to turn to a more fundamental criticism of the impartial perspective, one that raises doubts over its ability to formulate an adequate ideal for the entrance responsibilities of states. This is that the impartial view offers an incomplete and therefore misleading picture of the moral responsibilities of individuals and, derivatively, of states. Let us move towards this criticism by noting the key issue begged by impartialism: should the obligations we have to foreigners and those we have to our fellow citizens be weighed on a common scale? Or have we, for example, a special responsibility to our compatriots – such as to ensure they have access to a welfare state – that might trump the claims of the human community, considered impartially? To accept unamended the principle of impartiality in entry is to deny the validity of such special obligations – obligations that involve a bias to particular others, such as family members, neighbours or compatriots. It is, in the words of Michael Sandel, to insist 'that the more universal communities we inhabit must always take precedence over more particular ones' (1996: 343).

We need only consider the practical character of modern entry debates to see the strength of more particular obligations. Refugee and immigration debates in modern Britain, Australia, the US and Germany, as we shall see in later chapters, usually turn on complaints about the potential adverse effects of entry upon *citizens*. When politicians such as Enoch Powell, Pat Buchanan or Pauline Hanson rail against the perceived 'threat' of entry policies to the 'cultural homogeneity' of the nation; when hostile whites give tacit or sometimes active support to Neo-Nazis in Rostock in the belief that the entry of foreigners is placing pressure on an already extremely competitive and dilapidated housing market; and when large sections of the US Congress eagerly support new legislation mandating detention to prevent the 'security threat' that asylum seekers are seen as posing, these claims are not couched in impartialist terms. Rather, such claims appeal to the understanding that citizens' interests deserve priority in state deliberation and policy-making. Those who argue against entry assert that special responsibilities are owed to them by virtue of their citizenship; they reject out of hand the idea that the interests of outsiders should be considered on a par with their own.

It is easy to dismiss such complaints. They often are expressed in an appalling language of racial stereotype, or based on ignorance of the actual facts of immigration and of the hardships endured by refugees and asylum seekers. In many cases, these complaints are provoked by entry policies that are only minimally decent. But could we dismiss these complaints so easily if they were in response to entry policies that truly were indifferent to distinctions between the interests of members and those of strangers? Moreover, it seems difficult to reconcile the promotion of such indifference with other values that liberals cherish, including the principle of popular sovereignty, the right of the members of a political community independently to determine their collective future. What are we to make of this right if it does not mean that a group of people may make decisions that, while recognizing some limits, privilege their own concerns and interests rather than those of humanity as a whole?[11]

The conflict here between the force of general obligations (obligations to humanity) and the force of special obligations (obligations to compatriots) is usually brushed aside by impartialists. To the extent that special obligations are legitimate, impartialists argue, they can only be so when justified through a process of impartial moral reasoning.[12] But the conflict

[11] Preference towards fellow citizens is linked also to forms of national association with which liberals are less comfortable. The right of self-determination, for example, is often claimed by groups who desire a state that reflects their shared ethnicity. Significantly, this collective right is not reducible to more universalistic claims of basic security and respect for human rights. It might be possible for Palestinians or Kurds to have their human rights respected and their security ensured if they were resettled as refugees across a range of Western states. But this is not what the Palestinians and the Kurds want. They claim the right to have states of their own in which their people live together, privilege their common interests and maintain their shared identity.

[12] For example, Singer (1979) and Goodin (1988) do not advocate the rejection of all special obligations. But when they argue for these attachments they do so solely on the grounds that there are *advantages* in recognising responsibilities created by institutions such as the family. One such advantage is that, in Singer's words, it avoids the need for a 'large, impersonal bureaucracy' (1979: 172). Given that these forms of human attachment may well not be the most utility maximising distribution of human responsibility, this utilitarian defence of special obligations seems highly dubious. Moreover, this approach has been criticised by Williams, amongst others, for the way special obligations are 'put back' into moral theory. The argument that it is more 'efficient' if one is partial to one's family 'gets things back to front: my rights to my own children and my own time are

is, in fact, real. And we can best understand it – as well as the limitations of impartiality – by considering this conflict through the framework of what Thomas Nagel has described as the personal and the impersonal perspectives in political theory.

In his work, *Equality and Partiality* (1991), Nagel argues that one of the main problems facing political theory is its failure to identify a credible ideal by which to judge and assess current social and political institutions. The problem, he suggests, is that ideal theory fails to speak to the complexity of human moral experience. In particular, an adequate ideal needs to address itself to the fact that the ethical claims upon individual human beings emanate from two different sources: the impersonal perspective and the personal perspective. It is the resolution of the conflict between these two perspectives – a conflict rooted in a division in the human self – that Nagel sees as the central problem for ideal theory. I will now consider his argument in more depth.

According to Nagel, one common way of identifying the moral claims upon human beings involves adopting the impersonal perspective. Adopting this view, in order to gain insight into how we are morally required to act, we must 'remove ourselves in thought from our particular position in the world and think simply of all those people, without singling out as *I* the one we happen to be' (Nagel 1991: 10). After discarding our attachment to our own personal projects and concerns and those of the particular others with whom we share our lives, we realise that our own interests and projects are no more important than anyone else's in spite of their pressing importance to us personally. We become aware that everyone else in the world has a life to lead which is just as important to them as ours is to us (Nagel 1991: 11). If we assume the perspective of an impersonal observer, it is hard for us to deny that the life of everyone matters and matters equally. To act morally, then, is to act consistent with – or informed by – the principle of the equal moral worth of all individuals, regardless of their relation to us personally.

But, Nagel argues, the impersonal view does not exhaust our perspectives as moral agents. For while we are all capable of stepping back and seeing that the life of everyone matters equally, we also cannot help but acknowledge the pressing attachment we each have to our own projects and to the particular others in our lives (Nagel 1991: 14). Indeed, it is *because* of the value we attach to our own projects and concerns that it is so easy to recognise, when we adopt the impersonal perspective, how

not theirs to give back' (Williams 1985: 77). For an argument that presents a somewhat extreme critique of Williams, rejecting the moral force of special obligations altogether, see Belsey (1992: 40–2).

important the life plans of others must be also to them. Nonetheless, the personal perspective constitutes a powerful source of conflicting motivations for moral agents. We can never completely put to one side the special interest we have in how our own life goes, nor view with equanimity our relations with those particular others for whom we feel love, amity and reciprocity. This is not least because this special relation to our own concerns and to those of certain others in our lives is crucial in making us the kind of people we are: individuals with a distinct identity who can be moved, from time to time, by impartial considerations.[13] Significantly, from these special relations emerge a range of commitments and responsibilities that are often in competition with those that emerge from impartial reflection. For instance, we usually feel special attachments to our own projects and our family and friends which we could not justify impartially, and yet which are central to the way we conceive of ourselves.

The importance of this division in human morality lies not in its acknowledgement that individuals are driven, in turn, by personal and impersonal motivations. It is that both of these motivations can be sources of legitimate *moral* reasons for action. In this respect, Nagel's view of moral agency differs from some very strong currents in ethical theory which have reduced the personal view to egoism and self-interest, and, in doing so, seen its sources of motivation as inherently inferior to those which can be legitimated impersonally. But this approach can also be distinguished from recent efforts by political theorists who, recognising the force of certain particular attachments and their concomitant duties, responsibilities and rights, attach *derivative* moral significance to these relations, by arguing that it is possible to justify them impartially (Miller 1988; 1997).[14]

In the divided account of the sources of ethical claims just presented, however, the personal view has moral weight *independent* of its ability to be impartially legitimated; it can thus provide reasons for action which count against the demands arising from the impartial perspective. According to Nagel, 'morality allows compartments for individual pursuits, while defining their boundaries by general standards' (Nagel 1991: 25). These compartments set limits on the sacrifices that individuals can reasonably be expected to make for the sake of impersonal considerations – for the sake, in other words, of equality. In a conflict between the reasonable demands upon agents that issue from the personal view and those that

[13] Consider, for instance, Annette Baier's work, *Moral Prejudices* (1994). Baier argues that it is 'the natural virtue of parental love' (1994: 9) – an irredeemably partial attachment – which, above all else, forms individuals as trustworthy moral agents.

[14] For an example of the attempt to legitimate partial duties from the outside in, see Goodin (1988).

issue from the impersonal view, we should, argues Nagel, 'regard both of the elements that create the dilemma as *morally valid*' (Nagel 1991: 32; my emphasis).

The challenge for any convincing political ideal, aiming to inform agents of what they ought to strive for, is to acknowledge the moral importance of each of these perspectives in its prescriptions. To vindicate an account of political responsibilities in which the personal view completely overshadows the demands of impersonal morality is to suppress a key aspect of our identity as moral agents; to allow the demands of impersonal morality to ride roughshod over our personal claims, on the other hand, is to ignore the importance of the special commitments that make us the distinct individuals we are.

Does the conflict Nagel outlines have implications for the question of the responsibilities of states to foreigners wishing to enter? I believe that the competing accounts of the state responsibilities outlined in this chapter and the previous one mirror this ethical tension between impersonal and personal perspectives. Global liberal and utilitarian political theories – impartialist approaches – represent articulations of the impersonal perspective, stressing the universal moral claims of human beings to equal consideration by states. When applied to entrance policy, these theories severely restrict the grounds on which states are justified in denying admittance to foreigners. Communitarian and conservative political theories – partialist approaches – on the other hand, are manifestations of the personal view, stressing the particular moral claims of communities. When applied to entrance, these approaches usually uphold the rights of citizen-communities to wide-ranging control over who enters and becomes a member of the political community.

And, as with Nagel's broad contrast between personal and impersonal views, both impartial and partial viewpoints can be seen as representing powerful, ineliminable and conflicting moral claims. Partialism upholds the claims of justice of individuals as citizens with established expectations and entitlements (to a job, a certain standard of living, a culture, certain public goods). It emphasises people's right to reproduce the social and economic conditions which make possible the goods they currently enjoy. Impartialism upholds the claims to equal concern and respect of human beings *qua* human beings. It emphasises the entitlement of all individuals, regardless of citizenship, to have their security and welfare needs met and protected. Both of these claims to justice resonate in contemporary liberal-democratic thinking. On the one hand, widely held commitments to equal concern and respect undergird the provision to citizens of a welfare system and the recognition of rights of political participation in a democratic polity (the value of popular sovereignty). On the other hand, the same egalitarian values argue against the legitimacy of the state privileging the interests and rights of its own citizens over those of outsiders.[15]

Where, by way of conclusion, does this discussion leave us in relation to evaluating the impartial account of the responsibilities of states? If we accept Nagel's framework, and see entrance policy as a site of conflicting moral claims, then we have identified a problem with impartialism. For in failing to attach independent weight to the range of particular (and, in some cases, unchosen) ties that emerge in the course of our lives, impartialism, with its stress on equal rights and interests, can be accused of offering an incomplete account of the ethical considerations relevant to entrance decisions. The divided perspective I have outlined does not, of course, invalidate the existence of universal obligations, or the value of impartial perspective. Indeed, it suggests that these are key aspects of moral theorising. But it does suggest that the moral force of more particular attachments, such as those of citizenship, cannot simply be ignored, any more than partialists would be justified in failing to acknowledge universal responsibilities. An adequate ideal for responding to foreigners in entrance policy will need to find a way of integrating both universal and particular moral claims.

Conclusion

In this chapter and the previous one I have critically examined how two different ethical approaches deal with the responsibilities of states to foreigners in entrance. I have shown that together these approaches point to a real and pressing conflict between the claims of citizens (represented by partialism) and those of humanity (represented by impartialism). To demand that a (Western) state show equal concern and respect to those *beyond* the state is to ask it to pursue policies that in all likelihood would undermine those practices and institutions that make for a semblance of equality and social justice *within* the state, and would erode the meaningfulness of any political community's claim to democratic autonomy. Yet to vindicate the partiality of the modern state is to tolerate a world where differences in citizenship correspond to egregious differences in life quality and span.

The identification of this conflict is hardly an auspicious start for an attempt to outline an account of the responsibilities of liberal democratic

[15] Consider, for instance, the liberal theorist Joseph Carens' argument that in terms of its arbitrary distribution of life-chances, citizenship is the modern equivalent of 'feudal status' in the medieval world (Carens 1992: 26).

states to refugees. Yet acknowledging it does not leave us bereft of guidance on where we must head. For a start, the conflict suggests that while the partial and impartial approaches each capture an important moral claim raised by the current crisis, neither can be said to represent an adequate balance or integration of personal and impersonal moral claims. In the face of the huge numbers of official and unofficial refugees in the contemporary world, accepting the full logic of the impartial approach would lead to policies that undermine the conditions necessary for communal self-determination and the provision of public goods. Going with the full implications of the partial view, on the other hand, risks legitimating the current actions of states in paying scant regard to the claims of millions of aspiring entrants, many of whom are in great need, on the grounds of a right to communal autonomy. The knowledge that a convincing ideal must attend both to partial and impartial claims should at least make us very sceptical of global liberal and utilitarian and communitarian and conservative accounts of the responsibilities of states because of their exclusive emphasis on one or other side of the impartial/partial divide.

This is, admittedly, a very abstract response to the question of how we might formulate an ideal for the response of liberal democratic states in entrance. By way of conclusion, then, let me spell out an alternative ideal. An acceptable ideal would, I believe, see states as justified in restricting entry only in order to protect the institutions and values of the liberal democratic state, defined quite broadly to include not only civil and political rights, but also the kind of social rights associated with a generous welfare state that ensure some degree of economic justice amongst members. This ideal could be distinguished from partialism by its refusal to attach any intrinsic worth to the modern state as a site of cultural unity, legitimating a wide-ranging prerogative to control entrance. Unlike impartialism, as usually articulated, however, this ideal is consistent with recognising the strategic importance of reproducing peoples with a common identity. It would acknowledge that liberal egalitarian principles can only be realised in communities where relations amongst citizens are characterised by solidarity and trust, relations which develop over time and can be jeopardised by large, short-term changes in membership. This ideal would, furthermore, make the guarantee and protection of social rights, and thus protection of the welfare state, legitimate grounds for controlling entrance.

Because states would still, in this account, have some scope for restricting the admission of foreigners, the question of how liberal democracies should distribute scarce entry places arises. In the ideal I have presented, states would eschew cultural and ethnic grounds for admission and distribute entrance for membership and residence on the basis of need and familial connections. A plausible account of the responsibilities of states to foreigners under ideal conditions would, in my view, enjoin states to accept as many refugees as they can without undermining the provision of collective or public goods amongst their members.

Why would such an ideal state give priority to the claims of refugees? I have already suggested that global liberals, such as Carens and Dummett, fail to provide a rationale for privileging the needs of refugees over other entrants because there is nothing intrinsic in the idea of a general right of free movement that lends support to prioritising the claims of the needy. Once we recognise the moral importance of the conflict between impartial and partial claims, however, it is easier to see why the claims of refugees should be of special concern. For in the midst of huge numbers of needy immigrants in the modern world and a scarcity of entrance places imposed, *inter alia*, by the need to protect collective measures for equality, it makes sense to distinguish between those who can be helped *where they are* (for instance, through humanitarian aid) and those whose needs can only be met through the provision of a *new state* (Zolberg *et al.* 1989: 270–1). Thus the argument that states have a special responsibility for refugees and asylum seekers takes shape. For not only are these claimants for entry in great need, but, unlike other immigrants, there is only one conceivable way that their immediate needs can be addressed: through the provision of entrance to a new state.

3 The Federal Republic of Germany: the rise and fall of a right to asylum

> People persecuted on political grounds shall enjoy the right of asylum.
>
> Basic Law of the Federal Republic of Germany 1949

> There is no way we can process people at this rate. With every day we are falling further behind.
>
> Ulrich Kortmann, Cologne Refugee Centre 1992

> My responsibility as a politician is to optimise the conditions for the people who live here . . . It is not my duty to treat all problems in the world equally.
>
> Edmund Stoiber, Interior Minister of Bavaria (CSU) 1990[1]

In Chapters 1 and 2, I considered the question of responses to refugees from the viewpoint of ethical (or ideal) theory. In the next chapters I want to look at the actual responses of four liberal democratic states towards refugees and asylum seekers. By examining the recent behaviour of these states it is possible to identify both the ways in which the practices of states depart from the requirements of ideal theory and the range of real-world factors that currently shape and constrain how liberal democratic states respond to refugees. These factors will need to be taken into account in my attempt to furnish practical prescriptions for state behaviour in the final two chapters of this work. My examination of the practical responses of states, however, will begin, in this chapter, with Germany. I will then move on to consider the cases of the United Kingdom, the United States and Australia.

The Federal Republic of Germany has faced two daunting challenges brought about by the movement of refugees into its territory since the end of the Second World War.[2] The first occurred immediately after the end of the war and involved the resettlement of 10 million refugees of German nationality expelled from Eastern European countries and

[1] Quoted in Joppke (1999a: 128).

[2] By 'Federal Republic' I refer to the post-1945 West German state and, after unification in 1990, to the unified German state.

3.5 million evacuees from Soviet-controlled East Germany. It was a challenge that was met with dramatic success. With the help of a number of governmental programmes, and a rapidly expanding economy, these refugees were fully integrated into West German society in the two decades after 1945. Indeed, by the end of the 1960s, the success of this massive resettlement attempt, along with the country's uniquely broad constitutional article which recognised a right of asylum for all political refugees, had rendered the Federal Republic, in spite of its catastrophic past, something of a model for all states in the handling of refugees.

In recent years, however, the status of Germany as a role model has come seriously into question. The reasons for this lie with the way it dealt with its second refugee challenge. Between the mid 1970s and the mid 1980s, West Germany experienced a prodigious growth in the number of foreigners utilising its constitutional provisions to seek asylum in its territory. Between 1980 and 1993, the number of applicants for asylum rose by almost 8,000 per cent. Perhaps unsurprisingly, the inflow of huge waves of foreigners and the concomitant costs of providing housing, social services and of processing their claims (estimated in 1991 to be US$1.9 billion a year) provoked a reaction against both those seeking asylum and the laws that allowed them entry. Throughout 1992 and 1993 manifestations of this backlash ranged from violent attacks by hostile groups on the camps that house asylum seekers and the ominous growth of anti-foreigner parties to widespread calls by politicians for constitutional reform and high levels of discontent amongst broad sections of the German public with the entire asylum process. Tensions have eased in recent years (by 1996 asylum applications numbered 116,400 and by 2000, 78,000) largely due to constitutional change that has given officials broader powers to refuse entry to asylum seekers. Nonetheless, asylum remains a crucial and, in many ways, an unresolved issue in German politics, not least because the country still accepts an uncommonly large (by European standards) number of asylum seekers annually.

The refugee crisis of 1992–3 makes the Federal Republic a vital case study in any attempt to consider how states ought to act in the face of the current international refugee predicament. For the German state was for a long time one of the few states which through its law answered clearly and affirmatively a central question for both political theory and political practice, the question of whether necessitous people should be entitled to gain refuge in states of which they are not members. Through its adherence to a wide-ranging right of asylum, the Federal Republic of Germany went further than any other liberal democratic state in recognising the claims of refugees; yet its acknowledgement of this outsider entitlement placed it deep in political crisis. My aim in this chapter is to examine how this crisis came about and how it was resolved.

Because the Federal Republic's asylum imbroglio was part of a broader crisis of entrance policy, I will begin by examining those considerations which have been crucial to West Germany's decisions to admit and exclude non-residents since its formation in 1949. I shall discuss four distinct and influential features of the West German state in this regard: its foundation as a *Rechtsstaat*, its existence as a capitalist state, its role as representative of the nation and its location within a broader (and, in particular, European) system of states. The post-war policies of West German governments have been marked by an attempt to harmonise (often) competing demands which flow from these different features. Until the 1970s, I shall argue, governments managed to achieve considerable harmony between these different demands on entrance policy, but in the 1980s and 1990s changes in the international environment brought them far more sharply and publicly into tension than ever before. The consequence of this growth in tension was a crisis in asylum deeper than that yet experienced by any other liberal democratic state.

The state and entrance: 1949–70

What kinds of features of the West German state have shaped decisions on the entrance of foreigners since its formation as a state? In this section I will discuss four major features and consider the demands that have flowed from each of them, but first it is necessary to note that any attempt to outline the important characteristics of a state in this regard is unlikely to be comprehensive. The relevant aspects of any particular state in the modern world are simply too various and complex for a definitive account. That said, what I will discuss here are the most significant and unproblematical characteristics of the West German state that have played a role in determining post-war entrance policies. These characteristics are abstractions, and the boundaries between them are hard and fast neither in theory nor in practice. They are nonetheless exceedingly useful abstractions which, as I will argue in later parts, shed important light on Germany's current crisis. In this part, however, I will confine myself to discussing the nature of these features and their impact on Germany policy up to the late 1960s.

Rechtsstaat

The first characteristic of note has been the West German state's role as a distinctive kind of *Rechtsstaat* – a state governed by an extraordinarily comprehensive articulation of law. This has meant that certain decisions on the entrance of non-citizens – most notably in the area of asylum – have been subject neither to the discretion of the country's federal governments nor of its citizenry. The existence of the West German state as a modern *Rechtsstaat* has its origins in the Republic's constitution – the Basic Law of the Federal Republic of Germany (1949) – which was drawn up by a parliamentary council of German leaders under the inspection of the occupying Western military powers in the wake of Germany's comprehensive defeat in the Second World War. The Basic Law was designed as the consummate 'anti-Weimar constitution' (Sontheimer 1988: 229), one that unconditionally recognised basic citizen rights, empowered a strong executive (with built-in measures to militate against the chancellor being overthrown), protected against the centralisation of authority through the grant of important powers to the *Länder*, and established a constitutional court to ensure the legality of governmental legislation and activity. The aim of the constitution from the beginning was to ensure against a repeat of the failure and weaknesses of the Weimar constitution, which it was widely believed had allowed the rise of the National Socialists to power. Accordingly, the Basic Law constitutes the most rigid rule of law of any constitution in the world (Kielmansegg 1989: 176). Along with its comprehensive scope, the Basic Law contains provisions which make constitutional reform exceedingly difficult in the case of most of its articles, with the agreement of two-thirds of both houses of the German Parliament (the *Bundestag* and the *Bundesrat*) required for change, and absolutely forbidden for certain fundamental articles, specifically the basic citizen rights and those that ensure the maintenance of a federal and democratic state (Hucko 1989: 69–73; Sontheimer 1988: 230). In the way that it positively forbids constitutional change in some areas, and entrusts what change is allowed only to Parliament, the Basic Law can be seen as an anti-majoritarian constitution, one which is inherently hostile to the ideal of popular democracy (Kielmansegg 1989: 176).

To see how the German state as *Rechtsstaat* has influenced the position of successive governments on entrance decisions, it is not necessary to look any further than Section 16(2) of the Basic Law, which, until July 1993, read in full: 'Persons persecuted on political grounds shall enjoy the right to asylum.' This subjective right to asylum went well beyond the principles concerning refugees and asylum adumbrated in the 1949 UN Declaration of Human Rights and the 1951 Convention and 1967 Protocol on the Status of Refugees, which respectively recognize only the *state's* right to grant asylum and the principle of *non-refoulement*. For the Basic Law's provisions bound German authorities not only to consider the asylum claims of any applicant in its territory or at its frontiers, but allowed that person to remain in Germany as a matter of right if he or she satisfied the relevant criteria. This section, by recognizing asylum entitlements unrestricted by country of origin, vested rights in a potentially enormous pool of non-citizens. Moreover, by wrapping the principle of asylum in the constitution, and thus requiring the agreement of two-thirds of both houses of Parliament for change, the initial signatories to the constitution prevented entrance decisions in this area being determined by the expedience of government or the capriciousness of the electorate.

The motivation for the Basic Law's clause on asylum grew out of a significant and influential feature of the Federal Republic's post-war behaviour, the desire to make amends for the disastrous actions of the German state during World War II. In the treatment of refugees in particular, the framers of the constitution saw West Germany as especially indebted after so many people had been forced to flee Germany or face death in concentration camps under the Third Reich. Throughout the 1950s and 1960s, this unique sense of responsibility was worn lightly. While there was a steady stream of mostly Eastern Europeans who availed themselves of the country's constitutional right of asylum, a combination of factors including the congruence of accepting refugees from communism with West Germany's Cold War foreign policy objectives, and the economy's need for ever-increasing amounts of labour, meant that little controversy arose.

Capitalist state

The Federal Republic's status as a capitalist state attempting to rebuild itself and prosper in the post-war international economy has also heavily influenced the response of governments to the inflow of foreigners. The economic and infrastructural collapse that faced West Germany at the end of the war made a large supply of relatively cheap and versatile labour of supreme importance for rebuilding the economy and society. For the most part, in the six years after the formation of the Republic, that supply was guaranteed by the massive influx of expellees and refugees who came and continued to come after the war. But as the 'economic miracle' took hold – the incredible expansion in production in the West German economy in the middle to late 1950s – this abundant supply of labour started to dry up. By 1955, various sectors of the economy (first agriculture, and then industry) had begun urging the government to embark upon a campaign of recruiting foreign workers. This brought about the original labour recruiting agreements, which were signed first with Italy (1955) and then with Spain (1960), Greece (1960) and Turkey (1961) (Esser and Korte 1985: 170). When the Republic's main source of skilled and easily integratable labour was cut off by the erection of the Berlin Wall in 1961, an increased campaign of '[h]iring foreign workers, rather than shifting production abroad or accepting lower rates of economic growth, was . . . viewed in all political quarters as the only sensible response' (Katzenstein 1987: 214). Labour agreements were subsequently signed with Portugal (1964), Tunisia (1965) and Morocco (1963 and 1966) (Esser and Korte 1985: 170).

These agreements resulted in a massive inflow of workers. The total of foreign labourers in West Germany grew from 100,000 in 1955 to 500,000 in 1961 and had reached 1.3 million by 1967. During the recession of 1966–7 the government cut back sharply on the number of entrants, with the result that by January 1968 the number of foreign workers had fallen to less than a million. However, at the end of this short-lived recession, recruiting began again in earnest and by 1970 Germany's foreign labour force was over 2 million.

While the numbers of migrant workers grew during the 1950s and 1960s, domestic anxiety at their presence did not. The lack of tension can be attributed primarily to the fact that these workers were viewed as *temporary*, workers who would go back to their countries of origin after their period of labour had finished. This was certainly the outlook of the West German government. In 1966 it introduced the Aliens Act which aimed at providing a legal framework for making foreign labour a 'manoeuvrable resource', easily controlled and regulated, for the solving of economic problems and in particular, manpower shortages (Esser and Korte 1985: 170). This Act laid down restrictions on the residence of foreign workers by withholding from them any right to permanent settlement, introducing work permits, and giving discretionary powers to the government to assist it in regulating their stay (Esser and Korte 1985: 170). The Act reflected the widely held belief that the country's requirement of an inflow of people did not entail that West Germany become a country of immigration. It meant merely that residence would be allowed as long as foreign labour was conducive to the country's economic needs. As such, public anxiety over the entrance of such a large number of people in the two and a half decades after the war never became widespread or attained the status of an important political issue.

Nation-state

The Federal Republic's policies towards the entrance of non-citizens since 1945 have been profoundly influenced also by the state's role as representative of the nation and, in particular, by a distinctly German understanding of national membership. This understanding of membership in the national community has, according to Rogers Brubaker, historically been 'particularist, organic, differentialist and *Volk*-centred' (Brubaker 1990: 386). The nation has been conceived of as a kind of 'biological' entity, into which membership is gained at birth rather than acquired by non-citizens through accession. In a brilliant historical essay on the German conception of the nation, Brubaker proposes the following explanation for the distinctness of the German conception:

> Because national feeling developed before the nation-state, the German idea of the nation was not, originally, a political one, nor was it linked with the abstract idea of citizenship. The pre-political German nation, this nation in search of a state, was conceived not as the bearer of universal political values, but as an organic, cultural, linguistic or racial community – as an irreducibly particular *Volksgemeinschaft*. On this understanding, nationhood is constituted by ethnocultural unity and expressed in political unity. (Brubaker 1990: 386)

Defining national membership in ethnic rather than territorial terms has not gone unchallenged in West Germany during the post-war period, but it has nevertheless played an important part in shaping public attitudes and government policies towards the entrance of foreigners. Its influence has pulled in two opposing directions. On the one hand it has been a force for the *exclusion* of foreigners. The hostility towards the idea of integration inherent in the national conception came to be reflected in the belief that the Federal Republic should not become a country of immigration.[3] And the Republic's laws supported this anti-integration bias; West German citizenship was distributed only on the basis of descent (*jus sanguinis*) and not on the basis of birth in West German territory (*jus soli*). These laws ensured that residence in the Federal Republic could not become a pathway to full membership in the national and political community. It is significant that when an influx of people was necessary for economic reasons in the 1950s and 1960s, it was not a general immigration programme that was resorted to but the recruitment of temporary or guestworkers, upon whom heavy restrictions were placed to ensure that they did not become permanent residents. The guestworker programme was a classic example of the attempt to reconcile an anti-integration (and therefore anti-immigration) conception of national membership with the labour needs of the economy.

But the national conception has also been a force for the *inclusion* of certain types of non-residents. Those defined as members of the national

[3] A 1981 Christian Democrat resolution in the West German Federal Parliament accurately reflected this hostility towards integration: 'The role of the German Federal Republic as a national unitary state and as part of a divided nation does not permit the commencement of an irreversible development into a multi-ethnic state.' See Castles (1984: 46).

community might not have included everyone within the territory of the West German state, but it did include large numbers of people outside it. From 1949 ethnic Germans from Eastern Europe (*Aussiedler*) and from the German Democratic Republic (*Übersiedler*), possessed entrance and citizenship rights upon coming to the Federal Republic. These people, who were not considered foreigners (or even immigrants) by post-war West German governments, could claim residence under Article 116 of the Basic Law which accords German citizenship to the descendants and spouses of people settled in the frontiers of the German Reich as of 31 December 1937, as well as refugees and expellees of German stock (*Volkszughorigkeit*). The force for openness of this broad conception of the national community can be seen in the fact that from the 1940s, until the Berlin Wall was erected in 1961, these 'members' came to Germany in their millions (2.6 million East Germans had crossed into West Germany before 1961). Even after the erection of the Berlin Wall, a stream of *Übersiedler* and *Aussiedler* still flowed in to claim West German citizenship, and were integrated into West German society without major difficulty or great upheaval.

European state

A final feature of significance, one which militated against the West German government pursuing policies of closure in the 1950s and 1960s, was the state's role as a European state and, in particular, as a member of the European Economic Community. West Germany was a founding member of the Community as a signatory to the Treaty of Rome in 1957. The impetus behind membership, undeniably motivated in part by considerations of the value of stable and privileged patterns of trade with other countries of Europe, stemmed also from the desire of West German leaders to ensure that the disastrous events of Germany's recent past were not repeated. These leaders saw the formation of the EEC as providing an opportunity for the Federal Republic to transfer part of its sovereignty to a supranational institution, thereby placing important constraints on the power of the state. In this respect the Federal Republic's membership in the EEC was, as Kielmansegg has suggested, 'the logical conclusion of the founding of the West German state' (1989: 177). From the beginning, the EEC's commitment to the free movement of capital and goods between member states had an important corollary – to enable the free movement of labour between member states. West Germany could never be a totally closed political community after it had signed Articles 48 and 49 of the Treaty of Rome, which granted citizens of EEC countries the right to take up employment in any of the signatory countries (Castles and Kosack

1985: 43). This right was sharpened and reaffirmed by a number of European Acts throughout the 1950s and 1960s, and especially by Regulation 1612/68, adopted by the Council of Ministers in 1968. The cumulative result of the Acts and the Regulation was the abolition of work permits for EEC members and a commitment to the principle of non-discrimination towards nationals of member states in the competition for jobs. Under EEC regulations all citizens of member countries were to enjoy the same rights and conditions as nationals, with the exclusion of political rights.

How did the provisions for free labour movement in the EEC affect West Germany? Apart from placing constraints on the state's ability to apply the same residence restrictions on citizens of EEC countries working in the Federal Republic (mostly Italians) as it placed on other foreign labourers, the influence was minimal up to the 1970s. The number of foreign workers from most Community countries was not huge and residents tended to return home after short periods of labour. The real significance of West German membership – as would become obvious later on – was the way it enmeshed the state in a complex web of interdependence with other states. In the longer term, the EEC's commitment to free movement would ensure that the influence of West Germany's entrance and citizenship policies went far beyond its own borders.

It is apparent that in the years between the formation of the Federal Republic in 1949 and 1970, certain aspects of the West German state influenced the entrance policies of its governments. What was notable in these years was that the demands for entrance that flowed from these aspects of the state – the asylum law, the need for labour, the admittance of *Übersiedler* and *Aussiedler* and EEC membership – did not come into great conflict with the chief demand, for closure – the exclusive (anti-integration) element in the conception of the national community. Instead, all of the influences which emanated from the various characteristics of the West German state appeared to interact successfully: constitutional provisions enabled the entrance of ethnic Germans; the anti-integration ethos determined the form that labour migration took; and membership in the EEC was assisted by a constitution which enabled the ceding of sovereignty to supranational institutions. The explanation for this atmosphere of harmony amongst what were potentially competing influences appears to lie in the widespread social contentment that grew out of the country's massive economic expansion, the fact that the large influx of labour migration was considered temporary, and the relatively small numbers of foreigners utilising the country's asylum provisions. By the beginning of the 1970s the success of the Republic's governments in balancing the competing pressures for entrance and closure appeared hard to deny.

The emergence of a crisis: 1970–93

How did the Federal Republic degenerate into the political crisis of the early 1990s? The onset of Germany's imbroglio is best understood by considering the impact of three changes in the international environment during the 1970s: the slow-down of the world economy, the huge international growth in refugees and asylum seekers and the collapse of communism in Eastern Europe. Cumulatively, they brought the demands on entrance policy that flow from key features of the German state (the state as *Rechtsstaat*, as nation-state, as capitalist state and as European state) into radical tension, leaving Germany in a situation of growing crisis. In this part I shall discuss these changes in the international environment and show how they fed into almost unstoppable demands for reforming Germany's constitutional right of asylum.

Until the 1970s the presence of millions of guestworkers was, as Katzenstein has observed, 'remarkable for the lack of public debate it provoked' (1987: 213). The mood began to change in 1973. With the onset of world recession, provoked by the OPEC oil crisis, the West German economy suddenly found itself facing declining rates of growth and increasing unemployment and inflation. As a result, the government initiated a halt in the inflow of foreign workers, which has remained in force ever since. However, though the government could control the inflow of foreign workers, it was another matter altogether to persuade those foreigners already in West Germany to behave like 'good guests' and leave. While a small percentage of foreign workers emigrated as labour demand dried up, the vast majority stayed. Indeed, as a result of family migration and higher rates of birth amongst the foreign population, the total number of foreign residents in Germany by 1992 had actually increased by 2.3 million on 1973 levels to a total of 6.5 million. Clearly the international recession had both contributed to and demonstrated the failure of the Republic's temporary migration scheme. The recession had sapped the workers of any desire to return home. No matter how depressed the German economy was, things were unlikely to be any better in Turkey or North Africa. Moreover, the passage of time had enabled many of the guestworkers to put down roots in the Federal Republic and establish the kinds of social connections that make return onerous. The result was the slowly dawning reality for officials that Germany now had a substantial and permanent ethnic minority. By the early 1990s, foreign residents made up almost 8 per cent of the country's population, and of this percentage, the Turks, the 'last, poorest, and the most visible' (Martin and Miller 1990: 10) of all guest labourers, constituted one-third.

The economic recession brought into stark relief the conflict between the demands that emanated from the state's position as capitalist state and its role as representative of the national community. For while the conflict between capital's demand for labour in the 1950s and 1960s and the nation's anti-integration ethos had been reconciled before the 1970s through the employment of 'temporary labourers', international economic recession turned these people into permanent residents. The issue of ethnic integration could now not be ignored, not least because of widespread hostility towards these migrants from sections of the German working class, who saw them as 'competitors for jobs, housing and social amenities, and as a threat to security and life-styles' (Castles 1990: 15).

But hostility toward the continued presence of foreigners was not confined simply to the working classes. A succession of governments since the 1970s chose to maintain the fiction that Germany is 'not a country of immigration'. The disingenuousness of this approach was evident in policies by West German governments that simultaneously pursued the contradictory objectives of trying to encourage as many foreigners as they could to return home (often with financial assistance), while attempting to integrate those who remained. These efforts generally failed on both fronts. Few migrants wished to leave and, as many observers noted, full integration was impossible without access to citizenship. Procedures for the naturalisation of non-ethnic German residents remained both expensive and onerous (for instance, applicants had to have been resident for fifteen years even to be eligible).[4] The result was that Germany's large non-citizen population, despite important gains in the acquisition of social and civil rights during the 1970s and 1980s (Soysal 1994), were effectively deprived of political rights in their country of residence.

International economic down-turn also had a second, less obvious effect. It brought the demands emerging from the state's role as *Rechtsstaat* into conflict with those that grew out of its role as representative of the national community. As the barriers to entry for labour migrants from third-world countries went up from the 1970s, foreigners in need of employment found another avenue for entry into the Federal Republic through the country's asylum laws. The length of time taken to process asylum applications, as well as the fact that deportation was unlikely (even in the event of an unsuccessful claim) made this a rather certain, if not notably attractive way of gaining residence in the Republic. Thus throughout the 1980s and 1990s the ranks of asylum seekers in Germany

[4] Only approximately 2.9 per cent of Germany's Italian population, 2.8 per cent of its Spanish and 0.75 per cent of its Turkish population were naturalised citizens by the end of the 1980s (Räthzel 1991: 33). The rate of naturalisation of foreign residents in Germany was far lower than that of almost every other European country.

were swelled not only by people fleeing conflict and persecution, but also by those seeking to gain entry to the country for economic reasons. The appeal of this asylum-based entry route for Turks, amongst others, was further heightened by the presence of established migrant communities, formed after successive waves of labour migration in the 1950s and 1960s.

A second cause of tension was a marked change in the character and number of people seeking asylum in the West. Before the 1970s, asylum seekers in developed countries were chiefly people fleeing communist (and predominantly, Eastern Bloc) states. Their numbers fluctuated widely (increasing dramatically, for instance, after events in Hungary in 1956), but remained relatively limited due to tight exit restrictions imposed by East European states. After 1980, however, large numbers of what were dubbed the 'new asylum seekers' made their way to the frontiers of Western states. These applicants differed from the previous wave in a number of respects. First, they were predominantly people fleeing armed conflict (Lebanese, Tamils, and, by the early 1990s, citizens of the former Yugoslav republic), or non-communist countries that violated human rights (including Iraqis and Turks). Second, many originated from third-world countries, where economic underdevelopment and widespread poverty were defining features and their desire for entrance derived from a complex mixture of social, political and economic aspirations. Third, they were usually culturally and ethnically different from the majority populations of the countries in which they applied for entrance. Fourth, a significant proportion were 'jet age' asylum seekers. One of the effects of the frequency of modern international flight was to create a large pool of asylum seekers no longer forced to find refuge in countries that border their own. Instead they sought out secure and prosperous countries (often Western states) or countries with generous asylum policies that maximised their chances of success. For many richer states this meant that location far from the source of a refugee outflow was no longer insulation from its effects.

These changes were significant enough in themselves to transform the implications of offering a wide-ranging right of asylum. After the collapse of the Soviet Union in 1989, however, asylum pressures increased even further. In the early 1970s, the yearly total of asylum applicants in Western Europe averaged 13,000, but by 1992 the total of applicants had increased to 560,000 (see Meissner *et al.* 1993: 49).

The change in the number and character of the people seeking asylum affected no Western country more than the Federal Republic, which, by the early 1990s, was coming to terms with the social, economic and political challenges of reunification with the German Democratic Republic.

The constitutional right of asylum made Germany a magnet for asylum seekers genuine and spurious alike (Joppke 1999a: 122). The provisions of the law obliged officials to allow all applicants access to German territory where the asylee could exhaust the full panoply of review procedures designed to determine the validity of their claim. In 1973 only 5,595 applications for asylum were lodged in Germany. By 1980 the number had reached 107,818, and by 1992, 438,000. Germany received about two-thirds of all the asylum applications made to EU countries in the 1980s and 1990s. The bulk of these applications came from from nationals of Turkey, the former Yugoslavia, Bulgaria, Romania and Vietnam.

The emergence of the new asylum seekers created tension amongst the various state influences for openness and closure in two ways. First, it was another factor in bringing headlong into conflict the influences which flowed from the Federal Republic as both *Rechtsstaat*, and representative of the national community. The huge increase in asylum applicants and especially those, like the Turks and Vietnamese, culturally and ethnically distinct from the bulk of the German population, placed extreme pressure on the anti-immigration ethos of the national community. While the volume of applicants who actually attained refugee status could probably have been integrated into Germany with relative ease, pressure built up because most *un*successful applicants failed to leave or were not deported. By the early 1990s backlogs in asylum claims were growing at an alarming rate and applications were taking as long as three years to determine. This extended time period allowed asylum seekers to become firmly settled in the country, making deportation politically and ethically controversial.

A direct consequence of these problems was widespread public hostility towards a refugee system unable in practice to fulfil its role of distinguishing those entitled to protection from those (93.3 per cent by 1989) unsuccessful applicants who were not (Fullerton 1990: 394). Nowhere was this hostility more in evidence than in the economically depressed five new *Länder* in East Germany, which became part of the Federal Republic upon reunification in 1990. Here, economic hardship and high rates of unemployment fuelled immense antipathy towards the asylum seekers they had to accommodate (around 20 per cent of the country's total) as part of a quota system that allocated applicants amongst the provinces. Between August and November 1992 this discontent spilled over into violent attacks by Neo-Nazi and other right-wing groups on camps for asylum seekers across the east of Germany. By the end of the year, seventeen people had been killed and 598 injured in extremist violence. The murder of three Turkish women – two teenagers (both of whom had been born in Germany) and a grandmother – in November

1992, sparked a liberal response against the right-wing violence: 400,000 people subsequently marched against the rising tide of racism. Another nine people had become fatal victims of the violence by the following May.

Second, the world-wide increase in asylum applicants revealed conflict between the constitutional asylum laws and the German state's location within a wider system of states. The existence of jet-age asylum seekers enhanced the close interdependence of state action in the realm of refugee and migration matters. Moves to tighten up on asylum provisions in any one state, it was now obvious, could have dramatic consequences in other states. Germany was particularly vulnerable to the costs of this interdependence because of the way its asylum provisions were locked into its constitution, the Basic Law. When other Western countries, less constrained in asylum policy, implemented measures to restrict entrance, which they began to do in the early 1980s, the Federal Republic became an even more attractive destination for those seeking asylum; witness the increased number of applicants the Federal Republic received when Denmark and Sweden tightened up on refugee entrance policy (Hailbronner 1990: 346). It was partly cognisance of this interdependence that lay behind the Republic's failed attempt to create a general right of asylum under public international law in the late 1970s (Hailbronner 1990: 347). By 1993 Germany was embroiled in an international context in which states with the least room to manoeuvre in dealing with asylum seekers were likely to bear the biggest burden.

The third and final influential change in the practical environment was the collapse of communism in Eastern Europe in the late 1980s. The demise of regimes imposing tight exit restrictions on their citizens made possible the emigration of millions of Europeans. For Germany, the collapse had two major repercussions. In the first instance, it enabled the free flow of East Germans into the Federal Republic to take advantage of the fact that 'as far as citizenship law . . . [was] concerned, the division of Germany never happened' (Brubaker 1991: 13).[5] In October 1990 the German Democratic Republic and the Federal Republic were reunified, an act which brought to an end the separate state of East Germany, the largest single source of post-war migration to the Federal Republic. The second effect was to enable a large increase in the number of *Aussiedler* coming to Germany from throughout Eastern Europe. In 1991 some 200,000 ethnic Germans from the (old) Soviet Union, Poland and Romania, settled in the Federal Republic. By 1992, the government was

[5] As Brubaker notes, in just the first twelve days after the removal of the Berlin Wall, 55,000 East German resettlers flooded into the Federal Republic (1991: 13).

facing a backlog of 500,000 applications from ethnic Germans wishing to enter.

The large flow of *Aussiedler* into the Federal Republic, and the realisation of the possibility of increased numbers in the future, placed great pressure on the current German government to reduce the influx of ethnic Germans. Doubts emerged, in the aftermath of reunification, about Germany's ability to withstand the extra stress on the welfare system and on state infrastructure imposed by the absorption of large numbers of people.[6] In 1992 the Kohl government displayed the first real signs of action in recognition of these doubts, though its actions fell far short of reforming the inclusive definition of national membership that lay at the heart of the problem. The Christian Democrat government pledged financial support to assist in the creation of an independent republic for ethnic Germans located in the Volgograd region of the former Soviet Union. The government's unabashed intention was to dissuade the almost one million strong German community located there from taking advantage of their right to immigrate to Germany (Hyman 1992: 41–3).

The government's concern at the increased immigration of *Aussiedler* was also indicative of its fear that this inflow might lead to increased tension between the state's roles as member of the European Union and as representative of the national community. The Single European Act and the free movement provisions entailed in the Schengen Accord of 1990, both committed Germany eventually to end border controls with some of its neighbours. The issue of how Germany dealt with its externally located ethnic 'brothers and sisters' was thus becoming relevant to all EU states, as one of the effects of these free movement provisions would be to enable ethnic Germans, upon attaining citizenship in the Federal Republic, to move (subject to certain restrictions on the availability of work and other amenities) to any country in the Community (Rich 1992: 115). This was hardly a trivial matter: between 1990 and 1994, 238,000 ethnic German immigrants were made citizens of the Republic (*Economist* 1994: 55). Yet it was asylum that caused the most friction between Germany and its EU partners. At a Luxembourg summit in 1991 a proposal by the Federal Republic for EU states to harmonise their asylum policies to a level similar to Germany's gained little support (Bosswick 2000: 54). Germany's EU colleagues could not resist what Joppke describes as the profits of the status quo (Joppke 1999a: 128). A uniquely inclusive right of asylum in Germany meant lower asylum burdens for other European states.

[6] In 1989 alone the cost to the German government of resettling the *Aussiedler* was DM2,000 million. In addition to this cost, one could also add the social security payments to the almost 33 per cent of ethnic Germans, who after arriving in 1987 and 1989 were unemployed at the end of 1989. See Treasure (1991: 24–7).

The combination of huge and growing numbers of asylum applicants, violent incidents against immigrants and the fact that Germany had become, with great reluctance, one of the world's top immigration countries, did not leave the chancellor mincing words. By the early 1990s, Kohl was talking of a 'state crisis' (Thranhardt 1999: 33). His words did little to allay national anxiety, and probably exacerbated it. Nonetheless, the problems Germany faced were real and intractable. As the international environment had changed since the 1970s, the constitution's asylum provisions became a powerful constraint on the practical ability of German governments to control entrance. The recognition of a legally enshrined right of entry for asylum seekers had left Germany exceptionally vulnerable to the entrance decisions of other states as well as pressures for immigration that stemmed from deeply rooted international inequalities.

Withdrawing the right of asylum

The complex origins of Germany's crisis of entrance, emerging from a combination of the different features of its entrance policies – the capitalist demand for labour, the constitutional asylum provisions and the inclusive definition of national membership – did nothing to prevent most political attention focusing on the number of asylum seekers entering. To be sure, considerable financial resources were devoted to the task of encouraging resident guest-workers to return home, and discouraging the entrance of non-resident ethnic Germans. But these efforts paled into insignificance in comparison with governmental action in the area of asylum. Successive governments believed that reducing avenues for asylum was the key to easing Germany's imbroglio. This was reflected in the fact that, up to 1992, three major strategies had been used to break out of the constraints of the Constitution, the international practical environment and state interdependence.

The first was deterrence. Governments during the 1980s and early 1990s implemented a number of measures that aimed at discouraging potential asylum seekers from coming to Germany. The best known of these measures was the housing of asylum applicants in camps. This measure, introduced at the start of the 1980s, enabled the government to impose severe limitations on the movement of asylum seekers, and was intended to discourage 'economically motivated' entrants from using Germany's asylum laws as a vehicle for attaining a first-world standard of living. Further to deter asylum seekers, governments progressively toughened work restrictions on applicants over the 1980s. The period for which an asylum applicant was forbidden to work after arrival in Germany was, for instance, increased to five years.

A second strategy of governments was to speed up asylum processing. Legislation in 1986 introduced a category of 'manifestly unfounded' claims that curtailed the appeal rights of applicants fleeing countries involved in armed conflict or experiencing a general state of emergency. Further measures to expedite the assessing of claims became law in June 1992. These measures aimed at reducing processing time from an average of nine months to an average of six weeks by streamlining and centralising procedures. The time allowed in which to utilise appeal procedures was also reduced, as part of the government's general attempt to get unsuccessful applicants through the process and out of the country before they become a financial burden on the state.

The most effective strategy involved measures to stop potential asylum seekers from reaching German territory. The fact that the constitution's asylum provisions were triggered only when a person entered or reached the frontiers of the Federal Republic encouraged governments to impose barriers to stop potential asylum seekers reaching the territory of the state. Most commonly, the imposition of visas on the citizens of 'high-risk' countries (i.e., those with large refugee outflows) was the form these barriers took. Visa requirements enabled the country's overseas embassies to vet foreigners wishing to enter, and to refuse entry to potential asylum seekers before they reached the country's borders. From the early 1980s, when the Social Democrat (SPD)–Free Democrat (FDP) government introduced compulsory visas for Turkish citizens, they were required by an increasing number of entrants (Castles 1984: 41). To supplement their role, legislation was passed in 1986 that imposed heavy fines on carriers bringing passengers without the correct documentation (a valid passport or an appropriate visa) to the Federal Republic. But visas alone proved unable to 'solve' Germany's problems. They were helpless to stem the flow of applicants overland from countries such as Poland, or those who, like refugees from Bosnia, made it to the frontiers of Germany via Austria.

As another element in its attempt to prevent asylum seekers from reaching its territory, the Federal Republic had become a prime mover behind the 1990 Schengen Accord, signed by France, Benelux, Italy, Spain and Portugal. The Accord had the effect of abolishing almost all of the border controls between the signatory countries as a prelude to the abolition of borders across the EU. But the flip-side of a more open Europe was the construction of common, restrictive policies towards entrants coming from outside signatory states. A crucial implication of the Schengen commitment to the creation of an exclusive multicountry region in Europe, was that 'a refusal of asylum or entry to one country [in the Schengen group] . . . mean[t] refusal to all' (Mallet 1991: 115). The agreement worked out by these countries thus represented a way of dealing with asylum flows through collective action. There was no doubt that Germany saw the Schengen Accord from its first days as of value partly because it offered an opportunity to seal itself off from the flows of asylum seekers who pass through other member countries. Concerns that the European Union has transformed itself into a 'Fortress Europe' – a group of countries open to each other, but effectively closed to migration from non-member countries – largely grew out the Union's intention to use Schengen as a model for its integration process.

All of these preventative and deterrent measures, however, had failed to prevent the number of asylum seekers coming to Germany from reaching alarming proportions by 1992. Correspondingly, a widespread view developed – in, amongst other places, Helmut Kohl's Christian Democrat government – that these strategies were unable to get to the heart of Germany's current problem: the Basic Law's liberal asylum provisions. With public opinion firmly in agreement,[7] the government began to argue with greater force than ever the case for an amendment to the constitution. The most formidable barrier to the two-thirds parliamentary agreement necessary for constitutional change then became the opposition SPD, many of whose members believed that constitutional reform would damage Germany's international reputation. However, the events of August 1992 – violent xenophobic attacks on asylum hostels throughout the country, and the record number of asylum applicants for a single year already passed by the end of the month – began to shift the attitudes of the SPD leadership. When Christian Democrats began to suggest that every new asylum seeker could be blamed directly on the Social Democrats, the political pressure for change became impossible to ignore. Against substantial internal opposition, the SPD's leader, Björn Engholm, managed to win enough support at his party's national conference in mid November 1992 to enter into negotiations with the government on amending the constitution. The result was what became known as the 'asylum compromise'. In return for supporting the amendment of the right to asylum, the government pledged to the SPD that it would liberalise elements of Germany's citizenship requirements and make a number of other concessions in the sphere of migration (Steiner 2000: 65).

The constitutional amendment came into effect on 1 July 1993. The new provisions retained a general right to asylum but provided two new limitations. First, asylum applicants who had passed through a safe third

[7] An opinion poll quoted in *The Independent* newspaper taken in the aftermath of the August/September 1992 outbreak of xenophobic violence suggested that 60 per cent of all Germans favoured a 'provisional stop' on the entrance of asylum seekers into Germany. See, 'German Police Blame Violence on Social Strife' (*The Independent* 1992a: 7).

country, including any EU state, on their way to Germany could now be forced to return to that country. Second, a new streamlined and simplified recognition procedure would be introduced that would allow the authorities to reject immediately claims for asylum from individuals deemed to be from countries that did not persecute their citizens (Münz and Ulrich 1997: 89). The constitutional reforms of 1993 had a profound effect. They dramatically stemmed the tide of rising asylum applications. Within months of the new law, applications had fallen by almost a third on the previous year and by the end of 1993 the annual total was 322,600, a reduction of almost one-quarter on the level for 1992. By 1994 asylum applications had fallen to 127,200, a fraction of the 1992 figure.

The aftermath of reform

Since 1994 the Federal Republic has managed to keep asylum applications tightly under control. Only about 78,000 asylum applications were received in 2000 and the number was expected to fall further in 2001. The crisis of 1992/3 was now a thing of the past. Many have suggested that the changes of 1993 did not so much amend as completely neuter the right to asylum. Certainly, the constitutional changes made Germany's refugee obligations no more (and arguably something less) generous than the 1951 Refugee Convention commitments of any other Western state. The new laws prevented people from many countries with dubious human rights records, such as Ghana, the Czech Republic, Poland, Romania and Senegal from finding refuge (see Blay and Zimmerman 1994: 361–78). Furthermore, the safe country system, in conjunction with visas and carrier sanctions, made it virtually impossible to enter the German state by legitimate means. According to one recent estimate, in more than '98 per cent of all cases, access to the right of asylum is only possible by entering illegally and concealing the access route' (Bosswick 2000: 51). While applying for asylum in Germany is not illegal, it is virtually impossible now to gain protection without violating immigration laws.

Yet this dramatic turn-around was not due to constitutional change alone. Rather it was symptomatic of the degree of effort officials have marshalled since the early 1990s to build a regional context in which Germany is insulated from asylum claims. By the late 1990s, Germany had constructed what amounted to a buffer zone of surrounding states that made overland movement in search of asylum in the Federal Republic either impossible or illegal. Using carrot and stick measures that range from financial incentives, support for EU membership and money for increased border control, Germany has entered into a range of agreements to allow the deportation of migrants to so-called 'safe countries' including Romania in 1992, Poland and Switzerland in 1993, Bulgaria and the Czech Republic in 1994 and Vietnam in 1995 (Münz and Ulrich 1997: 90). The country has also paid DM120 million and 60 million to Poland and the Czech Republic respectively to boost the efficiency and effectiveness of their border controls (Münz and Ulrich 1997: 90). In coupling these measures with the first country of asylum provisions associated with the 1990 Dublin Convention and the Schengen Treaty, both of which are applicable to all of the accession states to the EU, Germany has completely reorganised the geography of asylum in Europe. The Federal Republic has transformed its position as a landlocked country in the centre of Europe from a disadvantage in terms of asylum-seeking into a huge advantage (Lavenex 2001: 148–99).

This highly dubious achievement has been matched by harsh policies towards asylum seekers and refugees who manage to have their applications heard in Germany. Officials use a very strict definition of eligibility for refugee status. Individuals persecuted by non-state agents, such as victims of the Islamic extremist opposition forces in Algeria, have been routinely denied Geneva Convention protection. Even those granted protection have not escaped the new restrictionism. No other Western European state showed as much alacrity in encouraging, and in some cases forcing, the return of refugees from the wars in FYR and Kosovo. While Germany granted temporary protection (asylum for the duration of the conflict) to a large number of victims of Europe's most brutal recent conflicts, many observers, including UNHCR, believe that the country showed an indecent haste in returning refugees from the Former Yugoslavia after the Dayton peace agreement (Gibney 2000b; Bagshaw 1997; Koser *et al.* 1998).

Conclusion

The constitutional right of asylum offered by Germany between 1949 and 1993 provided an entitlement for refugees in need of protection unparalleled amongst Western states. When the demands imposed by the recognition of this right were limited and relatively minor, political elites and the public at large were prepared to tolerate its existence. By the late 1980s, however, changes in the international environment created a large and growing gap between the volume of asylum seekers and refugees the public and officials were prepared to tolerate and the number of people entering to access that right. This gap continued to expand, like a rubber band stretched to breaking point, until the early 1990s. With constitutional reform in 1993, and a range of agreements with neighbouring countries, popular and elite expectations of asylum and actual avenues for entrance snapped back into closer alignment. The consequences for asylum seekers, both those with well-founded and those with weak claims to protection, were baleful. A dramatic assertion of popular sovereignty against established constitutional law rendered access to asylum virtually inaccessible, at least by legal means.

Could this backlash, this dramatic and painful recoil from an inclusive liberal entitlement, have been avoided? Many observers have argued that the Kohl government merely exacerbated public anxiety with its talk of an 'asylum crisis'. Some stress that the reactions of the Federal Republic's governments reflect a distinctively German form of illiberalism. In this view, there is a common thread that runs through the country's ethnic citizenship laws, the shoddy treatment of guestworkers, the Nazi experience, and the contemporary response to asylum seekers. As I have suggested in this chapter, certain internal features of German society (such as the embrace of an ethnic conception of citizenship) did feed the events of 1992–3. Yet, in the end, they were probably not the most important ones. We can make more headway into explaining the demise of asylum in 1993 by looking at how changes in the international environment (including the end of the Cold War, the Yugoslav refugee crisis and the rise of jet age asylum seekers) impacted on a uniquely inclusive entrance entitlement than by examining German perceptions of foreigners. For it is difficult to imagine any other Western country that would long have tolerated the number of entrants German experienced in the early 1990s. Certainly, it does not give much away about the chapters that follow to suggest that the UK and the USA would also have found themselves deep in political controversy if they had received 300,000 and 900,000 asylum applicants respectively in a single year – numbers which (adjusting for population differences) are proportional to Germany's 1992 total.

If we understand the crisis of 1992/3 with its sad legacy for asylum as a problem primarily of the supply side – the number of people accessing asylum – then what really made Germany's crisis one of unmanageable proportions comes much more clearly into view. Faced with increasing numbers of asylum applicants, the near-universal response of EU states was to impose tougher entrance restrictions and to scale down the availability of asylum. This technique was successful in reducing the number of asylum seekers *they* faced, but their success came at the cost of redirecting applicants to other states that, like Germany, enshrined inclusive entitlements towards refugees rigidly in law. If one wishes to find a culprit for the Federal Republic's 1992/3 imbroglio, one could do worse than to look at the actions of other European states which, by effectively 'opting out' of providing refuge for the new wave of asylum seekers, collectively created an environment that imposed enormous costs on states that recognise broad rights of entry for refugees. Ironically, German officials can claim the last laugh, if not the moral high ground. Many of the European countries, including Britain and the Netherlands, that could once count on a constitutionally constrained Germany to be the destination of the vast majority of Europe's asylum seekers now find the number of applicants they face growing.

4 The United Kingdom: the value of asylum

> [Britain has already experienced] a very considerable commotion [over immigration in the 1960s]. We've dealt with that problem and we don't wish to see it return.
>
> Douglas Hurd, British Foreign Secretary 1992

> The UK is taking the lead in arguing for reform, not of the [Refugee] convention's values, but of how it operates.
>
> Tony Blair, British Prime Minister 2001

> Only a few days ago I put a question to the Minister [Lord Rooker, Minister of State, Home Office] asking whether there was a legal way in which an asylum seeker could enter this country. He gave me a very blunt answer – 'No'.
>
> Lord Dholakia, House of Lords 2002

In May 2002 *The Guardian* newspaper reported that British Prime Minister Tony Blair had 'taken personal control of asylum policy' and was considering a range of radical new options to reduce the number of asylum seekers arriving in the UK. These options included mobilising 'Royal Navy warships to intercept people traffickers in the Mediterranean' (*The Guardian* 2002a: 1) and pursuing a far more aggressive policy on deportation. Few watchers of political events in the UK since 1999 could have been completely surprised by this development. The question of how to reduce asylum applications has been a hot political issue in recent years: the focus of two comprehensive pieces of legislation (in 1999 and 2002) since the Blair government came to power in 1997, as well as a major issue in the 2001 national election. Yet from a slightly longer historical perspective these events were indeed surprising. For between the early 1980s and the late 1990s, the UK appeared to be one European state that had avoided substantial numbers of asylum claimants, and thus the political controversy that seemed invariably to ensue.

In 1991, for example, Britain received 44,800 applications for asylum. This represented a substantial increase on the amount it received during the 1980s (when applications averaged about 5,000 a year), but this rise was hardly viewed as constituting – outside of at least the rather peculiar world-view of some of the popular newspapers – a crisis for the British state. And any tension that might have been present rapidly diminished when the number of applicants in 1994 fell substantially to 32,830. In 1996 the UK received only 27,932 applications for asylum. The contrast between the situations in the UK and in the Federal Republic of Germany raised an obvious but important question: how did the UK manage to escape the pressures brought about by an international environment favourable to the production and movement of increasing numbers of refugees and asylum seekers?

Answers were not in short supply. Some attributed the UK's success to geography, or the absence of a written bill of rights, or to the UK's early experience with New Commonwealth immigration. Yet by the late 1990s, it was not the UK's effectiveness in escaping the woes of many continental European states that was in need of explaining. Rather, as the Blair government discussed enlisting warships in the battle to defend the integrity of the UK's national borders, the question was, why had asylum emerged as such an important political issue?

In this chapter, I will trace the evolution of UK asylum policy since 1945 through the broader context of those forces that have shaped the admission and exclusion of immigrants by the British state over the last five decades. This examination is intended not only to highlight the political context within which current asylum policies have emerged, but also to provide insight into the question of how Britain remained insulated from the asylum challenges faced by continental Europe for so long and why it has recently come to find itself embroiled in problems similar to other Western states.

The state and entrance: 1945–75

To attain any kind of insight into how Britain has evolved in the realm of asylum policy it is necessary to understand those features of the British state that have influenced decisions on entrance and closure since 1945. For, like any modern state, the British state occupies a number of different roles from which flow complex and conflicting interests relevant to considerations of entrance. Some of these roles – its international commitments and its membership in the European Community – have only been acquired in the post-war period, but others – its position as a capitalist state, as representative of a distinct political community and as leader of the Commonwealth – have a far longer history. Post-war British governments have had to construct asylum policies in a context framed by these considerations. To suggest that they have attempted to *harmonise* the conflicting interests which flow from them would be perhaps too strong; it would be to imply that governments have possessed some kind of coherent vision of how the conflicting interests of the state could fit together. More accurately, governments have attempted to *lessen* conflict between these different interests as it has emerged, something which has given British entrance policy a remarkably reactive and *ad hoc* flavour.

Capitalist state

In the immediate post-war period the state's role as capitalist state was an important force for openness. While high unemployment in the British economy during the inter-war years had acted as a deterrent to large-scale immigration, the end of World War II found Britain faced with the task of rebuilding elements of the economy and infrastructure neglected or damaged by the war, and with a Labour government cognisant of the need to increase export production in order to achieve its election aims of full employment and 'fair shares' (Kay and Miles 1992: 40). But there was an immediate problem for the post-war government. It was clear that the traditional source of reserve labour for the British economy, Ireland, could not provide labour at a rate rapid enough for the state's needs, especially when its effect was mitigated by the continuing emigration of British citizens. The resettlement efforts of the government in relation to Polish refugees (specifically with the Polish Resettlement Act of 1947) helped to boost the supply of labour, but the government's main vehicle for satisfying the requirements of economic growth involved the establishment in 1946 of the European Volunteer Forces Scheme (EVF). Between 1946 and 1948 some 100,000 refugees from Lithuania, Ukraine, Latvia and Yugoslavia were recruited to work in labour-starved areas of the British economy, including agriculture, hospitals, and the textile, building and coal industries (Rees 1982: 81–2). The scheme was similar to European 'guestworker' migration; labourers were not free to sell their labour on the open market; they had to work in specific areas of labour shortage; and their presence was considered temporary. By 1948, however, the need for EVF-style schemes had diminished – and with it the need for direct government involvement in the recruitment of labour – as the economy's requirements were coming to be satisfied by a new external source: immigrants from the West Indies.

As Commonwealth citizens, West Indians were free to enter and gain work in the UK, under the provisions of the 1948 British Nationality Act. As has been shown by Ceri Peach, the West Indian workers, many of whom had been directly recruited for work by British employers, and in some cases by the British government, came to the UK primarily as a result of a 'single external stimulus' (Peach 1968: 93): the demand for labour in Britain. As such, the number entering Britain throughout the 1950s and 1960s ebbed and flowed according to changes in labour demand. And West Indian immigration represented only the beginning of capitalist-related migration to Britain. By the 1950s immigrants from other New Commonwealth countries, in particular, India and Pakistan, had joined the flow of workers to take up semi-skilled and unskilled positions in the UK economy. In overall terms, the number of New Commonwealth entrants was not large up to 1961: the UK's West Indian population rose from 15,300 to 171,800, its Indian population from 30,800 to 81,400 and its Pakistani population from 5,000 to 24,900, over the period 1951 to 1961 (Rees 1982: 83). The size of the flow of New Commonwealth immigration in this period indicated something of the weakness of the demand for labour in Britain relative to other West European countries. (By 1961 West Germany had already taken in 500,000 guestworkers.) Unlike these other countries, the UK's economic growth during the 1950s and 1960s was 'slow and punctuated by crises over the balance of payments and the role of sterling and by worries about inflation' (Layton-Henry 1985: 98). Nevertheless, the capitalist demand for labour acted as an important force for openness up to the start of the 1960s, and while governments played only a minor role in securing the supply of that labour and assisting the process of its settlement in the UK, they did not introduce entrance controls.

Commonwealth state

The unrestricted entrance rights of New Commonwealth citizens up to 1962 emanated from the state's role as head of the Commonwealth: the group of independent and semi-independent colonies and former colonies, states and territories which together had once formed the British Empire. In the immediate aftermath of World War II, British leaders viewed the Commonwealth not as a nagging reminder of a period of imperial expansion long past, but as a potentially lucrative network for mutual cooperation and economic growth which could offer Britain privileged trading relations, without diminishing its status as the leader of a substantial grouping of the world's states. The maintenance specifically of a right of entry for Commonwealth citizens was seen both as an important element in fostering the continued close relations between Commonwealth countries and as a unique responsibility of leadership, for no other member country allowed unrestricted access into its territory to all citizens of the Commonwealth. But in spite of the long history of this right, British leaders had no reason before the late 1940s to believe that it would actually be exercised by large numbers of non-white Commonwealth citizens. Before 1945, such immigrants had come to the UK only in very small numbers. When they finally did start entering in large numbers during the 1940s and 1950s, Britain's commitment to the Commonwealth was still strong enough (even if it was shared unevenly amongst the British elite) to militate against the introduction of entrance restrictions, though efforts were made by the Churchill government in the 1950s to pressure the governments of the countries concerned to discourage the flow. Early post-war governments were clearly not enamoured of the new immigration, but the view of the home secretary in 1954 that abandoning 'the old tradition that British subjects from any Colonial Territory can come freely to this country . . . would be to take a very drastic step' (Layton-Henry 1987: 65), still guided their response.

The maintenance of entrance rights for Commonwealth citizens did however point to a deeper historical problem in entrance policy for the British state which the collapse of the British Empire was bringing to the fore. Britain had never had an exclusive and clearly defined legal conception of citizenship for the members of its political community. As Rogers Brubaker has observed:

> The concept of citizenship as membership of a legal and political community was foreign to British thinking. Legal and political thinking were conceived instead in terms of allegiance between individual subjects and the King. These ties of allegiance knit together the British Empire not the British nation. (Brubaker 1989: 11)

The new British Nationality Act of 1948 did little to rectify this problem. The Act, like the one before it, still recognised British citizenship as something that accrued to all members of the British Commonwealth, Colonies and Protectorates, and accordingly granted all Commonwealth citizens the right to enter and settle in Britain. In doing so, it offered a right of entrance to almost 800 million overseas residents. In law, the situation facing Britain after 1948 was analogous to that of West Germany after 1948: British citizenship, like West German citizenship, was potentially claimable by huge numbers of people outside the territorial boundaries of the state. But there was an important difference. In Germany the political community had traditionally recognised non-resident ethnic Germans as their equals and as their own, and were amenable to their integration into the national community of the Federal Republic. The vast majority of the members of the British political community saw non-whites from the new Commonwealth as neither their equals nor their own, and this attitude reflected the implicitly racist ethos of the Commonwealth. Accordingly, there existed in Britain a large gap between those whom the law defined as legitimate entrants to the British polity and those whom the political community recognised as such. And the tension created by this gap came more and more clearly into view as New Commonwealth immigrants began to enter Britain.

Political community

While the notion of allegiance made the concept of British citizenship decidedly vague under law, the British state has still, throughout the twentieth century, occupied a role as representative of a distinctive, exclusive and predominantly white political community of those resident in the British Isles and (at least Northern) Ireland. And this political community has had an interest in decisions on entrance and closure which the British state and its governments have been unable to ignore. Before 1945 the views of the political community were most clearly reflected in legislation aimed at restricting the entrance of aliens (i.e., those not from countries of the British Empire or Commonwealth). Two important themes already established in entrance restrictions before 1945 were to have a powerful influence on entrance policy in the years after the war. The first involved the implementation of racial restrictions on entrance. This theme was reflected in the first modern restriction act – the Aliens Act of 1905 – which brought to an end the long history of *laissez faire* in British entrance policy. The Act came in response to a wave of anti-Semitic feeling which 'cut across the barriers of social class' (Holmes 1988: 70) in Britain and aimed to stem the flow of Russian Jews coming to the UK in order to escape Tsarist pogroms. A second, related, theme was most clearly perceptible during the inter-war years when large numbers of refugees from Nazi regimes attempted to come to the UK. The *Daily Mail* in 1938 captured this theme succinctly: 'once it was known that Britain offered sanctuary to all who were prepared to come, *the floodgates would be opened*, and we should be inundated by thousands seeking a home' (Holmes 1988: 84, emphasis added). The widespread fear that Britain as a tiny overcrowded island could easily be flooded by aliens if tight restrictions were not made on entrance, led to the imposition by the government of the day of visas for people (mostly Jews) coming to the UK from Germany and Austria.

It was into a country whose twentieth-century history had seen restrictions placed on entrance for reasons of race and overcrowding that West Indians began to enter in sizeable numbers after the war. Unsurprisingly in the context of that history, the Attlee and Churchill governments were immediately concerned about how the political community would respond to this new influx. As government documents from the time show, rather than recognising any potential for economic benefit from the influx of labour, government concerns, even when the size of the inflow was very small in the 1950s, lay with the possibility of emerging racial tension (Layton-Henry 1987: 64). These initial concerns were fuelled by the Notting Hill and Nottingham race riots of 1958, and by opinion polls which offered evidence of anxiety in the political community over the immigration. It was clear by the end of the 1950s, at least from the perspective of political leaders, that the same themes which had led to restrictions on the entrance of aliens in the first half of the century – racial harmony and the danger of the UK being swamped – were now present in much of the public reaction against New Commonwealth immigration. All the pressure on immigration flowing from the political community seemed to be pushing in the direction of restrictions on the entrance of New Commonwealth citizens.

State of refuge

A force for openness in British entrance policy throughout much of the period between 1900 and 1970 was the state's recognition of the principle of asylum for foreigners attempting to escape persecution in their home country. Before 1905 Britain had an international reputation as a place of refuge for the politically persecuted of Europe. This reputation was built not on any specific legal entitlement of asylees to enter, but on the *laissez faire* entrance policies of the British state of the time. After 1905, however, increasing restrictions were placed on foreigner entrance, and while there was some recognition of an entrance entitlement for political and religious asylum seekers, entry came increasingly to rest on the discretion of the Home Office and immigration officials. When new entrance restrictions were introduced in 1914 and 1919 under the guise of war-time security concerns, the residual generosity contained in Home Office discretion began to dry up. Thereupon began a period lasting until 1938 when no distinction was made in law and practice between immigrants and asylum seekers (Sherman 1973: 273). Throughout this period, asylum accrued only to those with enough wealth to satisfy normal immigration requirements. A 1934 joint conclusion by the Home and Foreign Offices captures the guiding theme – or more accurately, lack of one – in refugee admittance decisions: '[it would be] impossible to make any general statement as to when asylum would be extended to a political refugee, since a decision can only be reached in the light of the circumstances of any particular case' (quoted in Kaye and Charlton 1990: 9). The reluctance of governments to systematise and formalise refugee policy – which was heavily influenced by considerations of security and numbers – did not always lead to niggardliness in the granting of asylum, simply unpredictability. Between 1933 and 1939, despite visa restrictions, some 50,000 refugees from Germany and Austria were allowed entrance into Britain.

The combination of discretion and unpredictability continued to inform British policy in the early post-war era. Many thousands of refugees from Eastern Europe and the Baltic states were resettled in the UK after 1945, and by 1970 Britain had also accepted for settlement substantial numbers of refugees from Hungary, following the Soviet invasion of 1956, and from Czechoslovakia, after the crushing of the 'Prague Spring' in 1968. As in other Western countries, refugee and asylum admittance in Britain was closely aligned with foreign policy considerations, as a result of which refugees from the Soviet bloc formed the bulk of entrants. By 1970 Britain had signed the two major international agreements on the treatment of refugees and asylum seekers, the 1951 Convention Relating to Status of Refugees and the 1967 Protocol. These agreements turned the treatment of refugees into an international obligation; Britain had now agreed to respect the international law principle of *non-refoulement* and grant certain rights to individuals determined to be refugees. However, the Convention and Protocol were not immediately integrated into statute; they were simply acknowledged in the less legally binding statement of guiding principles for immigration admittance, the Immigration Rules, and then only in 1971. Thus, Britain's accession to these agreements did not fundamentally alter the way it treated refugees and asylum seekers nor lead to a substantial increase in the number of claims for entrance under the state's role as refuge.

European state

A final force for openness in UK entrance emerged from the state's location as part of the broader system of states of the European Community. Britain was a late-comer to the EC. It was only in January 1973 that it acceded to the Treaty of Rome. The tardiness of Britain's entry reflected its earlier reluctance to join moves towards economic cooperation in Europe. After World War II, the country's pride in victory, its traditional distrust of other European powers, and most significantly, the belief that its needs for privileged patterns of trade could be met more effectively through the Commonwealth, all combined to discourage British leaders from joining European discussions on economic association (Dummett and Nichol 1990: 213). By the 1960s, however, the continued value of British aloofness was questioned. The economic influence and prosperity of the EEC contrasted sharply with the slowness and crisis-ridden nature of British economic development. It was clear that the 'post-war view that the British economy was fundamentally stronger than any other in Western Europe had to be abandoned in the face of the evidence' (George 1990: 40). Hence, after two unsuccessful attempts at gaining membership, Britain finally joined in the early 1970s.

Membership immediately held out the prospect of fundamental changes in British entrance policy. Some 200 million EEC nationals now possessed the right to take up work opportunities in the UK. At a time when governments were busy trying to close off one wide-ranging entrance entitlement, Britain had committed itself to another. In practical terms, the initial effect of EEC membership was not great. The weakness of the British economy throughout the 1970s acted as a deterrent to European migration. In 1974 only 11,340 resident permits to EEC nationals were issued and only 6,940 in 1984, after a continuous downward slide in applications (Bevan 1986: 201). But the number of entrants failed to reflect the size of the leap Britain had taken. For EC membership meant that after 1973 Britain not only was forced to conceive of the entrance of certain groups of foreigners in fundamentally different terms – as a matter of right rather than discretion – but had enmeshed itself in complex and growing networks of collaboration with other European states which would later impact upon its provision of refuge and asylum.

Commonwealth versus political community: 1961–81

The demands for entrance and closure which emanated from the British state in the years up to the early 1970s did not sit comfortably together: the influence of capitalism (at least before the early 1960s), of Commonwealth leadership and of the refugee and asylum commitments dragged policy, to varying degrees, in the direction of openness; whereas the desires of the political community (permeated by considerations of race) required policies of closure. From the beginning of New Commonwealth immigration in the 1940s, the relationship between these different demands on entrance policy came more sharply into conflict. However, it was not until the start of the 1960s that a British government resorted to legislation to reduce the tension.

Why were entrance restrictions introduced in 1962? In an insightful recent examination of the subject, Randall Hansen has argued that before the early 1960s political elites were reluctant to alienate members of the Old Commonwealth (Canada, Australia and South Africa, etc.) by introducing entrance restrictions. As a result, they exhausted alternative means of controlling entrance, notably pressure on the New Commonwealth countries of origin to prevent departures (Hansen 2000a: 100), before resorting to entrance controls. When in 1961, however, the inward movement of Pakistanis and Indians experienced 'a very marked acceleration' (Smith 1981: 98) leading to an annual total of 130,000 new settlers, a consensus amongst elites emerged that controls were a regrettable necessity (Hansen 2000a: 19). At the same time, immigration had well and truly emerged as a key political issue, whose spoils were not going to be claimed by those in favour of keeping Commonwealth entitlements intact. With public opinion surveys showing the vast majority of the electorate in favour of the introduction of entrance restrictions, there was abundant evidence that immigration was already emerging as what Richard Crossman would later describe as 'the hottest potato in politics' (quoted in Holmes 1991: 219).

By the start of 1962 it was clear that the state's roles as leader of the Commonwealth and, to a far lesser extent, as capitalist state were directly in conflict with its role as representative of the British political community, and that something would have to give. It is worth considering here what was so distinctive about the UK situation that the pressure for controls on entrance emerged so early in its post-war history. Certainly there was nothing inevitable about conflict coming about through the large inflow of immigration into a Western country. The Federal Republic of Germany – a state not renowned for representing a political community with a more receptive attitude towards foreigners – allowed in many more non-residents during the 1950s and 1960s as a result of the demands of domestic capital. Yet it did not experience major social and political conflict, at least not until well into the 1970s.

Why was the UK different? There were a number of distinct features of the British situation which help explain the discrepancy. To begin with, British leaders, unlike German ones, never held a unanimous view of the economic value of immigration, and never attempted to assuage public concern by appealing to its economic benefits. This might in part be attributed to the state of British economic growth in the 1950s and 1960s, and concomitant rise in the general standard of living, which was not nearly as high, rapid or as steady as in Germany; in this context immigration simply appeared more likely to impose costs on the state's economic health rather than to play a great role in improving it. The economic problems Britain experienced in the early 1960s gave a veneer of respectability to this view. Second, the inflow of Commonwealth workers into Britain was widely and immediately seen as immigration for permanent settlement. It was apparent that the new immigrants would constitute an enduring part of the British political community, and that the community would be fundamentally changed by their arrival. In this respect, the British public were being asked to admit the immigrants as full members. By contrast, the labourers who came to Germany in the same period were perceived by both the government and the community as 'temporary' or 'guest' workers. Their ability to change the face of the nation would be minimised by the fact that they would be able to stay in the Federal Republic for as long and only as long as the country needed them. Thirdly and crucially, the New Commonwealth immigrants, unlike West Germany's *Gastarbeiter*, entered as a matter of right. As such, it was far easier to believe that British governments had lost control over their entrance, for the immigrants did not enter at the discretion of the state. Furthermore, it was obvious that as a prodigious number of Commonwealth citizens possessed this entitlement, the problem could, in the absence of legislative action, escalate dramatically.

If one takes seriously these three characteristics of New Commonwealth entrance, it is apparent that the German experience of labour migration in the 1950s and 1960s cannot be considered analogous. The situation which provides a far better point of comparison is the Federal Republic's 1992/3 asylum crisis. In both circumstances, the country concerned perceived a real economic cost as accruing because of the new entrants, the entrants were (at least if granted asylum in Germany) entering for permanent settlement, residence was ensured by virtue of a right and, most importantly of all, in both the tension between various aspects of the state (in Britain between the roles of Commonwealth and political community, and in Germany between *Rechtsstaat* and national community) held out the prospect of getting much worse. For in the UK in the 1960s and in the Federal Republic under Article 16 there existed an almost limitless supply of people who could take up a right to enter the country concerned.

But there was one vital difference in the British situation. The nature of the British state enabled governments to utilise legislation to ease tension between the conflicting features of entrance. Referring retrospectively to the preparations for the 1968 Commonwealth Immigrants Act the ex-Cabinet minister, Richard Crossman, suggested that they involved 'plans for legislation which we realised would have been declared unconstitutional in any country with a written constitution and a Supreme Court' (Robertson 1989: 317). In this sentence Crossman hit upon the key feature of the British state which enabled governments to evade the kind of protracted crisis that subsequently consumed Germany. For the British state was no *Rechtsstaat*; constraints on entrance policy were not locked into the structure of the state in a way that placed change out of the reach of the government of the day. In Britain, just what entrance policy would be at any particular time, and just who had an entitlement to enter, rested almost entirely on the balance of forces in the UK Parliament. As such, no outsider entrance entitlement was on a surer footing than the government of the day saw fit to place it on. Whereas the Federal Republic's Basic Law works to safeguard certain entrance rights from the capriciousness of government and public views on who shall enter, the sovereignty of the British Parliament – which in practice meant the sovereignty of the party of government (Ryan 1991b: 395) – made entrance entitlements far more precarious.

The theoretical manoeuvrability of British governments in the face of tensions between the state's demands for entrance and closure became practical during the 1960s. In 1962 the Macmillan Conservative government began a process of legislating out of existence the entrance rights of New Commonwealth citizens which would finally conclude almost twenty years later. The 1962 Commonwealth Immigrants Act, opposed by the Labour opposition of the time, introduced the requirement of work-vouchers for Commonwealth citizens coming to the UK to settle. The vouchers gave government the ability to control the entrance of semi-skilled and un-skilled entrants through the manipulation of the number of vouchers made available in any particular year. In the year immediately after the passing of the Act, these vouchers were allocated with some liberality, but when the net intake of immigrants from Commonwealth countries rose again in 1963–4, the number of vouchers made available was decreased (Smith 1981: 106). The bipartisan nature of entrance restrictions on immigrants from the New Commonwealth was indicated by the fact that it was the Labour Party that was responsible for the next major piece of restrictive legislation, the 1968 Commonwealth Immigration Act. The Act was introduced to stem the flow of East African Asian refugees coming to Britain to escape the 'Kenyanisation' policies of the Kenyan government, which imposed serious economic constraints on resident Asians and presaged mass expulsion. These Commonwealth citizens had not been subject to entrance restrictions because they travelled to the UK on British passports, retained after independence as a result of an offer by the British government. The number of Asian entrants rose from 6,150 in 1965 to 13,600 in 1967, and peaked in the first two months of 1968, when 12,823 arrived (Layton-Henry 1985: 104). In the midst of an at times overheated campaign against the immigration by Conservative politicians Duncan Sandys and Enoch Powell, and widespread public calls for action, the government rushed the 1968 Act through Parliament in three days.

The 1968 Act placed British immigration law on a new footing by introducing for the first time the principle of patriality. This principle required that all members of the Commonwealth who did not possess a substantial connection to Britain – who, in other words, did not 'belong' to the UK – by birth or blood (through descent from a parent or male grandparent) obtain an entry voucher before arriving in the UK. The effect (and, certainly for some, the deliberate intention) of the Act was to deprive non-white Commonwealth citizens (including those holding British passports) of the right to enter the UK, through the requirement of ties of blood to or birth in the UK's historically overwhelmingly white political community.

The 1962 and 1968 restriction Acts were superseded in 1971 by the more general and comprehensive Immigration Act, which laid down a systematic basis for future immigration to Britain. The Act enshrined patrials as the only Commonwealth citizens with an automatic right to enter and settle in Britain. In this respect, as Smith has observed, the Act 'effectively eradicated the long-standing differentiation in immigration law and practice between Commonwealth citizens and foreign nationals' (Smith 1981: 119).

But the 1971 Act was not only important in easing tension between the state's roles as Commonwealth leader and as representative of the political community. The clarification of the position of entrance-right-bearing non-residents in the 1971 Act was also necessary to defuse the potential for tension with the state's role as EEC member. The capacious conception of Commonwealth entrance rights that Britain had inherited from its imperial role was not a legacy which the states of Europe, mindful of the free movement provisions of EEC legislation, keenly welcomed. In the event, the category of patrial – which Britain used as its definition of a nationality for the purposes of the Treaty – helped it to by-pass potential problems (Rees 1982: 88). It specified a group of potential entrants not so open ended as to cause concern to other member states.

By 1981, through the British Nationality Act of that year, nationality law was adjusted to correspond with immigration law, creating 'a British citizenship exclusively for the United Kingdom' (Hansen 2000b: 43). Through this adjustment the British government breached the widespread state practice of first defining its own nationals and then constructing an immigration law to exclude certain categories of non-nationals (Dummett 1986: 145–6). British nationality law, however, simply confirmed what was by now established immigration practice by distinguishing between those persons:

> whose status was acquired by association with the United Kingdom and those whose status was acquired by association with the dependencies. The former were to be known as 'British citizens'. The latter were to be known as 'British Dependent territories citizens' or as 'British Overseas citizens', those two titles reflecting a distinction between associations with existing and former dependencies. (Plender 1988: 26)

The effect of the Act was to define British citizenship in a way that more closely resembled the perceptions of the political community. The gap which had existed between those whom the political community saw as legitimate members with a right of entry and those whom the law recognised as such was closed. As Ann Dummett observed in the wake of the new Act:

> [British governments have] drawn the lines in such a way that the vast majority of British citizens, free from immigration control, are white people (at a rough estimate 54 out of a total of 57 million) while over 95 per cent of the people in the four categories of British without right of entry are of non-European descent. (Dummett 1986: 146)

Ironically, the circumscribed citizenship mandated by the Act has, in the years since it was passed, proved too tough even for government intentions. In an interesting turn-around in 1983, an amendment was introduced to make Falkland Islanders full British citizens without even requiring them to register (Dummett 1986: 146). In a similar vein, the Thatcher government by-passed normal immigration restrictions in the late 1980s when it guaranteed a right of entry and settlement in the UK for some 50,000 of the more economically desirable residents of the colony of Hong Kong, which passed into Chinese hands in 1997 (Skeldon 1990/1: 512). In most respects, however, the new Act simply brought UK citizenship legislation into line with that of other Western states (Hansen 2000b: 43–6).

What then was the overall significance of the head-on clash between the roles of the British state as representative of the political community and as Commonwealth and capitalist state in the period between the late 1940s and 1981? First, it demonstrated how the structure of the British state (and, in particular, the principle of parliamentary sovereignty) could be used by governments to defuse a crisis brought about by the right-based entrance of substantial numbers of non-residents. Unlike Germany, British governments had the discretion fundamentally to alter and, where necessary, to eliminate undesirable entrance rights, through the use of a simple majority in Parliament. On the one hand, this enabled Britain to avoid protracted conflict between the demands which flowed from the different roles of the state, brought about by New Commonwealth immigration. On the other hand, this governmental discretion made British entrance policy exceedingly receptive to the capriciousness and narrow-mindedness of public opinion. This receptiveness was reflected in the fact that when the gap between those whom the political community saw as legitimate entrants and those whom the law recognised as such was closed, it was primarily non-whites that lost the entitlement to enter.

But something else of great significance emerged from this clash: the right-based inflow of New Commonwealth residents presented Britain very early on in its post-war history with a 'crisis of entitlement' potentially of the magnitude of the Federal Republic's situation in the early 1990s. The timing of this crisis taught the UK a lesson about the possible dangers of broad-based entry entitlement, and the uncontrolled inflow of what the political community perceived as 'foreigners', far in advance of other Western states.

Political community versus refuge: 1979–95

If, before the late 1970s, the major preoccupation of British governments in the area of entrance lay with ameliorating conflict between the state's role as Commonwealth leader and as representative of the political community, then by the 1980s increasing attention came to be focused on refugee and asylum matters. This shift in focus did not really reflect the existence of widespread discontent over refugee entrance policy amongst the British political community – it was in no way a key political issue, and there was little practical difference in policy between the major parties. What it clearly did reflect was governmental *apprehension* about the possibility of the uncontrolled entrance of foreigners: a desire not to repeat the controversy associated with the entry of the New Commonwealth immigrants in the 1950s and 1960s.

The new focus on asylum – on the potential for tension between the state's role as refuge and as representative of the political community – came to the fore because of three developments in Britain's practical environment that occurred in the 1970s and 1980s. The first was that the UK, like other Western states, found itself facing changes in the volume and national origins of those seeking asylum in its territory. While Britain received little more than a few hundred asylum seekers annually during the 1970s, in the 1980s they began to enter at the rate of around 5,000 per year. Moreover, the applicants were now coming from places such as Iran, Ghana, Sri Lanka, Pakistan, Zaire and Turkey rather than countries in the Soviet bloc. By 1992 56 per cent of all of Britain's asylum applicants came from Africa or Asia.

A second change concentrating government attention was economic down-turn in Britain in the 1970s. Unemployment rose from 3.0 per cent to 11.2 per cent between 1973 and 1986 in Britain (Brittan 1989: 23), while GDP growth dropped from an average of 3.0 per cent between 1950 and 1973 to an average of 1.1 per cent between 1973 and 1984 (Kirby 1991: 12). For British leaders this down-turn exacerbated traditional concerns about the potential economic and social costs of immigration. The new asylum seekers came to be perceived not only as taking advantage of traditional British hospitality to refugees, but as having a negative economic impact on employment levels and the provision of social welfare. Most asylum seekers, Home Office officials argued, were not 'genuine refugees . . . [but are] motivated primarily by a desire to circumvent normal immigration controls' (Amnesty International 1991: 3).

A final important change was the demise of New Commonwealth immigration in the 1970s. As legislative measures whittled away the entrance possibilities of Commonwealth citizens, other avenues of undesirable non-resident entrance and, in particular, asylum entrance, came under increasing governmental and public scrutiny.

The consequence of all these changes was to concentrate much of the free-floating anxiety of British political leaders, the press and parts of the general public over immigration matters onto asylum seekers. This anxiety was founded on very low numbers of entrants. Between 1981 and 1990 the total number of refugees resettled by the UK (including those granted asylum) was only 14,897 (Loescher 1993: 135) – less than 10 per cent of the respective totals of France, Austria, Sweden and Germany over the same period.[1] Moreover, Britain was also remarkably successful in insulating itself from asylum claims generally. While Germany's annual total of asylum applicants grew from 19,737 in 1983 to 121,318 in 1989, over the same period the UK's applicants grew only from 4,296 to 15,530. In 1993 the Federal Republic received over 320,000 applications for asylum compared to about 32,000 in the UK. How does one account for this discrepancy?

One reason has commonly been found in the eagerness of British officials from a very early stage to use legislative and administrative measures to block the arrival of claimants for asylum. Two complementary strategies were of immense importance in this regard. The first was the imposition of visas on countries that sent substantial numbers of asylum seekers to the UK. Just as a succession of barriers were placed in the way of immigrants from the New Commonwealth in the 1960s, so governments used visas to stem the flow of asylum entrants. A good example of their effectiveness was provided in the early months of 1985 when, faced with increasing numbers of Tamil applicants for asylum, the Netherlands government implemented a range of new restrictions that had the consequence of deflecting thousands of the applicants to Britain. The British government quickly imposed a visa requirement on those travelling to the UK on Sri Lankan passports, resulting in an abrupt halt in applications

[1] Most of those resettled by Britain (a few thousand) were Vietnamese refugees from detention camps in Hong Kong.

and the deflection of the applicants onward to other countries (Cels 1989: 182). The successful use of visas in this case encouraged their broad implementation in 1986 against citizens of India, Bangladesh, Ghana, Nigeria and Pakistan (Refugee Council undated: 13). In the first six months of these new visa requirements, 11,575 people were refused permission to travel to the UK (Robertson 1989: 321). By 1990 visa requirements had been imposed on the citizens of 98 countries, Commonwealth and non-Commonwealth alike (Refugee Council undated:13). In 1992 the British government decided to impose the requirement of visas on refugees from Bosnia fleeing civil war and repression associated with the break-up of Yugoslavia. This was clearly an anticipatory measure, as up to the point of the introduction of visas the UK had only received a few thousand asylum applicants from the region. The effectiveness of the visa requirement in this case was initially guaranteed by the fact that Britain had no embassies or consulates in Bosnia at which prospective asylum seekers could apply for entry.

A complementary strategy used by Britain was legislation to fine carriers who bring to the UK foreigners lacking the correct entrance documentation. The Immigration (Carriers Liability) Act of 1987 made it an offence for carriers to bring to the UK passengers who require but do not possess valid visas to enter the country, unless the passenger attains asylum status. According to Cruz, the immediate result of the legislation, which set fines at £1,000 per passenger, was a 50 per cent reduction in the number of asylum applications at British sea and airports (1991: 72). Continuing strict enforcement of the legislation had by August 1990 led to fines totalling £18.9 million on airlines alone (Cruz 1991: 72). The clear intention was to boost the effect of visas by dissuading airlines from accepting passengers about whom they are at all doubtful. The transfer of vetting would-be travellers to the UK onto airline staff was criticised in some circles as an example of the privatisation of immigration control, which involves profit-conscious airlines making decisions, in effect, on refugee status. The impact on the airlines was undeniable: in 1990 it was widely reported that British Airways refused to let three Sri Lankans disembark in the UK for fear of incurring fines under the Act. The airline subsequently flew the individuals concerned back to their original point of departure (Cruz 1991: 72–3).

While Britain may have begun using visas and carrier sanctions to prevent asylum flows earlier than most states, the use of these measures alone cannot explain Britain's success in avoiding high levels of unwanted migration, because virtually every other Western country was using the same measures by the start of the 1990s. Rather, Britain's distinctive advantage lay in geography. Separation from other countries by sea meant that external controls could be used with particular effectiveness. Asylum seekers simply could not reach the UK's frontiers unless they came on an air or sea carrier, and when visas were scarce, and airlines are fined for bringing people without them, the result was the establishment of a remarkably effective *cordon sanitaire* around the UK. Insulation by sea also meant that British officials could concentrate their finite migration control resources on closely monitoring the relatively small number of air and sea ports that aspiring migrants and asylum seekers needed to pass through in order to enter.

As well as having distinctive geographical advantages, the UK also possessed legislative ones. As we have seen, when faced with a crisis of entitlement over the entrance of New Commonwealth immigrants in the 1960s, governments, without the encumbrance of a written constitution, faced little difficulty in legislating these rights out of existence with a simple parliamentary majority. This kind of wide-ranging executive discretion or 'unbending sovereignty' has also, as Christian Joppke (1999a: 130) has noted, impacted upon British dealings with asylum seekers. It has done so, first of all, in the limited provision of procedural rights to claimants for asylum. Before 1993, avenues for review of unsuccessful asylum decisions were rare and determined by one's status upon entering the country. Those applicants who entered the UK illegally or who applied for asylum upon entering Britain and did not possess a valid visa or entrance authorisation (the vast majority of asylum-seekers) could only appeal against an unsuccessful decision *after* they left UK territory. The government's defence of this procedure was that 'there is no such right [of appeal] for the majority of passengers refused leave to enter on other grounds, and to single out asylum-seekers for special treatment would be to encourage applications for asylum' (Brownlie and Bowett 1991: 527). The discretion available to British officials, which ensured that illegal migrants and unsuccessful asylum applicants could be quickly removed, contrasted dramatically with that available to German ones. In the Federal Republic, officials were bound to recognise the array of review procedures available to asylum seekers right up to the Constitutional Court.[2]

[2] The difference reflected in large measure the fact that in the Federal Republic the nature of and grounds for asylum entitlement are clear and largely unambiguous because the entitlement forms part of the Basic Law. As Plender has observed, 'the Federal Constitutional Court has interpreted the right of asylum as one directly enforceable against the legislative, executive and judicial branches' (Plender 1988: 409). In Britain, however, the situation was quite different. Any kind of entry entitlement for refugees and asylum seekers has had a murkier character because any actual right of asylum for foreigners existed on a very shaky legal basis. Britain's commitment to asylum rested on the incorporation of the 1951 UN Convention and 1967 Protocol into the 1981 and 1983 Immigration Rules (which superseded the 1971 Rules). The Rules, as Goodwin-Gill noted, were 'of

The wide range of executive discretion also enabled British governments to rewrite the welfare entitlements of asylum seekers to deter supposed 'economic migrants' from coming to the UK. Legislation in 1996, for example, introduced an arbitrary distinction in the availability of welfare benefits to claimants for asylum on the basis of how quickly individuals lodged their asylum application. Those who failed to apply immediately upon arrival were rendered ineligible for welfare payments. In 1999, faced with rising numbers of asylum seekers, the Labour government passed legislation that abolished cash welfare payments for *all* applicants. Those claiming asylum in need of government support – the vast majority given that applicants were forbidden from working for six months after arrival – received vouchers that were transferable for food and other essential items.

Indeed, official powers have extended beyond the ability to shape the social rights of asylum seekers to their civil rights as well, notably their freedom of movement. Absent a bill of rights providing explicit limitations on state activity, officials faced few limits on their legal ability to detain asylum seekers. Up to the end of the 1990s, there was no real judicial oversight of decisions to detain asylum applicants on the basis of administrative convenience in jail or in immigration centres. Arguably more alarmingly, there was no statutory limit on how long such individuals could be held in custody (Ramsbotham 1998).

The political rise of asylum: 1996–2002

In spite of the advantages of executive discretion, historical experience and geography, it was clear by the latter half of the 1990s that Britain was facing asylum numbers in growing proportions. Indeed, the number of applicants rose sharply in the late 1990s, from 27,685 in 1996–7 to 51,255 in 1998–9 to 79,125 in 2000–1 buoyed by entrants from Kosovo, Albania, Iraq and Afghanistan (Home Office 2002). The increased volume, relatively low percentage granted refugee status (between 10 per cent and 17 per cent), and limited success of the measures (the end of cash benefits, compulsory dispersal of asylum seekers throughout the country) introduced under the 1999 Immigration and Asylum Act to stem new applications, combined to raise asylum's political prominence. Seizing the opportunity to find an issue that could place a wedge between the Labour government and his own Conservative opposition, William Hague and

doubtful legal standing, more like rules of practice than of law' (1983: 185). As such, claims to asylum made under them were not binding on UK courts, only on the Home Office bodies which assess refugee and asylum claims.

his shadow Home Secretary, Ann Widdecombe, accused the government of being 'too soft' on the asylum issue. In a speech entitled 'Common Sense for Asylum Seekers', Hague lambasted the government's failures in asylum policy and in particular large processing backlogs and a general failure to deport unsuccessful asylum applicants. The Tory leader announced that the 'next Conservative Government [would] detain all new applicants for asylum, whether port applicants or in-country applicants, in reception centres until their cases had been determined' (Hague 2000).

The Conservative attack added more heat to an issue already extensively – and at times, hysterically – covered in the tabloid press. The government responded by stressing the need to combat what it called the problem of 'abusive' asylum applications through European cooperation to seek reform of the 1951 Refugee Convention (Blair 2001: 18). The issue did not prevent the Labour Party from holding on to a huge parliamentary majority in the national elections of 2001. Yet the controversy reinforced deep anxiety in the Blair government about its vulnerability to the charge that the nation's borders were not under control. In late 2001, only weeks after the events of 11 September, new government-initiated legislation was passed, the Anti-Terrorism, Crime and Security Act of 2001, that boosted the Home Secretary's powers to detain and exclude from refugee determination processes individuals deemed to be terrorists. A few months later, early in 2002, a new asylum bill, foreshadowing government plans to introduce a nationwide system of accommodation centres, was introduced into Parliament. This legislative to-ing and fro-ing did little to quell public discomfort about rising illegal migration and the appearance of national borders under threat. In July 2002, *The Economist* published the results of a MORI poll in which the public listed immigration as the second most important issue currently facing Britain. Only the state of the health service generated more public concern (*The Economist* 2002).

How can we explain Britain's transformation from a country insulated from the political travails of asylum characteristic of other European states in the 1980s and 1990s to a country increasingly embroiled in them? We can move closer to understanding the contemporary state of asylum in Britain by considering the collective impact of four developments.

The first involves the diminishing insulation effect of geography. While Britain's island status and location away from the European heartland were once key advantages, the rise of organised trafficking and smuggling groups during the 1990s has undermined their importance. The worst consequences of such trafficking were laid out for public view in June 2000 when customs officers at the port of Dover in the south of England opened a refrigerated lorry to find the bodies of fifty-eight Chinese people who had attempted to secrete themselves into the UK. But such grim discoveries are (fortunately) rare compared to the number of people who arrive successfully to join the asylum queues or head underground. Perversely, Britain's location on the periphery of Europe has made it more popular with smugglers and traffickers, who have a financial interest in keeping aspiring asylum seekers moving from country to country, and thus using their services. In order to encourage migrants to head for the last stop on the 'European line', smugglers and traffickers often regale their consumers with stories of the extensive social services, high wages and relative security that will await them upon arrival in the UK, thus increasing the country's migration pressures. But Britain has not simply become more attractive to smugglers and traffickers recently, it has also become more accessible. The Channel Tunnel, opened in the early 1990s, has now become a popular way for asylum seekers to reach Britain. Throughout 2001 and 2002 hundreds of immigrants passing through France attempted nightly to sneak on to passenger and freight trains in order to arrive in the UK.

If Britain's geography no longer provides insulation from the effects of asylum seeking, neither does its traditional economic weakness. Once the economic laggard of Western Europe, the British economy has performed extremely well in recent years and, in certain low-wage sectors of the economy, the demand for labour is high. In the absence of a national identification card system of the type common in France and Germany, new entrants or illicit workers have found it relatively easy to take up formal and informal employment opportunities, even while their asylum claims are being processed (Gibney 2000c: 10). The strength of the British pound ensures, furthermore, that remittance money sent home to relatives is substantial. The attractiveness of the UK has also been increased by the value of acquiring English as a second language. Economic globalisation has placed a premium on those in non-English-speaking countries who can use the lingua franca of the world economy. Even asylum seekers or immigrants present in the country for a short period can acquire a skill that is likely to boost significantly their employment prospects upon return home (Gibney 2000c: 10).

A third development is of limited but arguably increasing significance, whittling away of the discretion of British governments by the courts since the mid 1990s. While Christian Joppke could confidently proclaim in 1999 that British sovereignty was 'unbending' (Joppke 1999a: 130), the incorporation of the European Convention on Human Rights into British law in the same year has somewhat blunted the power state officials can wield against seekers of asylum. Some of the most significant developments have occurred in relation to Article 3 of the European Convention on Human Rights (Lambert 1999). In *Chahal* v. *the UK* (1996) and *Ahmed* v. *Austria* (1996) the European Court of Human Rights interpreted the Convention as placing an absolute ban on the return of individuals to countries where they would face torture or inhumane or degrading treatment. The ECHR has also been used by national courts to challenge the British government's ability to detain asylum seekers for administrative purposes or over long periods. No one could claim that these developments have eliminated the potential for extremely harsh practices towards asylum seekers by the British state. But they may well signal the beginning of the end for the kind of discretionary authority that has been characteristic of state practice since 1945.

A final significant development is Britain's growing attractiveness as an asylum destination due to the increasing restrictiveness of continental European states. In the last chapter we saw how Germany had severely curtailed access to asylum since the early 1990s, thus reducing the number of applicants it receives. A number of other European states, including Denmark, France and the Netherlands, have also toughened up entrance policies over the last decade, some of them in direct response to asylum seekers deflected to their territory by the new German practices. In the midst of spreading restrictionism, the gap between the kinds of harsh preventative and deterrent policies operated by Britain and those of other states has closed. Thus, as Randall Hansen has observed, the popularity of Britain as a destination has risen because, from the perspective of asylum seekers, the UK now looks no less attractive than any other nation (Hansen 2003). There is a kind of rough justice in this state of affairs. For years Britain was a free-rider on the more inclusive policies of European states, particularly Germany. The UK's current annual level of asylum applications (around 70,000 to 90,000), it could be argued, represents little more than its rightful share of the European total.

Together these four changes have rendered Britain more attractive and accessible to asylum seekers and undermined the traditional claim of British exceptionalism with regard to migration movements. They have made Britain, the first West European country to experience a deep immigration controversy in the post-war period, the last to find itself enmeshed in an asylum imbroglio. As Britain has become less exceptional, a profound change in the attitude to the European Union has occurred. With its self-perception as uniquely able to filter and control the entrance of foreigners due in large measure to being an island state, UK officials were throughout most of the 1980s and 1990s hostile to or reluctant to be associated fully with measures by European states to coordinate or harmonise asylum policy. To be sure, there were moments of cooperation on various restrictive aspects of policy, such as the London Resolutions and the Schengen Information System. But the UK declined to take part in Schengen attempts to establish a fast track to a frontier-less Europe and opted in to the migration provisions of the Treaty of Amsterdam only partially. Even today the UK remains one of only a handful of European countries to retain the right to check the passports of entrants from other European Union states.

By 2001, however, Britain had begun looking to Europe to solve some of its asylum woes. The first real signs of this change emerged with British plans in 2000 to reform the 1951 Refugee Convention to process the claims of asylum seekers outside the European Union in warehousing countries (Blair 2001: 18). In 2002, conscious of the fact that many asylum seekers were passing through France (and in particular the Red Cross accommodation centre at Sangatte) to claim refugee status in the UK, the Blair government launched a concerted attempt with Spain and Italy for a tough new action plan to prevent illegal migration (2002b: 1). These measures, which included more active interdiction of asylum seekers and irregular migrants in the Mediterranean and the linking of EU foreign aid to attempts by migrant source and transit countries to prevent movement, were part of a new British strategy to 'force the pace of change' in EU asylum policy. Once the laggard in European cooperation on asylum matters, by 2001 David Blunkett, the Home Secretary, felt well-enough placed to outline what he considered to be the common migration challenge facing Europe's leaders. 'We need', he argued, 'to give confidence to people living in all EU countries that we are giving priority to these issues' (*Guardian* 2002b: 1).

Conclusion

In early 2002 the minister of state for immigration, Lord Rooker, reportedly answered a blunt 'no' to the question of whether there existed any legal avenues by which legitimate refugees might enter the UK. For a long time, the absence of legal ways for asylum seekers and refugees to enter Britain was reinforced by a range of practical barriers provided by geography, the absence of constitutional constraint and the policies of other European states that kept unwanted immigrants out. This situation was bad news for asylum seekers, as their prospects of finding protection and security in the UK were very low. Even at the height of the Cold War, when most Western countries were prepared to provide refuge to *émigrés* from the Soviet Bloc, Britain's niggardly attitude towards the claims of refugees manifested itself. Very few such individuals were accepted for entrance.

Since the mid-1990s, however, many of the barriers that once supported legislative restrictions have fallen away or become less effective. I have attempted in this chapter to explain the roots of the British state's desire to keep asylum seekers and refugees at bay and to understand why, in recent years, this desire has become less successful in translating itself into effective policy measures. One thing seems clear, the British government is more likely to supplement its armoury of restrictive measures in the years ahead than to diminish it. Carrier sanctions and other external migration controls might well be joined by the interdiction at sea and a greater use of detention. Indeed, the move towards a far more restrictive regime has already been clearly signalled (Home Office 2002).

It is not easy to judge the consequences that would flow from a completely different policy direction: the relaxation or elimination of measures to prevent or deter asylum claimants. British officials are wedded to the idea that the result of a less harsh regime would be increasing ethnic tension, disruptive for social order and fatal for their own political prospects. These are legitimate concerns that should be properly evaluated. Nonetheless, against the possible consequences of a more inclusive response, the costs of current practices need to be weighed. Externally, highly restrictive policies have fed the demand for traffickers and smugglers, encouraged refugees to undertake extremely hazardous journeys to the UK, and made the prospects of gaining protection in European states a lottery that has probably condemned some refugees to torture, imprisonment and even death. Internally, deterrence measures to control asylum have led to the development of increasingly illiberal measures, including the use of detention, voucher systems, involuntary dispersal and attempts to scale back the procedural rights of refugee status applicants.

These practices should worry anyone with a liberal conscience, even if one believes they might conceivably serve a legitimate state interest. They raise the question of whether British officials attach any real value to asylum. Admittedly, governments have displayed a general respect for international refugee and international human rights law obligations in their dealings with those refugees who manage to evade numerous barriers and obstacles to arrive on British territory. What seems lacking, however, is a dedication to the principle of asylum that is founded on an *ethical* commitment to alleviating the plight of refugees rather than simply a *legal* obligation to the minimal requirements of inherited international agreements.

Perhaps in order to show that it does attach some value to the institution of asylum, the British government announced in 2002 that its new asylum bill would introduce for the first time a refugee resettlement scheme to provide a 'gateway' so that 'legitimate refugees will no longer have to attempt hazardous journeys across the Channel' (House of Lords, February 2002). In an international context where there are tens of millions of people 'of concern' to UNHCR, such schemes are desperately needed. The government announced at the same time that it expected only about 500 people to enter annually under this proposal. Presented as a promising new direction by which Britain would respond to refugees, the scheme seems destined to provide further evidence of the low priority governments since 1945 have accorded to refugee protection.

5 The United States: the making and breaking of a refugee consensus

No Western country has accepted more refugees since the end of World War II than the United States (Holman 1996). Between 1946 and 1994 the US allowed almost 3 million refugees and other foreigners seeking protection access to permanent residence. While this remarkable inclusiveness has sometimes been attributed to a peculiarly American sensitivity to immigrants in need, less partial observers have seen it as evidence of the way refugee admissions have become entangled with foreign policy. As Kathleen Newland noted, refugee policy in the US has long been a 'handmaiden of foreign policy'. The belief that it would 'contribute to the overarching objective of damaging and ultimately defeating Communist countries, particularly the Soviet Union' (Newland 1995: 190) encouraged an openness that, at times during the Cold War, reached breathtaking heights. In 1965, President Lyndon Johnson issued an open invitation to Cubans discontented with Fidel Castro's rule to head for the US. Standing in front of the Statue of Liberty, he declared that all Cubans 'seeking refuge here in America will find it' (quoted in Masud-Polito 1988: 57).

Throughout much of the post-war period this inclusiveness has had a less admirable flip side: callous disregard for and even hostility to refugees fleeing right-wing dictatorships and other non-communist regimes. While all Western countries gave special preference to refugees from communist countries during the Cold War, no country knit together its definition of a refugee with escape from communism as tightly as the US. Before 1980, refugees from non-communist countries (with the sole exception of the Middle East) had no status under US law. Even after a more neutral refugee definition was legislated in 1980, Haitians, El Salvadorans and others from US-backed regimes found themselves unlikely to be granted refugee status. Of the 3 million refugees receiving protection before the end of 1994, well over two-thirds were from communist regimes (Holman 1996).

There is no doubting, then, that foreign policy objectives have profoundly shaped the evolution of US responses to refugees. Yet their influence is often exaggerated. In the early 1980s, the Reagan administration ignored the supposed foreign policy benefits of anti-communist refugees and began actively interdicting Cubans on their way to the US. Moreover, the US accepted more refugees during the 1990s than in any other decade since the 1940s, despite the end of the Cold War. If ideological and strategic considerations have always been important in refugee and asylum policy, other factors have also played a role.

As I will show in this chapter, the evolution of US refugee and asylum policy has, in both its inclusive and exclusive moments, been shaped by a diverse range of actors driven by an array of objectives. Empowered or weakened by specific events, the Executive, the courts, ethnic organisations, special interest groups within and without Congress, and the American public at large, have all struggled to influence the composition and volume of refugees and asylum seekers arriving in the US. Notwithstanding its distinctive status as a superpower, US policy and law relating to refugees has, as in other liberal democratic states, been shaped as much by domestic political considerations as foreign policy calculations.

In this chapter I trace the crooked path of US responses to refugees and asylum seekers since 1945. I begin by examining the origins of preferential policies for refugees as evidenced in the struggle over the 1948 Displaced Persons Act. I turn then to consider how, in the 1950s, refugee policy and the Cold War goal of fighting communism became increasingly entwined. This connection created a consensus that the Executive should have a free hand to enact highly inclusive policies towards refugees first from Hungary and then from Cuba. In the early 1980s, the consensus began to unravel. The arrival of large numbers of unplanned asylum seekers from Cuba and Haiti led, *inter alia*, to Congressional reassertion in refugee matters and the rise of the courts as a significant actor in policy evolution. I conclude the chapter by considering how these developments, combined with the end of the Cold War, impacted upon refugee resettlement policy and the responses to asylum seekers after 1990.

The aftermath of war and the origins of US refugee policy

The roots of contemporary US responses to refugees lie in the aftermath of World War II in Europe. In the final months of the war, the successful westward march by the Allied forces and the eastern movement by the Soviets overwhelmed the Axis forces, liberating millions of Europeans in the process. Liberation was, however, accompanied by unprecedented displacement, as large-scale property destruction, the end of Nazi rule and the need to flee oncoming conflict forced huge numbers of people on to the road. A 1945 US State Department report described the situation in Europe as 'one of the greatest population movements in history taking place before our eyes' (Loescher and Scanlan 1986: 1).

Those displaced or made homeless by the final months of the war constituted an extraordinarily diverse mass of humanity. These people included forced labourers from Central Europe, who had been brought to Germany and Austria to contribute to industrial production in the course of the war, as well as many who had fled the advance of the communists across central and eastern Europe in order to escape retribution for collaboration with the Germans or the prospect of Soviet rule. Significantly, the displaced comprised Jews and others who had been liberated by the Allies and the Russians from Nazi concentration camps. In the years immediately after the war, these victims of the worst that the Nazi regime could offer, were joined by thousands more Jews who fled post war pogroms in Poland and other countries (Divine 1957: 110–11).

The difficult question of how to respond to such widespread displacement weighed on the minds of Western leaders as the war in Europe entered its last stages. For many of the displaced, an answer to their plight could be found in integration into the communities in which they now found themselves. After the end of the war, this became the most viable option for the many millions of ethnic Germans (*Volkdeutsche*) who had fled central and eastern Europe. By the summer of 1945, the Allied forces found themselves the custodians of some 8 million people in Germany, Austria and Italy, many of whom were to be integrated locally. For the vast majority of the war's displaced, however, repatriation to their original homeland was both possible and desirable. To assist in this process, Allied forces established the United Nations Relief and Rehabilitation Agency (UNRRA) in 1943 (Loescher and Scanlan 1986: 3). From May to September 1945 alone, UNRRA repatriated some 7 million people (UNHCR 2000: 14).

The solutions of local integration and repatriation were not suitable for all. Even after widescale integration and repatriation a substantial core of displaced persons without an adequate resolution to their problem were left. Many of those who had fled the advance of the Soviets were justifiably reluctant to return to communist regimes. Germany and Austria, on the verge of famine in the winter of 1947, were ill-placed to satisfy the needs of more displaced people. Those who had been persecuted by the Nazis, Jews and other concentration camp survivors, faced an even more untenable situation. Camps had been established to deal with their short-term needs. However, as US President Harry Truman suggested, the Allied forces controlling the displaced person camps could not 'turn them out in Germany into the community of the very people who persecuted them' (US Government 1963: 328). The UN Special Committee on Refugees and Displaced Persons estimated that camps under Allied control in Germany, Austria and Italy held some 1,100,000 displaced persons as of March 1946.

Resettlement in countries outside Europe increasingly appeared the only viable option for those who remained displaced. By late 1945, lobbying by domestic Jewish organisations and a gradual realisation of the realities of the situation faced by those in the camps led to the formulation of a position by the US Executive favourable to the resettlement of displaced persons (Loescher and Scanlan 1986: 4–6). In December, Truman announced a new programme for the entrance of displaced persons, with the implicit intention of allowing the entry of Holocaust survivors (Loescher and Scanlan 1986: 6). Truman's programme, which was intended to avoid the need for new legislation, aimed to admit around 40,000 of the displaced per year to the US by reserving half the quotas for European settlers under established immigration legislation for those in the camps (Divine 1957: 113). The aims of this programme were conservative given the dimensions of the problem in Europe. In this they reflected the restrictiveness of US immigration legislation and American public opinion which, according to polls, was unenthusiastic about a large-scale resettlement scheme (see Simon 1996: 361).

Truman's programme proved inadequate to the task of resolving the displaced persons crisis. In the first nine months of 1946, only about 5,000 displaced persons were admitted to the US (Divine 1957: 113). To make matters worse, this resettlement did not even decrease the numbers of those in the camps. A steady influx of Jews from the east served to replenish the ranks depleted by those who had emigrated. By the end of 1946, it became evident that new legislation would be necessary if resettlement to the US was to make a significant dent in the population of the camps. In 1947 a new organisation, the International Refugee Organization (IRO), was formed specifically for the purpose of assisting with the resettlement of the displaced to countries such as the US, Canada and Australia. The issue by the end of 1947 was whether Truman and others supportive of greater inclusion could gather the political support necessary to put such an organisation to use.

The shape of immigration control

By 1948 the administration's efforts to secure legislation enabling the entry of refugees had borne fruit. Yet the relatively short time period between the proposals for legislation and their enactment by Congress belied the bitter political struggle over the new law. A range of different and conflicting factors fuelled this struggle. The lobbying of ethnic pressure groups, conflicting conceptions of national identity and views of the responsibilities of the US in the post-war world, and the institutional tensions between the Executive and Congressional branches of government, all shaped the legislation that ultimately emerged. I will now examine in detail the role that each of these factors played. This analysis will show that the battle for the 1948 Act was, in retrospect, a battle over nothing less than the complete transformation of US admissions policy. Moreover, many of the factors that shaped this struggle continue to influence the trajectory of US responses to refugees to the present day.

Ethnic pressure groups

While a number of factors combined to make the admittance of the displaced persons an important issue for the US government in the mid 1940s, chief amongst them was lobbying by Jewish pressure groups. The first stirrings of concern for the displaced were raised by American Jewish leaders who visited some of the European camps in 1945. After their visit, the leaders lobbied the US government for a coordinated resettlement policy, primarily to assist Holocaust survivors (Loescher and Scanlan 1986: 4–5). In response, Truman established the Harrison Commission in 1945, which ultimately recommended that the Administration embark upon a resettlement programme for those amongst the displaced who could not be repatriated or integrated locally (Loescher and Scanlon 1986: 5). When it became obvious that new legislation would be required for resettlement, two major Jewish lobby groups (the American Jewish Committee and the American Council on Judaism) pooled their efforts to create an organisation, the Citizens' Committee for Displaced Persons (CCDP), dedicated explicitly to promoting legislative reform. Using the media, public meetings and political lobbying, in addition to more than $1 million in funds, they attempted to soften hostile public and Congressional attitudes to the admission of those from the camps (Divine 1957: 114). They were rewarded for their efforts. According to Loescher and Scanlan, the CCDP managed to generate 'significant public support for the displaced persons and exert considerable pressure on Congress' (1986: 13). The Act that was passed in 1948 (and the Amendment which followed) was to no small degree a result of their efforts.

The success of groups like the CCDP in shaping immigration legislation was not unprecedented. The contours of US immigration law since the early 1900s owed much to the impact of pressure groups. The US political system had long provided ample opportunities for forms of 'client politics' in which well-organised interest groups had exerted an influence on the construction of immigration law well out of proportion to their numerical support in the electorate at large (Freeman 1995). However, the actors most adept at exploiting this influence had traditionally been those seeking to exclude immigrants. Nativist organisations, such as the Immigration Restriction League, Daughters of the American Revolution, as well as a range of patriotic and union organisations, were partly responsible for discriminatory immigration legislation of 1921 and 1924.

What was new in the activities of the AJC, the ACJ and the CCDP was that the influence was being exerted by non-Protestant and pro-inclusion groups. This development symbolised the growing political power of 'ethnic' lobby groups, composed of the offspring of immigrants who had entered in the great immigration waves at the turn of the century. American Jews, in particular, after decades of integration and access to education in the US, found themselves increasingly well positioned to tackle racist and discriminatory attitudes and policies (see Bolt 1984: 121–2; Dinnerstein 1994). The CCDP's success could thus be seen as a tracer of a broader political trend towards the empowerment and political maturation of the ethnic groups that had entered the US in the great migration waves earlier in the century. Yet Jewish lobbyists still looked out on an America where anti-Semitism was widespread. The CCDP was careful to present its campaign for the resettlement of those from the camps in such a way as to avoid any connection in the public mind between the admission of DPs and adding to the nation's Jewish population (Loescher and Scanlan 1986: 9).

National identity

The need to play down any link between the entrance of Jews and the resettlement of the displaced was required because the US was a sectarian and largely intolerant nation in 1945 (Loescher and Scanlan 1986). Jewish leaders were not the only ones to recognise this. Truman went out of his way to stress that the DPs were of 'all faiths' (and by implication not only Jews) when he called on an extremely reluctant Congress to pass new legislation in 1947 (US Government 1963:327). For large sections of American society, not least in Congress, opposition to entrance was linked to a broader vision of the proper composition of US society. In this vision, the US was rightly a racially and ethnically exclusive community dominated by white Anglo-Saxon Protestants. The aim of immigration control was to protect this dominant 'ethnic core' from 'external dilution' (Joppke 1999b: 23). Articulating the threat of 'external dilution' in its most extreme version, Representative Ed Gossett of Texas lambasted those in the DP camps as 'bums, criminals, black marketeers, subversives, revolutionaries, and crackpots of all colors and hues' unfit for

American society (Divine 1957: 118). Less specific, if no less hostile, was the National Commander for the Veterans Association, who described the DPs as 'the dregs of Europe' (Peters 1948: 107). Others couched their opposition in more reasonable terms by speaking of the need to maintain the integrity of the current immigration system. That system, it was argued, should not be amended to allow entry to one particular group of immigrants, however needy. In reality, though, this view was difficult to distinguish from more nativist ones. For contemporary immigration law was itself informed by a view of the nation as an ethnically exclusive community.

One major piece of law governed the entry of immigrants into the US in the early post-war period, the National Origins Act of 1924. This Act, and its predecessor of 1921, were both strongly influenced by principles of genetic selection designed 'to direct the future of America along safe and sound racial channels' (Morris 1985: 19). Both Acts attempted to ensure maintenance of the US's ethnic composition (and the dominance of Anglo-Saxon Protestants) by allowing for a quota system that admitted new immigrants from a particular country only in proportion to the number of immigrants from that country already resident in the US. The 1924 Act could rightly have been described as a particularly conservative, even discriminatory, piece of legislation even if its provisions linked immigration to the composition of the US population in the year of its enactment. But in a transparent attempt to preserve the dominance of the Anglo-Saxon Protestant population, the Act pegged entry levels to the make-up of the US population in 1890, before the mass immigration waves from central and eastern and southern Europe had reshaped American society. The legislation's quotas thus sharply limited the entrance of many European nationalities, including Italians, Poles and Greeks (Joppke 1999b: 24). After 1945, the quotas seriously constrained the number of displaced persons who could be brought to the US. Those in favour of more inclusive policies towards the DPs soon found themselves, however unintentionally, challenging more than hostile attitudes simply towards the displaced, but also the dominant vision of the proper role of immigration policy in US society.

Advocates for the displaced persons appealed to an alternative account of US traditions. In their account, the acceptance of large numbers of displaced persons from Europe was the logical corollary of the country's ideological commitments. Looking beyond the restrictions of the 1924 Act, advocates characterised hostility towards the displaced as unworthy of an American society that had committed itself in bronze to the poor, hungry and tired masses, 'yearning to breathe free'. An editorial in the World Report in June 1947 argued that 'American tradition, throughout most of US history, would support the idea of opening the door to the oppressed and the homeless of Europe' (Peters 1948: 114). The Harvard professor, Oscar Handlin, writing in *Commentary* in 1947, went even further, stating that the legal difficulties facing the entry of European displaced persons offered 'a pitiful commentary upon the reversal of historic American attitudes towards immigration . . . Four decades ago . . . this golden land stood forth as a refuge to the persecuted and exploited of all nations' (Peters 1948: 237). The idea that the US had a duty to the displaced persons based on its own immigration traditions was subscribed to by Truman as well. In August 1947, he expressed his confidence that Congress would construct the legislation necessary to protect the displaced persons 'for the simple reason that all of them are the descendants of the DPs – everybody in this country' (US Government 1963: 421).

This inclusive attitude had its limits. Few of the advocates of the displaced were ready to question the 1924 Act in its entirety. Truman constantly stressed that his aim was not to challenge the whole framework of American admissions policy; he aimed simply to gain entry for the small and limited groups of displaced persons left in Europe (US Government 1963: 328). But the credibility of this argument required showing that the US had a responsibility to the displaced persons distinguishable from that it had to other foreigners in need.

The responsibilities of leadership

The Administration used a range of different and not always complementary arguments to support its case for the admission of displaced persons. Truman, for example, argued that the US could not ignore its particular humanitarian responsibility to these refugees given the way that they had 'come into the hands of our own and the other Western Allied Armies of the occupation in Europe' in the midst of a war that the US had fought and won (US Government 1963: 325–6). Furthermore, after placing these people in camps and providing for their immediate needs, the US could not now deny some responsibility for their plight. These arguments for a particular moral responsibility to the displaced of the camps were greeted sceptically by those in the US with other interests to protect. William Floyd of the Veterans Association argued that the act of increasing the number of displaced persons entering would 'let down the millions of veterans who fought and won two wars at once for this nation'. Warming to his theme, he expanded, 'great and lavish promises were made to veterans . . . But now unemployment numbers in the millions, and housing for veterans and other citizens . . . appears not to have materialized' (Peters 1948: 110). This view was shared by some in

Congress. Speaking during the Committee stages of the Displaced Persons Act, one legislator urged that his fellow Congressmen, 'should not, in our zeal to fulfil our humanitarian responsibilities, forget our responsibilities to our own land and our own people' (Divine 1957: 122).

The humanitarian case for admission was thus of somewhat limited utility. Restrictionists, however, found it more difficult to repel another way of framing the resettlement issue. With the US embroiled in the reconstruction of Europe by the mid 1940s, issues of entrance policy and foreign policy became fused together in a new way. Even restrictionists could not completely ignore the question of what role immigration policy should play in servicing the goals of US foreign relations in the post-war world. The Administration was quick to emphasise the importance of resettlement to the country's own interests and to those of its allies. In terms of the former, Truman argued that the situation of the displaced needed to be resolved or Germany, which was 'already approaching economic suffocation', would become even more unstable and thus dangerous. If those in the camps were released into German society, not only would it be 'disastrous for them', he said, it would 'seriously aggravate' America's problems in Europe (US Government 1963: 328). In terms of the latter, Truman, speaking in 1948, stated that 'other nations have already provided homes for some of the displaced persons, but there is no prospect that all of them will be able to get a new start in life unless the US accepts its fair share' (US Government 1964: 115). In the idea of a 'fair share', Truman transformed the act of responsibility from a humanitarian duty owed to the refugees themselves into one owed to America's allies, who were, unlike the US, already pulling their weight.

Both of these arguments suggested that the issue of resettlement was not simply a matter of domestic policy to be governed by the traditional assumptions of immigration law, but, in Truman's words, 'an international problem' that 'will have to be worked out on an international basis' (US Government 1963: 248). Faced with a restrictionist Republican Congress, his arguments were of limited impact. However, from the middle of 1948, increasingly frosty US/Soviet relations had given the Administration and advocates for the displaced a new card to play in their efforts to secure more inclusive legislation. The 800,000 displaced persons still present in Germany, Austria and Italy were redescribed as 'heroes of democracy' unable to return home because they were 'anti-communist' and thus 'hate totalitarian governments' (US Government 1964: 288). The ideological implications were, for the proponents of the displaced persons at least, clear: the US must 'reward these people . . . for their opposition to communism' (US Government 1964: 288). This line of attack, which conjoined internationalism in foreign affairs and inclusive responses to displaced persons, did not automatically win over those who were in favour of restrictive entrance policies. However, Truman had now opened up a rich seam, which refugee advocates were happy to exploit, by connecting displaced person entrance to the campaign against communism.

'Ordered tension': the institutional framework[1]

The redefining of resettlement as a matter of international politics did more than simply provide new reasons for the admission of the displaced. By suggesting that resettlement touched upon issues of national interest, the Administration implied that the priorities of the Executive should trump those of Congress. This was not a shift in priorities that members of Congress were happy to take lying down. The US constitution's tripartite division of power between the Executive, Legislature and Judiciary, each with the power to check and balance the other, provided ample opportunities for Congress to frustrate the president's aspirations for new legislation, if it was so motivated. Congress, or at least a substantial proportion of the Republican dominated Congress of 1947–8, was so motivated.

The tension between Congress and the Executive is largely explicable in terms of the traditional roles of these branches of the US state. Before 1945, the Judiciary and the Executive had largely been content to let Congress determine the shape of immigration law (Morris 1985: 34; Schuck 1991: 9). The resulting legislation reflected the distinctive perspective of Congressmen and women on entrance issues. Dependent for their political survival on local constituencies and, in the case of senators, on their states, representatives tended to be highly sensitive to grass-roots opinion on immigration, which was often racist and exclusionary. On immigration matters Congressional members were naturally inclined to look inwards to focus on the potential domestic (social and economic) costs of immigration (Morris 1985: 35–7). This did not mean that Congress paid no attention to the international issues raised by immigration. But, as Morris has observed, 'To the extent that Congress did look abroad, it looked primarily for evidence to support its fears of inundation or subversion by immigrants' (Morris 1985: 36).

The Executive was different. With responsibility for foreign affairs, and with greater latitude to ignore grass-roots views, the Executive often adopted a more inclusive attitude towards immigration. Usually, this was for foreign policy reasons. Responsibility for international affairs left the

[1] I am grateful to Ray Nichols for the phrase 'ordered tension'.

Executive, and in particular the State Department, with the task of confronting the adverse diplomatic consequences of racist or discriminatory entrance laws (Morris 1985: 37–9). From time to time, the desire to avoid such consequences led the president into battle against Congressional legislation. In 1935, for example, Roosevelt tried to have legislation aimed at excluding Japanese immigrants defeated because of the adverse effect if would have on US–Japanese relations (Morris 1985: 38). His efforts ultimately failed.

Tradition dictated, then, that the displaced person issue would lead to a conflict between a Congress conscious of domestic hostility to the resettlement of Jews and Eastern Europeans and an Executive focused on the implications for foreign affairs of not resolving the issue of the camps. When it came to the Displaced Persons Bill, the 80th Congress pretty much stuck to the well-worn script. While restrictionists in Congress could not ignore calls for some new legislation to increase avenues for resettlement, not least because the president's views had been loudly declared, they still had some means by which to get their own way. First, they could delay the passing of legislation so that the number of refugees entering the US would not increase rapidly in the short term. Second, the restrictionists had the power to amend the original bill, and thus to add caveats, restrictions and qualifications to the legislation. Through this process, any bill could be made a mockery of its initiator's original intentions. Congressional opponents of resettlement used both means at their disposal.

The 1948 Displaced Persons Act and beyond

Out of the tensions and conflicts between these various features of the US polity, the 1948 Displaced Persons Act was born. The Act did not bear the signs of its mixed paternity lightly. The legislation allowed for the entry of some 200,000 displaced persons, as well as 2,000 Czech refugees and 3,000 orphans (Divine 1957: 125–6). Yet while the Act appeared quite inclusive, the restrictionist forces in Congress had left their imprint. The Act limited eligibility for resettlement to those amongst the displaced who had entered Germany, Austria and Italy on or before 22 December 1945. According to critics, this requirement was intended to prevent Jews (and, as Truman claimed during the 1948 presidential campaign, Catholics) from entering (US Government 1964: 383; Dinnerstein 1994: 161). Most concentration camp survivors who had entered the refugee camps before December 1945 had already been resettled in the US or elsewhere. It was refugees from eastern and central Europe, a proportion of whom were Jews fleeing pogroms, who had entered after this date, who were most in need of resettlement. Another feature of the Act ensured the continued dominance of Congress in matters of admission. Entrance places allocated to displaced persons were not new places as such. Rather, they were charged against the future immigration quotas of the countries from which the displaced persons originated. Furthermore, a maximum of 50 per cent of any country's quota could be 'mortgaged' to provide entrance for displaced persons in this way. The legislation thus operated within the restrictive and discriminatory framework of the 1924 National Origins Act.

Truman and those who lobbied hard for new legislation despised the Act, seeing it as a victory for bigotry and exclusion. Upon signing it into law in 1948, the president stated, 'It is a close question whether this bill is better or worse than no bill at all' (US Government 1964: 382). But the bill was better than nothing, even if this was to become clear only in retrospect. The fight for and the passage of the new legislation highlighted three developments of great significance for the evolution of America's response to refugees in the post-war period. First, the Act distinguished conceptually for the first time in law refugees from other immigrants. In the new legislation, displaced persons were now eligible for different treatment than other entrants, even if they were not completely freed of the requirements of the National Origins Act. Second, the struggle for the bill challenged traditional assumptions about the role of the presidency in legislation relating to foreigner admission. There was, to be sure, nothing new about presidential involvement in immigration legislation *per se*. Presidents in the past had taken an active role in vetoing laws that conflicted with their foreign policy interests. What was distinctive about the DP issue was the role played by the Executive in *initiating* legislation. Third, in the process of arguing for resettlement, a new, seemingly cogent, rationale for linking humanitarian concern for certain groups of refugees with the interests of the US state had emerged. By the time the Act was passed, refugees had come to be seen less as victims and more as allies in the country's struggle against the Soviet Union.

In retrospect, these developments gave strong reasons for seeing the 1948 Act as a turning point in US responses to refugees. But the new legislation did not represent anything like a clear victory for the proponents of inclusion, let alone an end to the tensions – structural and ideological – that had made the refugee resettlement such a hard-fought issue. The continuing struggle was evident in efforts to get the Act amended, which began almost as soon as it had been passed. In 1950, largely as a result of Democratic inroads into Congress in the 1948 elections, a more liberal act came into law. The amendment extended the cut-off date for eligible displaced persons and a select group of other entrants without regard to criteria of national origin, race or religion, allowing some 300,000 refugees to be admitted. The legislation would, it was widely thought, bring an end to the displaced person problem once and for all. By the end of the 1948 Act's term in 30 June 1952, four years after the initial legislation, some 337,244 displaced persons had been resettled in the US, along with 80,000 other Europeans expelled from their countries.

The large volume of entrants was undoubtedly a victory for Executive authority in refugee admissions. Truman's success fuelled a radicalisation in his desire to shape entrance policy to serve the state's foreign policy ends. But there still remained a substantial gap between the ambitions of the Executive and its political capabilities. At no time was this more evident than in 1952 when the McCarran–Walter Act was passed. The Act, which bore the names of two of the most skilled restrictionists in Congress, was a major piece of immigration legislation that represented the antithesis of foreign-policy-informed immigration law. Passed over Truman's veto, the Act reasserted the domestic concerns of Congress by re-entrenching the divisive National Origins systems, albeit while making a cursory gesture towards relaxing restrictions on the entry of the Japanese (Zucker and Zucker 1996: 28). More importantly, from the perspective of the White House, the Act did nothing to recognise the need for provisions to allow entry to refugees. Despite the fact that (contrary to predictions) there were still thousands of displaced persons in Europe, and that the 1948 Act had now come to an end, the law made no specific allowance for resettlement. Refugees would have to satisfy the stringent requirements of general immigration law if they were to find haven in the US.

The administration's hostility to the Act ran deep, as Truman's veto symbolised. In criticising the Act, Truman revealed how much his views on entrance policy had changed since he had first proposed legislation in 1947. While originally suggesting that the resettlement of refugees was an exceptional act, and no challenge to the traditional legislative basis of immigration control, by 1952 Truman had come to see the National Origins system as a problem in its own right. In vetoing the bill, he stated that the quota system's 'country by country limitations create a pattern that is insulting to large numbers of our finest citizens, irritating to our allies abroad, and foreign to our purposes and ideals'. Expanding on the theme, Truman argued that the concept of discrimination that underpinned the National Origins system 'violates the great political doctrine of the Declaration of Independence that "all men are created equal"', and 'repudiates our basic religious concepts, our belief in the brotherhood of man' (Tyler 1956: 97–8).

Another feature of the Act notably demonstrated the contingent origins of the relationship between the prosecution of the Cold War and inclusive refugee policies. Reflecting the spirit of the Internal Security Act of 1950, the McCarran–Walter Act contained security provisions designed to prevent communists and – importantly from the administration's viewpoint – former communists from settling in the US. The provisions were a blunt instrument, excluding refugees who had defected from entering the US, as much as spies and real national security threats. The Administration and those in the State Department associated support for defectors and refugees from the Soviet Bloc with weakening the ideological legitimacy of communist regimes. Many on the right, however, feared that allowing defectors from communist countries to enter would make the US vulnerable to spies and those who had been indoctrinated by the Soviets (Divine 1957). To some degree, these arguments were fictions used to justify greater inclusion or greater restriction in immigration. Restrictionists, for example, could use anti-communist rhetoric to make more palatable arguments based on exclusion for reasons of race or ethnicity in an era when the question of civil rights was beginning to gain momentum. But the threat of communist subversion through immigration was taken seriously in many circles. When in 1957, for example, Vice President Richard Nixon wrote a report, published in the *New York Times*, on his visit to camps for Hungarian refugees in Austria, he was anxious to assure readers that 'if the screening process which is presently in effect is continued, the Hungarian refugees who are admitted to the United States will present no significant risk of internal subversion in this country' (Branyan and Larsen 1971: 681).

The debate over the direction of US responses to refugees was highly acrimonious in the wake of the McCarran–Walter Act. But the degree of acrimony could not obscure a growing consensus on the principle that the proper yardstick for evaluating refugee policy was its contribution to the struggle against communism. This consensus had important implications; for it symbolised that many of the old fears of ethnic invasion had given way to concerns over communism in immigration policy (Divine 1957: 163). This was good news for those promoting inclusion, including Republican President Dwight Eisenhower. Now those in favour of more liberal refugee policies could concentrate their energies on one issue. Nonetheless, the problem of conflicting accounts of the utility to the anti-communist cause of refugee admissions remained. The deadlock was eventually eased in a way that gave victory to the Executive and those supporting inclusion. While restrictionists could question the credibility of using refugees who had been indoctrinated by communism as ideological weapons, it was more difficult to deny that the US had some responsibility to admit those from the Eastern Bloc who had risked their lives as spies or informers, or those in the public at large who had revolted against their oppressors, partly because of radio-transmitted encouragement by the American propaganda machine (Loescher and Scanlan 1986). As the US became more deeply involved in the Cold War struggle in Europe, the claims of such men and women became increasingly pressing.

The Cold War and the politics of inclusion

If there is a moment when a new consensus congealed – when domestic and foreign policy, Congress and president, and different visions of US responsibilities fused together – it was in 1956. In that year an uprising to demand free elections and an end to forced industrialisation occurred in Hungary. The revolt against the communist regime, encouraged in part by a US propaganda campaign, was brutally suppressed by Soviet troops (UNHCR 2000: 27; Loescher and Scanlan 1986: 53). More than 200,000 troops invaded Hungary, enabling Moscow quickly to take control of events and execute or deport dissident leaders. The severity of the Soviet backlash prompted a mass exodus from the country. In a period between 23 October 1956 and the end of the year, about 155,000 people crossed the border into Austria and Yugoslavia (Branyan and Larsen 1971: 681). Under a relief operation coordinated by the fledgling United Nations High Commissioner for Refugees, Western countries acted quickly to allow the resettlement of Hungarian refugees. Within just over two weeks of the Soviet attack on Budapest, Hungarian refugees were being resettled in the US. By mid 1958, the US had allowed entry to about 38,000 Hungarian refugees (UNHCR 2000: 32).

The Administration's success in speedily resettling large numbers of the refugees was largely attributable to the popularity of the refugees themselves. Their plight was extensively and sympathetically documented by American television networks. It was due also to the difficulty of building a case for preventing the entrance of refugees whose plight the US had clearly had a hand in creating. Here was the first real example of refugee admission based upon, in the words of Loescher and Scanlan, 'the politics of failed revolution' (1986: 50). The Hungary crisis set in train a period during which the US would use refugee admission as a reward for those who battled unsuccessfully against communist regimes. But the real significance of the events in Hungary lay less in the unprecedented level of political support garnered for the refugees, than in the institutional innovation the crisis brought about.

As refugees poured out of Hungary, the US Administration faced the traditional problem of how to respond to the need for mass resettlement without violating the restrictions of the National Origins system. With Congress in recess, and the Hungarian quota under the 1924 Immigration

Act already mortgaged until 1990, experts from the State and Justice Departments set to work looking for avenues through which the president could ensure entry for the refugees (Binsten 1958: 50–2). Ironically, the means they hit upon came from the McCarran–Walter Act. Under the Act, the attorney general had a power of parole, the authority to 'parole' or temporarily release aliens for entry into the US. The original rationale for this power has been the subject of dispute.[2] Perhaps the most convincing explanation for its existence is that the power was inserted into the law to enable the government to prevent the deportation of the small number of individuals from communist regimes who landed on US territory. The original provision had been prompted by a particular incident in the early 1950s in which a group of escapees from communism had arrived on US shores in a small boat from Scandinavia (Binsten 1958: 54). Nonetheless, the provision was never intended to serve as the basis for the resettlement of large numbers of refugees into the US, without the consent of Congress. This, however, became its major use.

Much has been written on the importance of parole power to Executive dominance in matters of refugee entry. But it is possible to overestimate the significance of this power. Parole allowed the attorney general to grant admission and that was all. The consent of Congress was necessary if the refugees concerned were to regularise their status, let alone claim citizenship (Loescher and Scanlan 1986: 50). Moreover, the Executive's willingness to use the provision reflected a more significant shift in Congress towards giving the Executive a freer hand in matters of entrance policy connected to Cold War objectives. Even then, the Administration felt the need to shape public and Congressional opinion in order to dispel concerns that refugee policy might be a route for the entry of potential subversives and the economically undesirable. The Administration provided a steady stream of sympathetic media stories on the refugees' plight, conducted tight screening procedures for those refugees eligible to enter and assured the public that there would be economic advantages in the entry of the Hungarians (Branyan and Larsen 1971: 681).

In the end, the Administration's response to the Hungarian refugees was not overly generous. In total, only 38,000 of the 171,000 refugees who left after the uprising found asylum in the US. But the US response did herald the confluence of a range of factors: a newly compliant Congress, a novel institutional mechanism for escaping the strictures of immigration law and an ideology in the Cold War battle with the Soviet Union that could be used to justify refugee entry. Refugee policy had now been

[2] For differing accounts of the origin of parole power, see Binsten (1958: 220) and Martin (1982: 92).

liberated from immigration policy. By the end of the Hungarian crisis, the fierce battles over entrance policy that had so marked the early post-war period were a thing of the past. Around two-thirds of all immigrants entering the US between 1952 and 1965 were admitted outside the terms of the National Origins quota system, almost all of them entering as refugees (Briggs 1996: 105).

The majority of these new entrants were neither displaced persons nor Hungarians. They were Cubans. In 1959, Fidel Castro's communist forces seized power from the corrupt autocracy of Batista, sparking the flight of many of Cuba's elites. From the earliest days, the US Administration chose to tolerate the movement of Cubans into the US, and later to try to organise the movement. The decision to remain open to the refugees was not taken rashly (Masud-Piloto 1988: 33). The circumstances that had led to the refugee movement and the profile of refugees both played a role. The Administration believed that the presence of the Cubans in the US would be only temporary (Loescher and Scanlan 1986: 62). Most Latin American revolutions were short-lived events, especially those that incurred the hostility of the US government, and there was little reason to believe that Castro's reign would be any different. Furthermore, the grant of asylum was seen as a way of hastening the regime's rapid demise. The departure of refugees was understandably viewed as a haemorrhaging of the country's best and brightest that would prove fatal to the regime. Indeed, in the late 1950s and early 1960s Cuban refugees were commonly referred to as the 'golden exiles' because their ranks were made up of the educated classes: doctors, teachers and other professionals (Briggs 1992: 90). It was reported in the early 1960s that over half of the University of Havana's faculty was living in or near Miami (Mitchell 1962: 5). As well as serving the strategic goal of weakening the regime, the Administration saw in the acceptance of Cubans an opportunity for ideological point scoring (Dominguez 1992). The departure of the refugees offered strong evidence of the brutal implications of communist regimes whether they came to power in Europe or the Caribbean. How could any but the most barbarous regimes create such an exodus?

The rationale for accepting Cuban refugees changed over time, just as the flows and character of the entrants did. Between 1 January 1959 and 1 April 1961, approximately 125,000 Cubans arrived in the US, almost half of whom settled in southern Florida. Many of these entrants already had permanent residence status in the US or had entered the country on tourist, business or student visas and were eventually legalised through grants of permanent residence (immigration) visas (Holman 1996: 7). To assist with resettlement, the Eisenhower Administration established, and Kennedy's Administration oversaw, the establishment of the Cuban Refugee Center in Miami that provided healthcare, welfare and education to the Cubans. The programme provided a level of services for Cuban refugees that was at the time unprecedented even for US citizens (Masud-Piloto 1988: 54; Dominguez 1992: 39.) Furthermore, federal funding for the programme took the pressure of hosting the refugees off local and state budgets, thus defusing the potential for political hostility to their residence.

In 1961, the US government's isolation of Cuba led to the termination of direct flights, as well as consular and diplomatic relations, between the countries (Holman 1996: 8). Migration to the US subsequently dropped off to around 35,000 annually. Those leaving now had to travel to a third country before they could be parolled into the US (Zucker and Zucker 1996). But if the departure of Cubans slowed, the welcome extended by the US remained strong. The failed Bay of Pigs invasion in 1961, when Cuban exiles backed by the CIA tried unsuccessfully to overthrow Castro, further entrenched a moral commitment by the US to aid Cuban refugees. Here was another example of the principle of 'failed liberation'. Yet events in the Bay of Pigs also challenged the common assumption that the Castro regime was weak and vulnerable.

The welcome extended to Cubans reached its apogee in 1965. The end of direct flights between the US and Cuba, and the imposition of greater restrictions on emigration, had boosted the number of people attempting to flee Cuba on makeshift rafts and boats across the Florida Strait. Stung by criticism that the deaths that inevitably resulted were caused by his restrictions, Castro unexpectedly announced a change in policy. Exiles with relatives in Cuba would be able to come to Cuba by boat and take them to the US. President Johnson responded to Castro's proposal in October of 1965. Standing in front of the Statue of Liberty, the president made an open commitment of unprecedented proportions: 'I declare this afternoon to the people of Cuba that those seeking refuge here in America will find it. The dedication of America to our tradition as an asylum for the oppressed is going to be upheld' (Masud-Piloto 1988: 57).

Johnson's pledge resulted in a chaotic movement of people out of Cuba by sea. Attempting to create some order in the movement, the US signed an official memorandum of understanding with Cuba, allowing for regular flights between the countries. The flights allowed for the entry to the US of around 350 refugees a month (Holman 1996: 10). The opportunities for leaving on regular flights virtually ended the small boat crossings. In 1973 Castro finally closed the door on the possibility of exit from Cuba. The 'aerial bridge' (Zucker and Zucker 1996) between Cuba and the US established under the memorandum had allowed more than

265,000 refugees to settle in Miami and another 200,000 of them to join relatives in other parts of the country (Holman 1996: 10).

The admission of such large numbers of Cubans had little to do with providing asylum to individuals escaping violence or persecution. After 1965, most of the Cubans entering the US were seeking better economic opportunities or reunification with their relatives (Loescher and Scanlan 1986: 74–5) and little attempt was made to determine whether they faced harm at the hands of the Cuban regime. Indeed, it was telling that the memorandum ensured that many of those who best fitted the criteria of a refugee, including political prisoners, were explicitly excluded from the ranks of those allowed to leave Cuba (Loescher and Scanlan 1996: 75). Refugee policy, initially formed to bypass the stringent requirements of immigration control, had by the early 1970s become a vehicle by which Executive-favoured immigrants from communist countries could enter the US.

The end of Cold War consensus

Belying its humble origins in disputes over the entry of thousands of displaced persons in the immediate aftermath of World War II, refugee policy had become a key factor in the shaping of America as an immigrant society by the early 1970s. The expansion in refugee admission over such a short period of time was nothing short of dramatic. Yet the level of the increase could easily obscure the fact that this growth in admissions was built on a number of contingent attributes of the 1950s and 1960s political landscape. The Executive had been given unchallenged priority in refugee entrance decisions; asylum for refugees was widely viewed as serving foreign policy goals and could be managed so as to assuage the potential for domestic political anxiety; and, finally, it was assumed that only communist regimes generated refugees. By the early 1980s, all of these assumptions would be under challenge, consigning the period of the Cold War consensus to history, long before the Cold War had itself been brought to a close.

The reassertion of Congress

While the airlifts from Cuba that began in 1965 arguably represented the pinnacle of presidential supremacy in refugee admission decisions, in the same year the beginnings of a Congressional backlash became evident. Congress's reassertion took the form of a new Immigration Act. The Immigration Act of 1965 was notable mostly because (in the civil rights spirit of the time) it abolished the discriminatory National Origins admission system (Bach 1990: 141–2). In place of the old system, new immigration to the US was to be based largely on family reunification. But the Act also furnished for the first time a general framework for US refugee admissions (Briggs 1996: 113). A statutory definition of a refugee was provided in the Act, which entrenched the priority accorded to those fleeing communist regimes. Refugees were defined as persecuted people who had fled a communist state or a communist-dominated area or persons who had fled countries in the Middle East (Briggs 1996: 113). The Act also specified the number of visas that would be set aside annually for the entrance of refugees. A total of 17,400 slots per year, or 6 per cent of the total migration pool, would be allocated annually, far fewer than the average annual admissions for the preceding 15 years (Briggs 1996: 113). In specifying such an allocation, Congress's aim was to provide a grounded alternative to the parolling of refugees at the Executive's discretion. The committee reports associated with the new legislation made it clear parole could no longer be used as a way of admitting refugees (Martin 1982: 94).

As an attempt at Congressional reassertion in refugee matters, however, the 1965 legislation was something of a false start. Johnson boldly ignored the Act in his decision to open the doors of the US to Cubans in 1965, though he did at least gain bipartisan support for this move (Martin 1982: 93). By 1973, however, the welcome towards Cubans was becoming strained in Congress, not least because there appeared no end in sight to the immigration. The discontent was only beginning to gain force when Castro, with perfect timing, placed new limits on departures. Nonetheless, the strains created by the admission of Cubans, particularly by the use of parole power, did have implications for the Executive. The White House faced increasingly acrimonious parole hearings throughout the 1970s, and President Nixon even apologised for using the provision at one point (Martin 1982: 94–5). The tense relationship between Congress and the Executive did not prevent Ford and Carter using parole to allow the admission of some 430,000 refugees from Vietnam after 1975. But the huge number of refugees admitted outside of the Act demonstrated with great clarity that the 1965 legislation had failed to provide a working framework for refugee admissions. By the late 1970s, there was widespread agreement in both branches of government on the need for a specific refugee act to guide the resettlement of refugees.

The Refugee Act of 1980 was passed in an attempt to find once and for all a way of accommodating the conflicting needs of the Executive for flexibility in admissions with Congress's desire for predictability and control (Martin 1982). The statutory formula of this accommodation granted the president the right to fix annual admission refugee ceilings, but only after consultation with Congress on the composition and level of admissions. The Act, furthermore, restricted parole by specifying in statute that the power be used only when 'compelling reasons in the public interest with respect to that particular alien' pertain (Holman 1996: 14). Along with the attempt to curtail Executive authority, the new legislation aimed to bring US responses to refugees into line with international law. To this end, the statutory definition of a refugee in the US was disentangled from its Cold War origins. The UN definition of a refugee as an individual with a 'well-founded fear of persecution' was incorporated into the law, along with the 1967 UN Protocol. While refugees were now defined independently of the ideological hue of the regime from which they emanated, the Act still made room for the entry of those whose admittance served foreign policy goals. A new category of refugee, those of 'special humanitarian concern' to the US, was created to enable the entry of those who could not meet the standards of the UN definition.

The 1980 Act also contained another important change, though its full significance was not appreciated straight away. The incorporation of the 1967 Protocol into law created a duty incumbent on the US state not to return (*refouler*) anyone with a well-founded fear of persecution at or within US territory. Unsurprisingly, this new obligation raised few eyebrows when Congress considered the Act. The vast majority of refugees entered, like the Vietnamese had, through planned resettlement schemes after extensive overseas screening processes. Very few applicants sought refugee status upon or after arrival. But the implications of this legislative commitment were about to become impossible to ignore.

The decreasing utility of the Cold War refugee

The 1980 Act's freeing of the refugee definition from its traditional ideological connotations was partly the product of increasing scepticism in Congress on the role of refugees as Cold War weapons. Congress's new attitude reflected in turn changing attitudes towards the strategic and ideological value of admitting Cuban refugees. This scepticism deepened over the 1980s and spread to the Executive. The weakening of the strategic rationale for admission could be traced to the failed Bay of Pigs invasion in 1961, which showed the US Administration the difficulties that faced any attempt by exiles to overthrow Castro by force. By 1965, the strategy of depleting the country of its professional classes through the acceptance of refugees seemed equally questionable. It became hard to imagine why Castro would allow mass emigration, let alone sign an agreement with the US organising orderly departure, if he expected the departures to damage his regime. While it was unclear that the emigration was harming Castro, it was becoming obvious to the US government that the Cuban refugees were turning into permanent immigrants. The 1966 Cuban Adjustment Act, which allowed Cubans access to permanent residence in the US, was probably the only humane way for the US government to address the lack of status amongst Cuban refugees. But as critics noted at the time, it did nothing to motivate American-based Cubans to overthrow Castro (Dominguez 1992: 43).

From the US perspective, any strategic rationale for allowing entrance to Cubans had vanished by the early 1970s. But the Cuban point of view was different. Not long after the passage of the 1980 Act, Castro turned the tables by once again allowing emigration. All Cubans wishing to go to the US were free to depart from the port of Mariel (Holman 1996: 15). His declaration unleashed a frantic flotilla of boats commandeered by Cuban Americans to pick up relatives. More than 94,000 new *émigrés* entered the US in the period between 21 April and end of May 1980. As well as opening the country's doors, Castro had opened Cuba's jails. Much to the anger of US authorities, some 8,000 criminals and others considered undesirable by the Castro regime were amongst the departing Cubans. There could now be no question of which country was benefiting most from the open door policy. A White House official summed up the Administration's reaction, 'Castro, in a way, is using people like bullets aimed at this country' (Alpern 1980: 22). Within just over two years, the Reagan Administration had turned the traditional logic of refugee policy on its head. Intervention in Central America to prevent the rise and consolidation of left-wing regimes was defended by the government not simply as a way of containing communism, but in order to prevent, in Reagan's words, a 'tidal wave of refugees swarming into our country' (Ferris 1987: 129).

The ideological case for refugees was less prone to contradiction by practical events. Nonetheless, the ideological utility of refugee admissions tended to diminish over time. The unattractiveness of Castro's Cuba could only be underlined so many times. By the 1970s, the days of using refugee policy for ideological point scoring were numbered. The large volume of Vietnamese refugees who came to the US after the fall of Saigon in 1975 certainly sent out a negative message about the regime from which they fled. But the liberality of the US response was driven primarily by considerations of maintaining stability in the South East Asian region (Loescher and Scanlan 1986: 102–46) and the fulfilment of a moral obligation forged through the involvement in the war. It was left to the Mariel boatlift, however, to deliver the *coup de grâce*. The public backlash against the entry of Cubans during the Mariel crisis made it clear that the ideological benefits of maintaining the US image as sanctuary for the oppressed were more than matched by the domestic political costs of appearing to tolerate uncontrolled migration.

By 1981, the Reagan Administration, acting on this new cost/benefit analysis, began doing the unthinkable: it reached an agreement with Castro and started sending unwanted Marielitos back to Cuba.[3] Relatively inclusive policies towards Cuban and other communist refugees remained throughout the rest of the 1980s. But things had changed. When Nicaraguans attempted to enter the US after 1981, they did not receive the kind of privileges traditionally accorded to anti-communist refugees, in spite of their departure from a government the Reagan Administration was attempting to overthrow (Dominguez 1990: 160–1). During the Solidarity crisis of 1981, the Administration made it clear that, unlike with Hungarians in 1956, it would not grant mass asylum to Poles struggling against the Soviet-backed regime (Zolberg 1994: 342). After Mariel, departure from a communist regime was still the main currency for refuge in the US, however, it had been sharply devalued from the highs of the 1950s and 1960s.

The US as a country of first asylum

The breakdown in the policy consensus over refugees resulted, above all else, from the US transition from a country of resettlement to one of first asylum. While the US had long been the first port of call for Cubans and Haitians, before 1980 it had been able to evade the political controversy resulting from this role. As I have already shown, by enlisting the cooperation of the Cuban government, the Johnson Administration had been able to manage the resettlement of refugees from Cuba in 1965, preventing a disorderly rush to US shores. The entry of Haitians had also been controlled, though by somewhat less benign practices. While a steady exodus of elites had been allowed to enter the US after the right-wing dictator François Duvalier's accession to power in 1957, once boats full of ordinary Haitians began appearing off the Florida coast, in September 1963, the welcome mat was pulled away (Stepick 1992: 129–31). The summary rejection and return of Haitian asylum seekers put an end to the movement of Haitians to the US for almost a decade. However, in 1972 boats from Haiti once again started arriving in the US (Stepick 1992: 133). Between 1972 and 1980, around 30,000 Haitians landed on US shores, about 25 per cent of whom were granted asylum

[3] By 1984 the US Administration was actually arguing in court that its policy of deporting certain groups of Marielitos was justifiable because they would have their human rights respected if returned to Cuba (Dominguez 1990: 160).

(Loescher and Scanlan 1986: 80). Most of the others were denied a formal hearing and sent back to Haiti with little formality (Loescher and Scanlan 1986: 80–1).

By 1980, the traditional methods US governments had used to control the entry of asylum seekers were proving inadequate to the task. The Mariel crisis unfolded at a speed that made a resettlement-based response redundant; 80,000 Cubans arrived in the US within six weeks of Castro's announcement. To make matters worse, Haitian asylum seekers began arriving in the very same month as the Cuban crisis occurred. Around 40,000 claimed asylum. Numbers of asylum seekers were also boosted by the arrival of what were to become known as 'jet age asylum seekers', refugee applicants who travelled intercontinentally to claim asylum in Western countries. While the volume was still relatively low in 1980, the rise of those intercontinental travellers in pursuit of asylum added to the feeling that US borders were under siege. The problem was not simply a matter of numbers, however. The incorporation of the 1967 UN Protocol into US domestic law in the 1980 Refugee Act made the summary exclusion of asylum seekers a violation of the international law principle of *non-refoulement*. For the first time, government officials could not ignore the fact that Haitian asylum seekers, along with others from non-communist countries, had a legal right to have their claims for asylum heard. Summary exclusion was still possible, but only if the Administration was prepared to violate the law.

Added to this combination of factors, the newly passed 1980 Act, drafted on the assumption that most refugees entered the US through resettlement schemes, offered little guidance on how to deal with large numbers of onshore applications for asylum. The result was a public and Congressional perception of a border control crisis, with anxiety fuelled by concerns that asylum was becoming a vehicle for the entry of criminals and illegal migrants. Little wonder that the legal scholar David Martin would later describe 'the taming of the asylum process' as the 'major unfinished business left by the Refugee Act' (Martin 1982: 116).

From being perched high in the realm of national security, the events of 1980 dragged refugee policy back into the maelstrom of domestic politics. And President Carter's response did little to dampen political controversy. He offered neither Cubans nor Haitians refugee status. Instead, drawing upon the attorney general's parole authority, a new status, 'Cuban/Haitian Entrant', was created. His compromise resolved the immediate problem, but further politicised refugee policy. Excluding the entrants from refugee status decentralised the costs of resettlement, making them a local responsibility (Ferris 1987: 115). Residents in Florida, already concerned about an influx of large numbers of working-class Cubans, now had another reason to resent the arrival of boat people (see Alpern 1980: 28). After his failed 1980 campaign for re-election, Carter pointed to the Mariel incident as an important factor in his loss. 'The refugee question', he said, 'has hurt us badly. It wasn't just in Florida, but it was throughout the country. It was a burning issue. It made us look impotent' (quoted in Dominguez 1990: 155). Once a sign of the Executive's strength, refugee policy now showed that it could weaken presidents too.

Unequal protection and the rise of the courts

As much as the movement of Haitians and Cubans in 1980 raised border control issues, it also raised questions of justice. Human rights advocates had long pointed to refugee policy as an area where the kind of discrimination, expunged from immigration policy by the 1965 Immigration Act, lingered on. With its whiff of racism, the widespread exclusion of Haitians was viewed as particularly odious. Yet it was only in 1980, when Cubans and Haitians began making their way to Florida simultaneously, that these concerns were echoed in a larger and more influential audience.

The Carter Administration saw itself facing a number of stark choices in 1980. Was it to continue to accept Cubans for asylum while denying entry to Haitians in obvious need? If so, how could such action be reconciled with the demands of the 1980 Refugee Act, which incorporated a refugee definition of universal applicability? On the other hand, did not conceding the necessity of equal treatment mean leaving the US open to the claims of millions of immigrants from the Caribbean and Central America who also might come in search of asylum? Carter's 'Cuban/Haitian Entrant' status got around the most obvious criticisms of bias, without creating a precedent for the granting of refugee status. However, the status did not grant permanent residence. This hardly mattered for Cuban entrants who, after one year's residence in the US, were eligible for permanent residence under the 1966 Cuban Adjustment Act (Gordon 1996: 344). Haitians, on the other hand, had to apply for asylum if they were to adjust their status and escape eligibility for removal.[4]

The next Administration, Ronald Reagan's, which came to power in 1981, showed little interest even in the appearance of even-handedness. Throughout the 1980s, Haitians were viewed – almost *en masse* – as economic migrants, and consequently subjected to harsh treatment. Those

[4] As it turned out, the Immigration Control and Reform Act of 1996 changed the status of the Haitians, leading many to gain permanent residence, though outside the refugee system (Gordon 1996: 344).

who managed to avoid being interdicted at sea and summarily returned to Haiti, could expect to be detained upon arrival in the US for an extended period, before being rejected for asylum, if they were lucky enough to be given access to determination proceedings (Schuck 1991: 9). They were not the only ones on the receiving end of such hostility. Central Americans fleeing right-wing dictatorships in Guatemala and El Salvador entered the US illegally in large numbers during the 1980s. Around 100,000 El Salvadorans alone entered during the decade (Gordon 1996: 345). Those who trusted their plight to the asylum system were bound for disappointment. Through State Department opinions, the ideological predilections of the Administration found their way into Immigration and Naturalization Service (INS) asylum decisions (Ferris 1987: 126). The results spoke for themselves.

> In 1981, 2 Salvadorans were granted asylum (and 154 denied); in 1982, 74 were granted asylum (and 169 denied); in 1983, 230 were granted asylum (and approximately 4000 denied). In 1984, the government granted 328 Salvadoran asylum claims and denied 13,045; only 3 Guatemalan claims were accepted and 753 denied. (Ferris 1987: 126)

Refugees from communist countries and other regimes considered hostile to the US had somewhat more success in gaining asylum In 1984, 1,018 Nicaraguans had their asylum claims accepted, while 7,274 were rejected. In the same year, 5,017 Iranians were accepted, 3,216 were rejected (Ferris 1987: 126).

The rejection figures for asylum seekers from dictatorships such as El Salvador simply 'could not withstand the common-sense test of public scrutiny' (Meissner 1990: 134). Summary and discriminatory treatment mobilised refugee advocates and other human rights groups, including the churches. Aware of the difficulties of achieving legislative reform, they took the INS to court with increasing frequency in the early 1980s. Their successes were few compared to the volume of cases fought. But their efforts bore some fruit. In an increasing number of decisions, Federal Court justices showed themselves willing to draw upon administrative and constitutional law norms that had long been influential in other policy areas in ways that recognised asylum seekers as rights-bearing subjects protected by considerations of due process (Schuck 1991: 9–10). The legal victories that resulted eased the standard of proof required to gain refugee status, upheld the asylum claims made by those who had been politically neutral, and forced change in the INS's practice of withholding work authorisation for certain groups. Federal Courts had now begun to abandon 'their traditional deference to the INS' (Schuck 1998: 215). In the words of Peter Schuck, a 'more detailed supervision of the Agency's administration of the law' now became the order of the day (Schuck 1998: 215).

Constitutional scrutiny brought a new branch of government into play in the evolution of US refugee policy, the Judiciary. Partly in response to this new atmosphere, a series of reforms was implemented by the Justice Department in 1990. These reforms moved the asylum system closer to political impartiality, and thus nearer to the expectations of the Refugee Convention, by establishing a new corps of asylum officers trained in international law and required to be independent of State Department prerogatives (Joppke 1999b: 53). When, in that same year, the INS settled a broad challenge to its asylum procedures out of court, allowing for the claims of some 150,000 Guatemalans and Salvadorans to be reheard (Schuck 1991: 10), it appeared that a new era beyond the traditional 'double standard' had been ushered in (Joppke 1999a: 119–20). The reality was somewhat more complicated. The Executive still had enormous discretion to choose who amongst the world's vast number of refugees located outside US territory would be resettled in the US. Nonetheless, for those inside or at the borders of the charmed circle of US territory, the odds that having a well-founded fear of persecution would qualify one for asylum were better than ever before.

The new era in responses to refugees

The cumulative effect of these changes was to make US refugee policy a very different beast by the early 1990s. Not only had the major ideological compass directing responses to refugees – the Cold War – disappeared, but the range of actors with a stake in influencing policy had expanded to include the judiciary, civil rights groups and larger sections of the electorate. As a result, refugee issues had simultaneously diminished and grown in political significance. On the one hand, the end of the Cold War had devalued refugee policy. It was difficult now to consider refugee admissions as an urgent matter of national interest. On the other hand, the rise of mass asylum seeking had made refugees an extremely volatile electoral issue, raising questions about the state's ability to exercise border control. As Carter's experience with Mariel had shown, the political consequences of not 'taming' asylum could be extremely negative.

The rise of mass asylum seeking also brought about another change. Policy responses to refugees became divided by the early 1990s (Joppke 1999a: 115–19). Large numbers of spontaneous arrivals, and the incorporation of the 1951 Refugee Convention into the 1980 Act, bifurcated refugee policy, creating two distinctive policy realms: asylum policy (responses to claimants for refugee status at or within US borders) and resettlement policy (the organized admission of refugees located in other countries). Each of these realms was now governed by a distinctive dynamic. In order to understand the evolution of US responses to refugees over the last decade, it is thus necessary to consider resettlement policy and asylum policy separately.

Resettlement

One way of characterising the difference between resettlement and asylum policies since 1990 is to say that US resettlement policy has been generous but not humanitarian, while asylum policy has been humanitarian but not generous. The case for describing resettlement policy as generous is fairly easy to make. Year after year the US government has made available resettlement places to large numbers of refugees in accord with the demands of the 1980 Act. Indeed, no other Western country has accepted more refugees for admission since the beginning of the 1990s. Between 1991 and 1994, the volume of refugee admissions to the US continued to resemble the levels of the late 1980s (Gordon 1996: 346), with some 110,000 refugees resettled annually, in spite of the demise of a cogent national security rationale for entrance with the end of the Cold War. In 2000, the US resettled 72,515 refugees.

Impressive as these figures may be, they are a tribute to the strength of partial attachments as much as impartial concern based on need. Despite the fall of the Berlin Wall in 1989, the major beneficiaries of refugee resettlement programmes till the mid 1990s remained people from the countries of the former Soviet Union and Eastern Europe. When immigration officials moved in the late 1980s to cut back entry places from these countries, their efforts were strongly resisted by well-developed and influential lobby groups (Meissner 1990: 136). American Jewish groups and evangelical Christian organisations actively campaigned for a continuation of the Cold War admission policies despite the move to democratic governance across the former Soviet Union. Their lobbying of Congress yielded impressive fruit. A legislative amendment to the fiscal year 1990 Appropriations Act eased the standards required to prove eligibility for refugee status for Soviet Jews, Poles outside Poland, Soviet Evangelical Christians, Ukrainian Catholics and Orthodox and a range of Indochinese entrants (Meissner 1990: 136; Schrag 2000: 12). The Amendment passed the Senate unanimously and, after further extensions, remained in force until 1994 (Schrag 2000: 12).

The degree of influence exercised by lobby groups, particularly those representing Jewish, Christian and Cuban immigrants, has not pleased all legislators. In the late 1980s, Senator Alan Simpson decried 'gimmickry in the use of the word refugee'. It is necessary, he argued, 'to distinguish between the right to leave the Soviet Union and the right to enter the United States' (quoted in Briggs 1996: 146). Bitter criticism of such 'gimmickry' has also come from a more unlikely corner. In the late 1980s the Israeli government complained that the inclusiveness of US refugee law was discouraging Soviet Jews from settling in Israel (Briggs 1996: 145). There is, to be sure, nothing new in special interest groups determining the composition and character of refugee admissions. The very foundations of US refugee policy, as I have shown, lay in such a connection. What is significant, however, is that there has been no move in resettlement policy to correspond with the attempt to expunge political preferences from asylum policy in the early 1990s. As a discretionary policy, the composition of resettlement policy remains highly responsive to political bargaining.

Foreign policy considerations have also continued to play a key role in refugee resettlement over the last decade. The origins of many of the refugees resettled in the US since the early 1990s pretty much track the countries in which US troops have been deployed since the end of the Cold War. Between 1992 and 1998, 269,068 people from the Soviet Union were resettled in the US, along with 23,584 from Cuba, 23,127 from Iraq, 27,369 from Laos, 24,745 from Somalia, 157,479 from Vietnam and 83,141 from the former Yugoslavia (INS 2002). Of the 85,006 refugees the US resettled in the 1999 fiscal year, the vast majority came from Bosnia, the former Soviet Union, Kosovo and Vietnam.

There have, however, recently been signs that Executive and Congressional support for resettlement as an all-purpose foreign policy tool may be waning. The number of refugees resettled annually has declined steadily since the early 1990s. Moreover, despite its role in the mass exodus of Kosovans in 1999, the US was reluctant to take Kosovans for permanent settlement. The Administration eventually accepted a little over 14,000 refugees. This was lower than the number taken in by Germany. The US's modest response was the result of a number of factors, including a desire not to play into the hands of Serbia's 'ethnic cleansers' by reducing the number of Kosovan Albanians residing in Kosovo. Nonetheless, the low intake was seen by some observers as signalling a new reluctance to take in refugees (*The Economist* 1999: 26–8). The US response to the bombing of Afghanistan in the aftermath of 11 September 2001 has added weight to this interpretation. Despite the provision of a substantial amount of aid, there were no moves to relieve Pakistan and Iran of even part of their refugee burdens through resettlement. It is possible that the Executive, in future years, may become less interested in determining the composition of US refugee admissions. It is unlikely that this will make refugee resettlement redundant. More likely, it will leave greater room for immigrant lobby groups to determine the shape of admissions.

Asylum

In principle, asylum policy should be insulated from the kinds of political pressures that have shaped resettlement. The incorporation of the Refugee Convention's Protocol into the 1980 Refugee Act bound the US to an obligation not to *refoule* any person at or within its borders with a legitimate claim to refugee status. While this is not an obligation to grant asylum *per se*, the difficulties of gaining protection for refugees in other countries usually makes it a *de facto* duty.

Of course, as we have seen with the Cuban/Haitian double standard, US practice has tended to depart a long way from the principle. By the early 1990s, however, largely as a result of judicial intervention, the US found itself edging towards a non-discriminatory and politically independent system of asylum provision (Joppke 1999a: 117–20). In the last decade, this movement has continued. But it has not on balance resulted in more inclusive responses to asylum seekers, though the doors of the US did become more open for a brief period in the early 1990s (Joppke 1999a: 120). Rather, the move towards asylum based on need has been accompanied by two highly restrictive developments: the dismantling of the *ancien régime* of welcoming asylum seekers from communist countries and the increasing use of deterrent and preventive measure designed to impede access to asylum. These two developments have resulted in an asylum system that is humanitarian but not generous.

The erosion of the *ancien régime* began, as we have seen, in the early 1980s, with the Reagan Administration's reluctance to grant refugee status to asylum seekers from socialist regimes in Central America. The case for ending the privileged status of anti-communist refugees became even stronger after the Cold War's end. As a consequence, Cubans in particular began to feel the heat. In 1994, Castro seized the opportunity to increase the refugee pressure on the US, already facing boatloads of Haitian refugees, by allowing the departure of Cuban rafters (*balseros*). When *balseros* started to head to the US in large numbers that summer, the Clinton Administration adopted tactics unprecedented in their harshness. The president suspended the Cuban Adjustment Act, ordered the prosecution of all US captains picking up Cuban immigrants, and requested that the Coast Guard send all Cubans picked up at sea to a new US-constructed refugee camp at Guantanamo Bay on the island of Cuba in anticipation of their return home (Olson and Olson 1995: 111). After a period of months, many of the Cubans sent to Guantanamo found their way to the US. The Administration was not better than its predecessors at avoiding the temptation to sign agreements with Castro to allow for orderly immigration to the US. In spite of the outcome, the Administration's attempts to prevent the spontaneous arrivals of Cubans had now been ratcheted up. A message had gone out that spontaneous arrivals would not be tolerated and that message was heard, initially at least. Between January and October 1996, the US Coast Guard reportedly intercepted only 278 rafters from Cuba (Reimers 1998: 77).

Despite harsher treatment for Cubans, Haitians still fared worse. Haitian boat people were also sent to Guantanamo during the mid 1990s. They were much more likely, however, to end up back in Haiti, and many intercepted by the Coast Guard faced immediate return home. In the midst of a deepening human rights crisis in Haiti in 1994, brewing since the ousting of its democratically elected leader, Jean-Bertrand Aristide, in a military coup in 1991, returning Haitian refugees became politically untenable. Democratic members of Congress, led by the Black Caucus, pressured Clinton either to admit Haitian boat people or to intervene militarily to restore Aristide to power (Perusse 1995: 75–6). Fearing electoral backlash in Florida if large numbers of Haitians were admitted, Clinton reluctantly chose the latter course of action. On 15 September 1994 Clinton announced in a televised speech the reasons for US intervention in Haiti, citing the desire, amongst other things, to 'protect the integrity of US borders'.

The tough measures visited on Cubans may have helped to equalise opportunities for asylum. But the motivating force behind these measures was not justice. Rather, the Administration wanted to prevent a political backlash from an electorate increasingly sensitive to migration issues. It also wished to avoid placing more pressure on an already overloaded asylum system. By 1994, rising numbers of 'jet age asylum seekers', the new requirements of due process, and lack of bureaucratic resources, had led to a backlog of some 400,000 asylum claims. As a result, applicants could expect to wait years for a final decision. These delays created their own problems. Economic migrants wishing to work and remain in the US now had a strong incentive to use the asylum route as a way of bypassing normal immigration control, further boosting the number of asylum applicants (Joppke 1999a: 120; see also, Martin 1998).

In 1995, the Clinton Administration implemented a number of reforms aimed at clearing the backlog and reducing the attractions of entering via the asylum route. The most significant reform limited the rights of asylum seekers to work, requiring a wait of at least 180 days before permission would be granted. Yet the most effective (and politically prudent) way of limiting asylum claims was to prevent foreigners accessing US territory.

Accordingly the US, like most other Western countries, also beefed up its means of exclusion – visa controls, carrier sanctions and interdictions at sea – during the 1990s, in recognition of this fact.

Of these preventative practices, interdiction was the most dubious from a legal perspective. However, it passed judicial muster in a famous 1994 decision that appalled refugee activists. In the 1994 case, *Sale* vs. *Haitian Centers Council*, the US Supreme Court ruled six to one that interdicting Haitian boats before they reached US territorial waters and returning the occupants to Haiti, without assessment of their asylum claim, was not a violation of domestic US or international law. The implications of the ruling, which appealed to an arcane and highly dubious interpretation of what it is to '*refoule*' a refugee, denied that the US had any legal responsibility to refugees who were not within or at US borders, even if they were prevented from arriving at those borders by deliberate US action. Another judicial decision brought bad news for asylum seekers held at Guantanamo Bay. In 1999, the Eleventh Circuit Court of Appeals determined that these aliens 'had no legal rights under the domestic law of the US or under international law' because such rights were available only to persons on US territory. The court found that Guantanamo Bay, while under US 'jurisdiction and control', was not US sovereign territory (Jones 1995: 498–505).

The courts, the site of such important victories for the rights of asylum seekers in the 1980s and early 1990s, showed themselves in these decisions reluctant to constrain the state's treatment of asylum seekers outside US territorial waters. The rationale behind this judicial deference was complex; courts defended their actions through their own interpretations of the 1951 Convention and the intentions of Congress during the passage of the 1980 Refugee Act. But, significantly, the Supreme Court also found itself in *Sale* vs. *Haitian Centers Council (1994)* reluctant to construe extraterritorial obligations to treaty and statutory provisions 'that may involve foreign and military affairs for which the President has unique responsibility'. The judiciary, through an appeal to the foreign policy prerogatives of the Executive, indirectly gave its imprimatur to a double standard of growing significance. Asylum seekers within US territory would enjoy the rights and protections of US law, while those outside territorial waters could be treated summarily by the US state.

By 1995, even the rights of asylum seekers *within* the US appeared to be contracting. Between 1990 and 1993, the problem of asylum was seen largely in bureaucratic terms. How does one create a system of refugee determination that respects the limited rights of asylum seekers to a fair and impartial assessment of their claim while discouraging abuse of the system? After 1993, the problem of asylum came to be seen in a more insidious and darker light. The key event in this transition was the bombing of the World Trade Center in New York City in 1993. When a foreigner in the process of applying for refugee status was charged with plotting the bombing, the asylum process came under intense political and media scrutiny. Public scepticism of asylum, fuelled by a more general backlash against illegal migration originating in California and media-recounted tales of asylum abuse and laxity, made some kind of legislative backlash inevitable. Seizing the opportunity to capture public concern, the unabashedly ideological Republican Congress began the task of rewriting the country's asylum and immigration laws.

The 1996 Illegal Immigration Reform and Immigrant Responsibility Act was signed by President Bill Clinton on 24 April 1996. The Act 'essentially wipe[d] out asylum as we know it' (Fragomen 1997: 43) by reasserting political control over asylum, illegal aliens and aliens convicted of committing crimes at the expense of the courts. The scope of the new Act was wide-reaching. Applicants for asylum now had to lodge their asylum claim within one year of entering the US; new restrictions were placed on repeat applications; the grounds for rejecting asylum claims were expanded, codified and made mandatory, giving authorities more scope to remove those suspected of having committed serious, non-political crimes before entering the US or being involved in terrorist activities. Most controversially, the Act introduced a system of 'expedited removal' that gave immigration officers the authority to remove 'improperly documented aliens' arriving in the US 'without further hearing or review'. While an exception has been made for those who indicate their desire to apply for asylum (who must be referred to a trained asylum officer), those found to lack a 'credible fear' of persecution are subject to immediate removal. Detention was made mandatory during the process of determining whether an applicant has a credible claim to asylum.

In general, the Act has made applying for asylum more onerous and exclusive. The United States Committee for Refugees reported in 1999 that some 89,521 migrants were removed through the expedited process, an increase of 15 per cent on the previous year (US Committee for Refugees 2001). Another 86,000 were removed in 2000 (US Committee for Refugees 2001). Advocates for refugees worry that a substantial percentage of those removed may have made a credible claim to asylum but never make it past control-minded immigration officials, eager to explain the penalities for unsuccessful asylum applicants, to see a trained asylum officer (Schmitt 2001). Another consequence of the 1996 Act has been an increase in the number of asylum applicants in detention, a proportion of whom spend long periods in custody. The use of detention has an incalculable deterrent value in reducing overall asylum claims, probably pushing some potential asylum seekers into other (in some cases illicit) entry channels. Asylum applications to the US have fallen substantially in the aftermath of the 1996 Act. In 1997 the US received 84,839 applications for asylum, followed by 54,952 and 41,377 for 1998 and 1999. In 1999, 38.2 per cent of applications for asylum were successful. The main source countries for asylum seekers were China, Somalia, Haiti, El Salvador, Guatemala and Mexico (US Committee for Refugees 2001). The US received 48,054 claims for asylum in 2000.

Despite the fact that some of the Act's most egregious features have been challenged successfully in the courts, and that the California-led backlash against illegal migration disappeared as quickly as it arose, US asylum policy still finds itself living under the shadow of the 1996 Act. By 2001, asylum, the unruly child of the 1980 Act, had been well and truly 'tamed'. The transition to an era of restrictive and (for the most part) non-discriminatory asylum policy had been achieved, though at a cost to the spirit of the 1951 Geneva Convention. One thing seems clear. There will be no let up in the tight control currently exercised over asylum in the years ahead. The terrorist attacks of 11 September 2001 in New York, Virginia and Pennsylvania have once again focused attention on the adequacy of asylum procedures. While none of the terrorists involved in the attacks had passed through the US asylum system, the adequacy of border controls is now a key security issue. Legislation passed in the aftermath of 11 September empowered the Justice Department to detain, deport and exclude, with limited or no judicial scrutiny, foreigners within or attempting to enter the US suspected of being associated with terrorist groups or activities. These changes do not dramatically affect opportunities for asylum. Five years before the events of 11 September, the 1996 Act had put in place a legislative framework for asylum that anticipated many of the measures now being applied to immigrants generally. Nonetheless, the events of that fateful September day will ensure that any future attempts to liberalise asylum policy are likely to founder on the rocks of preserving the security of US citizens.

6 Australia: restricting asylum, resettling refugees

> It is our duty to present to the world the spectacle of a rich country with a great people, with an adequate population – with a population which may say justly to the rest of the world: We are here; we propose to maintain our integrity as a nation; and our warrant for that is that we are using the resources which God has given into our hands. The case for migration on a great scale is indeed an irresistible one.
>
> Robert Menzies, Prime Minister of Australia 1950

> Australia's interests [fall] . . . in three broad categories: geo-political or strategic interests; economic and trade interests; and the national interest in being, and being seen to be, a good international citizen.
>
> Gareth Evans, Australian Minister for Foreign Affairs 1991

> If the view becomes entrenched around the world that it's easy to get into this country, we will have an enormous problem . . . We will have an unbelievable problem trying to control our borders.
>
> John Howard, Prime Minister of Australia 2001

In 1991 Australia's Minister for Foreign Affairs, Gareth Evans, stated that fulfilling the duties of a 'good international citizen' was one of the major objectives of Australian foreign policy (Evans and Grant 1991: 34). International citizenship, he claimed, involved demonstrating a readiness to tackle some of the vast range of global challenges currently confronting the international community. One challenge singled out was solving 'the world-wide problem of refugees' (Evans and Grant 1991: 35). Here, Evans argued, Australia would continue to make a particularly important contribution.

The minister's choice of Australia's treatment of refugees as a way of highlighting the country's preparedness to accept the obligations of membership in the international community was in no way surprising. Between 1945 and the early 1990s Australia had accepted well over 500,000 refugees and other displaced persons for entry, including some 137,000 Indochinese refugees, the highest number per capita of any Western country (Robinson 1998: 151). Since the mid 1970s, the country had also engaged in resettlement programmes, over and above its obligations not to return (*refouler*) refugees under the 1951 Refugee Convention, allowing between 9,000 to 20,000 refugees and others in like situations to enter annually.

Yet Evans' view that Australian responses to refugees bolstered the country's claim to be a good international citizen would soon look deeply ironic. Within a year of his statement, Australia would put in place the toughest and most wide-ranging system in the world for the detention of asylum seekers. Within a decade, the country would turn around asylum seekers on boats, redefine in legislation the definition of Australian territory for immigration purposes, and house asylum seekers on the remote and barren island of Nauru, all to prevent the country from incurring claims under the 1951 Refugee Convention. While it was still possible in the early 1990s to consider harsh treatment of asylum seekers as a sideshow to the country's overall response to refugees, the *Tampa* incident of 2001 had, above all in the eyes of the international community, made Australia's restrictive policies the main event.

In this chapter, I will trace the evolution of Australia's responses to refugees through a series of transitions. Over the last 100 years, Australia has moved from being the country of the infamous 'White Australia' immigration policy, to one with a plausible claim to be a model international citizen in its response to refugees, to its current incarnation as arguably the most unwelcoming country towards asylum seekers in the Western world.

Throughout these different historical incarnations inclusion and exclusion of immigrants and refugees have gone hand in hand: the ability to exclude non-whites was premised upon the need to attract large numbers of European migrants; the embrace of Indo-Chinese refugees for resettlement in the early 1970s was driven by a belief that the employment of such schemes would prevent the spontaneous arrivals of such refugees; current policies which interdict boat arrivals, which have their origins in the 2001 *Tampa* incident, are justified by what the government characterises as the availability of 'legitimate' entrance routes. The paradoxical nature of Australian policy towards refugees and asylum seekers makes it extremely difficult to judge the country's overall contribution to refugee protection.

I will begin this chapter by examining the factors that have influenced the Australian state's entrance policies since 1945. In the first part, I consider the forces that made possible the mass migration programme that led Australia to accept almost 2.5 million immigrants for entrance between 1947 and the early 1970s. In the second, I consider Australian policy between 1975 and 1996. I show how responses to refugees and asylum seekers were affected by changes in the fundamental assumptions that had guided Australian entrance policy during the mass migration period, as a result of economic downturn, the rise of multiculturalism and challenges to the traditional idea of control. In the final section, I turn to the evolution of policy under John Howard's Liberal government, which came to power in 1996. Through the perspective of the *Tampa* incident of 2001, I examine whether recent developments represent a new departure in Australian policy-making. I conclude by assessing the defensibility of key aspects of the current government's policies.

The state and entrance: 1945–75

Any attempt to understand Australia's current response to refugees needs to consider the range of factors that led to the post-war mass migration programme which lasted until the early 1970s. Throughout much of the last fifty years, refugees have been the fortunate beneficiaries of a general programme of immigration that was motivated by the security and economic needs of the state. Current refugee policy has recently developed a distinct logic of its own, but its fate is still closely connected to that of immigration in general.

What factors influenced the state's response to the admission of outsiders between 1945 and 1975? I shall now outline four features of the Australian state that were crucial in this regard: its quest for international legitimacy; its role as a provider of security; its existence as a capitalist state; and its role as the representative of a political community.

The quest for legitimacy

Britain's initial claim to the territory which was to become known as Australia rested upon the view that the land 'discovered' by James Cook in 1770 and settled by Governor Arthur Phillip eighteen years later was officially unoccupied or *terra nullius*. The claim, which dramatically swept aside any Aboriginal entitlement to the land they had inhabited for thousands of years, rested upon the natural law argument that primitive nomadic peoples who lacked recognisable social structures and failed to cultivate land had no right to object to the appropriation of their territory by those who could use it to support a greater population. Accordingly, New South Wales was, from the perspective of natural law (as interpreted by the British), 'uninhabited' when British representatives laid initial title to it. From the landing of the First Fleet in 1788, the territory passed into the hands of the British sovereign.

The natural law justification for occupation had important implications for the question of who should be allowed to reside in the state. For the cogency of the European claim that the Aborigines had no right to 'Tracts of ground' that were 'more than the people who dwell on it do or can make use of' (Locke 1964: book II, sec. 45) suggested that white settlers needed to make good use of the land if they were to be justified in excluding others. The ease with which the previous inhabitants had lost control of the territory testified starkly to the importance of populating Australia if the British were to possess the moral right as well as the practical ability to exclude.

Before the 1850s, peopling the territory was not a matter of great urgency, largely because there were no serious challengers to the legitimacy of the British claim. The continent of Australia was insulated from uncontrolled migration by two geographical realities which have strongly shaped the entrance of new settlers in the years since. First, Australia's location 12,000 miles from Europe enabled British and, afterwards, colonial governments stringently to control the flow of settlers to the territory. Second, as an island continent, Australia was protected from the flow of large movements of unwanted people overland. Nonetheless, if geographical destiny had helped insulate Australia, by the 1850s it was clear that it had also thrown forth one serious challenge: the proximity of Asia. The discovery of gold in 1851 led to large flows of entrants from sources more diverse than previously, most notably immigrants from China, whose numbers had reached some 50,000 by the 1880s. The reaction to the Chinese on the gold-fields was hostile and violent: racially restrictive entrance policies were quickly (but often ineffectively) legislated by colonial governments. This legislation was to be the first in a long line of immigration laws reaching up to the 1960s, specifically designed to keep the 'teeming millions' of Asia from Australia's shores.

Early attempts to control migration could not help but raise awkward questions about 'white Australia's' occupation of the land:

> Were they to exclude the people of an industrious and civilised race, who in their own country were often exposed to want which was partly the result of a teeming population? The British took this land from the native inhabitants because they could make it more valuable to human beings. By what right did they now attempt to exclude the Chinese from coming for the same purpose? (Willard 1967: 30; original edition 1923)

These sharp questions were not successful in making the country's leaders think again about admitting Asians; one of the first Acts of the Australian Federal Parliament was the Immigration Restriction Act (1901) which provided the initial framework for the unofficial 'White Australia' Policy that operated until the late 1960s. But they did provide governmental officials with the challenge of showing that the land was being used to its fullest advantage. Australia's leaders chose to meet this challenge, and thus to dampen international criticism, by encouraging the entrance and settlement of British immigrants and by tolerating the entry of settlers from other, less desirable parts of Europe. Increasing the rate of immigration was, by the early twentieth century, a matter of national concern. It was important enough for the Australian prime minister, W. M. Hughes, to remark in the period immediately after the end of World War I:

> Australia needs a much larger population. World opinion will not tolerate much longer a dog-in-the-manger policy. We must choose between doing the thing ourselves in our own way, or letting others do it in their way. Our choice lies between filling up spaces with immigrants from Britain, and, if needs be, other countries, and having the matter taken out of our hands and being swamped by the rush of peoples from the over-crowded countries of the world. (Quoted in Willard 1967: 213)

Hughes's remark exemplified the paradox that prevailed in Australian immigration policy in the period leading up to World War II: mass migration was necessary to legitimate the state's exclusion of certain types of outsiders. Once the post-1945 mass migration scheme began, criticism of Australia's right to exclude needy outsiders from entrance became rarer. It was now more difficult to criticise white Australia for failing to use the land at its disposal. Even when the programme was in full swing, however, anxiety about the territorial legitimacy of the Australian state did not completely disappear. No less than Robert Menzies, the man who was to become Australia's longest-serving Prime Minister, argued in the 1950s that a large migration intake was necessary in order to show to the world 'that we are using the resources that God has given into our hands' (quoted in Crowley 1973b: 219).

State of security

William Hughes' concern that questions of entrance might be 'taken out of Australia's hands' did not only reflect the dubiousness of the Australian state's right to exclude; it also reflected doubts as to Australia's practical ability to restrict entrance. His anxiety exemplified another influential factor in Australia's recent entrance history: the need for a population large enough to ensure the nation's military security. Until 1945, Australia was viewed by its leaders as 'a lonely outpost of Western civilisation in a profoundly alien sea. Too far from Britain for easy succour . . . perilously near the . . . storm centres of the world' (Harris 1938: 125). Given this view, it is not surprising most of Australia's apprehensions with regard to security centred directly upon the Asian region to its north. Attempts to restrict Chinese and later Japanese entrants in the late nineteenth and early twentieth centuries were not only a product of racism. At their most powerful, they reflected a belief that Australia's survival could be threatened 'by the implantation on Australian soil of Asian minorities' (Freeman 1993: 91). These settlers, it was argued, were of dubious loyalty and could well be used as a pretext for intervention in Australian affairs by Asian powers (Freeman 1993: 91).

The long history of Australia's anxiety towards Asia reached its apogee during World War II when Japanese forces swept through South East Asia occupying the island of Timor and landing troops (which were subsequently repelled by Australian forces) on the north coast of New Guinea. While Australia was not invaded, bombs were dropped on Darwin by Japanese forces and a small number of mini-submarines penetrated Sydney Harbour. Moreover, Japan's capture of Singapore vividly demonstrated the vulnerability 'of the British security system in the Pacific on which . . . [Australia] had so long relied for protection' (Hawkins 1991: 31).

The war-time experience convinced political leaders that a population of 7 million was too small to deter or repel any hostile army intent on invasion. With an eye to these concerns, the ruling Labor Party government created Australia's first Ministry of Immigration in 1945. Arthur Calwell, its first minister, was charged with the task of boosting Australia's population through a programme of mass immigration designed to increase the country's population by 1 per cent per year. In November 1946 he outlined his reasons for a huge expansion in migrant intake:

> There was a time just four years ago when Australia faced its gravest peril. Armies recruited from the teeming millions of Japan threatened to overrun our cities and broad hinterland. They were so many. We were so few . . . The call to all Australians is to realise that without adequate numbers this wide brown land may not be held in another clash of arms. (Quoted in Crowley 1973b: 158–9)

The implementation of Calwell's programme needed the agreement of the other major parties if it was to be accepted by the Australian public. The link between immigration and the nation's security was crucial in gaining the programme that consent. When the Labor Party lost office in 1949, the incoming Liberal government pursued the attempts to expand Australia's population with equal vigour.[1] By 1978 over 3.5 million immigrants had settled in Australia. The country's population had doubled

[1] In January 1950, the new Prime Minister, Robert Menzies, stated: 'There is one thing upon which we can all agree . . . and that is, that the attack made upon the problem of immigration in this country under Mr Chifley and Mr Calwell deserves the deep gratitude and warm praise of every Australian' (quoted in Crowley 1973b: 218).

within the space of thirty years. There could be little doubt that Australia with a population of 14 million presented a more daunting challenge to any aggressor nation.

Capitalist state

The Australian state's role as a capitalist state, attempting to manage class conflict and ensure economic development, has also influenced its historical response to entrance. The political strength of labour unions (formalised in the world's first Labour Party) and the highly centralised nature of wage bargaining (Freeman and Jupp 1992: 14–17), brought forth policies which protected the Australian economy from foreign labour and goods throughout much of the twentieth century. As Robert Birrell has argued, early restrictions on the entrance of Asians were:

> linked to a distinctive feature of the working class accommodation with capital at the beginning of the century. Capital would retain ownership of the productive process, but, in return, workers would be guaranteed work under fair wages and conditions. The outcome was a protected economy – and immigration restrictions to protect against low-cost labour. (Birrell 1994: 108)

Asians were not, however, the only ones restricted from entering in order to protect living standards. *All* migration, even that from Britain, was curtailed during times of economic recession and depression. Hence, periods of low immigrant inflow, such as those between 1890 and 1905, 1929 and 1947 and mid 1974 to 1979, closely corresponded to periods of economic downturn (Freeman and Jupp 1992: 2).

But if governments were not slow to restrict entrance during times of economic recession, they also recognised the importance of expanding the labour supply in order to maximise economic growth. Security reasons alone could not explain the alacrity with which Australia's leaders greeted mass migration programmes in the post-war period. As well as contributing to the country's security, increased migration would, in the words of Calwell, lead to 'the fullest expansion' of the Australian economy (quoted in Hawkins 1991: 32). The desire to supplement the labour force grew out of an awareness in the immediate post-war period that Australia's economy was exceedingly vulnerable to fluctuations in international commodity prices because of its overdependence upon the production of primary goods. A larger supply of labour was necessary if the nation was to construct a strong manufacturing base. In 1947, the immigration minister flew to Europe to recruit immigrant labour. Australia subsequently struck a deal with the newly formed International Refugee

Organization (IRO) to resettle large numbers of European war refugees, including displaced people from the Baltic states. As a direct result of these arrangements almost 200,000 refugees arrived in Australia between 1947 and 1952 (National Population Council 1991: 66), 'the largest planned intake of non-British in Australia's history' (Freeman and Jupp 1992: 5). The Australian government ensured supplies of migrant labour afterwards through intergovernmental agreements with Malta (1948), Italy and the Netherlands (1951), West Germany, Austria and Greece (1952), Spain (1958), Turkey (1967) and Yugoslavia (1970). In addition, refugees were accepted from Hungary in 1956 and Czechoslovakia in 1968 (Freeman and Jupp 1992: 5).

There is little doubt that the post-war migration was generally beneficial to the Australian economy. Migrant labour led to an expansion in the country's manufacturing base and, according to the immigration minister in 1951, 'greatly assisted in breaking bottle-necks in the production of iron and steel, bricks, tiles, cement and other building materials' (quoted in Crowley 1973b: 239). The fact that early migrants signed agreements with the government to undertake directed labour for the first two years of their residence maximised these benefits. Indeed, directed labour offered advantages similar to Western European guest-worker schemes; under both, migrant labour could be used as a 'manoeuvrable resource'.[2] Economic expansion during the 1950s and 1960s was far greater than in the first half of the twentieth century; GDP rose at a rate just below 5 per cent, which was higher than corresponding rates in Britain and the US, though lower than that achieved by West Germany (Bolton 1990: 90). Moreover, any adverse effects of the migration were muted by low unemployment (it was never higher than 3.2 per cent and as low as 1.2 per cent in August 1965) and a rapid expansion in average weekly earnings (these grew at 4 per cent in real terms, five times the average rate between 1901 and 1940) during this period (Bolton 1990: 90).

Nation-state

I have already noted how until 1945 entrance policies were constructed with the specific intention of excluding non-European and, to a lesser extent, non-English-speaking migrants. This exclusionist tradition was underpinned by a particular vision of Australian society whose two major elements came together in the idea of a 'White Australia'. The founders of

[2] It also assuaged union fears that the incoming labour would depress wage levels. This was a particularly important consideration for Labor governments.

Australia aimed to create a society that while clearly British in its culture and institutions strove to realise a distinctively egalitarian and demotic ideal. Robert Birrell accurately captures the dominant ethos:

> the White Australia Policy was an expression of the social aspirations of both Liberal and Labour leaders who dominated Australian politics during the foundational years of the Federation which extended from the 1890s to World War I. Their central idea was the creation of a nation free of the old world social and religious cleavages in which all could live a dignified lifestyle. It was believed that the importation of migrants who were Asian and Pacific Islanders would undermine these ideas by degrading the dignity of manual labour. (Birrell 1994: 107–8)

The creation of an exclusively 'white Australia' was viewed by its defenders as a necessary prerequisite for a socially progressive society sensitive to the needs of the ordinary 'working man' and not simply a statement of racial superiority. Importing non-British stock would undermine civic equality and, through the availability of cheap labour, lower the Australian standard of living, such that, according to one Labour leader, 'in a very short time social legislation would be ineffective' (quoted in Crowley 1973a: 15). In this view, it was 'the forces of Toryism and reaction' (*The Worker Magazine* quoted in Crowley 1973a: 14) and not the general public that had an interest in non-discriminatory immigration policies.

Early immigration policies were thus designed to ensure the survival and development of a socially progressive 'British' nation in an unfamiliar and seemingly hostile environment. Essential to the realisation of this goal was the state's provision of subsidised travel arrangements to British settlers. Before 1945, those coming from other European states were rarely prevented from entering, but they did not receive assisted passages. When this changed in the 1940s, however, so did the cultural trajectory of Australian society. Rising employment opportunities in Britain at the end of the war meant that the UK could not supply enough immigrants to satisfy Australia's post-war needs. If these needs were now to be met, the Australian government would have to actively recruit immigrants from the non-English-speaking countries of Northern, Central and Southern Europe. The economic and security needs of the state and the desire for a British political community were potentially in conflict. The government's response was to try to reshape public opinion in order to avoid the potential for a backlash against the new migration. It launched a range of campaigns which publicised the benefits of mass migration and, in a 'remarkable piece of innovation' at the time (Hawkins 1991: 32), it encouraged local community participation in bodies (such as the 'Good Neighbour' Councils) that helped integrate the new settlers. Both of these measures proved remarkably successful.

The architects of the post-war scheme did not believe that the mass migration would jeopardise the Britishness of Australian society (Jupp 1991: 96). Throughout the 1950s and 1960s immigrants were encouraged and expected to assimilate as quickly as possible into Australian ways and customs. The Immigration Minister in 1969, Billy Snedden, bluntly expressed the official view:

> We must have a single culture . . . if immigration implied multi-cultural activities within Australian society, then it was not the type Australia wanted. I am quite determined that we should have a monoculture, with everyone living in the same way, understanding each other, and sharing the same aspirations. We don't want pluralism. (Quoted in Bolton 1990: 106–7)

By the early 1970s, however, it was quite clear that, for better or for worse, pluralism was what Australia had got. The government had abandoned the policy of assimilation by the mid 1970s because of its unpopularity amongst immigrant groups. As an alternative, the Whitlam government embraced a rather vague multicultural vision of Australian society which stressed (not strongly enough according to its critics) shared civic values but celebrated the different cultural backgrounds of citizens.

How are we to explain Australia's extraordinary success in integrating huge numbers of immigrants and refugees between 1945 and 1975? It is evident, first of all, that the various *roles* occupied by the state in the post-war period were favourable to a policy of mass (European) migration. Forceful arguments could be made from the perspective of the state's security (because of the World War II experience); from the capitalist perspective (because of structural weaknesses in the Australian economy and the strong economic growth that occurred during the 1950s and 1960s); and from the perspective of the state's desire to legitimate its appropriation of the continent to justify its exclusion of non-European migration. Furthermore, the political community, that had previously been hostile to non-British migration, had many of its concerns assuaged by an interventionist state keen on using a range of measures to convince the public of the necessity of increased numbers of immigrants and refugees. The case for embarking upon a programme of mass migration in the 1940s and 1950s was, if anything, overdetermined.

Another essential element was the stringent *control* governments exercised over who entered during the programme. This control was practised in two primary ways. The intake of new migrants, first of all, specifically excluded those of non-European ancestry. There was nothing coincidental about the fact that state officials eager to boost migration pursued the White Australia Policy with increased vigour during the 1950s and early

1960s (Bolton 1990: 56). They wished to send a message to the public that the programme would not threaten the European-ness of Australian society. Governments also made sure that migrants accepted for entrance would not be a burden on the community. Only those young and fit enough to contribute to the nation's economic development were recruited, and once they arrived they were often required to undertake directed labour. Clearly, the success of these aspects of control was greatly assisted by the favourableness of Australia's geographical isolation, which insulated the country from the overland movement of people.

Australia's achievement in combining mass migration with tight entrance control between 1945 and 1975 contrasts strongly with the post-war experiences of Britain and Germany. In Germany there were certainly influential forces acting upon the state, particularly those deriving from the desire for economic expansion, which encouraged immigration. But these forces were not powerful enough to neutralise the country's exclusionist conception of nationhood. What resulted was the compromise position of temporary worker migration – foreigners were allowed to work in Germany but not to become citizens. Like Germany, Australia had an exclusionist national ethos but, unlike the Federal Republic, it needed to boost the size of its labour force *and* (for security reasons) the size of its citizenry. While Australian entrance policy aimed for mass migration along with racial restriction, Germany wanted to increase its labour supply without gaining permanent settlers. The Federal Republic failed to achieve this objective because, while it could control the entry of migrants into the state, liberal democratic norms constrained the ability of governments to ensure their departure. The failure of the *Gastarbeiter* programme left the Federal Republic with a substantial ethnic population that its governments had made no attempt to integrate into the political community.

Britain was a different case altogether. Its experience of immigration in the 1950s and 1960s was the result not of the active recruitment of migration but of changes in the international environment that interacted with established entrance provisions. Correspondingly, the state was widely and for the most part correctly perceived by the public as lacking control over the flow of the immigration. New Commonwealth immigrants arrived in a political community that was unprepared for their arrival. Under these circumstances, it is perhaps not surprising that many in the political community, often influenced by racism, viewed the new entrants as a threat to their own interests. Britain did, however, share one thing in common with Australia – governments had far-reaching legislative powers with which to change immigration law. By the late 1960s, UK governments had aggressively used this power to wrest back control over entrance.

Responses to refugees between 1975 and 1996

So far I have said little about Australia's dealings with refugees. This is not because the state failed to respond to their plight during the post-war period. Indeed, between 1945 and 1975, well over 350,000 refugees (broadly defined) and displaced persons were accepted for entrance (Price 1981: 101). The Australian government had been one of the first countries to sign the 1951 Refugee Convention in 1954 and acceded to the 1967 Protocol in 1973, thus committing itself legally to respect the principle of *non-refoulement*. Moreover, by 1975, Australia had given substantial financial support to the Intergovernmental Committee for European Migration and the UNHCR (National Population Council (NPC) 1991: 66–7).

Yet the history of Australia's responses to refugees was more mixed than these actions suggest. The country had done little in the face of Nazi Germany's persecution of the Jews, arguably the twentieth century's most devastating refugee crisis. Australian officials rejected requests to take large numbers of refugees at the 1939 Evian conference with the response, 'we have no racial problem [and] we are not desirous of importing one by encouraging any scheme of large-scale foreign migration' (NPC 1991: 65).[3] Furthermore, while Australia was a signatory to the UN Refugee Convention, the Article 33 prohibition of *refoulement* had virtually no effect on its policies. The Refugee Convention was not incorporated in domestic law (Goodwin-Gill 1983: 167). Geographical isolation made the prospect of applications for asylum at the border nugatory, and virtually all of the refugees accepted by officials entered pre-screened, as part of broader resettlement schemes that the government was free under international law to operate at its discretion.

Accepting large numbers of refugees, moreover, did not prevent the motivations of government officials being called into question. In the late 1940s, Australia was criticised by the International Refugee Organization for being 'less interested in helping the unfortunate than in finding healthy and industrious "factory fodder" for its population and development programmes' (Price 1981: 101). But if economic and demographic reasons encouraged a response to the plight of refugees, so also did ideological and strategic concerns. The entry of substantial numbers of refugees from the Soviet bloc, notably from Hungary and Czechoslavakia, was a sign that Australia was, like other Western countries, prepared to play its part in the Cold War struggle against the Soviet Union in return for protection under the US's security umbrella.

[3] Under a great deal of international pressure, Australia eventually accepted 15,000 refugees for entrance.

When the needs of refugees and the economic, demographic or foreign policy interests of the Australian state parted company, the contingent commitment of officials to refugees became apparent: non-European refugees, the aged and the infirm, typically were excluded from entry. If European states are justified in describing as 'bogus refugees' economic migrants who claim asylum, Australian officials could be said to have operated a bogus refugee policy. Hundreds and thousands of forced migrants, to their good fortune, were simply swept along by a wave of state interests that made mass migration profitable.[4]

The admission of large numbers of refugees before 1975, then, posed no threat to the consensus that governed broader post-war Australian immigration policy. Indeed, it was easy to see the entry of refugees as reinforcing three pillars of the implicit pact on immigration between government and the public: refugees contributed to the state's economic, demographic and foreign policy goals; they did not challenge the state's national identity as a European country; and they entered in a manner that could be strictly managed and controlled, namely, through resettlement programmes.

The consensus was not to last, however. Two years after US forces had pulled out of Saigon in 1975, signalling the victory of the communists of the North in the Vietnam war, a small boat of Vietnamese refugees arrived in the waters of northern Australia. The boat had, remarkably, navigated its way across the hazardous South China and Timor seas in search of its destination. By the middle of 1978 a total of fifty-one boats carrying over 2,000 boat people arrived on Australia's northern shores (Robinson 1998: 152). A number of other boats made similar trips over the next four years, bringing to northern Australia some 2,000 Indo-Chinese refugees, without visas, passports or entry permission.

The arrival of the Vietnamese, which signalled the early stages of the movement of more than 1 million refugees out of the now-communist country, quickly rekindled long-established public concerns over Australia's ability to insulate itself from the 'poor and overcrowded' nations of Asia. Popular newspapers, conservative commentators and sections of the Labor party did not greet the entrants warmly, for an array of reasons ranging from concerns over diminishing sovereignty, the putative conservatism of those fleeing from a communist regime and the belief the Vietnamese refugees were primarily the US's responsibility (Viviani 1988: 174–6).

In the face of a highly anxious public, however, the Fraser government's response demonstrated a good deal of *sang-froid*. Recognising in

[4] Until 1975 there were no settlement programmes specifically for the purpose of taking refugees (NPC 1991: 121).

part a duty to respond to refugees whose plight had been inextricably connected to Australia's through involvement in the Vietnam war, the government 'spearheaded' international discussions with the UNHCR and the United States to resettle refugees from Thailand and later Malaysia (Robinson 1998: 153; NPC 1991: 76). These discussions, which led eventually to the establishment of an orderly departure programme for Vietnamese refugees, attempted to prevent future arrivals by boat by giving potential boat people an official route to enter Australia, along with other Western countries, notably the US. By 1981, around 50,000 Indo-Chinese had been allowed to enter Australia as refugees. The government had also committed itself to accepting approximately 15,000 more annually (Viviani 1988: 177).

The experience with the Vietnamese brought about a new era in the understandings governing Australian responses to refugees, and to immigrants more generally. From the moment of their arrival, immigration and refugee matters became more divisive subjects in Australian society, paving the way for the *Tampa* controversy of 2001. The landing of the Vietnamese boat people in 1976 was, in some respects, analogous to the US's Mariel boat crisis of 1980, which transformed American attitudes to Cold War refugees. The arrival of the Vietnamese in Australia challenged, and ultimately resulted in the reformulation of, the pillars of the post-war migration consensus.

A European nation?

The refugees from Vietnam (and those who arrived later from Cambodia) posed an obvious challenge to those who viewed Australia's national identity purely in European terms. To be sure, on the official level the presumptions and policies of White Australia had been publicly renounced in 1973, and much of the machinery allowing racial discrimination in admissions discarded some years before. But the immediate effect of the end of the 'White Australia' policy was not a profound transformation in the character of migration to Australia. Indeed, the number of overall immigrants accepted by the state fell after Whitlam's declaration of White Australia's demise to their lowest levels in years, partly due to the country's poor economy. The arrival of Indo-Chinese boat people was thus a first visible sign to many Australians of the implications of ending racial discrimination in entrance.

Significantly, Indo-Chinese migration also emerged at a time when the ethos behind integration policies towards immigrants in general was in flux. The Labour government of 1972–5, assisted by its flamboyant immigration minister, Al Grassby, had officially renounced the complete assimilation into a predominantly British national culture as a goal for new immigrants. The policy of assimilation (or 'monoculturalism' to use Snedden's term) had not been considered a success, often serving to alienate new migrants from the public culture. In its place the Whitlam government advocated a way of cultural integration which stressed 'the contribution of migrants to Australia . . . and the need to recognize, rather than dismiss, their distinctiveness' (Collins 1988: 232). The next government, that of Malcolm Fraser, also embraced multiculturalism. As a matter of policy, it 'officially encouraged assisted migrants in maintaining their distinctive cultural identities, including languages, and declared that Australia was a multicultural society' (Freeman 1993: 94).

As an idea and a policy, multiculturalism proved a 'lightning rod' (Freeman 1993: 98) for criticism. Concern was expressed throughout the 1970s and 1980s that the concept of multiculturalism reflected the overweening influence of ethnic lobby groups, militated against a set of civic principles pertinent to all Australians, or was simply vacuous (Betts 1993: 223; Jupp 1993: 215–17). Much as debate had already raged before their arrival, the acceptance of the Vietnamese, by promising an even more ethnically diverse society, served merely to deepen controversy about the terms on which migrants should be integrated.[5]

By the beginning of the 1980s, immigration had become synonymous with the entrance of Asians for some sections of the Australian public. The number of Asians entering was multiplied by the fact that Indo-Chinese refugees used family reunion entitlements initially devised for Southern European migrants to bring their relatives to Australia, as did new migrants from the Philippines and Hong Kong. By the mid-1980s, immigrants from Asia (including business migrants) had come to comprise almost 40 per cent of all new entrants.

Asians still constituted a very small proportion of Australian society (by the early 1990s, 600,000 Australian residents were of Asian descent, 3.5 per cent of the total population). But this did not prevent the well-known historian Geoffrey Blainey from sparking a debate in 1984, which rumbled throughout the rest of the 1980s, when he criticised successive governments for allowing Asians to enter at a rate far in excess of what the public would tolerate (Collins 1988: 212–21). There was little doubt that Blainey's comments tapped into the feelings of discomfort over immigration policy felt by substantial sections of the public, not least in rural areas. It was less than clear, however, what proportion

[5] The 1988 report on immigration commissioned by the Australian government, which become known as the 'Fitzgerald report', was particularly critical of the government's implementation of multiculturalism arguing that most citizens saw it as 'something for immigrants and ethnic communities only, and not for the whole of Australia' (CAAIP 1988: 10).

of the public was hostile to immigration on the grounds of racism, rather than antipathetic to high levels of immigration in general (Collins 1988: 304–5).

Despite a brief flirtation with restrictions on Asian migration by the conservative Liberal opposition, the major political parties were reluctant to pander to discriminatory views, or to call into question the central principle of White Australia's abolition, the rejection of racial discrimination in entrance policy. Indeed, a year before the debate had begun in earnest, in 1983, Bill Hayden, then the Minister for Foreign Affairs, argued that it was both inevitable and desirable that Australia would eventually become a 'Eurasian country' (Sherington 1990: 170). His comment was one of the first articulations at high level of a vision of Australian identity that challenged the Europeanist view.

By the beginning of the 1990s, there was little evidence that the Australian public was solidly behind Hayden's new conceptualisation. Yet no one could disagree with Nancy Viviani that 'something of a revolution' (Viviani 1988) in Australian entrance policy had occurred since the mid-1970s in terms of Asian migration. It was clear that the social and political goal of preserving a singularly European (and, even more so, British) identity had given way first to principle (in the abandonment of White Australia) and now to reality (in the existence of a substantial and growing Asian–Australian minority). Nonetheless, the lack of agreement on an alternative vision of national identity was obvious.

National interests and refugee admissions

While European refugees after 1945 had benefited from the fortunate coincidence that their need for protection served Australia's security, economic and demographic interests, the Vietnamese boat people could not rely on such good fortune. By the late 1970s, the traditional arguments in favour of mass migration had become dubious, raising the question how – if at all – the admission of refugees could be justified in this new environment.

When the Australian economy was performing well in the 1950s and 1960s, there was no reason to doubt the existence of a favourable causal relationship between immigration and living standards. From the early 1970s, however, Australia began experiencing, like other OECD countries, sustained periods of low economic growth and high rates of inflation and unemployment. Consequently, governments began to vary immigration levels. In the mid to late 1970s, consecutive Labor and Liberal governments reduced new settler intake to its lowest levels since 1945 (Viviani 1983: 136).

Immigration rose again, averaging almost 100,000 annually during the 1980s, largely due to the continued influence in official circles of forceful economic arguments.[6] However, dissenters, particularly from the ranks of environmentalists and economists, could increasingly be heard. These critics linked high levels of immigration to ecological damage and 'capital shortage, a reduced standard of living, inflation and balance of payments difficulties' (Collins 1988: 101). More important in influencing government policy was hostility from the general public to high levels of immigration during periods of substantial unemployment. As unemployment figures spiralled upwards from the beginning of the 1990s – in 1992/3 unemployment was nearly 12 per cent – the Keating Labor government began to cut immigration levels drastically.

If the economic benefits in favour of refugees became more disputed, the security and demographic ones receded entirely. While deterring an enemy invasion was a pressing reason for Australia boosting its intake in the immediate post-war period, population growth in the years since then has undoubtedly increased the country's security. By the beginning of the 1970s, Australia's population was already almost twice as large as in 1945; by the mid 1990s, it was 17.5 million, two and a half times the post-war level. Furthermore, as numbers grew, developments in military technology reduced the importance of population size to national security. Katherine Betts has noted that a range of influential reports on Australian security in the 1970s and 1980s showed that '[d]efence experts did not foresee any shortage of manpower for the armed forces' and argued that Australia's population was more than adequate to meet its security needs '[g]iven the technological basis of modern warfare' (quoted in Freeman 1993: 88). As a result, security arguments ceased to provide support for high immigration levels.

The demise of traditional justifications brought to the fore new reasons for accepting immigrants and refugees. The importance of establishing good relations with other Asian countries has been one such reason. The end of 'White Australia' in the early 1970s reflected more than simply a moral awakening on the part of the Australian community to the evils of racism. The viability of 'White Australia' had always depended upon Australia's key economic and security interests being tied to Europe and North America. By the beginning of the 1970s, however, with Britain a member of the EEC and with the US reluctant to intervene further in Asia after Vietnam, Australia's connections to the Northern Hemisphere weakened. Simultaneously, Asia commenced its rise to global political

[6] The Fitzgerald report, for instance, came out strongly in favour of using mass migration to boost the amount of skilled labour in Australia (CAAIP 1988).

and economic prominence as the region's newly independent states began 'the most intense episode of economic growth the world has ever seen . . . [turning] East Asia, within four decades, from one of the world's problem regions . . . into one of the world's three greatest centres of economic production and trade' (Garnaut 1994: 227).

Australia turned increasing attention towards Asia in response to the rise in the region's fortunes. It hoped to reap some of the area's abundant opportunities for trade and investment by becoming more politically and economically integrated into the region. Integration did not prove easy. The need to overcome long-established mutual suspicions and cultural differences made it crucial that Australia show that it had left behind the racism that had tarred its immigration policies historically and that it was willing to share some of the region's burdens as well as its benefits. Here, the resettlement of Vietnamese refugees took on great significance. For Australia's inclusive response had the advantage of challenging the country's image as racist while simultaneously illustrating to powerful Association of South East Asian Nations (ASEAN) members (like Thailand, Malaysia and Indonesia) that the country was willing to cooperate to resolve the region's problems. By the mid 1990s, 53 per cent of all Australia's trade was being done with Asian countries. Good relations with its regional neighbours did not always benefit refugees, however. Australia was reluctant to recognise as refugees those fleeing oppressive rule in East Timor and Irian Jaya so as not to offend Indonesia (Ayling and Blay 1989: 263–5).

The role of regional interests as a motivating factor for accepting refugees should not be overstated. During the 1980s and 1990s, refugees from all around the world benefited from Australia's resettlement policies, as public justification for accepting refugees began to be more closely tied to the virtues of humanitarianism. Between the mid 1980s and mid 1990s, in spite of wide variations in the rate of unemployment, Australia took in between 10,000 and 12,000 refugees each year. This was somewhat down on the number of admittances in the early 1980s (at the peak of the boat people crisis), but it represented a significant increase on the kind of numbers entering in the mid 1970s.

It was evident by the early 1990s that Australian governments had pulled off quite a remarkable feat. They had in little more than a decade managed to disentangle refugee policy from its traditional security, economic and demographic justifications and provide it with a humanitarian rationale, albeit one that was supported by a range of new regional interests. The influential Fitzgerald report of 1988 gave its imprimatur to this transformation. It found 'no significant opposition to refugee resettlement' in its wide-ranging submissions and consultations (CAAIP

1988: 69). The foundation for the country's responses to refugees was, the report found, that 'helping refugees is part of Australians' view of themselves' (CAAIP 1988: 69).

Controlling entry

If two of the pillars of the post-war immigration consensus had been refashioned by the middle of the 1990s, the promise of control remained. When faced with the unplanned arrival of the Indo-Chinese boat people from 1976, the Fraser Liberal and later the Hawke Labor governments, anxious to placate public concerns, sought a compromise. In agreements that called upon Thailand and Malaysia not to deflect boat people on to Australia (the Orderly Departure Programme of 1979) and for Vietnam to crack down on illegal departures (the Comprehensive Plan of Action of 1987), these governments pledged to resettle Indo-Chinese refugees. Recognising the value of the appearance of order, government officials accepted large numbers of quota refugees in return for actions that would prevent unplanned boat arrivals.

The trade-off appeared to work. Throughout most of the 1980s, boat arrivals at Australia's northern shores were few, and refugees from Indo-China benefited from being able to claim refuge in a Western country without travelling enormous distances by boat. But by the end of the decade, 'on shore' asylum claims began to grow again. Whereas in the three years between 1982 and 1984 only 520 such claims were made, the number rose to 27,117 between 1989 and 1991 (JSCMR 1992: 38). The dramatic rise was partly due to a large one-off offer to consider for refugee status Chinese students living in Australia in the aftermath of the massacre at Tiananmen Square. However, it was evidence also that Australia was not immune to the rising numbers of 'jet age' asylum seekers that had generated controversy in Europe and North America. Refugees from as far afield as Somalia, Afghanistan, Ethiopia and Iran were now seeking asylum in Australia (JSCMR 1992: 36).

No one could say that these numbers constituted a challenge of German proportions. But the upward trajectory in asylum claims did alarm the government. When asylum numbers were boosted by the arrival of more boat people, this time Cambodians in 1989, it was apparent that the hope that Australia could buy itself out of first asylum duties through resettlement quotas was in tatters. In response to rising claims, governments cut back on refugee resettlement entries (JSCMR 1992: 37) and attempted to control entry through harsh new prevention and deterrent measures.

In 1991 the Hawke government created a new detention facility for asylum claimants in the remote town of Port Hedland in Western Australia. A year later the Labor government propelled the 1992 Migration Amendment Act though Parliament. The Act contained highly illiberal detention powers, requiring that 'any person who arrived by boat in Australia after November 19, 1989 . . . be kept in custody until he or she left Australia or was given an entry permit' (US Committee for Refugees 2002). The new focus on preventing Australia from becoming a country of first asylum did not spell an end to the use of resettlement schemes. Throughout the 1990s, these schemes continued to allow entry to around 10,000 refugees and other humanitarian cases per year, many of whom were selected because they had preexisting ties with Australia or were sponsored by relatives. Increasingly, however, the existence of resettlement served as an excuse to criticise asylum seekers as 'queue jumpers', pushing their way past other refugees waiting to enter Australia legitimately. The 1992 Act, the immigration minister of the time proclaimed, 'puts it beyond all doubt' that if you want to come to Australia 'you'll have to enter in a proper way' (quoted in ABC 7.30 Report 2002).

If the 1992 Act was motivated by an attempt to win back control over entry from asylum seekers arriving spontaneously, it also signalled government intentions to constrain the power of the courts in immigration matters. Before the 1980s, the decision-making authority of the Department of Immigration was subject to very little judicial constraint. The 1958 Migration Act did not detail selection criteria for entrants, enabling governments to change 'policy at will, often without informing the public' (Birrell 1992: 25). Indeed, when the Vietnamese boat people initially arrived on Australia's shores the Immigration Minister had no domestically enforceable legal obligation even to hear their claims. Primarily to tackle the bureaucratic challenges of dealing with the volume of new claims, the Liberal government established the Determination of Refugee Status Committee (DORS) in 1977 to advise the minister on claims for protection under the Convention (Crock 1998: 127).

The establishment of DORS coincided closely with a wide-ranging overhaul of administrative law in Australia, designed to make government bureaucracies more open and accountable. The Administrative Decisions Judicial Review Act of 1977 gave the courts new powers to oversee that state decision-making was consistent with standards of procedural fairness and natural justice. The implications of these reforms for decision-making in refugee matters were not immediately obvious. However, it soon became apparent that, in spite of their uncertain status, asylum seekers would now have 'real and viable' (Crock 1998: 38) access to the courts to appeal unfavourable decisions. A steady rise in the number of reviews of refugee status decisions in the courts ensued.

Judicial intervention in refugee matters did not reach its apogee until 1989, however, when the courts called into question the criteria on which officials determined refugee claims. In that year, the High Court ruled in *Chan* vs. *Minister for Immigration and Ethnic Affairs* that the government had interpreted eligibility for the UN definition of a refugee too narrowly. In a 'change from the test being applied by the DORS committee in the late 1980s', the court found that in order to meet the standards of 'well-founded fear' of persecution to receive refugee status it was necessary only that the applicant face a 'a real chance of persecution' and that could be 'as little as a 10 per cent chance' (Crock 1998: 136).

The increasing involvement of the courts in the asylum process enraged governments. The whittling away of the traditional discretionary powers of the minister was interpreted as a challenge to the public desire for strict control over the entry of asylum seekers and illegal migrants. As well as calling into question established practices, the access to review procedures for applicants made the processing of asylum claims more time-consuming and expensive. In 1992 the secretary of the Immigration Department estimated that processing an individual asylum claim in Australia cost Aus$28,000, one hundred times more than the cost of processing one overseas (*The Age*, 22 June 1992). The legal empowering of asylum seekers was viewed as frustrating the state's attempt to deter unwanted arrivals.

Learning from previous failures, governments began to craft legislation with an eye to reducing the room available for judicial interpretation of legislation. The 1992 Migration Amendment Act was the apotheosis of such new law. Not only did the legislation spell out explicitly the procedures that needed to be followed by asylum decision-makers in order, according to the Labor government Immigration Minister of the time, Gerry Hand, to 'replace the somewhat open ended doctrines of natural justice and unreasonableness' (quoted in Ruddock 1997), but, in requiring mandatory detention for asylum seekers, it forbade courts to order the release of individuals so detained (US Committee for Refugees 2002).

In 1996 the government of Paul Keating lost office, bringing to an end thirteen consecutive years of Labor governments begun by Bob Hawke. These governments – and the Fraser government of 1975–83 that had preceded them – had a mixed legacy in terms of asylum and immigration policy. They had, on the one hand, reconstructed aspects of the post-war migration consensus. Australia's transition to a multicultural society with a strong Asian influence was, by the beginning of the 1990s, undeniable, even if it was not welcomed in all quarters; the argument for accepting refugees had come to rest on a humanitarian footing, in public justification, if less so in reality. These were important developments and, in many respects, achievements.

Yet the governments of this period continued to embrace the assumption that Australia should, under no circumstances, become a country of first asylum, particularly to boat arrivals. However, the kind of measures governments were prepared to use to avoid taking on such a role evolved dramatically. In the transition from Fraser to Hawke to Keating, government measures to prevent unplanned arrivals became increasingly harsh and illiberal, culminating in mandatory detention. The defeat of Keating's government brought to power the Liberal government of John Howard, and a continuation in the trajectory of government practices.

Tampa and beyond

Despite Australia's considerable achievements in building a multicultural society and in resettling refugees, it seems likely that international attitudes towards the country will, for the foreseeable future, be defined by a singular act of exclusion. The government's refusal to allow the Norwegian freighter, MV *Tampa*, carrying a few hundred Iraqi and Afghani asylum seekers, to land in 2001 brought Australia's response to asylum seekers to international attention. And the image beamed to the world was one of a country extremely hostile to refugees.

Upon taking office in 1996, the Howard government inherited the same focus on control as its predecessors. But its focus was sharpened by a vivid lesson in the politics of immigration. Between 1996 and 1998, Pauline Hanson, a former Queensland shopkeeper, and her 'One Nation' party led a populist political campaign centred on the putative injustice of 'special services' for Aborigines and immigrants and the failure of governments to construct immigration policies consonant with the wishes of the Australian public. 'We are', Hanson argued in her maiden speech to Parliament, 'in danger of being swamped by Asians . . . They have their own culture and religion, form ghettos and do not assimilate . . . I should have the right to have a say in who comes into my country' (Hanson quoted in Jupp 2002: 130).

Hanson's campaign appealed to limited constituencies, never gaining great support in Victoria or Tasmania. Yet in 1988 Federal elections for the Senate, One Nation gathered around 1 million votes, establishing itself as the most successful party behind the Liberals and the ALP (Jupp 2002: 135). As is common with anti-immigration parties, One Nation was soon beset by internal divisions and leadership scandals that reduced its capacity to garner votes. By the end of the 1990s, it was in serious, arguably terminal, decline. However, the party's (albeit short-lived) success had shown that hostility to immigrants and asylum seekers played very well with parts of the electorate. Moreover, the blunt language of its representatives had created a new space to express views on immigrants and asylum seekers that bordered on the racist.

The peak of One Nation's success in 1998 came just before a new stream of boat arrivals. Between 1999 and 2001 over 10,000 asylum seekers, mostly Iraqis, Afghans and Turks, made their way to Australia (Hugo 2002: 37). The Howard government's response was nothing if not forceful. New regulations were introduced in October 1999 to mandate that 'unauthorised arrivals' in Australia determined to be refugees would no longer receive permanent residence. Instead, they would be eligible only for temporary visas, enabling them to work but not to apply for family reunion or long-term stay.[7] In the 1999 Border Protection Amendment Act, the government added to its powers to prevent arrivals by enabling itself to reject the claims to asylum of those arriving in Australia who could have applied in what was deemed a 'safe third country' (US Committee for Refugees 2002). Philip Ruddock, the Immigration Minister, defended the legislation as necessary to prevent Australia from being viewed as a 'soft target by forum shoppers and the increasingly sophisticated people smuggling rackets' (Ruddock 1999). Despite the new measures and Ruddock's uncompromising style, the boat arrivals kept coming.

The Tampa *incident*

It was in the context of the dramatic election successes of One Nation a few years before, a growing sense by the government that previous policies had proven inadequate in deterring boat arrivals, and near the start of a new Federal election campaign that another boat of asylum seekers set off from Indonesia in August of 2001. The 20 metre wooden fishing boat was soon in serious distress and, after responding to an alert by Australian coastal officials, a Norwegian freighter, the MV *Tampa*, rescued the 438 asylum seekers on board. The freighter, now carrying a human cargo well beyond its safe capacity, initially headed for Indonesia, but, at the request of its new passengers, turned around and charted a course for Christmas Island, where the asylum seekers would be able to make a

[7] The operation of the Kosovan refugee programme, while involving resettled refugees, gave some indication of the government's seriousness. While the initial entry of some 4,000 Kosovans between May and June 1999 was trumpeted as an act of humanitarian concern, when conditions were deemed safe for return, the government applied direct and indirect pressures, ranging from the cutting of services and threats of removal to detention centres, to get the refugees to leave (US Committee for Refugees 2002).

demand for asylum incumbent upon Australia. Wishing to prevent just such a scenario, Australian government officials telephoned the captain and warned him not to enter Australia's territorial waters. The captain, in charge of a dangerously overloaded and underresourced ship, ignored the requests and entered Australian waters. Within hours, forty-five SAS troops from the Australian Defence Force boarded the ship. The ensuing stand-off (resulting from the refusal of Australian officials to let the ship land) attracted international attention. Defending Australia's actions, the Prime Minister, John Howard, stated that 'we simply cannot allow a situation where Australia is seen around the world as a country of easy destination' (BBC News 2001a).

After several days a resolution of sorts was achieved when the asylum seekers were forcefully transferred to another ship that took them to Papua New Guinea and the barren and impoverished Pacific Island of Nauru. The Australian government had reached a financial deal for these countries to hold the asylum seekers until other states could be convinced to give asylum to those determined to be refugees. In the event, only New Zealand and Ireland agreed to resettle the asylum seekers. The government's efforts to resolve the crisis by drawing upon resettlement options in other states became known as the 'Pacific Solution'.

Throughout the events surrounding the *Tampa*, public support for the government's position was extraordinarily strong. In one poll for the *Sydney Morning Herald*, 77 per cent of respondents expressed support for the government's policy of refusing the asylum seekers entry (Burke 2001: 323). While the issue provoked sharply divided reactions, the vast majority of the public accepted government characterisations that the boat people were 'queue jumpers' (bypassing the normal route of entry via refugee resettlement schemes) and the thin end of a great wedge of asylum seekers ready to enter Australia's territory with the help of smugglers.

The strong public reaction enabled the government to enact legislation to provide retrospective legitimacy to its actions in preventing boats from landing. In addition, new legislation 'excised' a number of Australian island territories (Christmas Island, Ashmore Reef and Cocos Island) from the country's 'migration zone'. Asylum seekers landing on these territories would no longer be deemed to have landed in Australia for the purposes of immigration law, denying them access to the protection of the Australian courts.

The chord the actions of the Howard government struck with the public was evident on election day, 10 November 2001. The government comfortably defeated the ALP, reversing a huge deficit in the polls before the *Tampa* incident. The ALP opposition, led by Kim Beazley, had supported the principles surrounding the government's response to the *Tampa*, though it did challenge specific aspects of the government's legislative proposals. The mood of the time, however, was unfavourable to nuance. The Liberal Party's unequivocal position enabled them to ride the anti-asylum seeker wave to electoral triumph.

A sea change?

The policies of the Howard government have been widely characterised as constituting a radical departure – a 'sea change' (US Committee for Refugees 2002) – in Australia's responses to asylum seekers. Yet, as we have seen, consecutive governments have consistently rejected the mantle of Australia as a country of first asylum since the mid 1970s. The 'Pacific Solution' simply represented a new solution to an old problem. While the previous government of Paul Keating had attempted to deter asylum seekers by making detention mandatory and reducing the prospects for judicial review, the Howard government, finding policies of deterrence inadequate, shifted its response to the direct prevention of arrivals through interdiction. This was a cruel development for the asylum seekers concerned. But the movement from deterrence to direct prevention was perfectly consistent with the trajectory of policy-making since the late 1970s.

Arguably more remarkable was the way the Howard government used the *Tampa* issue as a tool to garner support and ultimately achieve electoral victory. In recent years, asylum has tended to find its way into the domain of the electoral politics of Western states because opposition parties have seized upon a particular crisis or rising numbers as a way to criticise the policy-making failures of governments. The asylum issue has thus typically placed governments on the defensive and given them an interest in taking it off the political agenda as quickly as possible (to wit, the Carter Administration with the Mariel incident in 1981; the Clinton Administration with Haitian boat people in the mid 1990s; and the Blair government during the 2001 UK election).

The events of 2001, however, departed from this script. For it was clear from early on that the Howard government saw public anxiety over the boat people as something it could use to its own electoral advantage. Through a combination of its tough stance, extremely negative characterisations of the asylum seekers concerned and illiberal policies, the government grasped a political opportunity to fuel a widespread public view that the asylum seekers constituted a serious threat to the Australian nation. The strategy was amazingly successful. Not only did it twist the ALP in knots, but it established the Liberals as the party for the million or so voters who three years before had voted for Pauline Hanson and One Nation (Jupp 2002: 1999). The Australian elections of 2001, in other words, were the site of a new government-led *offensive* politics of asylum.

The question of justifiability

Were the Howard government's response to the MV *Tampa* and its new strategies of prevention justifiable? The government put forward a number of reasons in defence of its policy of not allowing the boat people asylum in Australia. It argued that 'queue jumpers' should not be rewarded when there existed legal ways to enter the country. Officials also stressed the importance of not allowing human smugglers successfully to ply their trade or doing anything that might encourage other asylum seekers (already milling in Indonesia, according to Ruddock (BBC 2001b)) to embark upon potentially perilous boat passages to Australia. At other times, it was claimed that the asylum seekers should have applied for asylum in other safe countries they had passed through (most commonly, Indonesia). After 11 September officials even hinted at the need to prevent boat arrivals to protect the country from infiltration by terrorists.

Many of these arguments have drawn the scorn of more critical observers. Government worries about terrorism were risible because the policy of mandatory detention gave officials more than enough time to screen new arrivals before release into the community. The argument that the asylum seekers should have sought protection in Indonesia is weakened by the fact that as the country is not a signatory to the 1951 Refugee Convention and has a poor human rights record, it seems ill-placed to be able to provide refugee status determinations of high quality (Crock and Saul 2002). Characterising boat arrivals as 'queue jumpers' conveniently, as William Malley has pointed out, ignores the fact 'that there is no "queue" in the international refugee system to jump' (Malley 2002: 7). The resettlement system operated by Australia is not a proper substitute for claiming asylum in-country because officials use characteristics in addition to need to choose entrants (preference goes to 'the educated rather than the skilled, the healthy rather than the disabled, the quiescent rather than the "troublesome"', as Malley has put it (2002: 7)). Finally, the vision of unending flows of asylum seekers making their way to Australia's northern shores encouraged by the successes of others seems hard to credit given the relatively small numbers that have followed the route over the last twenty or so years.

These rebuttals are strong and, in some cases, compelling. Equally, there is no doubting that the Howard government, while arguably staying within the boundaries of international refugee law, demonstrated an insouciance towards asylum seekers worthy of condemnation. Nonetheless, critics of the government's response often ignore the difficult questions posed by boat arrivals. In the face of rising numbers, even a government far more sensitive to refugees would have faced an agonising choice about whether to put in place preventative strategies if they truly believed that their policies were encouraging increasing numbers of people to head towards Australia on dangerously unseaworthy craft. Moreover, while specific aspects of the 'Pacific Solution' raise genuine human rights (and even *refoulement*) concerns, it is an interesting question whether, if circumstances more favourable to asylum seekers could have been arranged, it is legitimate for rich countries, like Australia, to pay poorer ones temporarily to host asylum seekers and refugees. Finally, the *Tampa* incident brings home powerfully the question of the ethical legitimacy of Australia's trade-off between resettlement and first asylum. It is true that Australia's current resettlement scheme is so permeated by morally irrelevant considerations that it provides an imperfect substitute for on-shore access to asylum. But would such a trade-off be justifiable if need was made the only consideration, or if the number of refugees accepted through such schemes was to be dramatically increased?

Conclusion

When considered together with the United States, Australia's dealings with asylum seekers over the last few decades provide ample evidence for the view that traditional countries of immigration are as hostile to becoming countries of first asylum as their European counterparts. Indeed, if the case of Australia is representative, immigration countries may see themselves as justified in implementing even harsher deterrent and preventative policies than 'non-immigration' countries because they offer (on paper at least) avenues through which refugees might enter legally.

Yet if the specific policies employed by Australia appear harsher than those of European countries, the difference is mostly one of degree. The trajectory of Australia's asylum policies since the 1980s (when it became clear that resettlement would not put an end to all spontaneous arrivals) may have been one of increasing radicalisation in the measures used to deter and prevent arrivals, particularly of boat people. But this kind of radicalisation in the face of policy measures deemed ineffective has been evident in every country we have looked at. Germany moved from mild reforms in its asylum procedures in the early 1980s to whole-scale constitutional change in the early 1990s; in the 1960s, the US tried to manage Cuban arrivals with organised resettlement schemes but, by the 1980s, was employing interdiction. The UK, faced with unprecedented numbers of asylum seeker arrivals after 1999, stated that, in addition to continuing its policies on detaining and restricting welfare to asylum seekers, it was now considering the 'Australian style' turning back of 'illegal' migrants in the Mediterranean.

What, then, is distinctive about the Australian response to refugees? It could be argued that while all of the countries we have looked at have gone through asylum 'crises' and used fairly similar measures to reduce entrant numbers, Australia is remarkable because so few asylum seekers were needed to provoke a 'crisis'. Whereas the US, Germany and the UK have faced tens of thousands of applicants or more on an annual basis, Australia has at most faced a few thousand. Australia's particular historical fears about invasion from the populous nations to its North no doubt played a part in explaining the degree of controversy generated in 2001, as perhaps do lingering doubts about the legitimacy of European claims to the land. Another distinctive feature of the Australian case has been, as I have suggested, the appearance of a new type of government-led, *offensive* politics of asylum. Other administrations (notably the Kohl government in Germany in the early 1990s) have flirted with using the asylum issue as a way of exposing the weakness of their opponents. But no Western government in recent decades can claim as direct a link to their re-election and the issue of restricting asylum-seeking as the Howard government in 2001.

By way of conclusion it is worth mentioning one other notable feature of the Australian case. Discussions of asylum in Australia have been peculiar for how little importance has been attached to the distinction between 'economic migrants' and 'genuine refugees'. While debates in most liberal democratic states have generally turned on the 'abuse' of refugee systems by economic migrants, in Australia asylum seekers have more commonly been characterised as 'queue jumpers'. This sobriquet takes for granted that asylum seekers are in fact refugees (and hence should join the 'official' queue). Notwithstanding problems with the term's accuracy, the Australian approach has its virtues. For, unlike European governments that pretend that their preventative policies impact only upon economic migrants, Australian officials have been ready to admit that all unauthorised entrants are unwelcome, regardless of whether or not they are refugees. This is honesty, albeit at its most brutal.

7 From ideal to non-ideal theory: reckoning with the state, politics and consequences

I started this work by arguing that any critical standard for the entry policies of liberal democratic states needs to possess ethical force (be informed by a convincing value) and be sensitive to the practical reality of the agent whose action it aims to direct (have realistic expectations of what states can do). In this chapter, I will illustrate the complications and challenges of moving from ideal ethical theory to practical prescriptions for actually existing states in their dealings with refugees and asylum seekers, partly by drawing upon the experiences of Germany, the UK, the United States and Australia. But before undertaking this task, it is important to remember where we have been.

In the first part, I illustrated the difficulties of outlining a compelling ideal for state responsibilities in entrance. It was apparent that none of the established accounts of the responsibilities of states – communitarianism, conservatism, nationalism, utilitarianism or global liberalism – had a convincing claim to be the single authoritative standard for the assessment of the entry policies of states. Partialists and impartialists gave contrasting responses to the nature of the state's duties to outsiders. The partial view, which attached ultimate value to the entitlement of people to act collectively to sustain cultural communities of membership, argued that states were morally entitled to distribute membership and admission largely according to their own criteria. The impartial view, by contrast, argued that states are obliged to take into equal account the interests (utilitarianism) or rights (global liberalism) of the human community in its entirety in decisions on entry, leading to the conclusion that individuals be entitled either to move freely between states or to settle where they desire as long as doing so does not reduce global total utility.

I argued, using the framework of Thomas Nagel, that these ethical approaches illustrate a conflict between two very powerful claims: the right of a political community to provide for its own members, and the right of all human beings to equal concern and respect. One implication might be that political theory has no light to shine that can help us navigate between these claims. It might well be that *both* the Chinese woman who undertakes a life-threatening journey across the European continent in the back of a lorry in an illicit attempt to make Britain her home *and* the UK border guards whose job it is to track down such hopefuls and upon finding them alive deport them back to China, have right on their side. But I concluded my discussion of value by suggesting that the tension between these two ideals could be reduced (if not completely dissolved) with an ideal that would see states as justified in restricting entry only in order to protect the institutions and values of the liberal democratic state, defined quite broadly to include not only civil and political rights, but also the kind of social rights associated with a generous welfare state that ensures economic justice. This state would, I argued, prioritise refugees in the distribution of scarce entrance places because of their pressing need.

In the second part, I turned to consider the practical experiences of Germany, the UK, the US and Australia in asylum and refugee policy to gain insight in how much state practices departed from what would be ethically ideal. In moving from the realm of ethical theory to examine actual state behaviour, the limited recognition of ethical obligations to refugees was startlingly apparent. To be sure, state policies were not completely lacking an ethical anchor. The principle of *non-refoulement*, as expressed in the 1951 Refugee Convention and in other international and national legal instruments, is the legal manifestation of what many consider a fundamental moral duty. Yet the evolution of responses in recent years to refugees owes much to a range of other influences, including the dynamics of electoral politics, economic interests, and foreign policy and security concerns. These influences, moreover, have increasingly pushed governments towards restrictive asylum policies and thus further away from attaching the kind of importance to the claims of refugees demanded by the ethical ideal I outlined above.

The result is of course an international system that currently fails to meet asylum challenges on a number of grounds. First, the present response of states is inadequate to deal with, and makes no attempt even to consider, the claims of large numbers of people in need of a new state. The use of undiscriminating deterrent and preventative measures militates against the gaining of refuge by the most needy of claimants every bit as much as the least deserving, leaving large numbers of people in acute danger. Second, the current system results in huge inequalities in the burdens of individual states. The tyranny of geography, as the case of Germany shows, can lead to some states accepting very large numbers of asylum seekers, while others, like Australia, take far fewer. Third, the current system saps some of the world's wealthiest and most influential states of any motivation to contend with the actual *causes* of refugee movements. Those states that can successfully use the measures currently at their disposal are apt to ignore the real problems of refugee creation. For each of these reasons there exist good grounds for rethinking the response of liberal democratic states to refugees.

Challenges of agency: from ideal to non-ideal theory

What we have, then, is a large and growing gap between what is ethically ideal (a far more inclusive response to refugees and other immigrants in need) and the current practices of liberal democratic states (which are increasingly restrictive towards refugees both in resettlement and asylum policy). The existence of this gap raises questions about the adequacy of current responses towards refugees by liberal democratic states. But it does not in itself show that governments are failing to live up to their moral responsibilities. This is because while we have determined what would be morally ideal, we have yet to specify how particular agents stand in relation to the realisation of this ideal.

In ideal theory, the question of what is morally desirable is usually considered independently of questions of agency. The agent or agents (citizens? governments? international organisations?) responsible for realising the ideal are generally left unspecified. But when we turn to scrutinise and improve the behaviour of actually existing states, questions of agency require much greater precision. In our case, *governments* are, above all else, the agents of most import; they are the actors that typically initiate and oversee the implementation of policies towards refugees. However, now that we have identified the agent concerned, it is necessary to consider the question of capabilities. If it is to have any critical force, our statement of the responsibilities of states must take into account the practical constraints that a morally informed government would face in moving the world closer to our ideal.

So, what kind of responsibilities towards refugees – what kind of balance between partial and impartial claims – do we have good reason to demand that real governments facing a non-ideal world adhere to? In this, the final part of this work, I want to move towards an answer to this question. In the remainder of this chapter, however, I will bring practice to bear on ethical theorising by presenting three constraints that shape or limit the ability of liberal democratic governments to respond inclusively towards refugees. These constraints, derived from the earlier discussion of the US, the UK, Germany and Australia, illustrate the difficulties of moving between theory and practice. The first constraint is *structural*, and concerns the need to acknowledge the fact that the state is a particularistic agent, with a primary responsibility to promote the interests of its own citizens. The second is *political* and involves the role that politics plays in limiting the ability of governments to bring about a morally defensible response to refugees and asylum seekers. The third is *ethical*, stemming from the difficulties of predicting the societal costs of applying a particular normative standard in entrance. Once I illustrate the nature of these constraints, the criteria for an adequate account of the responsibilities of governments will become clearer.

The institutional challenge: reckoning with the character of the modern state

The first constraint on governments emerges from their location within a particular structure of political authority, the modern state. This structure sets important limits on governmental action that need to be taken into account in prescriptions for action. We see its impact in one feature of states evident from the case studies. In spite of their very different situations, and diverse immigration policies and structures of entitlement, none of the states we examined considered the needs of outsiders as at all approaching a par with those of its own citizenry. Everywhere entrance policies were different, and yet everywhere such policies were constructed, implemented and maintained by states through a deliberative logic that attached priority to the interests of their own citizenries.

From the perspective of ideal theory, the existence of this deliberative logic is typically ignored. States are assumed to be completely in the service of moral theory, capable of replacing their current responsibilities with ones more consistent with the findings of moral reasoning. To be sure, a state's current responsibilities ultimately may be vindicated through the process of moral reasoning: Carens, Dummett and the Singers, for instance, all view states as morally justified in restricting entrance if it jeopardises the security of the state's citizens. But the relevance of these current responsibilities rests entirely on whether they can be vindicated in global liberal or utilitarian theorising. The question is whether any real world government could put to one side its responsibilities in this manner.

Is a bias towards the interests of its own citizens, then, simply a contingent feature of the modern state? We can make some headway into this question, and in turn explain the remarkable commonalities in state consideration of the claims of outsiders, by examining the history of the idea of the state. Drawing upon a detailed discussion of the way the authority of the state has been conceived and developed over time, I will suggest that the state is at base a particularistic agent, defined by a responsibility to privilege the interests and concerns of its own members. This character of the state places important limitations on the ability of governments to respond to refugees.

The idea of the state

As Quentin Skinner has shown, the term 'state' was first used in its fully modern sense in the sixteenth and seventeenth centuries by Jean Bodin and Thomas Hobbes (Skinner 1989). These two theorists used 'state' to describe and advocate a common and exclusive structure of political authority linked to, but not reducible to, the rulers or representatives in charge of it at any particular point in time, the human community over which it claimed authority, and the territory that it held. As such, the initial use of the term 'state' marked an important break with previous conceptions of coordinated political authority used by writers in the 'republican' and 'free state' traditions. While the writers in these traditions conceived of public power largely in 'personal and charismatic terms' (Skinner 1989: 90), the fully modern use of the term 'state' identified a uniquely abstract entity characterised by its altogether impersonal nature.

The key problem of political authority which the construction of this common, independent and abstract centre of authority was meant to solve is particularly clear in the work of Hobbes. He saw the modern state as the essential answer to the problem of order in the context of the civil strife of seventeenth-century England. This type of centralised authority structure offered the only hope of cutting through the myriad claims and counter-claims to authority, and the corresponding and conflicting sets of duties and obligations that flowed from these diverse authority sources. Such claims, vividly evident in the period's battles between monarchists and republicans, were inevitably rooted in the immutably idiosyncratic nature of moral belief (Tuck 1989: 165–78). Only a modern state with its monopolistic claim both to authority and the use of coercive force could concentrate the loyalties and duties of the people in a particular territory upon a single centre. As Skinner has observed, Hobbes believed that 'if there is to be any prospect of attaining civil peace, the fullest powers of sovereignty must be vested neither in the people nor in their rulers, but always in the figure of an "artificial man"' (Skinner 1989: 121).

How was the creation of such a monopolistic structure of authority to be justified? Why would people be obliged to follow its dictates? For Hobbes, the state had a central and compelling justification which connected the destiny of individual human beings to its unique authority structure: the human interest in self-preservation. The continuance of the disorder of seventeenth-century England (a practical manifestation of the

State of Nature's War 'of every man, against every man' [Hobbes 1968: 184]) was in no one's interest because this kind of environment placed in jeopardy the most fundamental of individual goals – and the most natural of individual rights – the individual claim to self-preservation. Radical differences in individual judgement concerning people's exercise of their right to act to preserve themselves led to perilous insecurity in the State of Nature, as each individual was rendered vulnerable by the potentially capricious security judgements of other individuals. Such a state of unremitting insecurity generated, according to Hobbes, a common motivation for individuals to align their judgement – that is, to submit their right to judge and their ability to act to ensure their own preservation – to a common and independent political authority charged with the task of defending them 'from the invasion of Forraigners, and the injuries of one another' (Hobbes 1968: 227). The state's monopoly of authority and coercive force was thus underpinned not by an extravagant picture of the ends of civil and political association, but by the achievement of an altogether more basic and secular goal – the maintenance of individual and collective security.

But if, for Hobbes and Bodin, the modern state originated through the concatenation of the authority of individuals, the nature of the political authority created was not simply a vehicle which expressed 'the powers of the people in a more convenient form' (Skinner 1989: 113). According to its initial defenders, the creation of the state came about not through the *delegation* of the individuals' authority to determine how best to preserve themselves, but through 'the "alienation" or renunciation of that authority' (Skinner 1989: 117). This common authority was thus originally conceived, in contradistinction to the work of John Locke, not as a 'trust', but as an agent unto itself. The state emerged as a concentrated form of power and authority that, while connected to the human population that originally brought it into being, was not reducible to that population. While the state's coercive power derived from its ability to ensure the security of its citizenry, it had interests of its own – most particularly, an interest in ensuring its continued reproduction – and could call in times of crisis upon the loyalty of both the people and the rulers to assist it in the defence of those interests (Skinner 1989: 112).

This conception of the state as an agent unto itself was a crucial element in the vision shared by Hobbes and Bodin of a structure of authority able to concentrate human bonds and imaginative energies. The modern state was viewed as an entity which would appropriate all rights of political agency for the human community over which it held sway. In active hostility to the seventeenth-century revival of republican conceptions of political authority, which placed a premium on a key role for the people or *demos* in determining just what the political community would do over time – how it would act and what goals it would pursue – the modern state was conceived as an entity which would, as John Dunn argues,

> deny the very possibility that any *demos* (let alone one on the demographic scale of a European territorial monarchy) could be a genuine political agent, could *act* at all, let alone act with sufficiently continuous identity and practical coherence for it to be able to rule itself. (Dunn 1992a: 247)

Hobbes and Bodin saw the modern state's combination of the features of abstraction, independence and irreducibility as providing a bulwark against the potential for capricious judgement in the human community over which it ruled; the distinctive features of this entity would ensure that its population could not act in such a way as to endanger the state or its interests. The task of attaining and maintaining political order in the context of multifarious conceptions of the good demanded, for these political theorists, not only an entity with a monopoly claim to the utilisation of coercive authority, but an entity which possessed a monopoly claim to collective political agency.

What the modern state offered to its original defenders was therefore an answer – a curt, secular and absolutist answer – both to the problem of political obligation and, consequently, to the question of the ends of civil and political association. For while the state emerges as an entity unto itself with a monopolistic claim to authority, the use of force, and the ability to do what was necessary to ensure its own survival and reproduction (a range of attributes distilled in the expression, *raison d'état*), any authority it possesses ultimately emanates from its protection of the security needs of a specific human community. The state emerges as an entity charged with the task of ensuring the security of, and maintaining order in, the human community over which it rules.

What is important for our purposes is that this way of conceiving the authority of the modern state has some crucial implications for the relationship between the political community and outsiders. First, the emergence of the state concentrates the obligations and duties of individual human beings upon the state by sapping life and relevance from other potential sources of authority that lie beyond the state. The state makes a claim to exhaust the obligations of its citizens. Second, the state emerges as an entity that is responsible exclusively to its own citizenry. Thus, what is patently clear in this original conception is whom the state is *for* – itself and its citizenry. The state emerges as an intractably *particularistic* agent, one informed by a rationale for action that has as its goals both the protecting of the security needs of its citizens and the ensuring of its own reproduction. It is by acting in pursuit of these ends that the state derives and maintains its authority. Consequently, for the state to cater for the needs of outsiders would constitute a misuse of its authority, especially if the pursuit of the interests and needs of outsiders came at some cost to the interests of the citizenry over which it has charge. As Richard Tuck observes of Hobbes:

> In *Leviathan* . . . [Hobbes] frequently talks of the sovereign acting in some sense on behalf of his citizens, and seems to regard it as rational for a sovereign to do whatever he sincerely believes conduces to his own preservation and that of the people he represents. *For the sovereign to do anything else, he repeatedly says . . . would be 'a breach of trust, and of the Law of Nature'.* (My emphasis; Tuck 1989: 184)

The practical limitations of the modern state

What is the relevance of the idea carved out by Bodin and Hobbes to the kind of states we find ourselves confronted with today? Clearly the idea of the state as a definitive answer to the problem of political obligation has taken something of a battering since the tumultuous period of the seventeenth century. The idea that the state would constitute a single centre of will, aptly demonstrated in Hobbes' use of the metaphor of a single person to describe its concentration of sovereignty, seems hard to reconcile with the huge bureaucratic structures, complex separation of powers and federal organisation of many contemporary states. Equally, Hobbes' assumption of an intimate connection between the interests of the sovereign authority (the interest in preserving the state) and the interests of its citizenry (the interest in being secure) has been challenged in practice throughout the twentieth century, not least by the emergence of prodigious numbers of refugees across all parts of the world. The existence of so many people who need to flee their state of normal residence is indicative not merely of states' neglect in catering for the basic security requirements of their residents, but of the brutal fact that the perceived interests of many states seem to lie in the persecution, or worse still, the elimination of those sections of its human community which are deemed to be of the wrong race, religion or political persuasion.

The key assumption of both Hobbes and Bodin that the state could be some kind of independent entity – disinterested with regard to the conflicting interests within the human community over which it rules – has also rightly been attacked since the seventeenth century. Writers from Marx onwards have assailed the state's claim to be a dispassionate observer in the battle between the interests of capital and those of labour, which has characterised modern capitalist societies. Indeed, so deeply was the modern state implicated in these exploitative processes for Marx, and many of his subsequent followers, that no kind of human emancipation could be achieved without the complete withering away of the state as a form of coercive and monopolistic authority (Aveneri 1968).

However, the Marxist critique was on one level simply representative of a broader dissatisfaction, reflected in political theory since the formation of the modern state system, with the state as the best possible form of civil and political association. From Kant (1795 [1991]) to Sidgwick (1891) and on to many contemporary theorists including Beitz (1979) to Held (1998) and Linklater (1998), the state's claim fully to exhaust the moral and political obligations of citizens has been seen as problematical, not least because it has clashed with the explicit universalism of the legacy of Judaeo-Christian ethics. As Andrew Linklater has observed, tension between the state's particularism and the universal applicability of moral obligations 'has persisted because the notion of the state's answerability to universal principles has been an ineluctable feature of the modern state system' (Linklater 1990: 207). While writers in this broad tradition have recognised the lack of institutional forms for the concrete manifestation of duties beyond the state, each has argued either that human beings are obliged to work towards the development of such institutions or that the steady advance of universal moral awareness would engender in human beings the motivation for their creation.

These arguments for a more capacious conception of the duties of human beings have coincided with, and drawn strength from, changes in the international environment over the last 300 years that have brought into question both the efficacy and adequacy of the style of particularistic collective agency which the modern state champions. The movement towards increasing state economic interdependence, regional political integration and other forms of inter-linkage has been a discontinuous feature of the international state-system since the 1600s (see Bull 1977; Krasner 1993, 1999). But it cannot be denied that at least since 1945, the world's states have become increasingly bound together through the development and implementation of new modes of transportation, telecommunication and economic and political integration (Held 1991). The international landscape in which states are located is now radically different to that which existed at the time of Hobbes.

It is not easy to discern the full impact of these recent changes on the state as agent. What is evident, however, is that the range of factors that states need to consider in the struggle to define and pursue their own interests has become far more varied and complex. Many states are no less effective at achieving their goals. Large bureaucracies and enhanced technological capacity arguably make contemporary liberal democratic states better equipped to face an uncertain international environment than ever before (see Krasner 1993). Indeed, one of the ways that states have responded to these new complexities has been by forming or joining collective institutions (of which the EU is the most prominent example), which aim to align state action in such a way as to enable individual states to achieve more effectively their traditional goals. But the international system has also thrown forth over the last fifty years a range of far more radical problems of world significance and dimension that fundamentally challenge the efficacy of the state's brand of particularistic agency. The questions of international distributive justice, of global ecological crisis, of the dangers of nuclear arms proliferation, of terrorism by non-state agents, and of the international refugee problem itself, all point to inadequacies in the modern state and the type of international system that it generates. For the modern state as agent, informed as it is by a logic dominated by its own interests and those of its citizenry, seems unable to move ahead with the kind of speed and decisiveness to address these pressing global issues, which demand consideration of the needs of humankind as a whole.

The adapting agent

But if the authority of the state has not gone unchallenged, if the idea of the state has lost some key political arguments, and has been deprived of some of its normative force on the way to the twenty-first century, it still remains the world's dominant form of political authority. The modern state is still the central political reality in the lives of the world's human population, and it remains firmly at the heart of both the claims of refugees for a secure place of residence and of the entitlement, wielded by those already resident in prosperous and secure states amongst others, to restrict entrance. Indeed, since the post-war period, the number of the world's states has dramatically increased, partly as a result of the process of decolonisation, but more recently as a result of the demise of communism in Eastern Europe which presented the UN with an array of new states. How has the idea of the state managed not only to survive attacks on its authority and dramatic changes in the setting in which it is located over the last 300 years, but to prosper to a point where states so comprehensively dominate the political and geographical landscape of the modern world?

At least part of the explanation can be found in a range of innovations in the state's claim to authority which have enabled the relationship between the state and its human community to become one of increasing intimacy. It can in particular be found in the way the state's connection to its citizenry has been bolstered on three distinct fronts since Hobbes first conceived the idea of the state. While originally the link between the state as agent and its citizenry was defended on the grounds of security, each of these changes has either extended or recharacterised the agency of the modern state; and in so doing has bound the state and citizens more closely together.

National agent

The first of these innovations has been evidenced in the rise of national identity as a powerful legitimating force for states since at least the late eighteenth century. A nation may be said to exist when, as John Stuart Mill argued, a distinct group of people

> are united amongst themselves by common sympathies which do not exist between them and any others – which make them cooperate with each other more willingly than with other people, desire to be under the same government, and desire that it should be a government by themselves or a portion of themselves exclusively. (Mill 1958: 229)

These common sympathies have usually been brought about by ethnic, linguistic, cultural or political and historical affinities. Virtually all modern states now claim to be the proper representatives of more than just a political community of individuals bound together by nothing other than a common desire for security; they claim to be the active representatives of (or agents for) a distinct 'people', who feel it right that they should be together, a people who are entitled to a state of their own.

Throughout the twentieth century, and across the globe, nationalism has been an immensely successful and powerful force for challenging the legitimacy and practical survival of established states. But this is hardly the full story of its impact. Successful attempts by states to mould the communities over which they rule into distinct nations have often served to multiply the reasons why citizens believe they need a state. Where national feeling is present, the objectives of state agency are often expanded to include the goal of preserving the distinct culture or 'way of life' of those whom it represents against the encroachments of outsiders. And even where nationalism has challenged established state authority on the grounds that a section of the state's human community have a right to a political community of their own, it has never been an enemy of the state as a way of organising political authority; on the contrary, as Gellner has suggested, nationalism holds that the state and the nation 'were destined for each other' (Gellner 1983: 6).

If one considers the state's responsibility to accept outsiders for entrance, nationalism can be said to have played a role in recasting the state as an even more particularistic entity. In relation to long-established states, there is evidence to suggest that as these states have come increasingly to be identified in terms of the nation they represent, more ethnically and racially restrictive entrance policies have followed (Dowty 1989: 57; Hammar 1985: 239–42), though exclusivist impulses have always had to compete with economic needs. At the very least, the development of the idea that the human community over which the state rules is more than simply a random collection of individuals, has almost always relied on making the distinction between citizens and outsiders a far sharper and more politically resonant one (Smith 2001). The effectiveness of most anti-immigrant campaigners, from Enoch Powell in Britain in the late 1960s to the more recent efforts of Pauline Hanson and Pim Fortuyn in Australia and Netherlands respectively, has rested not solely on their portrayal of immigration as responsible for increasing unemployment or population pressures, but on the threat that it was assumed to pose to the survival of the 'distinctive' culture of the national community. Arguments for cultural and ethnic preservation have also played a powerful role in states that are often associated with the repudiation of a single ethnic or racial identity, such as the US. Not only did arguments in support of cultural and ethnic homogeneity (however bogus) influence US entrance policy up to the 1960s, resulting, *inter alia*, in tight restrictions on Asian migration, they have emerged in one of the most popular works on US immigration policy to appear in recent years, Peter Brimelow's *Alien Nation* (1995: 9–11; but compare Zolberg 2001).

In newly established states, the use of national consciousness for political goals has also played a part in shaping state practices and policies towards outsiders. This has been brutally apparent in the way many twentieth-century refugees have emerged from attempts to make states and nations compatible. The European Jews in the 1930s and 1940s, the Ugandan Asians in the early 1970s, and the victims of 'ethnic cleansing' in Bosnia in the early 1990s, even the treatment of Kosovan Serbs since the end of the 1999 war, all testify to the fact that victory for the nation often comes at the price of making some residents misfits. This is equally – if normally less brutally – on display in the way newly formed states (Australia in 1901; the new states of Europe created by the demise of the USSR; South Africa since the demise of apartheid) immediately attempt to seize control over entrance after gaining independence, usually on the grounds of preserving the 'way of life' which the nation claimed it needed the security of a state to protect in the first place.

In summary, it can be said that while the rise of nationalism has posed a very practical threat to many established states, where present it has reinforced the kind of particularistic agency which the modern state practises.

An essential element in nationalism's claim has been that the human communities over which states preside require protection not only from the threat outsiders might pose to their physical security, but from the threat they might pose to the identity the citizens claim to share. The rise of nationalism has required that modern states convincingly portray their agency as informed by the needs of the nation.

Democratic agent

The second innovation which has bolstered the authority of the state *vis-à-vis* its citizenry since the time of Hobbes is the development of a closer relationship between the state's role as agent and the claims and interests of its citizenry. The near-universal rise of the principle of democratic governance – of the view that, in the final instance, the sovereignty of any political community lies not in the state as an independent entity, or in its rulers, but in its people, who exercise sovereignty through representative democratic institutions – has been an important factor in the continued legitimacy of the state as an entity which claims political authority on behalf of its human population. While, for Hobbes, defending the unique authority and agency claims of the state involved a self-conscious repudiation of the idea that the state was simply a trust – an entity whose interests were reducible to the individual wills which originally brought it into being – no contemporary state can afford to describe its agency in anything less than Lockean terms: '[w]hat modern state agency legitimately consists in is the collective agency of its own citizenry' (Dunn 1990a: 1).

If it is a difficult task to assess just what kind of a difference the rise of democratic forms of state legitimation has made to the *internal* practices of states, at least one can feel confident that the rise of the *demos* must have made *some* difference, if only by encouraging states to act more carefully and thus more humanely towards their members (see Dunn 1992a). When, however, one attempts to assess the impact of the rise of democracy on the *external* behaviour of states – how states treat outsiders – it is hard to muster even this confidence. Has the advance of the *demos*, where it has occurred, made the state a less particularistic agent?

There is a cogent and persistent school of thought in the realist and 'society of states' traditions of international relations which argues that the ideology or form of government within a state makes virtually no difference to how it acts externally. It is an argument to which Hedley Bull appeals when he criticises those who feel that more cosmopolitan conceptions of duties towards outsiders and more pacific behaviour by states would result if all states shared a common ideology. For, he argues, these people naively ignore 'the argument that Hegel made in his critique of Kant that it is the state *qua* state that is the source of [international] tension and war, not the state *qua* this or that kind of state' (Bull 1977: 247). The argument of this school of thought can be criticised for drawing too strong a distinction between the domestic form of the state and its external behaviour (Bobbio 1987: 41). The emergence of a *demos* in many modern states has affected the way these states treat outsiders, but its effect has been highly ambiguous and double-edged.

There is an array of evidence to suggest that the existence of an active and informed citizenry can lead to widespread criticism of and discontent with the state's treatment of outsiders, and that this criticism and discontent can influence state action. The American public's response to the Vietnam debacle as seen on television *did* affect how US officials prosecuted this war. The moral outrage of the citizenry of many Western states at the appalling sight of media-selected human victims of famine, civil war or genocide *has* from time to time pressured states into humanitarian action – the US in Somalia and the Former Yugoslavia; many European states in Kosovo – though citizen outrage has, admittedly, rarely been the only consideration in state action (see Wheeler 2001). A democratic state is usually more vulnerable, in the short term, to the existence of a gap between the moral expectations of its citizens and the way it acts, because it claims merely to be an entity for putting into practice the collective views and interests of its citizenry.

At the same time, widespread moral criticism of how the state responds or fails to respond to outsiders is relatively rare in Western states, and the influence of such condemnation has at least to be balanced against the role that the *demos* has historically played in encouraging the state to act in a particularistic way. Nowhere has this less edifying role for the *demos* been more often on display in the West in recent years than in the area of entrance policy. It was British public opinion that eventually triumphed over government intransigence and paved the way for tight entrance restrictions on immigrants from the countries of the New Commonwealth during the 1960s (Hansen 2000a), and, as we have seen, vociferous public hostility towards asylum seekers that made the left-wing opposition parties buckle under to new restrictive asylum legislation in Germany in 1993 and Australia in 2001 respectively. While the realist approach can be accused of overlooking the dual-edged effect of the influence of the citizenry on the democratic state, it does still capture the fact that the dominant logic of the agency of even the democratic state in the modern world is (at least over the medium and long term) strongly particularist.

In some respects, the fact that the rise of democracy has not fundamentally challenged the particularism of state agency should not be surprising. Modern representative democracy is an ideal that is deeply implicated in the modern state as a structure of political authority (Dunn 2001: 280–7). Representative democracy's fundamental claim, since its emergence within the confines of the eighteenth and nineteenth-century territorial state, has been that the members of the state's human community have the right to decide amongst themselves – through representative institutions – which interests the state will pursue. Consequently, representative democracy has never been hostile to the state's right to be the citizenry's sole political agent, only to the state's traditional prerogative to decide *which* interests of the human community it would act to promote and defend. The rise of the democratic state represents a change in how the particularistic agency of the state is legitimated, not a challenge to the idea that the state should be a particularistic agent.

There is a second, related aspect to the close connection between representative democracy and the modern state. If the members of the *demos* have the right to decide the interests the state will pursue, then it can be argued that they must also have the right to decide these interests amongst themselves free from the direct participation of outsiders. Thus the emergence of representative democracy has been highly compatible with another principle – the right of a political community to democratic autonomy. For many of the defenders of this right, only the protective confines of a modern state – with, above all else, the ability to control entry and settlement – can provide the stable and secure environment in which a democracy can properly function (see Walzer 1983; Black 1991). In practice, it is clear that the modern claim to democratic autonomy is an updated expression of the traditional claim of the state to sovereignty (of its right to be free from internal interference by other states). The state's right to autonomy is now legitimated through the democratic rights of its people, hence the claim of 'popular sovereignty'.

The principle of popular sovereignty for a state's citizens is very much in tension with the practical realities of the contemporary interdependent world. As David Held noted not long after the fall of the Berlin Wall, '[n]ations are heralding democracy at the very time when changes in the international order are compromising the very viability of the democratic state' (Held 1991: 197). The interdependence and interconnectedness of the current international system results in a situation in which, while: 'territorial boundaries provide the basis on which individuals are included in and excluded from participation in decisions affecting their lives . . . the outcomes of these decisions frequently "stretch" beyond national frontiers' (Held 1991: 204). But it is, at the same time, worth remembering that in some respects the problem identified here – the fact that many people profoundly affected by the decisions of a *demos* are outsiders who have no right to participate in the making of these decisions – is as old as democratic politics itself. Policies on entrance and citizenship have from the Greeks onwards traditionally formed a range of democratic decisions which, while dramatically affecting the life-chances of outsiders, have historically been defended as the prerogative of the *demos* to fashion largely as it pleases.[1]

Economic agent

A third innovation has bolstered the state's relationship to its citizenry since the time of Hobbes. Modern states, and particularly the wealthy industrialised democracies of the West, now claim to offer their citizenries a great deal more than simply a guarantee of security over time in return for obedience. If, as Poggi has observed, states have come to see themselves as justified by the services they render (Poggi 1990: 28), then a crucial justification for states is their ability to guarantee for their citizens a certain standard of living or life-style, a situation of at least stable, and normally improving, life-chances (see Dunn 1993b). This new-found responsibility has played an important role in the transformation of the modern state into an economic agent since the seventeenth century. For the task of ensuring a certain standard of living in addition to basic subsistence requirements for their citizenries has required that modern states take an active interest in the maintenance and reproduction of conditions both within and without their territory conducive to economic growth and development.

The inclusion of economic advancement as one of the major goals of state agency has been crucial in generating the tight interdependence of the modern international system. In the realms of trade, finance and investment, the economic responsibilities of states have enmeshed them in complex, mutually dependent and competitive relations. One must therefore add to the state's roles as provider of security, and national and democratic agent, that the agency of the state is also actively shaped by the pursuit of conditions favourable to the maximisation of its own (and its citizenry's) economic interests. No matter how much a modern state plays down citizen expectations, it cannot actively disavow a crucial role

[1] This is not to deny that the patterns of interconnectedness in the modern international system have resulted in a whole range of new areas where the decisions of any one democratic community can have major repercussions for the members of others. But it is to point out that there is a deep and long-established conflict of ideals here.

in acting both domestically and internationally to ensure and implement conditions conducive to economic growth.

The roots of the state's foray into ensuring the living standards of its citizenry lie in changes in the seventeenth century when European states required commerce to build up income in order to finance defence and military expenditure (Hont 1990: 42–3). But if this was the way that economic goals came first to be embedded in the state's *raison d'état*, it has become evident in the years since then that the state's economic agency has come to have something of a life of its own, driven less by security needs than the life-style expectations of its members.

The expansion of state agency to include economic goals over the last three centuries has not threatened the deliberative rationality of the modern state; it has merely expanded the realm of action where this rationality is applied. This is apparent in the contemporary world where each state entering into international negotiations on everything from fishing rights, to trade deals, tariffs and even environmental protection, carries with it the weight of the economic interests of part or all of the human community it represents. What legitimises the state's role as economic agent is just what legitimises the state's role as security-maximising agent: the claim that it is acting to maximise the short, medium or long-term interests of its citizenry.

But this role brings its own problems. The state's involvement in commercial interaction and exchange has made it dependent upon the capriciousness of international markets, a force which no state could be confident of shaping to its wishes, in order to ensure conditions for economic growth and development. An important element in the state's claim to authority has thus come to rest upon the claim that it can guarantee a certain standard of living for its citizenry, while it is clear that no single state can possibly control the range of economic forces necessary to be able to discharge such a commitment (Dunn 2001: 251).

How much does this tension within the state's claim to authority affect its ability to act as a particularistic moral agent? It is hard to predict how this tension will work itself out in the long term. But if the human communities over which Western states preside have to lower radically their life-style expectations, at least some of the cogency of the modern state's claim to authority is likely to be lost. In the shorter term, the picture looks clearer, but unthreatening to the particularism that characterises modern state agency. In times when Western states are finding it increasingly difficult to live up to the expectations of their citizenries, states are under more pressure than ever to show clearly and unambiguously that the interests that they pursue are those of their citizens. In this kind of environment, states are unlikely to expand their responsibilities towards outsiders. Indeed, as the increasing restrictions on the entrance of refugees into Western states since the 1970s show, many states faced with an unfavourable international economic environment are more inclined to contract their responsibilities towards necessitous strangers.

Implications of the state as a particularistic agent

In the last 300 years the way the state is legitimated has undergone considerable transformation. Normative defences of the state no longer hinge solely on the state's satisfaction of the brute security needs of its subjects. Modern states now also claim to be agents for the protection of the way of life of the human community over which they rule (national agents) and actors in the pursuit of their citizens' economic welfare (economic agents). These changes are not unrelated to a broader development in the relation between citizen and state: the modern state's role as democratic agent. Increasingly, the authority of the modern state has come to rest upon the claim that its actions and goals reflect not only the needs of its citizenry but also their wishes as expressed through a representative democratic process.

Despite these transformations, one feature of the defences of the state has remained constant: the claim that the state's authority is derived from the human community over which it holds sway. The modern state has survived the last 300 years because it has generally been successful in linking its authority to act to the interests and needs of the human community over which it presides. In many cases the success of the state in negotiating this practical feat might be attributed more to citizen gullibility than to a serious concern on its part for the needs of its human population – after all, the state has always had interests of its own to protect. But there is no doubting that the state as an idea still exerts a powerful force on modern consciousness as well as political reality.

Above all else, then, the state is fundamentally an answer to the question of who is responsible to whom in the modern world: states are responsible to their own citizens. The survival of the state as an entity over time rests, moreover, on its ability to portray itself convincingly as an answer to such a question. As a consequence, the claims of outsiders are assessed by states, including liberal democratic ones, through a logic that deprecates the interests and needs of outsiders – a logic that is exceedingly sensitive to the potential damage to its own authority involved in forcing its citizens to incur costs for the sake of strangers. Modern states are highly resistant to the moral claims of outsiders.

The analysis of the idea of the modern state presented here provides strong reasons for believing that states could not be the kind of cosmopolitan moral agents demanded by many ideal theories, including impartialist ones. Criticising the state for putting the needs and interests of insiders first is like criticising a public company for seeking to make a profit for its shareholders – in neither case is one's criticism likely to offend the institution in question. To expect it to do so is fundamentally to misunderstand the nature of the agent concerned. While most states are responsive to the needs of outsiders *in extremis*, they do not equate the needs of outsiders with the needs of citizens. When states accept refugees, they are responding to extremity, not equality. The extreme need of outsiders never dislodges the fundamental relationship between citizen and state; it never challenges the state's claim to be the state of a particular human community. If this special relationship were to be transcended – if people or governments were in a position to charge the state to act impartially between their own interests and those of outsiders – we would have transcended the need for the modern state. We would be ready for world government.

What implications does this finding have for ideal theory? The desirability of an ideal does not depend on the existence of an agent ready, willing or able to implement it. Moreover, it's perfectly within the realm of ideal theory to demand that we create new institutions capable of implementing cosmopolitan moral values. But the preceding analysis does have important consequences if we wish to give an account of the responsibilities of governments located in the world as we currently find it. For the ability of these governments to implement more inclusive – and thus morally defensible – policies towards refugees will depend on their maintaining the support of (at least a substantial proportion) of their citizenries.

The political challenge: avoiding a backlash

I have suggested, then, that the state is a particularistic moral agent, one constituted by a set of duties owed to its citizens that are integral to its authority to act. The classical formulation of these responsibilities lies, as we have seen, in the idea that states have a duty to ensure the security and provide for the welfare of their citizens. In recent times, however, all liberal states have come to see themselves as bound by a more stringent duty: to act in accordance with the wishes of their citizens, as expressed through regular elections. At least in principle, it is now the *demos* who decide which objectives the state will pursue.

Acknowledging the state to be a particularistic agent is perfectly consistent with recognising that states have duties to provide protection to outsiders in need. All liberal democratic states publicly avow the principle of *non-refoulement*, and, to a large though probably diminishing extent, ensure in practice that it is not violated. But the inherent particularism of a state's form of agency does suggest that how much any state – or to be more specific, any *government* – can do for refugees will be determined largely by the possibilities afforded by its domestic political environment, and that environment will be shaped by a changing array of social, institutional and economic forces, both domestic and international in origin.

The need to judge the political limits of refugee integration is thus the second challenge for an account of the responsibilities of governments to refugees. It is a crucial challenge because state action will always be potentially endangered by the possibility of political backlashes that set back attempts to implement and maintain morally defensible practices. Germany's ill-fated experience with a wide-ranging right of asylum shows powerfully the need to provide an account of the responsibilities of liberal democracies that is attentive to the range of real world forces that are likely to frustrate and hinder the attempt to implement and maintain morally superior practices. In order to meet this challenge, we need to consider the range of factors that are likely to shape or reproduce a political consensus favourable to the integration of refugees. I will now draw from the recent experiences of liberal democratic states to outline the factors that are likely to be of critical importance in affecting the ability of liberal democracies to respond inclusively to refugees.

The needs of the claimants

A potential entrant's reason for seeking residence will be important in any attempt to prise open the gates of the state. Moral beliefs are a force in shaping the attitudes of citizens towards entrants. Thus some entry claims are easier to deny than others. If it is clear that refusing entry will result in the loss of a person's life, or in great physical harm being visited upon them, then a strong case can be made by governments for entry. The individual's claim will be even harder to resist if the costs of allowing entry to that person are low and, as I have argued earlier, if either of the following conditions hold: (i) the person in desperate need is inside or at the borders of the state, or (ii) the applicant's parlous situation has been brought about by the state he or she is attempting to enter. In both cases, there exists an obvious *connection* between the needy claimant and the state. It is evident from current practices that the existence of some connection of this kind is often crucial to the state's acknowledgement of responsibility. It is not coincidental that it is the principle of asylum or *non-refoulement* – a duty to those at one's borders and not the existence of a general obligation to help all refugees – that has come to be accepted as the standard practice for states in dealing with refugees. The presence of an asylum seeker at its border makes it difficult for a state to deny a responsibility to this particular individual. Yet when numbers climb, public anxiety can make even the recognition of this responsibility hard. Clearly, while the sympathy of the general public for refugees and asylum seekers has limits, governments can do much to expand the boundaries of moral concern by conveying the sheer desperation of the plight of refugees. Here, advertising and stressing the importance of the ethical (and political) issues at stake in inclusive asylum policies can prove helpful. To put the same point negatively, a government that fails to counter fallacious and negative portrayals of the real plight of refugees cannot be said to be taking the life and death claims of legitimate refugees seriously.

Determining who is a refugee

The preceding argument is dependent upon states being able to distinguish those who are refugees from those who are not. However, as we have seen, in the case of asylum seekers, this is often no easy task. Refugee determination is complicated by the need for lengthy and costly procedures (including review mechanisms) to decide whether applicants come within the ambit of the UN definition. The complexity and inefficiency of these procedures has led to large asylum backlogs in Germany, the UK and the US in recent years. In addition to leaving many asylum seekers in an agonising state of limbo, long processing times increase the costs of housing and supporting applicants. Moreover, as the US case shows, the consequent backlogs can attract asylum seekers with dubious claims to a country, further exacerbating lengthy delays. Under such circumstances, asylum inevitably becomes a lightning rod for political criticism and the space for inclusive policies contracts.

The desire by governments in liberal democratic states to reduce the costs associated with refugee determination has in recent years spawned a range of measures – from the speeding up of determination procedures to eliminating avenues for review – many of which have proved ineffective. Perhaps more worryingly, some measures widely seen as effective – such as detaining asylum seekers, a practice that by 2002 was mandatory for certain classes of entrants in the US and Australia – involve the state resorting to highly illiberal measures which raise genuine concerns about civil liberties.[2] Until alternatives that address these problems are found,

[2] Compare the recent controversy in Australia over the imprisonment of 'boat people' while their claims for residence are processed, discussed in Chapter 6.

the imperfect ability of states to determine refugee status will constitute a significant constraint on their response to the current predicament.[3]

The wealth of the state

Many recent accounts of the responsibilities of states to refugees assume that Western states are best placed to shoulder the costs of resettling refugees due to their relative wealth. While this assumption is initially plausible – refugee resettlement often involves substantial costs incurred through the provision of housing, language lessons, social security and education – the link between wealth and resettlement ability is often exaggerated. The economic costs of integrating outsiders have to be considered in terms relative to the state. Refugees accepted by Western states must be provided with the goods necessary to a style of life that is far more expensive in absolute terms than equivalent goods provided in less-developed states: housing, education and food all cost a great deal more in the West. Moreover, from a liberal egalitarian perspective many of these costs are inescapable. The high price of asylum guards against the emergence of long-term, second-class members excluded from the kinds of rights and goods (welfare, public housing, education, etc.) available to other members. Recently many Western governments, including the UK, have, however, tried to roll back the social rights of asylum seekers, partly to discourage asylum claims. But even where this has been done, governments have not been able to escape the steep costs associated with legal representation, housing and social provision (even when it is in the form of 'in kind' benefits.) It is thus still true to say that the wealth or GNP of a state is an inadequate indicator of a state's ability to settle refugees or handle asylum claims.

Unemployment and housing

Far better at indicating absorptive ability is the relative buoyancy of a state's national and local markets for housing and labour. The recent trajectory of German asylum and Australian, amongst other states, entrance policy suggests that a state's level of unemployment and rate of economic growth are important in determining how electorates respond to new entrants. While some hostility towards foreigners usually exists during periods of economic growth, the demand for entry restrictions

[3] Various aspects of the problem of squaring the rights of asylum seekers and other immigrants with citizens' desire for tight entrance control are discussed in Joppke (1999a) and Gibney (2004).

during such periods is usually weak (witness the Federal Republic during the 1960s and Australia between 1950 and 1970). In periods of economic contraction, however, especially when accompanied by widespread unemployment, greater austerity in the provision of public goods, or a decrease in the availability of cheap housing (Germany and Australia after 1973; Britain during the 1960s), calls for restriction gain force. In unfavourable economic conditions, some citizens invariably come to view new entrants as competitors for jobs, housing and public goods, regardless of the refugees' actual contribution to economic growth. This is perhaps unsurprising as it is often much easier to point to the costs of newcomers (increased pressure on public housing, schooling, etc.), than to the economic benefits (disputed as they are by economists themselves), especially in the deprived areas where refugees and asylum seekers are often forced to settle. A government's prospects for bringing under control the economic forces that lead to this constraint on entry appear bleak. Even the most advanced and powerful liberal democracies have so far found no way of avoiding the fluctuating economic fortunes associated with the business cycle. Yet governments can take measures to minimise hostile responses to asylum seekers and refugees. At the very least, they can compensate local communities for hosting asylum seekers and refugees by ensuring that any public expenditure benefits long-term residents as well as the newcomers. The principles of burden sharing are applicable within states as well as between them.

Ethnic affinity

Ethnic affinity often has the strength to override perceived economic interests in entry decisions. Some outsiders are seen by electorates not as potential competitors for resources, but as part of what is viewed as the state's 'extended family'. This is commonly the case with outsiders who possess religious, racial or linguistic links to the state's dominant ethnic group. Germany (with *Aussiedler*), Australia (with the Irish), and the United Kingdom (with, for example, white Rhodesians), have all managed to integrate substantial numbers of new entrants, in spite of unfavourable economic conditions, because of the existence of affinities of this sort.[4] More broadly, it was surely not a coincidence that Kosovans elicited in Western countries the most public support of any refugee group of recent years. Western publics related to the experience of refugehood

[4] Israel exemplifies this point quite remarkably. In spite of its small population and relatively weak economy it managed to resettle over 200,000 Soviet Jews in 1992 (Weiner 1992/3: 104).

of white Europeans in a way that confounded established expectations (Gibney 1999b).

If the presence of such affinities can expand moral boundaries, however, their absence can also contract them. The long history of Australian, Canadian and US restrictions on Asian immigration, and the measures introduced by Britain in the 1960s to stem West Indian and Asian and East African refugees and migrants, are indicative of the judgement that maintaining ethnic and racial homogeneity is for large sections of the public a higher priority than the humanitarian or economic benefits that migration might bring. There is no reason to believe that prejudices of this type constitute an insuperable barrier to refugee resettlement. As Myron Weiner has observed, just who amongst outsiders is considered capable of being integrated is a social construct which changes over time.

> Australians and Americans, for example, redefined themselves so that Asians are no longer excluded as unassimilable peoples. Who is or who is not 'one of us' is historically variable. To many nineteenth century American Protestants, Jews and Catholics were not 'one of us' and today, for many Europeans, Muslims are not 'one of us'. (Weiner 1992/93: 105)[5]

But the current perceptions of citizens are usually crucial in determining how many new entrants a state will be able to accept in the short term.[6] While political leaders can have some success in eroding established prejudices over the medium to long term, the biases of a political community cannot be ignored in any assessment of the political limits on integrating refugees.[7]

Integration history

The role played by immigration in the history of a state is often a key indicator of its likely success in absorbing new entrants. It cannot be denied that there is something disingenuous in the claims of some European states that they are 'not countries of immigration'. No liberal democracy has remained completely sealed off from migration over the last twenty

[5] For an interesting account of the way nineteenth-century Britons redefined their national identity to include Catholics, see Colley (1992).

[6] Though different ethnic groups within a state often have conflicting ideas about who amongst outsiders is an economic, political or cultural threat. Compare, for instance, the reaction of Christians in France and Britain to immigration from Islamic states to the reaction of Muslims already settled in those states (Weiner 1992/3: 105).

[7] And it is often dangerous to ignore them. There is always the possibility, as the cases of Britain in the late 1950s and Germany in recent years show, that large influxes of unwelcome (from the perspective of current residents) immigrants will prompt a violent backlash from current residents that will make integration virtually impossible. There are also real dangers, however, in yielding to racial – and extremist – violence.

years. Every Western European state has relied to some extent on the labour of illegal migrants and accepts substantial numbers of new entrants through family reunion programmes. Nonetheless, there *is* a fundamental difference, if only one of attitude, between most European states for whom immigration has, in recent decades at least, been incidental to their historical development and the states of the New World. The latter have either been constituted as nations by diverse immigration (like the US) (Brubaker 1989: 7), or (like Australia, Canada and Israel) are still in the process of being so constituted. In these 'integrationist' states, immigration is often crucial to national myths that create and sustain citizen solidarity, as is clearly demonstrated in the US's national motto 'E Pluribus Unum'.[8]

There are two reasons why this overt and widely accepted role for immigration is relevant to the task of shaping the politics of refugee admission. First, its existence diminishes the force of exclusionist claims that certain outsiders are inassimilable. Justifications for exclusion on cultural, racial or linguistic grounds are still made, as the speeches of Pauline Hanson testify, but they are more likely than in European states to come to grief in battle against the view that what separates outsiders from insiders is that outsiders *are* immigrants, and insiders (or their forebears) *were* immigrants. For instance, one Australian observer responding to complaints about Vietnamese boat people in 1999 made the obvious point that 'Non-Aboriginal Australians *are all boat people* in this southern land on the extremity of Asia' (my emphasis, Pybus 1992: 15). Harry Truman, as we saw earlier, made a very similar claim about the backgrounds of members of Congress in his struggle to pass displaced persons legislation in the 1940s. These attitudes do not gainsay the ongoing force of the distinction between citizens and outsiders in immigrant societies. But, as I suggested in my discussion of partiality, the acquisition of citizenship in these states usually requires only a commitment to widely shared civic values, and not to membership in a particular ethnic group. Accordingly, arguments for restrictions are less likely to turn on the cultural consequences of migration.

Second, an integrative history suggests experience in dealing with new entrants. Integrationist states, such as Australia, have built up over many years the necessary infrastructure (government departments, legislation, community organisations, etc.) to ensure that entrants are transformed

[8] For insightful discussions of the way immigration policies in America have been shaped by both nationalist *and* integrationist ideals, see Schuck (1984); and Smith (1988). For an enlightening discussion of the historical 'meaning' of citizenship in America, see Shklar (1991).

into citizens with relative ease. In many European states, the processes for being accepted into citizenship have traditionally been extremely complex and only available to those who have been resident for many years. It is certainly possible for governments in states historically opposed to the admission of large numbers of new entrants to begin the process of building a more avowedly diverse society, as the recent changes in Germany's citizenship laws show. But the full success of these measures is dependent upon the support of citizens, which is often slow in coming.

The actions of other states

The policies and intentions of other states can also dramatically affect a government's ability (and willingness) to respond to asylum seekers. At one end of the spectrum, a hostile state can use asylum policies to 'dump' unwanted and undesirable members of its citizenry (such as political opponents or criminals) on another political community. Western states accused Vietnam of acting in this way in the late 1970s, when they claimed that it was helping dissidents flee the country by boat; as we have seen, Cuba actively encouraged the emigration of its citizens in the early 1980s as a way of pressuring the US government, partly in order to protest against economic sanctions. More recently, the Serbian government forced the flight of Albanians from Kosovo in 1999 in order to fulfil its aim of 'ethnically cleansing' the region.[9] When faced with this kind of deliberate displacement, it can be wise for a host state to restrict entry because the main beneficiary of its asylum policies is likely to be the repressive regime.[10] Moreover, the consequence of a particular state continuing to accept refugees released with the deliberate intention of causing it harm is to bring the provision of asylum in general into disrepute.[11]

At the other end of the spectrum, the success of the Comprehensive Plan of Action for Vietnamese refugees in the 1970s shows how states can

[9] For discussions of the legal and political issues raised by the actions of Vietnam in assisting with the departure of refugees, see Johnson (1980); for the case of Cuba and the US, see Mitchell (1992: esp. 452.) On the broader question of the responsibility of states of refugee outflow to those political communities forced to take their citizens, see Ayling and Blay (1989).

[10] Obviously the moral dilemma here becomes more intractable when the repressive state is not the *only* beneficiary of asylum laws; when, that is, those being assisted in fleeing have very powerful reasons to leave (e.g., if they risk being harmed by the state). In this situation, third country resettlement may be one of the few acceptable options.

[11] One (albeit imperfect) way of responding to this type of situation is to look to third parties to settle the asylum seekers. During 1994 the US paid Latin American states to temporarily house Cuban and Haitian refugees.

mitigate a refugee crisis by coordinating their actions. This kind of cooperation is still, however, the exception. Current state interactions with refugees are primarily determined by the capriciousness of geography and locale rather than the result of a collective determination of what constitutes a fair share of the refugee burden, notwithstanding the fact that in 2000 EU states committed themselves to a European Refugee Fund to financially compensate member states for refugee burdens. Under conditions of very limited cooperation, it can become difficult for even well-intentioned governments to operate inclusive policies. The case of Germany showed the difficulties of maintaining a wide-ranging right of asylum in an environment in which neighbouring states are increasingly restricting access to entry. The state's burden quickly becomes a rallying cry for politicians and citizens who ask why their state should shoulder a disproportionate share of refugees. Sometimes this leads politicians to place pressure on other states to accept more refugees (as in the case of German and Austrian pressure on Britain to accept more of those fleeing Bosnia in early 1993). But more often it results in the demise of the liberal policy, or efforts to restrict the workings of the 1951 Convention, such as those advocated by British Prime Minister Blair in 2001 (Blair 2001). As another state with broad entitlements buckles under, the pressure on any remaining states to become more restrictive is further increased.

What, then, are the prospects for securing the kind of 'effective and trustworthy international co-operation' (Dunn 1993b: 14) amongst states that would enable a sharing of the current burden? In the absence of the acceptance of duties in entry other than *non-refoulement*, a collective response is dependent upon a convergence of state interests. This is not completely implausible because the interests of states need not be identical. As Loescher and Scanlan have argued, when states cooperate to deal with refugees

> Their interests frequently differ and, indeed, may be of entirely different orders. Thus, for example, one nation may be interested most in solving the practical problems occasioned by the sudden arrival of thousands of ill-fed and desperate people on its borders, whereas another nation may be most concerned by the regional instability created by such a flow, or may be seeking some symbolic advantage from its act of kindness. (Loescher and Scanlan 1985: 3)

However, a convergence of state interests does not of itself guarantee humanitarian assistance. States often see it as more in their interests to cooperate to *insulate* themselves from refugee flows. The recent attempts by EU states to harmonise their asylum policies present a sobering reminder of the current appeal of this option (Harvey 2000; Geddes 2003).[12]

Control

The number of new entrants (or, to be more exact, the *perceived* number of entrants) almost always influences the degree of community hostility towards the reception of refugees and asylum seekers. As Western European states have discovered over the last two decades, it is one thing to respect a duty of asylum when the number of applicants constitutes a few thousand annually and they can be settled at relatively little cost. It is quite another thing to respond in a similar fashion when the number of applicants is in the tens or hundreds of thousands. Under these new conditions, respecting long-established entry entitlements takes on an entirely new political significance, and the claims of citizens and those of entrants are increasingly likely to come into conflict.

That said, perhaps the most important constraint on a government's ability to operate inclusive policies lies not so much in the numbers entering, as in maintaining the appearance that the admission of asylum seekers and refugees is orderly and controlled. The harshest pieces of restrictive legislation of recent years have coincided with periods when governments were perceived as having lost control of inward movement. The entrance of New Commonwealth immigrants as a matter of right in 1960s Britain and the experience of Australia with asylum seekers coming by boat, particularly in 2001 and 2002, gave birth to strong public pressure to restrict entrance, despite the relatively small numbers entering in each case. Public concern was fanned by the fear that the foreigners arriving (or attempting to arrive) were merely the thin edge of what was likely, if left unchecked, to be much larger movements.

Control is a key issue largely because refugees and asylum seekers are commonly viewed as something to be feared. This is particularly apparent since the terrorist attacks of 11 September 2001 focused attention on the various ways that terrorists might enter Western states. But concerns about asylum seekers and refugees have also focused in recent decades on their impact on the welfare state and increasingly, after the electoral successes of Jean-Marie Le Pen in 2002 in France, on crime and personal security. Many of these connections are greatly exaggerated: a tribute to

[12] Moreover, commitments to other states (for reciprocally open borders, for instance) can actually *constrain* a state's ability to accept outsiders, as the pressure EU states have placed on accession countries to tighten their border controls illustrates.

the enduring force of stereotypes and the vulnerability of new entrants rather than a victory for objective data. Any government serious about preserving asylum must actively combat such stereotypes with a more accurate account of the realities and simultaneously remind the public of the vital human interests at stake in asylum. It is necessary to concede, nonetheless, that even the most morally enlightened of governments will find their ability to act inclusively towards refugees limited by public concerns over entrance control and security.

The factors I have outlined above cannot be taken as a definitive list of what shapes the political limits of any government's attempt to move towards the implementation of more inclusive asylum policies. Yet even this abridged version shows clearly that the practical ability of governments to respond to refugees is going to be shaped by a large range of factors that vary across countries and over time and that are the product of both domestic and international forces. We might regret that some of these factors (ethnic affinity, the pursuit by states of their national interest) will influence the possibility of successful resettlement. But the judgement that these factors are highly likely to influence the success or failure of morally informed action by states constitutes a powerful reason why we cannot construct a critical account of how states should act independently of them.

The ethical challenge: unintended consequences

The third and final constraint that shapes the ability of governments to respond inclusively to refugees is the difficulty of predicting the consequences of asylum policies. Virtually all of the ideal theories we examined in the first part of this work saw consequences as relevant to the issue of how states should respond to refugees. The utilitarian attempt to align the marginal utilities of citizens and strangers was driven quite explicitly by the potential or actual consequences of allowing entry to outsiders. But even the deontological global liberalism of Carens, Dummett and Ackerman sets some limits on the costs they saw states as obliged to bear.[13] While impartialists differed amongst themselves in how and where they set the limits of state responsibility, all shared the view that states are entitled to restrict entry in the face of imminent social and political chaos. I have already suggested that impartialism is sapped of some of its ethical appeal because its demands end up submerging the claims

[13] For instance, Bruce Ackerman argues that 'the *only* reason for restricting immigration is to protect the ongoing process of the liberal conversation itself' (1980: 85). Other liberals like Dummett and Carens also see threats to the survival of liberal institutions as justifying restrictions on entry.

of citizens. However, another important difficulty with ideal theory as a guide for actual governments stems from our real world ignorance of the consequences of adopting far more inclusive policies towards refugees. Impartialists and other ideal theorists who stress the importance of consequences often assume a knowledge of the likely effects of population flows that is simply unavailable to contemporary governments.

Evidence of the unintended and unforeseeable consequences of refugee law and policy (as well as immigration generally) can be gleaned from each of the states I have examined. In 1949, Germany's enactment of a wide-ranging right of asylum seemed a perfectly reasonable (if minor) response to its behaviour during the 1930s and 1940s. The entitlement was intended to cater for the security needs of the relatively small numbers of refugees fleeing the Eastern Bloc. At the time, no one could have guessed the changes in the international environment which would make the restriction of this entitlement a key political issue some forty years later. Most ironically of all, nobody could have predicted that changes in the state's asylum laws would become a rallying cry for newly revived extremist right-wing groups.

Similarly, few could have foreseen the changes that British society would soon undergo when the Attlee government routinely reconfirmed the entry right of all Commonwealth citizens in the 1948 Nationality Act. Within two decades, British leaders would respond to race riots and widespread hostility towards West Indian and Asian migration by enacting entry legislation that disposed of this central Commonwealth right and blatantly discriminated against non-white entrants. Britain's transformation into a multiracial society in the years after 1945 was brought about less by governmental choice than by the maintenance of traditional policies in an environment that suddenly became more favourable to immigration from the countries outside the West.

The acceptance of a substantial number of refugees from Vietnam in the late 1970s and early 1980s has had a similar, if less profound, effect on Australian society. A relatively generous family reunion policy (allowing for the unification of siblings in addition to other immediate family members) has resulted in Vietnamese migration taking on something of a life of its own. Family reunion entitlements have allowed decisions made in the late 1970s to continue to shape Australian entry policy. By 1991, the state that had once claimed the right to practise racist entry policies was accepting 11 per cent of its annual migration intake from Vietnam alone (Castles and Miller 1993: 101).

The US also experienced difficulties of a similar sort. Policy-makers of the late 1950s could not reasonably have expected that allowing entrance to Cubans would over time become a way of strengthening rather than weakening the Castro regime, thus laying the groundwork for increasing numbers of desperate immigrants making their way after the late 1970s. This is true not least because the changing effect was due to a combination of factors, including growing diversification in the composition of the *émigrés* (from elite to middle-class to poorer Cubans), the magnet effect of vibrant Cuban communities in Florida, and the economic appeal of life in the US, especially to Cubans suffering under US sanctions.

The persistent difficulty in foreseeing the consequences of refugee policies poses a serious problem for conceptualising the duties of states in entry.[14] For if one accepts that there are limits to the responsibilities of states – thresholds beyond which it is supererogatory or even morally undesirable for the state to go – then one has no right to expect states to transgress these boundaries. But if we cannot be sure of the consequences of any substantial flow of foreigners, how can we know whether or not a particular theory is asking states to step over the threshold?

This problem is not unique to asylum or indeed immigration policy generally. Recent 'humanitarian interventions' in Somalia in 1993 and Kosovo in 1999 have quickly turned sour as a result of the difficulties of controlling the consequences of using military force. In spite of these difficulties, one might still argue that states have a responsibility to assist outsiders in situations where it is overwhelmingly likely that the negative consequences of intervention will be low. This is, I think, a convincing response. But one must acknowledge that the problem of predicting consequences is *particularly* acute in the case of entrance. This is a result of differences both in degree and in kind. In terms of degree, entrance duties can, when the numbers involved are large enough, reshape the face of the nation, influencing the welfare state, social order and the outcomes of democratic political systems. It is difficult to think of another area where the acknowledgement of duties to outsiders could so profoundly influence a political community.

What differences in kind are pertinent? Two particular problems make predicting the consequences of entrance policy a particularly formidable task. First, in some situations, entry policies can 'snowball', multiplying the number of people entering the state. This 'snowball effect' not only confounds all attempts to predict the likely number of entrants under a particular policy, but makes it extremely difficult for a government to exercise border control. There are three major ways that policies can bring about this effect.

[14] For discussion of the failure by the Western states who operated guestworker schemes to anticipate the full consequences of allowing entry to temporary labourers, see, amongst others, Tapinos (1983); and Castles (1986: 761–78).

(1) Inclusive asylum policies, as the Federal Republic of Germany and the US discovered in the 1990s and the 1960s respectively, often *create* demand for entry rather than simply satisfying the needs of people already on the move.[15] Recent changes in technology have given far wider publicity to the entry policies of particular states, and enabled the rapid movement of large numbers of people over long distances. The more inclusive a state's asylum entitlements – for instance, the greater the chance of a successful application – the more they are likely to encourage those dissatisfied with their state of citizenship for reasons other than persecution to emigrate. Western officials quite justifiably turn pale at the thought that their asylum policies risk encouraging the movement of people from economically deprived states. Yet there is some evidence that restrictive asylum policies can also generate perverse effects. In particular, as we have seen, some observers have suggested that there is a link between the closing down of asylum options in the UK and increasing numbers of illegal migrants (Gibney 2000c; Morrison and Crosland 2001).

(2) New entrants often affect the refugee policies of states through political pressure on governments once they are admitted as members. This is most evident in the US, where successive generations of Cuban exiles have lobbied hard for the maintenance of the double standard in US policy favouring *balseros*, efforts that reached their apogee during the Elian Gonzales affair of 2000. But it is also evident in Australia, where successive waves of migrants, including refugees, have lobbied governments to widen family reunion schemes. These pressures are hardly unique to Australia. All liberal-democratic states operate family migration schemes, and consequently receive large flows of new entrants, derived from long-ended primary migration. Moreover, the political consequences of this migration are likely to continue to shape Western states far into the future. For the end of one cycle of reunification often allows a new one to begin.[16] Myron Weiner has argued that it is the ability of new entrants to shape the politics of receiving states which is at the heart of the distinctiveness of modern immigration: 'what is unique about international migration . . . is that it changes the very composition of one's population and therefore one's domestic policies; it brings the outside in, as it were, and it involves sending a piece of one's nation to another society' (1985: 453).[17] Even

[15] Compare Hailbronner (1990: 341–60) and (1993: 31–65).

[16] Suppose, for instance, one migrates to a Western country. One might be entitled to be joined by one's sister who in turn is entitled to be joined by her husband. One's sister's husband is then entitled to be joined by his siblings, and so on.

[17] For an insightful discussion of the political influence on the migration and foreign policies of receiving states, see Weiner (1992: 452ff.).

very small numbers of primary settlers can lead over time to profound changes in the 'face of the nation' (Fitzgerald 1996).

(3) Refugee flows, like other migration movements, open up chains of connection between states and migrant source countries in ways other than through family reunion. As one observer has noted, 'immigration flows are not random. They track close connections that have been established, often decades ago, between and among nations' (Meissner *et al.* 1993: 8). The establishment of new ethnic communities in a foreign state often acts as a magnet for nationals at home. The respective histories of Pakistani and West Indian settlement in Britain during the 1940s and 1950s, Cuban migration to the US from the late 1950s to the present, and Vietnamese settlement in Australia since the late 1970s provide ample evidence of the way early settlers reduce the cultural disincentives of international migration by establishing a foothold within the state for their particular ethnic group (Barry 1992: 281–2). When the new communities are composed of nationals from states with large numbers of people who wish to migrate, the demand for entry often exceeds the number of places (Birrell 1994). While states faced with such strong entry pressures move to restrict legal avenues for entry, this often results only in an increase in illicit migration or asylum applications, which creates new problems, as Germany's experience with Turkish migration after 1973 and the UK's with Kosovan migration after 1999 testify.[18]

Second, a state's success in integrating refugees without social disruption or great domestic hostility depends upon a range of factors whose relative weight over time is often difficult to determine. For instance, it is safe to say that the ability of the Australian state to integrate immigrants without great social tension will depend at any particular point in time upon changes in the rate of unemployment. But who could predict with any confidence the level of unemployment in Australia (or anywhere else) in one, two, five, let alone ten years' time? Another crucial determinant of the consequences of pursuing a particular entry policy, the actions of other states, is similarly hard to predict in advance. This is largely because of the tendency of states to adjust their entry policies to take advantage of, or 'free ride' on, the actions of states more principled or constrained than themselves. This type of behaviour was, as we saw,

[18] The difficulties states have in controlling borders once movements of people have started are further evidenced in the way impending restrictions can generate new entrants. In Britain in the early 1960s, the mere discussion of entry restrictions on New Commonwealth immigrants was enough to increase numbers dramatically (Walvin 1984: 112). More recently, impending restrictions on the entry of Nicaraguan refugees into the US prompted a 'squalid sprint' for the borders (Mitchell 1992: 294).

one factor responsible for Germany's disproportionate share of the EU asylum burden throughout much of the 1990s. If the aim of articulating an account of responsibilities to refugees is to guide the actions of states over time, then our ignorance as to how the various causal factors which determine consequences will influence future events provides a serious constraint on any attempt to specify how states should act.

Above all else, these difficulties in determining consequences pose serious problems for the type of moral brinkmanship in entry demanded by utilitarian and global liberal theorists. These approaches require that states accept refugees or other immigrants up to the 'brink' – up to the point, that is, where taking any more would either threaten the viability of the state as a site of liberal values, or extract such costs from residents that the addition to marginal utility in keeping immigrants out is greater than that of allowing them in. The main weakness of these arguments is that the ideal limits they specify are, at best, useful guides to action only for ideal agents. Faced with the real and unremitting uncertainties of practice, no state could (or should) risk going right up to the brink of social disharmony, for instance. The poor record of states in controlling entrance once it has started suggests that few states can be confident of their ability to grind things to a halt right at the edge of severe social problems.

These problems suggest two possible responses for ideal theorists concerned with directing state action. One, they can be reckless in the advice they give as to how states ought to act. They can ignore the possibility of unpredictable consequences and demand that states enact and maintain policies that take them perilously close to a morally undesirable state of affairs, regardless of the risks. Or, two, they can temper their demands and acknowledge the need for states to be cautious in entry, perhaps by giving them more latitude to decide which policies they should pursue. The difficulty with the first approach is that it wilfully disregards possible consequences in a way that appears to jeopardise what ethical force the directions might have. The problem with the second is that it leaves one to wonder whether this approach would mandate policies very different to those currently favoured by Western states. For instance, how would such a tempered approach have judged Britain's actions during the 1960s, when it restricted the entry of New Commonwealth immigrants in an atmosphere of widespread community antagonism, sporadic racial riots and economic difficulties? Does it make any difference that these actions were prompted by only a relatively small number of entrants (at least in proportion to Britain's overall population)? Entry policy is a particularly hazardous realm of state action to theorise, even when that theorisation is accompanied by a detailed consideration of the integrative abilities of particular states. This reality suggests that, in the absence of secure knowledge of the likely consequences of action, some caution is in order.

Conclusion

This chapter has analysed the challenges associated with moving from a statement of what would be an ethically ideal response to refugees and asylum seekers to the question of what kind of actions we should demand of any actually existing government to meet the needs of these desperate men and women. Drawing upon the practical experiences of liberal democratic states, I argued that prescriptions for governments must take into account two major considerations. First, how the capabilities of governments in asylum policy are (for the most part) politically constructed within a structure – the modern state – that demands that governments legitimate their actions to the members of their state. Second, prescriptions must be informed by a realisation of the difficulties of predicting the consequences of different policy responses.

These challenges must surely dampen our expectations of the kind of guidance normative theory can provide for improving the current responses of states. Yet any theory that ignores them in pursuit of what would be ethically ideal is likely to purchase its moral purity at the cost of practical relevance. If we are to respond to the great urgency of the claims of refugees we must aim to direct the actions of governments through the hazardous and unpredictable circumstances within which they actually operate. To do otherwise is to allow normative theory to drift loose from the real world of political debate, choice and, ultimately, action. In the final chapter of this work I will show how the principle of humanitarianism makes headway in meeting these challenges I have outlined.

8 Liberal democratic states and ethically defensible asylum practices

For such things homelessness is ours
And shall be others'. Tenement roofs and towers
Will fall upon the kind and the unkind
Without election,
For deaf and blind
Is rejection bred by rejection
Breeding rejection,
And where no counsel is what will be will be.
We must shape here a new philosophy.

Edwin Muir, *The Refugees* 1960

If the provision of protection for refugees is its central goal, then the system of asylum offered by Western states is currently in deep crisis. Over the last few decades, liberal democratic states have put in place barrier after barrier to prevent the arrival of rising numbers of refugees, as well as individuals on the move to escape grinding poverty or lack of opportunity. These barriers may well be justified in order to prevent the arrival of economic migrants, but they also halt the movement and punish the entry of those fleeing persecution and great danger. Perversely, that some lucky individuals manage to slip through the net of restrictions and ultimately gain refugee status (or some other form of protection) is taken as evidence by governments that the institution of asylum is alive and well; or, just as erroneously, that their ethical (and legal) responsibilities to assist refugees are being met. Yet the current response of Western states to refugees and asylum seekers is characterised by a kind of 'organized hypocrisy'.[1] Liberal democratic states publicly avow the principle of asylum but use fair means and foul to prevent as many asylum seekers as possible from arriving on their territory where they could claim its protections.

Edwin Muir's call for a 'new philosophy' in dealings with refugees seems more relevant than ever forty-four years on. Yet, as I have shown in

[1] I have borrowed this term from Stephen Krasner (1999) who has recently used it to describe the principle of state sovereignty.

this work, a forceful account of how and why governments can and should improve things requires a convincing statement of the ethical responsibilities of states. There are two major challenges associated with providing such a statement. First, at the ethical level, there is the need to identify a convincing ideal for state action – a desirable goal. As we have seen, different ethical theories present contrasting accounts of what that goal should be. The partial view brings to the fore the claims of citizens to maintain self-determining political communities which sustain their collective way of life; the impartial view highlights the claims of human beings in general – and refugees in particular – to equal consideration. Each of these views captures an important moral claim at issue in the current asylum crisis. Yet these views are in tension with each other. While accepting the full logic of impartialism might lead to policies which would undermine the conditions necessary for communal self-determination and the provision of public goods, adhering to partialism risks sacralising entrance policies that attach little weight to the claims of refugees. A credible ideal needs to take seriously both the claims of citizens *and* those of refugees. I have suggested that one way of integrating these claims is to require states to accept as many refugees as they can without undermining the civil, political and, importantly, the social rights associated with the liberal democratic state.

This requirement, however, tells us only how it would be ideal for states to respond to refugees. A second important challenge is to spell out the implications of this ideal for what any government should actually do. In order to provide this we need to understand those forces that shape state agency in the area of refugee and asylum policy. Drawing upon the case studies, I suggested that unifying theory and practice requires taking account of a range of structural, political and ethical challenges faced by governments. I concluded by suggesting that prescriptions for action must not only strike a compromise between partial and impartial claims, but also recognise that governments operate within the structure of the modern state, find their capabilities politically constrained by democratic politics, and have only a limited ability to determine the costs of entrance policy in advance. This is a tall order indeed.

My aim in this, the final chapter of this work, is to put forward a way of thinking about the responsibilities of liberal democracies to refugees that is both ethically informed and politically relevant. I will propose the *humanitarian principle* – an old and, in many respects, conservative principle – as the best way of capturing current responsibilities to refugees. In what follows, I will explain the nature of this principle and how it differs from other accounts of responsibilities to refugees. I will then move to spell out its practical implications. As well as demanding respect for the principle of *non-refoulement*, humanitarianism directs Western states to boost efforts to resettle refugees. Over the longer term, the principle also requires more determined efforts by states to create a more favourable national and international environment for refugees by, *inter alia*, promoting positive public attitudes and securing international cooperation on asylum issues. There are, however, limits on the ability of states to respond to refugees and asylum seekers. And I will conclude this work by considering two important questions that are likely to impact upon the future direction of asylum in the West. The first concerns the justifiability of policies (such as detention or 'temporary protection') that trade the rights of asylum seekers or refugees for the sake of increasing or preserving the availability of overall refugee protection; the second discusses the question of how one should balance the needs of refugees and asylum seekers against the national security interests of states. In each of these cases, I will propose some standards for assessing the legitimacy of policy measures.

Defining humanitarianism

We can begin the task of moving towards superior policies to refugees by identifying an appropriate principle to govern the actions of liberal democratic states. In my view, that principle should be the principle of humanitarianism. Humanitarianism can be simply stated: the principle holds that states have an obligation to assist refugees when the costs of doing so are low. This responsibility recognises, like impartial theories, the existence of duties that stem from membership in a single human community. However, it is less comprehensive in scope than most impartial theories – specifying obligations only to those in great need. It is also not as onerous in its demands as impartial accounts. For the conception of 'low costs' suggests that states (or individuals) have room to protect other valued interests or obligations to which they attach significant value.

The humanitarian principle is not new. It has found perhaps its best-known historical expression in the Biblical parable of the Good Samaritan. In that parable, a Samaritan comes across the victim of an attack who lies hurt and vulnerable at the side of the road. The 'Good Samaritan' does not simply pass the stranger by, like the priest and Levite, but lends him assistance by binding his wounds, taking him to an inn and paying for him to convalesce there. The duty of humanitarianism, which the actions of the Samaritan exemplify, has commonly been formalised in the principle that there is a duty incumbent upon each and every individual to assist those in great distress or suffering when the costs of doing so are low. Significantly, this is a moral principle that holds between *strangers*, those sharing in common nothing more than their humanity.

While the humanitarian principle has often been formulated in terms of the responsibilities that hold between individuals, it has long been viewed as having implications for state behaviour to foreigners. The principle, for example, has informed the work of virtually all the great natural law theorists including Grotius, Locke and Vattel. The idea of a duty of charity that transcends both political boundaries and current property appropriations is central in the work of John Locke, for instance:

> And therefore no Man could ever have just Power over the Life of another, by Right of property in Land or Possessions; since 'twould always be a Sin in any Man of Estate, to let his Brother perish for want of affording Relief out of his Plenty. As *Justice* gives every Man a Title to the product of his honest Industry, and the fair Acquisitions of his Ancestors descended to him; so *Charity* gives every man a Title to so much out of another's Plenty, as will keep him from extream [*sic*] want, where he has no means to subsist otherwise. (Locke 1964: first treatise, sec. 42)

Humanitarianism has direct implications for relations between states and refugees.[2] For the refugee has long been seen as a fitting analogue of the hurt and vulnerable stranger left lying by the side of the road. Moreover, many states, as I will argue, could clearly do a great deal for substantial numbers of refugees at little cost to their important interests. Indeed, as Michael Walzer has observed, with reference to the analogous principle of 'mutual aid':

> [this principle] is more coercive for political communities than it is for individuals because a wide range of benevolent actions is open to the community which will only marginally affect its present members considered as a body or even, with possible exceptions, one by one or family by family or club by club. (Walzer 1983: 45)

The early theorists of international law recognised that humanitarianism had implications for those who were vulnerable because they lacked the protection of a political community. Hugo Grotius, for instance, suggested that:

> A permanent residence ought not to be denied to foreigners who, expelled from their homes, are seeking a refuge, provided that they submit themselves to the established government and observe any regulations which are necessary to avoid strifes. (1925: book II, ch. II, sec. 16)

[2] See also Andrew Shacknove's essay (1988) which also appeals to the principle of humanitarianism to determine the responsibilities of states, specifically the US, to refugees.

Even Emmerich de Vattel, who accepted that each state should have a broad-ranging prerogative to decide who should enter and reside in its territory, placed some limits on the rights of states in line with the humanitarianism principle. Entrance decisions, he claimed,

> should not take the form of suspicion nor be pushed to the point of refusing an asylum to the outcast on slight grounds and from unreasonable or foolish fears. It should be regulated by never losing sight of the charity and sympathy which are due to the unfortunate. We should entertain these sentiments even for those whose misfortune is their own fault; for by the law of charity which bids men love one another we should condemn the crime but love the victim of it. (Vattel 1916: book I, ch. XIX, sec. 231)

The appeal to humanitarianism has been echoed in more recent times by communitarians such as Michael Walzer. In *Spheres of Justice* (1983) Walzer argues that while states are generally free to construct entrance policies according to their own criteria, in dealing with refugees they are bound by the requirements of the humanitarian or, in his case, the mutual aid principle. According to Walzer, states are obligated to accept as many refugees as they can without disturbing the cultural life (what he calls, after Clifford Geertz, the 'way of life') that their citizens share.

The belief that states have a responsibility to alleviate the suffering of refugees when the costs of doing so are low provides a realistic alternative to the more onerous demands of both utilitarians, who argue for entrance policies that maximise total utility, and global liberals, who demand a basic right of free movement. Furthermore, humanitarianism represents a clear and minimal statement of responsibilities in contrast to those partialists who view states as entitled to well-nigh complete discretion in entrance.

The advantages of humanitarianism

Humanitarianism makes significant headway in meeting the three challenges for a critical standard outlined in chapter 7. First, it offers a response to the difficulty of incorporating the competing moral claims of citizens and foreigners. Humanitarianism *concentrates* the responsibilities of states by specifying that positive duties of assistance to outsiders are owed exclusively to those in great need. When applied to entrance, humanitarianism provides grounds for attaching priority to the claims of refugees (i.e. those whose needs can be satisfied only through resettlement) in a way that global liberalism, for instance, with its concern for rights of free movement does not. Humanitarianism is, moreover, attentive to the modern state's kind of agency. Its requirements are consistent with the belief that states have interests and priorities of their own which are of ethical importance. The principle certainly places moral side-constraints on the freedom of states to pursue their own interests. But the duties it mandates are not so demanding that they overwhelm the commitments (such as to ensuring the security and welfare of their own citizens) that governments already have. As the cost of assisting outsiders comes increasingly to impinge upon these commitments, a state's duty to help outsiders correspondingly decreases (Shacknove 1988: 134).

Second, humanitarianism is well placed to take account of the way that the integrative abilities of states are politically constructed. If we understand 'low costs' as a way of keeping the sacrifices required of citizens at a minimum to reduce the likelihood of backlash, humanitarianism is able to align the moral demands upon states with what politics makes possible at any particular point in time. Humanitarianism's generality also means that it is flexible enough to be applied to very different states. The proviso 'if the costs are low' can be fleshed out with reference to the circumstances that prevail in a particular country, thus allowing that the potential for a political backlash against admitting new entrants might be greater, for example, at a time of rising unemployment.

Third, humanitarianism is *cautious* in the demands it makes of states. Like the ideal theories I have discussed, humanitarianism demands that states accept new entrants up to the point that certain costs are incurred. But unlike these theories, the costs it expects states to shoulder are minor. Because humanitarianism does not demand that states go right up to the edge of a morally undesirable state of affairs (such as where the viability of liberal institutions is threatened), it lessens the potential hazards of addressing this crisis. This means that the principle is less vulnerable to kinds of unintended consequences resulting from fluctuations in social, political and economic forces, which confound other attempts to theorise state responses.

Objections to the humanitarian principle

Any appeal to humanitarianism does, however, face some obvious objections. The first concerns whether embracing this principle involves accepting the validity of the partialist and, in particular, the communitarian account of responsibilities to outsiders. Communitarians, it will be remembered, claimed priority for the right of political communities to self-determination, as a way of respecting the cultural claims of citizens. Their advocacy of the humanitarian principle was thus premissed on a view that attached great moral significance to the distinction between citizens and strangers on cultural grounds. Are we, then, in embracing humanitarianism, simply brought back to the position of Michael Walzer (1983), who argued that states are required to accept refugees and asylum seekers while doing so does not jeopardise the political community's shared culture?

The case I have put forward for the humanitarian principle is, I believe, quite different. What makes humanitarianism a compelling standard in my account is the ethical and political problems states acting in a non-ideal world face in assisting refugees and asylum seekers. The distinctiveness of this case for is significant. Global liberals and utilitarians are unlikely to accept an argument for the principle reliant, like Walzer's, on the claim that states have a moral right to preserve their culture. But they will find it harder to ignore a case constructed around the difficulties of translating what would be morally ideal in terms of treatment of refugees into practical policy prescriptions for states. Such difficulties, moreover, confront any approach that would see a substantial increase in the intake of refugees by liberal democratic states as morally desirable. Impartialists thus have reason to accept humanitarianism as a pragmatic and contingent accommodation to the world as we find it, one that commits them neither to a view of what behaviour would be ideal in a context where states were more effective agents than they currently are, nor to a belief in the cultural rights of states. Humanitarianism might therefore be considered a rallying principle for partialists and impartialists alike: the site of an 'overlapping consensus'[3] on the minimal responsibilities of states.

A second objection might be that such a minimal account of state responsibilities fails to reflect the fact that Western states are often deeply implicated in the production of refugees through their economic and military activities (Castles 2002; Chimni 2002). In this view, a more radical – but typically unspecified – account of state responsibilities is in order, perhaps even a duty to end all immigration controls. There is no doubt that, as I noted in Chapter 2, responsibilities to prevent and redress harms exist and, in recent years, liberal democracies have incurred them (for example, in Vietnam, Kosovo and Iraq). When Western states fail to acknowledge and act upon such responsibilities they are rightly the object of criticism. At the same time, not all of the world's refugees are victims of the actions of liberal democratic states, considered individually or collectively; even in our globalised world, some injustices are simply local.[4] An account of responsibilities based on harms therefore does not

[3] The term is, of course, John Rawls'. See Rawls (1996: 3–15). See also Anthony Appiah (2003) for an enlightening discussion of the possibilities of reaching agreement from different starting points and assumptions.

[4] It not at all obvious why Western states should be seen as implicated in the plight of North Korean refugees who have crossed into China in recent years. Moreover, responsibility for

obviate the need for an answer to the basic question, what obligations do liberal democratic states have to refugees *qua* refugees? This is exactly the question to which humanitarianism – with its minimal account of responsibilities – is a response.

The practical requirements of humanitarianism

Perhaps the most serious question raised by the humanitarian principle is whether it has the critical teeth necessary to evaluate the actions by states towards refugees. Is the standard 'if the costs are low' too plastic to assess state action? After all, virtually all governments in liberal democratic states would claim to be doing 'all they can' to assist refugees within current constraints, and thus satisfying the demands of the principle. Can humanitarianism defend itself against the subjective interpretations of those whose actions it claims to judge?

There are real limits on what can be said about the specific requirements of humanitarianism in abstraction from an appreciation of the empirical circumstances that confront particular states. In contrast to a right of free movement, for example, humanitarianism mainly offers a *framework* within which a state is required to assess and defend its response to refugees. Significantly, however, the acceptance of this framework places the onus on state officials to give a *reasoned* defence of why they believe that their current policies are satisfying humanitarianism's requirements. While we may contest the validity of these reasons,[5] the acknowledgement of the validity of the principle still ensures that any ensuing debate proceeds on the assumption that states have responsibilities to refugees that it is wrong for them to ignore.

That said, I want now to offer my own interpretation of the implications of the humanitarian principle for Western states like Germany, Australia, the US and Britain. Humanitarianism, I will argue, gives rise to two general responsibilities. First, it requires that governments scrutinise their own policies to search for ways that, *subject to the political environment they currently face*, more protection could be provided to refugees at low cost. As a way of fleshing out the practical implications of this principle, I will argue that states could assist greater numbers of refugees at low

the harms done to particular groups of refugees differs across liberal democratic states. The US and the UK certainly had an obligation to resettle Kosovan refugees in 1999, as they participated in the bombing of the beleaguered territory. But on what grounds could we argue that New Zealand had a similar obligation?

[5] There are, of course, many grounds – economic, political, social – on which one might challenge a particular state's interpretation of whether it is meeting the humanitarianism standard. Governments are rarely afraid to exaggerate the costs involved in increasing the number of refugee entrants.

cost by boosting refugee resettlement programmes. Second, the principle enjoins states to work, over the longer term, towards *reshaping the political environment they face* in ways more conducive to the protection of refugees. In practical terms, I will suggest that governments should, *inter alia*, encourage more receptive public attitudes to refugees and greater international cooperation in the area of burden sharing. I will now explore each of these responsibilities in more depth and explain how their recognition could lessen the kind of organised hypocrisy that blights the current responses of states.

The first responsibility: humanitarianism within current constraints

The first responsibility of liberal democratic states under the humanitarian principle is perhaps the most obvious. Humanitarianism asks that we examine whether, under the constraints they currently face, states could do more to boost the protection they offer to refugees at low cost. In answering this question, we need to take account of the fact that refugees can make moral claims on Western states in two primary ways: first and most obviously, as asylum seekers, as applicants of indeterminate status claiming refugee status at or within their territorial borders; and second, and less directly, by virtue of being individuals stuck in insecure and interim arrangements of refugee camps in the developing world. I want to argue that while states have responsibilities to both of these groups of claimants for protection, if we want to maximise the amount of protection offered by states under the humanitarian principle, far more attention needs to be given to the resettlement of refugees in camps. In what follows, I will argue, first, that respect for the humanitarian principle does *not* necessarily oblige states to dismantle non-arrival measures or significantly increase the number of asylum seekers they enable to arrive. But the lack of this obligation in no way frees states from a responsibility to expand significantly the resettlement of camp refugees and others in need of asylum beyond their borders. I will, then, show why I believe the UK, Australia, the US and Germany could undertake such an expansion at 'low cost'.

Humanitarianism and the claims of asylum seekers

Does respect for the humanitarian principle require that states dismantle the preventative and deterrent measures they have erected in recent years to prevent the arrival of asylum seekers? The gains from such a move appear straightforward. These measures serve to contain legitimate refugees in unstable and insecure regions of the world, and mock the obligations of states under the *non-refoulement* principle by preventing the arrival of those in need of protection. Dismantling them would clearly improve the *access* of many people in great need to liberal democratic states. But would it be consistent with the dictum of 'low costs'?

Refugee advocates are usually sanguine about the consequences of ending non-arrival measures. Typically, they argue that the volume of new applicants would not rise sharply or that any increase would not have serious implications if more resources were put into making asylum determination systems speedier and more effective. By contrast, government officials claim that non-arrival measures are essential if asylum seeker numbers are not to snowball and overwhelm determination procedures. Public confidence in asylum, they believe, could not withstand the large movements of people that would arrive under a more liberal regime, as Germany's experience in the early 1990s testifies. Some states, notably the UK and Australia, have also recently argued that the partial abolition of non-arrival measures would merely create greater misery for asylum seekers themselves. Under a less restrictive regime, more people would be tempted to use the services of smugglers and embark upon the kind of hazardous sea crossings undertaken to reach Australia in recent years by Vietnamese, Afghan, Cambodian and Iraqi refugees.

This dispute reveals the difficulty any moral principle for the current asylum situation in the West faces. Even if governments and refugee advocates could be brought to agree that the humanitarian principle represents a convincing account of the duties of states to refugees, profound disagreement would still persist in their respective assessments of the wisdom of different courses of action. This is partly a matter of conflicting interests. Governments, always conscious of the next election, are usually reluctant to take risks for the sake of refugees; advocates, working directly to improve the plight of refugees, have little reason to concern themselves with the electoral viability of their demands. Yet, above all else, the conflict reflects the fact that no one really *knows* what the consequences of ending non-arrival measures would be. The results of a freer 'market' in asylum seeking can only be guessed at.

In the midst of this uncertainty, I think it is very difficult to argue that states have an obligation to abandon non-arrival measures completely. The consequences of such a move might well be uncertain. But there is a possibility that, given the current interconnections between movements of asylum seekers and global inequalities, and the evident lack of cooperation amongst states to deal justly with refugee burdens, a state undertaking such a move would soon find itself overwhelmed. As I will argue below, this does not mean that governments do not have an obligation to work towards building an international system where the elimination of non-arrival measures is possible. But if we take the political constraints seriously in prescriptions for action, we need to look for ways refugees might be assisted that minimise the political and social risks associated with large-scale movements of asylum seekers.

Humanitarianism and the issue of resettlement

While the most common way of assisting refugees is for states to allow entrance to people at or within their borders, another way is for states to arrange for refugees to be brought to their territory. Such refugees are typically those residing in camps or other temporary accommodation in overloaded countries of first asylum or in transit countries. Orderly resettlement schemes of this type are currently operated by a number of traditional countries of immigration, notably the US, Canada and Australia, on the basis of annual quotas. Other liberal democratic countries have used resettlement on a more *ad hoc* basis to respond to specific emergencies, including the conflict in the Balkans in the 1990s (Van Selm-Thorburn 1997). All of these schemes, however, share in common the fact that in the perception of states and under international law they are considered supererogatory acts: burdens that states undertake separately from their duties under international law and, less explicitly, common morality.

There are, however, a number of powerful advantages in seeing the resettlement of refugees as a way that states might fulfil some of their responsibilities under the humanitarian principle. First, the status of those entering the country under resettlement programmes can be determined before they arrive in the country. Thus the financial costs associated with processing refugees in Western countries are lessened or avoided and political debates over whether asylum seekers are economic migrants are defused. Second, resettlement programmes allow governments to manage their refugee commitments with greater predictability and less risk. While *non-refoulement* is, to all intents and purposes, almost unlimited in the obligations it imposes – and this is one reason why states artificially cap it through the use of non-arrival measures – resettlement allows precise determination of how many refugees will be admitted in a particular year.

Finally, more than simply minimising political risk, resettlement schemes might address some of the ethical and practical problems associated with *non-refoulement*. The principle of *non-refoulement* represents the fusion of two separate ideas – the recognition of an obligation to provide assistance and protection to refugees in need *and* the belief that this obligation is owed only to those at or within the state's territorial boundaries. While the *non-refoulement* principle enjoys the unwavering support of refugee advocates, there is no getting around the fact that this fusion is a dubious one from an ethical perspective. For it raises the question of why one should see states as having a stronger obligation to refugees at their territorial boundaries than they do to those at risk far from their borders. This kind of bias is hard to square with the humanitarian principle. Humanitarianism has no respect for distance; it is owed to all refugees on the basis of need alone.

Historically, the linking together of duties of assistance with considerations of location made sense because states lacked the technological capability to alleviate the suffering of strangers far away. The states that Grotius or Vattel addressed had no choice but to exercise any universal obligations they had to refugees locally. But the technological capabilities of states are now vastly different. Modern states have the ability (if not always the legal and moral right) to intervene rapidly and directly in other societies across the world to protect foreigners. Kosovan refugees in Macedonia in 1999 could be airlifted to Australia in a way that the natural law articulators of the right of asylum could not have imagined. Universal obligations to refugees can now be exercised universally.

The changing capabilities of states have taken on even more significance in recent years because the negative consequences of the way *non-refoulement* currently operates are so stark. Distributing refugee claims on the basis of proximity gives rise, as we have seen, to enormous disparities in state burdens, inefficiencies in resource allocation exemplified by the fact that much of the money spent on the world's refugees goes into operating determination systems in Western states, and a bias in favour of those refugees with the contacts, resources and youth to embark upon hazardous journeys to the richer states.

None of these limitations undermine the *practical* importance of *non-refoulement*. Unless states of first asylum recognise a duty not to return those claiming asylum, refugees are unlikely to be able to find real or lasting protection. Respect for the *non-refoulement* principle in some shape or form is an integral part of any international system to protect refugees. But these limitations do suggest that the reasons for supporting a greater commitment by states to resettlement might be as much ethical as practical. Resettlement, under the right conditions, might be a way of ensuring that those most in need of protection receive it, regardless of location.

Practical implications

How, then, should we view the practical requirements of humanitarianism for liberal democratic states? One can, I believe, derive two requirements for a legitimate asylum policy from the humanitarian principle. The first and primary requirement is that any liberal democracy must ensure the protection of all refugees who arrive at the borders of the state, either by providing them with asylum or arranging for another safe country to do so. This requirement is primary not for the reason that states have a greater moral responsibility to refugees at the border than to refugees in other countries. But because until states agree on a system for distributing refugees based on considerations less arbitrary than proximity (e.g. wealth, integrative history, etc.), it would be extremely imprudent to abandon the one basis for allocating refugees between states that is widely accepted.

Acting on this proposal does not, as I have already suggested, require the abolition of all non-arrival measures. A reasonable fear that ending such policies would lead to a backlash resulting in more restrictive policies, or encourage the embarkation of large numbers of asylum seekers on life-threatening journeys, or play into the hands of leaders intent on 'ethnic cleansing' *might* constitute a valid reason for continuing to employ these measures.[6] However, a state that uses non-arrival policies has a responsibility to ensure that it is not complicit in *refoulement*. Any government has the duty to ensure that asylum seekers it interdicts on the high seas (or in the airports of foreign countries) have their claims closely examined. Any asylum seeker whose claim is found to be credible must be granted asylum either by the interdicting state or by another safe country.

Largely because states will continue to operate non-arrival measures, the demands of humanitarianism are likely to require further actions on behalf of refugees by liberal democratic states. Even if a state fulfils its responsibilities to asylum seekers, that is, there will probably be a window to do more for refugees at low cost. The real question is how states ought to take advantage of it. This leads to a second feature of a requirement for states – serious engagement in resettlement programmes for refugees.

How many refugees would a state need to resettle in order to live up to the demands of humanitarianism? The volume should, of course, be determined by the 'integrative ability' of the state in question. But now we are drawn back to a difficulty that is a central theme of this work – that the integrative abilities of states are politically constructed. The ability of any government to integrate refugees depends on a range of factors (economy, national history, public affinity for particular groups of refugees), some of which are not under the control of political leaders (in the short or long term) and which vary considerably across states.

[6] What might constitute a 'reasonable' fear? This is something that needs to be worked out in the course of public debate.

The search for some objective, cross-national standard is thus likely to be fruitless. How can we get around this problem?

In the absence of objective standards, the best way of determining integrative abilities is, I think, to look to the judgements states themselves make of their own capabilities. These judgements can be gleaned from their current immigration commitments; that is, the number of immigrants they plan to accept for settlement in a particular year. One can assume that these judgements provide a reasonable (albeit subjective) indication of the total volume of new entrants a state is capable at a minimum of integrating; it is, after all, the level that the government itself has chosen.

Once we have estimated the volume of entrants capable of being integrated, we can turn to the question of the composition of entrants. Here, ethical considerations come into play. Currently, the total volume of new admissions for residence in Western states is made up of three major groups: economic migrants, family reunion cases and refugees. We need to consider the kind of weight given to resettled refugees in this mix. In other words, have states got the *composition* of entrants right from an ethical point of view? It seems reasonable to assume that a state taking the claims of refugees seriously would treat them as at least *on a par* with the other entrants. But in order to feel confident of this position, we need to consider the ethical force of competing claims for entrance.

Despite the fact that they arrive in much greater volume than resettled refugees in all of the countries under examination, *economic migrants* appear to have a much weaker claim for entry. Indeed, the whole discourse of asylum in the West is built around the view that their needs are not as pressing – and thus do not deserve the same consideration – as those of refugees. Why else do Western governments rail so loudly against 'abusive asylum applicants' entering the refugee determination system with purely economic intentions? One could respond, however, that the justification for allowing economic migrants to enter lies not in the benefits to the migrants themselves but in the advantages they bring to the host state. Economic migration might help boost economic growth or enlarge the skills of the workforce. Consequently, it's possible that reducing economic migration levels for the sake of refugees could result in costs to the society in question that go beyond the demands of humanitarianism. This argument might well justify allowing a proportion of entry places to be reserved for economic migrants. However, given that these societal gains from economic migrants are far more speculative[7] than the certain

[7] This is even more the case because the economic benefits of migration are often hotly contested and when they are evident are spread unevenly amongst state members. The

gains to refugees of entrance (they are saved from persecution or even death), the greater weight attached to economic migrants over refugees by Western countries seems hard to justify.

What of *family reunion* entrants? Family entrants represent the partial view at its most forceful; few things are more important for individuals than being allowed to reside with one's spouse and dependent children. To require a state to curtail their entrance would be to ask it to bear a very heavy burden. Even refugees themselves would be hard pressed to deny the force of the claim of families to be together. That said, the entrance policies of many liberal democracies (including the US) sometimes allow admission not only to the closest family members of citizens, but also to citizens' non-dependent children and siblings (and the families of these relatives in turn). These people may also have some moral claim to enter. But it is reasonable to believe that their claim lacks the force – the necessity – that lies behind the claim for entry of the refugee.

There is, then, a strong *prima facie* case for liberal democracies giving refugees at least as high a priority in entrance decisions as regular and family migrants. In no Western state (not even the US) do refugees currently constitute one-third or more of all new settlers. We can thus conclude that the more even allocation of admission places between the three different groups of entrants demanded by humanitarianism would result in refugee intakes rising, sharply in some countries and prodigiously in others. And it is significant that reaching this conclusion does not involve accepting any of the following propositions: (1) that the claims of refugees are *more important* than those of immediate family members or economic migrants; (2) that states should increase the *total* number of entrants they currently accept; (3) that determining the *absolute* integrative ability of individual states is the only way of responding to their different resettlement capabilities. The tens or hundreds of thousands of new refugee places that would be made available demonstrates that even adherence to the seemingly modest principle of humanitarianism would have profound implications for the distribution of protection.

Humanitarianism and the duty to challenge current constraints

So far I have shown how the humanitarian principle might lessen some of the worst effects generated by the 'organised hypocrisy' of current responses to refugees. But what I have outlined represents only a

benefits to a refugee of being allowed entrance are, on the other hand, both enormous and virtually certain.

conservative reading of humanitarianism. It is conservative because it takes the 'costs' central to humanitarianism as something almost entirely outside the control of states. Governments have largely been assumed to be passive actors in the face of constraints set by public opinion, the expense of determination systems and the actions of other states, etc. This, to be sure, is how governments often portray themselves. Most politicians, including those in the current Labour government in the UK, claim that electoral realities prevent them from implementing more inclusive policies.

Nonetheless, governments can and do play an important role in shaping the social and political environment in which they are located. They may not have the ability to refashion that environment *de novo*. But in the way that they characterise and respond to refugees and asylum seekers, political leaders influence both how the public counts the costs of responding to refugees, as well as the volume of refugees able to receive protection. This suggests that the conception of 'costs' at the heart of humanitarianism is partly a social and political construct. If this is right, and we concede the moral importance of the claims of refugees, then it makes sense to see humanitarianism as imposing on governments an additional responsibility – a duty to work towards *reshaping the political space* in which they find themselves in ways more conducive to the reception of refugees and asylum seekers. To put it another way, states not only have an obligation to accept refugees when the costs of doing so are low; they also have a supplementary duty to do what they can to create a domestic and international environment in which the amount of protection provided for refugees at low cost will be maximised.

How might liberal democracies fulfil this duty? I will now outline three ways that governments can work towards making responses to refugees and asylum seekers less hypocritical, more effective and more in tune with the moral significance of providing protection than current practices. None of these activities involves states accepting more refugees or asylum seekers immediately. But each of them should contribute towards creating a domestic and international environment where this is possible in the longer term.

Reshaping public opinion

In democratic states, the costs that any government will be willing to bear for refugees and asylum seekers will be greatly affected by public attitudes. And, as even the most casual observer will have noticed, these attitudes are, with occasional exceptions (e.g., Kosovan refugees in 1999) often quite hostile or insensitive to the claims of asylum seekers and refugees.

Such restrictive (and sometimes outright racist) public attitudes exist in part because of the behaviour of irresponsible political elites prepared to use every card in the deck to stay in or to come to power. Examples of politicians whipping up hostility towards asylum seekers are not hard to find, as the actions of the Liberal government during the 2001 Australian election and, to a lesser extent, the Conservative Party in the UK election of the same year show. But as much as political parties can play a role in fomenting hostile attitudes to asylum seekers and refugees, they are just as often at the mercy of them. In some cases, proffering inclusive policies to an electorate can amount to political suicide. Kim Beazley's opposition Labor Party had very little alternative but to propose asylum policies as restrictive as the Howard government's during the 2001 *Tampa* Affair; the Blair Labour government has attempted to impose a tough line on asylum seekers since coming to office largely to ward off potentially damaging criticism from the tabloid press.

The central political problem of asylum is not that leaders have an inflated sense of their own electoral vulnerability on the issue. Most electorates simply *are* intolerant of grievous lapses in border control, or asylum systems that allow economic migration by stealth, and they are prepared to punish governments accordingly. It is that politicians generally have a very narrow view of how their vulnerability might be reduced. They believe that ever more restrictive measures will eliminate public discontent. And, in the short term, they may well be right. But, in the longer term, a better way (and certainly one more consistent with the spirit of humanitarianism) of tackling public volatility might be by increasing people's sense of the moral value of the institution of asylum. If publics could be brought to see more clearly the ethical importance of saving strangers from persecution and danger, they would probably be more inclined to tolerate the inevitable imperfections associated with asylum policies (e.g. large annual fluctuations in entrance numbers, unfounded claimants, problems with removal, etc.). Governments would have more latitude to reform asylum policies in inclusive ways without electoral risk.

An important question, then, is how governments might impress upon their constituents the moral importance of asylum. There are a number of ways to proceed. First, public campaigns and statements that promote the obligation of granting asylum, if conducted with sensitivity and an unpatronising attitude could be highly effective. (This, it should be noted, is a different requirement than professing how wonderful our state is for accepting refugees throughout its history.) Second, political leaders could attempt to establish greater political bipartisanship on asylum issues in order that the minimum requirements of humanitarianism can be met. The costs able to be borne for refugees are likely to be greater in a state where there is a political consensus not to exploit asylum for electoral gain than in one where it is seen like any other issue. And, third, leaders could commit themselves to supporting broader campaigns to combat xenophobia and racism. These forms of prejudice often stand in the way of seeing the central moral issues posed by asylum seekers and refugees.

Of course, none of these efforts are guaranteed to be successful. One cannot count on everyone supporting the humanitarian principle and publics are often highly resistant to any whiff of moral didacticism in their political leaders. Nonetheless, one would expect any government committed to the humanitarian principle to at least try measures of this sort as a way of bearing witness to the importance of the claims of refugees.

Participating in resettlement sharing

As well as attempting to change public attitudes, a state committed to humanitarianism should encourage international cooperation when this will boost the availability of protection for refugees. We have already seen that the limitations of the current international response are rooted in the fact that states have failed to agree upon fair terms for the distribution of responsibility for refugees (resulting in huge inequalities in state burdens) and that most states are content to 'free ride' off countries that have more inclusive asylum policies (increasing the likely costs of dismantling non-arrival measures). If we are to rid the international system of organised hypocrisy, greater cooperation is a precondition (Loescher 2001: ch. 10; Helton 2002: ch. 9).

Cooperation could boost the effectiveness of the humanitarian principle in two major ways. First, if it resulted in a more equitable distribution of refugees between states, it could take some of the heat out of domestic political debates on asylum, which are often based around a sense of grievance that the state is taking more refugees than its fair share. A well-publicised and transparent system for dealing with refugee burdens could only add to the legitimacy of international arrangements for protecting refugees, particularly in the eyes of publics currently dealing with large refugee burdens. Moreover, as a sense of injustice usually limits popular tolerance for refugees, a fairer system would be likely to expand the political prospects for protection. Second, burden sharing is also likely to reduce the costs associated with the humanitarian principle through gains associated with greater efficiencies. As Gil Loescher has recently commented, 'international co-operation and collective action through resettlement sharing' would have the benefit of enabling 'clarity, consistency and lower transaction costs' for states (2001: 367). One obvious way it could do this would be by reducing the need for expensive refugee determination systems to be replicated across states.

Apart from some impressive achievements in response to particular emergencies (including the Vietnamese boat people crisis of the 1970s and 1980s and the war in the Balkans in the 1990s), ongoing forms of sharing burdens remain relatively underdeveloped at both the regional and international level.[8] This is despite the proliferation of influential regional fora (above all, the European Union) that cooperate on other issues of common concern, including economic and strategic matters. States appear to lack the kind of common interest in responding to refugees positively that might outweigh the short-term advantages of current unilateral arrangements. Yet governments that claim that they recognise the moral importance of asylum – that are, in other words, respectful of the humanitarian principle – have a strong *ethical* reason for participating in and promoting cooperative schemes when and where they are possible.

Tackling the causes of forced migration

A final way of transforming the costs of providing asylum involves addressing the reasons why people are forced to leave their countries of normal residence. There is clearly no more effective way of reducing the political and financial costs of asylum than by reducing the need of refugees to call upon it. Arthur Helton has recently argued that 'the traditional tools of humanitarian response – provision of basic material assistance, asylum, and resettlement – are just the beginning of a set of policy tools which decision makers need to respond' to the complexities of forced migration in the contemporary world (Helton 2002: 266).

It is fairly easy to identify the proximate causes of forced migration: human rights abuses, lack of economic opportunities and civil and international conflict. Yet, as Sarah Collinson has noted, international migration is, not a 'discrete phenomenon', but 'only one component of much broader processes of political, economic, social and cultural change . . . [which] varies as much as the processes which give rise to and result from it' (Collinson 1993a: 88). To the extent that she is right, the implications are somewhat depressing. For if we concede that forced migration is rooted in deep elements of the structure of international society (the nation-state system, the global economy, etc.), the chances of achieving positive and lasting reform seem slim.

[8] For a recent discussions of the legal and political issues associated with burden sharing in Europe, see Hurwitz (2002) and Thielemann (2003).

This is partly because Western states are unlikely to put the time, effort and financial resources into addressing these complicated causalities. Driven by the short-term electoral incentives associated with controlling asylum seeking and illicit migration, governments are usually reluctant to invest in long-term solutions to the forces that create forced migration. The disincentives are even greater when the institutions in need of reform, such as the world economy, are ones that they currently benefit from. But it would be less than honest to ignore the fact that the problems are also rooted in disagreement about how to tackle the complicated and interconnected forces generating forced migration. This is most evident in the area of protecting and promoting human rights. Is it justifiable for Western states to use sanctions against tyrannical regimes? Under what circumstances, if any, is military intervention to prevent forced migration – or even its causes – warranted? Many well-intentioned and well-informed commentators differ on these questions (Todorov 2003; Wheeler 2001). There are also difficult issues associated with ensuring stable and productive economic growth. Many of the factors essential to economic development are internal to states (a modicum of political stability, for example, or the necessary natural resources) and thus cannot be imposed from the outside. Moreover, powerful as they are, Western states possess no magic wand that can ensure successful economic development or insulation from the business cycle.

As unlikely and difficult as structural reform might be, there are still plenty of things that a state aiming to live up to the humanitarian principle could do to reduce the likelihood of forced migration. The provision of well-targeted development aid, bans on the small arms trade, allowing greater access to Western markets for third world producers and, in some cases, the entry of economic migrants (who might generate remittances) are some of the forms that positive action might take. The moral reasons for reducing forced migration are powerful on their own. But they can be bolstered by compelling pragmatic ones. The very existence of refugees indicates that the political, social or economic problems of one state have spilt over into a matter of international concern. It would be naïve to think that the direction in which these human victims spill ignores the uneven distribution of security and prosperity across states. As Powloski has perceptively noted, in the modern world asylum seekers and refugees are like a tax on wealthy and prosperous states (quoted in Soguk 1993: 9). Over the next few decades, the importance of liberal democratic states paying this tax in ways other than through entrance will almost certainly grow if efforts are not undertaken to deal with the causes of forced migration.

These, then, are simply three possible ways that one might get 'more bang for the buck' from the humanitarian principle. There may of course be other valid ethical and practical justifications for these three measures, but responding in a morally defensible way to the issue of asylum is justification in and of itself. We get a sense of the ethical importance of these measures by thinking through what was so reprehensible about the Howard government's response to asylum seekers during Australia's 2001 *Tampa* crisis. Here the government actively reshaped its political environment in a way that created even greater public hostility to asylum seekers (many of whom were genuine refugees). The government may not have been motivated solely by malevolence or the prospect of electoral advantage. But, at the very least, it presented the asylum issue in a way that negligently ignored the central issue of protection. Ultimately, the Howard government's claims to value the institution of asylum were mocked both by its actions and their consequences. Yet just as actions that carelessly reduce political support for protection mock asylum, so those that deliberately aim to create a more receptive political environment for refugees laud it. The recognition by governments of the duty to work towards creating a domestic and international environment favourable to refugees and asylum seekers is simply the logical corollary of taking humanitarianism seriously.

Rights versus asylum

As a consequentialist principle, humanitarianism outlines the limits of what one can reasonably demand of states in their responses to refugees and asylum seekers. I have now considered ways that governments might act to extend these limits in their dealings with refugees. But the principle of humanitarianism's consequentialism also requires that we explore whether there are any limits on how refugees and asylum seekers can rightfully be treated. Many recent government policies raise the question of whether (or to what extent) it is justifiable to trade off rights-respecting treatment for asylum seekers and refugees for the sake of preserving or maximising refugee protection. A range of different policy measures have been justified on these grounds, including temporary protection, the use of detention, restrictions on welfare and unemployment, and international schemes that trade financial resources for asylum. Yet these measures have also been criticised for not taking rights seriously enough. How do these disputes look from the perspective of an ethics of asylum that remains politically relevant?

The first thing to say is that the conflict between respect for the rights of asylum seekers and refugees and the provision of asylum is real. Just as rights impose constraints on what can legitimately be done *to* refugees, so they place limits on what can be done *for* them. Rights constrain the ability of states to respond to refugees and, by doing so, to maximise the provision of protection. Two forms of constraint are particularly pertinent. First, rights have *financial* implications. The provision of access to public welfare, including living allowances or housing, is expensive, as is the operation of the kinds of quasi-judicial refugee determination systems required by respect for due process rights (Holmes and Sunstein 1999). As is often noted, the total bill for refugee determination systems in Western Europe, which cater for only a small proportion of the world's refugees, vastly exceeds UNHCR's total annual budget for operations across the globe. Second, rights can also impact upon a state's *integrative ability*. Recognition of the right of family reunion, for example, can mean that grants of refugee status not only allow the asylum applicant to remain, but also allow close or extended family members, who may not be refugees, to enter. In an international context where asylum is a scarce good, opening the doors to family members may limit the ability of the state to accept refugees. Furthermore, rights to procedural justice (such as appeal rights) and rights to employment and welfare can attract migrants with weak or baseless claims to refugee status hoping to find an alternative route to working or residing in a Western country. These claims can serve further to clog up asylum systems and add to the financial costs of their operation.

Talking about the costs of rights understandably makes refugee advocates nervous. Even if one concedes that scaling back rights might free up resources, can one really trust governments to use such resources to advance asylum? As I have shown in previous chapters, in recent years asylum seekers and refugees in the West have been detained with greater frequency, deprived of the right to work for part or all of their stay, and subjected to harsher welfare regimes than those of nationals. Yet the quality of refugee protection inside and outside the West has not improved. The words of Hannah Arendt seem particularly apt here: 'It's true that you can't make an omelette without breaking a few eggs but you can break a great many eggs without making an omelette' (quoted in Nagel 1991: 7). Nonetheless, is it justifiable to curtail the rights of asylum seekers or refugees if we *are* confident that doing so would advance asylum?

Any answer to this question must depend in part on the importance of the right under consideration. In recent discussions of asylum, three rights have been the topic of particular debate. The first is the right of liberty for the duration of the asylum-processing period. Governments in Australia, Britain and the US have all justified detention for asylum seekers on the grounds of deterring fraudulent asylum claimants and thus preserving the integrity of the institution of asylum.[9] The second

[9] In the case of Australia, other arguments, as we have seen, have also been used, including deterring asylum seekers from entering the country through unofficial routes.

is the right of refugees to reside permanently – and thus to rebuild their lives – in the state that they find asylum. The right has come into question with the rise of 'temporary protection' regimes across Europe and beyond since the early 1990s. Governments have argued that their ability to take refugees is greater if refugees admitted return home once the reasons that originally forced them to flee (e.g., civil war) no longer exist. A final right in dispute is the right of individuals to choose the country in which to claim asylum. International agreements, such as the Dublin Convention, have been established by most states over the last decade to prevent 'asylum shopping' and to ensure that asylum seekers claim protection in the first country they pass through upon fleeing. These agreements usually have very little to do with improving the quality of overall refugee protection; they are more about 'burden shifting' than 'burden sharing'. However, legal scholars such as James Hathaway (Hathaway and Neve 1997) and Peter Schuck (1997) have recently outlined proposals for improving the quality of global refugee protection by distributing refugees amongst states in a more rational and equitable manner. These proposals are driven by the idea that if refugees are divided up between states on the basis of explicitly agreed-upon criteria (for example, integrative ability or financial incentives), the volume of asylum available internationally could be significantly increased. Critics have countered that these proposals 'commodify refugees'; they subordinate the right of refugees to seek asylum where they wish to considerations of financial or political expediency (Anker, Fitzpatrick and Shacknove 1998).

It is beyond the scope of this work to offer a detailed examination of the acceptability of these practices. In order to judge specific state policies adequately one needs to factor in a great deal about the particular circumstances in which they will be enacted. For example, even if one accepts 'safe third country' agreements as valid in principle, whether or not any particular agreement should be affirmed will depend on empirical judgements on the safety of the 'third country' in question. But if there is no substitute for using practical reason to decide specific cases, it is still possible to identify some key principles that are helpful in evaluating the moral status of practices that involve curtailing the rights of refugees or asylum seekers. These principles can be encapsulated in the form of three questions, which I shall now outline.

Is the right tradeable? There are certain individual rights that are endowed with an iconic status so great that no state that systematically violated them would be worthy of the description 'liberal democratic'. One effective way of preventing bogus asylum claims might be to cut off the hands of anyone whose claim to refugee status was rejected. But how could any humane government deliberately inflict such injury in the name of a moral good? Some rights, such as the right not be tortured, killed, *refouled*, enslaved or arbitrarily deprived of liberty, are so fundamental that it seems wrong to put them up for grabs in any discussion of how to boost prospects for asylum. By contrast, the right to choose one's country of asylum, or being allowed to reside permanently in a country of asylum, is qualitatively different. These rights certainly touch upon important interests, but failing to respect them is unlikely to inflict existential damage on the individuals concerned.[10] Yet if we consider the arbitrary deprivation of liberty as an impermissible violation of a human right, what should we make of the detention of asylum seekers? Detention is defended by governments on a number of grounds, including the risks of terrorism, to prevent absconcion and to deter further asylum applications. All of these grounds appeal to the idea that the social good served by detention outweighs any liberty violation involved. Such trade-offs are by no means reserved only for non-citizens; the mentally ill are occasionally detained simply to prevent them harming themselves and others, and most countries have legislation that allows for criminal suspects to be held for a legally specified period without charge. What is distinctive about the treatment of asylum seekers in some countries (notably Australia and the UK) is that the process of detention has been subject to very limited judicial review. The power to detain in these countries is thus for the most part limited only by the availability of detention spaces and the political will to fill them, making asylum seekers vulnerable to the powers of the state in a way that contradicts basic liberal principles. If the right to liberty is to be traded for a greater good, a minimal requirement must be that the judiciary supervise the terms of the trade.

Is the sacrifice of the right commensurable with the benefit that would result? The test of commensurability demands that we consider the likely benefits to asylum overall from the withholding of a particular right. The restriction of rights is usually justified either because it will preserve the integrity of asylum or because it will increase the number of refugees who receive protection. The former justification – used to legitimate detention, restrictions on the right to work and access to welfare payments – is extremely vague in formulation. How do we determine whether or not the restrictions on rights are successful in maintaining 'integrity'? The latter

[10] Of course, in practice, these rights are sometimes difficult to separate from other rights that do involve fundamental interests. For example, while asylum seekers might not have an absolute right to choose their country of asylum, they should be recognised as having a fundamental right to claim asylum in the same country as their immediate family. Moreover, the right to reside permanently in the asylum country becomes, with the passage of years, a fundamental (non-tradeable) right simply because it is inhumane for states to have long-term residents who contribute as members but have no say in the political structures that govern them (cf., e.g., Walzer 1983: 52–61).

justification is less vague in specification; the test is that more refugees would find protection than otherwise would have been the case. But the question of what 'otherwise would have been the case' is a counterfactual open to widely different interpretations. What can we conclude? Where the right in question involves a tradeable right, such as the right to choose one's country of asylum or reside permanently in an asylum country, there is no reason to reject out of hand measures that curtail the right to improve the overall welfare of refugees. As long as *refoulement* is guarded against, the desire of asylum seekers to go to the country of their choice, for example, should not scupper all proposals for international burden sharing on grounds such as the 'commodification' of refugees.[11] When the right in question is a more significant one, however, such as the right to liberty, the standards required for showing that the benefits override the costs are going to be much more difficult to meet. We should expect virtual certainty that significant benefits will result. It is notable that no Western state that uses long-term detention has so far provided anything more than the flimsiest evidence to show that this practice has any effect on asylum seeker numbers, even less that it increases public faith in the integrity of asylum systems.

Is the violation of the right necessary? Even if we find a particular right to be tradeable and believe that important gains would result from trading it, we still need to ask whether the sacrifice of the right is *really* necessary. There may be other ways in the short, medium or long term to bolster the possibilities of protection for refugees either at home or abroad that do not involve curtailing rights. For example, it seems unlikely that there is no alternative to Australia's mandatory detention policy. At the very least, the government could allow for 'credible fear' hearings, along US lines, enabling the release of individuals with plausible claims. More generally, the goals of maintaining the integrity of asylum and increasing receptiveness towards refugees might be best served by reforms that leave rights untouched. Speeding the process of determining asylum through increases of resources, public campaigns to stress the importance of protecting refugees, and activities to stem human rights violations in countries of origin might all take the pressure off asylum systems. These, of course, will be familiar as the type of measures demanded by respect for

[11] There may well be other grounds for rejecting such a scheme, notably that it will not really improve protection for refugees overall, etc. However, I think a good case can be made that Germany's use of temporary protection in the case of refugees from the Former Yugoslavia in the early 1990s was an ethically defensible response by a country already facing very large numbers of asylum seekers. Other aspects of its treatment of these refugees were, however, much more dubious, see Bagshaw (1997) and Gibney (2000b).

the humanitarian principle. This is exactly the point. The proper way to think about restricting the rights of asylum seekers and refugees is to see this move as a last resort for states that are already fulfilling the demands of this principle.

The three questions I have posed should be seen as hurdles that any proposal or practice that curtails a right traditionally held by asylum seekers or refugees needs to clear before it can be deemed justifiable. I have commented only briefly on the implications of these questions for current state policies. Nonetheless, it is clear that certain practices, notably the mandatory or unsupervised use of detention, are deeply problematical and in need of significant reform if they are to pass ethical muster. By contrast, there is nothing unsound in principle with measures with temporary protection or refugee burden-sharing regimes, as long as they contribute to boosting the overall quantity of refugee protection. Obviously, there are limits – political, financial and practical – on the ability of liberal democracies to expand out the protections they guarantee to their citizens to everyone who might set foot on their territory claiming asylum. These limits are particularly apparent in an international system, like the current one, where states are reluctant to join in cooperative arrangements to share refugees on an equitable basis. Even so, liberal democratic states are bound by their own stated values to respect the fundamental rights of asylum seekers and refugees. In addition, they should ensure that these men and women possess the rights that permanent residents have, at least when doing so is consistent with maximising overall refugee protection. To ensure anything less is likely to degrade not just asylum seekers and refugees, but the guarantee of rights that lies at the centre of liberal societies.

National security versus asylum

After the events of 11 September 2002 no discussion of the politics and ethics of asylum in Western states can be concluded without considering the vexed issue of national security. As we saw in the preceding chapters, in the wake of the terrorist attacks of 11 September a wide range of restrictive legislation has now come to impact directly on asylum policy in Western states. The view that asylum policy might have implications for security was, however, established long before the events of 11 September. The latest incarnation of asylum as a security threat is rooted in a range of developments since the mid 1980s including the abolition of border controls between European Community member states, the end of the Cold War, and the increasing involvement of the UN Security Council in conflicts generating refugees. But the movement towards a new security perspective on forced migration really picked up pace, as we have seen, in the wake of actual terrorist activity. The bombing of the World Trade Center in 1993 in New York by Islamic extremists, one of whom had an asylum decision pending, and, of course, the events of 11 September 2001, by foreigners on visitor and student visas, demonstrated that security talk actually corresponded to an empirically verifiable threat. These attacks spawned a range of new restrictive laws and policies across Western states, and particularly in the US, where the Illegal Immigration Reform and Immigrant Responsibility Act of 1996 made detention mandatory for most asylum seekers. There now exists an unprecedented consensus amongst states on the following issues: that refugees generally constitute as much a threat than an asset; that the dangers posed by asylum seekers are arguably more diverse and variegated than ever before; and that there is a need for international cooperation to deal with these new security risks.[12]

This account of the growing link between asylum, refugees and security captures elements of what some have called a new security paradigm in state responses to forced migrants (Chimni 1998b). However, this characterisation tends to blur together a number of different *reasons* why states and their citizens have come to perceive the existence of a threat. These reasons must be disaggregated if we are to move towards outlining an ethically defensible approach to security in the realm of asylum. There are three major reasons why states have come to see asylum seekers and refugees as a threat in recent years: reasons of *volume*; reasons of *character*; and reasons of *anonymity*.

The claim that refugees might be considered a threat by virtue of *volume* is generally of least concern to Western states. This reason is typically invoked in situations called 'mass influx', where tens or hundreds of thousands of refugees attempt to cross into another state in a very short period of time. In such volume, refugees can destabilise the countries they enter. They might be a catalyst for ethnic conflict (as with Kosovan refugees in Macedonia in 1999) or anxiety over the distribution of scarce resources. The results of such tensions can even spread into other neighbouring states, provoking regional security concerns. Located, as they usually are, far from the sources of most refugee conflicts, Western states can normally insulate themselves from such large short-term movements of people. Moreover, it's hard to see how the threat of terrorism – the recent focus of Western concerns – makes the likelihood of such movements greater.

[12] For detailed discussions of the implications of transforming migration into a security concern, see Jef Huysmans (1993) and Ole Waever *et al.* (1993).

A far more powerful influence over official and informal perceptions towards asylum stems from what I consider to be concerns over the *character* of refugees and asylum seekers. This view is deeply rooted in common understandings towards foreigners. When the English political philosopher, Thomas Hobbes, set out to justify obeying the modern state to a conflict-ridden and deeply divided seventeenth-century English audience, he placed, as we have seen, the state's role in delivering security at the centre of his argument. The sovereign, according to Hobbes, shall do 'whatsoever he shall think necessary to be done . . . for the preserving of Peace and Security, by preventing discord at home and Hostility from abroad' (1968: 232–3). In the contemporary age, characterised by judicially specified limits on state authority, few would grant the state the prerogative to do 'whatsoever [it] shall think necessary' to ensure peace at home. Yet, where the treatment of foreigners – 'Hostility from abroad' – is concerned, almost anything goes. Expanded detention, new deportation procedures for foreigners, and the Bush Administration's suggestion that military trials will be used for some of the Taliban fighters held at Guantanamo, are simply cases in point.

Widespread public indifference to such discretionary treatment is closely linked to a general view of the foreigner as threat. Yet the refugee is no ordinary foreigner. There is something deeply ironic in seeing him or her as a threat. For the refugee is, by definition, a person who is a victim of insecurity. Their very search for protection vindicates the importance of security. But this is only one side of the coin of refugeehood. By virtue of being escapees from violent conflict and human rights violations, refugees are also (albeit unwilling) representatives of these phenomena. They are human examples of how states can sink into violence, torture and oppression. As representatives of these undesirable features of social life, it is not surprising that refugees are often construed as carriers of the instability and insecurity that led to their initial departure. As in the case of those fleeing a plague, reactions to them typically involve a mixture of sympathy for their plight and concern that they might be the carriers of the disease that wracked their own societies. There is, then, something discomforting in the very character of the refugee. And this sense of discomfort translates easily into concerns over security.

A third and final reason for seeing refugees as a threat can be found in their *anonymity*. In this view, asylum seekers might be considered dangerous because states lack knowledge of their backgrounds and intentions. Now this concern is different from the view that refugees are threatening due to their character. For the concern over the anonymity of refugees, or more accurately asylum seekers, is rooted *not* in something intrinsic to refugees *qua* refugees, but in their mode of entry to Western states.

Asylum seekers generate concerns, that is, because they are foreigners a state is obliged (under international law) to accept for entrance, even if it has not yet had the opportunity to vet, screen or examine their intentions. States may of course do so after they have been admitted. But concerns remain that some ill-intentioned individuals will slip through the security net, giving them the opportunity to wreak havoc. It is unsurprising, then, that asylum has for this reason attracted the attention of those concerned with maintaining state and societal security.

How, then, should we account for security concerns in the responses of liberal democratic states to asylum seekers and refugees? We need to begin by ensuring that a generalised fear of refugees based on *character* is disentangled from potentially more legitimate concerns about asylum seekers based on *anonymity*. This process of disentangling, I am going to suggest, requires that states subject their own security concerns to the same kind of scrutiny as they currently apply to the claims of asylum seekers. However, let me work towards this conclusion by saying a little more about security.

Security is, for the most part, an instrumental value. That is, we want it because it enables us to realise other values, such as freedom, peace of mind, justice. However, its instrumental role suggests that the value of any gain in security is not absolute; it needs to be weighed against the costs it might have to the other important values. This has important implications. For example, we could ensure that the type of terrorist attacks that occurred on 11 September could not happen again, if we were prepared to ground all planes permanently. Few of us, however, would be willing to tolerate the consequences of this move. The cost in terms of our freedom to move alone would far outweigh the added security this measure would bring. But the trade-offs associated with increased security are not only shared out amongst citizens. Importantly, as we have seen, the security of foreigners, like refugees in search of a secure place of residence, is sometimes traded off against the interests of citizens. At times of high national drama, the consequences for foreigners of these trade-offs are rarely a matter of great public debate. Yet, from an ethical perspective, the interests of outsiders must count for something. In the aftermath of 11 September, many officials and public figures have called for new restrictions on asylum with barely a passing mention of the effect of these measures on the lives of refugees.

The unspoken truth is that, as shocking as the recent terrorist attacks in New York, Pennsylvania and Virginia were, the number of people killed by them is dwarfed by the number of people whose lives are saved from death and torture annually as a result of the asylum policies of the US, Canada and other Western countries. Even if there are good moral reasons for prioritising the needs of one's compatriots, the value of these lives saved cannot be completely written off.

One reason we can be sure that the costs of making asylum more restrictive would be more death and suffering is because the claims of refugees are subjected to rigorous scrutiny. Rather than take their claims at face value, Western states, as we have seen, put refugees through an elaborate set of procedures to make them prove that their security would really be under threat if they were returned. The aim is to sort out those who really need protection from those who would use asylum to serve other, less urgent or less morally compelling, ends. A refugee must establish that their fear is 'well founded' and that this fear applies to them as an individual. This process of establishing the credibility and applicability of a claim to refugee status is both expensive and resource intensive. Yet, officials argue, it is necessary if the integrity of providing protection is to be ensured.

Here we have a powerful model for how states should deal with their own security concerns in the wake of 11 September. For just as Western states do not take an asylum seeker's claim to be threatened at face value, so they should not take the act of exclusion on security grounds as self-justifying. Especially at the current time, when terrorist attacks have made our governments more prone to exclusion, we need to apply some rigorous criteria for determining the validity of security threats.

There are three questions that we can draw from current asylum practices that are helpful in this regard. First, are we applying a clearly stated standard for what constitutes a security threat (an analogue to Article 1A of the Refugee Convention)? Second, is there a procedure for investigation as to whether claims to exclude on security grounds are 'well founded' (an analogue to current refugee determination systems)? Third, has a personal link between the individual seeking entry and the supposed security threat been established (an analogue to the reluctance of states to give blanket protection to asylum seekers from particular countries)?

These questions may not provide a blueprint for dealing with all the thorny issues raised by security in entrance. But they indicate clearly enough a general principle: that the standards states use for evaluating security threats to their own societies should resemble those demanded of individual asylum seekers wishing to be admitted. They need not be exactly the same; the damage (in terms of human lives) one ill-intentioned terrorist can do is potentially much greater than the cost of sending an individual refugee back to persecution or death. Yet in order to avoid unnecessary suffering – as well as the charge of hypocrisy – liberal democratic states must avoid blanket exclusions of certain nationalities from refugee protection. Moreover, the determinations of individuals as security threats need adequate and independent processes for review to ensure legitimate claims for protection are not being ignored.

Conclusion

The response I have offered in this work to formulating the duties of liberal democratic states has been a modest one. It is painfully evident that even if liberal democratic states satisfied all of the requirements of humanitarianism, the claims of many of the world's refugees to a safe place of residence might well go unmet. Adherence to humanitarianism would certainly represent a dramatic improvement on the current responses of the liberal democracies. But with more than 20 million people in refugee-like situations in the world, the costs of providing asylum to all or even the bulk of these people extend far beyond what could be reasonably demanded of Western states under this principle.

Moreover, even if large numbers of refugees were to be resettled, new ones would continue to emerge from the complex political, social and economic milieux that fuel the violence and political instability that make day-to-day living exceedingly dangerous for millions of people. An attempt to counteract the *causes* of refugee generation is clearly necessary. A duty to address causes, I have argued, can and should be derived from the humanitarian principle. Yet there are no simple answers to the mixture of problems – war, ethnic hatred, political instability, economic failure – that force people from their homelands, nor any simple routes to eliciting the international political will needed to ameliorate them.

If the limitations of humanitarianism are obvious, it's important to remind ourselves of why we have been driven towards this relatively sober and incremental account of state responsibilities. In this work I have argued that asylum exposes a profound *conflict of value* between the legitimate claims of citizens and those of refugees. This conflict is exacerbated by the *scope* of the contemporary problem. What makes asylum such a difficult issue is not simply that refugees exist in large numbers, but that their plight is often so difficult to uncouple from the much greater problem of a world of deep inequality in the provision of security and welfare across states. In such a world, asylum policies will inevitably attract those on the move in search of better opportunities for themselves and their families as well as those fleeing violence and persecution. Finally, there is the challenge of transforming any reconciliation of this conflict at the theoretical level into actual *prescriptions* for governments. If prescriptions are to have any force they must take into account real world constraints (electoral, economic and international) on the ability of governments to implement more inclusive refugee policies.

It is possible, of course, to provide a more radical account of the responsibilities of states. Indeed, as I have shown in this work, some observers have argued that border controls are immoral and that freedom of movement is a moral imperative; others would see states as ethically bound to dismantle all non-arrival measures to ensure an international right of asylum. Advocates of these positions are often very persuasive in defending their claims and usually have an element of right on their side. Yet their prescriptions brush aside the conflicts of value and difficulties of policy-making that have been central considerations in this work. As Joseph Carens (1998) has argued recently, the detached perspective of the 'philosopher', in which all or most obstacles to what is practically possible are removed, can give us a critical perspective that is simply unavailable to policy-makers. But the problems with such 'other-wordly' theorising is that it is often unclear to whom its conclusions are addressed and what force they can have for actors in the real world. Inevitably, such theorising cannot reckon with the kind of challenges that the humanitarian principle takes as its starting point.

Humanitarianism is not, to be sure, the last word in the responsibilities of liberal democracies to refugees. An appeal to this principle cannot free us from the need to reckon with the political forces that shape and constrain what states can do; nor can it completely satisfy the ethical aspiration that states (or indeed some other form of political organisation) may some day be brought to act upon a far more expansive set of duties to foreigners in need. There is little chance that adherence to this principle will on its own 'solve' the problem of refugees in the contemporary world. Humanitarianism arguably falls short of providing the kind of 'new philosophy' that Edwin Muir called for in the poem that began this chapter. Yet, by requiring that the governments of liberal democracies take the moral claims of refugees and asylum seekers more seriously, the humanitarian principle might move these states closer to realising the values they claim to live by now.

References

ABC 7.30 Report 2002, 'Immigration Causing Nightmares for Labor', transcript. Accessed at: http://www.abc.net.au/7.30/s471733.htm

Ackerman, Bruce 1980, *Social Justice in the Liberal State*, New Haven, Yale University Press.

The Age 1992, 22 June, Melbourne.

1994, 28 December, Melbourne.

Aleinikoff, T. A. 1989, 'Federal Regulation of Aliens and the Constitution', *American Journal of International Law* 83, 4 (October): 862–71.

Alpern, D. M. 1980, 'Carter and the Cuban Influx', *Newsweek*, 26 May: 22–8.

Amnesty International [British Section] 1991, *United Kingdom: Deficient Policy and Practice for the Protection of Asylum Seekers*, May.

Anker, Deborah, Joan Fitzpatrick and Andrew Shacknove 1998, 'A Reply to Hathaway/Neve and Schuck', *Harvard Human Rights Journal* 11: 295–310.

Appiah, Anthony K. 2003, 'Citizens of the World' in Matthew J. Gibney (ed.), *Globalizing Rights, Oxford Amnesty Lectures 1999*, Oxford University Press.

Arendt, Hannah 1986, *The Origins of Totalitarianism*, London, Andre Deutsch.

Attfield, Robin and Barry Williams (eds.) 1992, *International Justice and the Third World: Studies in the Philosophy of Development*, London, Routledge.

Avineri, S. 1968, *The Social and Political Thought of Karl Marx*, Cambridge University Press.

Ayling, D. C. and S. K. N. Blay 1989, 'Australia and International Refugee Law: An Appraisal', *University of Tasmania Law Review* 9, 3: 245–77.

Bach, Robert L. 1990, 'Immigration and US Foreign Policy in Latin America and the Caribbean' in R. W. Tucker, C. B. Keely and L. Wrigley (eds.), *Immigration and US Foreign Policy*, Boulder, Westview Press.

Bader, Veit 1995, 'Citizenship and Exclusion', *Political Theory* 23, 2 (May): 211–46.

1997, 'Fairly Open Borders' in Veit Bader (ed.), *Citizenship and Exclusion*, London, Macmillan.

Bagshaw, Simon 1997, 'Benchmarks or Deutschmarks? Determining Criteria for the Repatriation of Refugees to Bosnia and Herzegovina', *International Journal of Refugee Law* 9: 573–4.

Baier, Annette C. 1994, *Moral Prejudices: Essays on Ethics*, Cambridge, MA, Harvard University Press.

Barry, Brian 1973, *The Liberal Theory of Justice*, Oxford, Clarendon.

1983, 'Self-Government Revisited' in David Miller and Larry Siedentop (eds.), *The Nature of Political Theory*, Oxford, Clarendon.

1991, *Liberty and Justice: Essays in Political Theory II*, Oxford, Clarendon.

1992, 'The Quest for Consistency: A Sceptical View' in B. Barry and R. Goodin (eds.), *Free Movement: Ethical Issues in the Transnational Migration of People and Money*, Hemel Hempstead, Harvester Wheatsheaf.

1995, *Justice as Impartiality*, Oxford University Press.

Barutciski, Michael 1998, 'Tensions Between the Refugee Concept and the IDP Debate', *Forced Migration Review* 3: 11–14.

BBC News, 2001a, 'High Stakes for Howard', 30 August. Accessed on line at: http://news.bbc.co.uk/1/hi/world/asia-pacific/1517183.stm

2001b, 'Australia Defends Asylum Stance', 31 August. Accessed on line at: http://news.bbc.co.uk/1/hi/world/asia-pacific/1629745.stm

Beitz, Charles 1979, *Political Theory and International Relations*, Princeton University Press.

1988, 'Recent International Thought', *International Journal* 43, 2 (Spring): 183–204.

Belsey, Andrew 1992, 'World Poverty, Justice, Equality' in R. Attfield and B. Williams (eds.), *International Justice and the Third World: Studies in the Philosophy of Development*, London, Routledge.

Betts, Katharine 1993, 'Public Discourse, Immigration and the New Class' in J. Jupp and M. Kabala (eds.), *The Politics of Australian Migration*, Canberra, Australian Government Publishing Service.

Bevan, Vaughan 1986, *The Development of British Immigration Law*, London, Croom Helm.

Binsten, M. A. 1958, *Escape from Fear*, New York, Syracuse University Press.

Birrell, Robert 1984, 'A New Era in Australian Immigration Policy', *International Migration Review* 18, 1 (Spring): 65–84.

1992, 'Problems of Immigration Control in Liberal Democracies: The Australian Experience' in Gary Freeman and James Jupp (eds.), *Nations of Immigrants: Australia, the United States and International Migration*, Melbourne, Oxford University Press.

1994, 'Immigration Control in Australia', *Annals AAPSS* (July): 106–17.

Black, Samuel 1991, 'Individualism at an Impasse', *Canadian Journal of Philosophy* 21, 3 (September): 347–77.

Black's Law Dictionary: Definitions of the Terms and Phrases of English and American Jurisprudence, Ancient and Modern, 1968, St Paul, MN, West Publishing Company.

Blair, Tony 2001, 'Immigrants Are Seeking Asylum in Outdated Law', *The Times*, 4 May, p. 18.

Blay, S. and A. Zimmerman 1994, 'Recent Changes in German Refugee Law: A Critical Assessment', *American Journal of International Law* 88, 2 (April): 361–78.

Bobbio, Norberto 1987, *The Future of Democracy: A Defence of the Rules of the Game*, trans. Roger Griffin and ed. Richard Bellamy, Cambridge, Polity.

Bolt, C. 1984, 'Ethnic Pressure Groups in the Twentieth Century' in A. Babrook and C. Bolt (eds.), *Power and Protest in American Life*, Oxford, Martin Robertson.

Bolton, Geoffrey 1990, *The Oxford History of Australia, Volume 5, 1942–1988: The Middle Way*, Melbourne University Press.

Booth, William James 1997, 'Foreigners: Insiders, Outsiders, and the Ethics of Membership', *Review of Politics* 59 (Spring): 259–92.

Bosswick, Wolfgang 2000, 'Development of Asylum Policy in Germany', *Journal of Refugee Studies* 13, 1: 43–60.

Branyan, R. L. and L. H. Larsen 1971. *The Eisenhower Administration 1953–1961, Volume 1: A Documentary History*, New York, Random House.

Briggs, V., Jr 1992, *Mass Immigration and the National Interest*, Armonk, NY, M. E. Sharpe.

1996, *Mass Immigration and the National Interest*, 2nd edn, Armonk, NY, M. E. Sharpe.

Brilmayer, Lea 1989, *Justifying International Acts*, Ithaca, NY, Cornell University Press.

Brimelow, Peter 1995, *Alien Nation: Common Sense about America's Immigration Disaster*, New York, Random House.

The British Refugee Council (undated), *At Risk: Refugees and the Convention Forty Years On*, London.

Brittan, Samuel 1989, 'The Thatcher Government's Economic Policy' in Dennis Kavanagh and Anthony Seldon (eds.), *The Thatcher Effect*, Oxford, Clarendon.

Brownlie, I. and D. W. Bowett (eds.) 1991, *The British Yearbook of International Law 1990*, Oxford, Clarendon.

Brubaker, William Rogers 1989 (ed.), *Immigration and the Politics of Citizenship in Europe and North America*, Lanham, University Press of America.

1990, 'Immigration, Citizenship and the Nation State in France and Germany: A Comparative Historical Analysis', *International Sociology* 5, 4: 379–407.

1991, 'Frontier Theses: Exit, Voice and Loyalty in East Germany', *Migration World* 18, 3/4: 12–17.

1994, 'Are Immigration Control Efforts Really Failing? in Wayne Cornelius *et al.* (eds.), *Controlling Immigration: A Global Perspective*, Stanford University Press.

Bull, Hedley 1977, *The Anarchical Society: A Study of Order in World Politics*, London, Macmillan.

Burgess, D. 1991, 'Asylum by Ordeal', *New Law Journal*, 18 Jan.: 50–2.

Burke, Anthony 2001, *In Fear of Security: Australia's Invasion Anxiety*, Annandale, NSW, Pluto.

Burke, Edmund 1969, *Reflections on the Revolution in France*, ed. Conor Cruise O'Brien, Harmondsworth, Penguin.

Carens, Joseph, H. 1987, 'The Case for Open Borders', *The Review of Politics* 49 (Spring): 251–73.

1988a, 'Immigration and the Welfare State' in Amy Gutmann (ed.), *Democracy and the Welfare State*, Princeton University Press.

1988b, 'Nationalism and the Exclusion of Immigrants: Lessons from Australian Immigration Policy' in Mark Gibney (ed.), *Open Borders? Closed Societies?: The Ethical and Political Issues*, Westport, Greenwood.

1992a, 'Migration and Morality: A Liberal Egalitarian Perspective' in B. Barry and R. Goodin (eds.), *Free Movement: Ethical Issues in the Transnational Migration of People and Money*, Hemel Hempstead, Harvester Wheatsheaf.

1992b, 'Refugees and the Limits of Obligations', *Public Affairs Quarterly* 6, 1: 31–44.

1995, 'Complex Justice, Cultural Difference and Political Community' in David Miller and Michael Walzer (eds.), *Pluralism, Justice, and Equality*, Oxford University Press.

1998, 'The Philosopher and the Policymaker: Two Perspectives on the Ethics of Immigration with Special Attention to the Problem of Restricting Asylum' in K. Hailbronner, D. A. Martin and H. Motomura (eds.), *Immigration Admissions: The Search for Workable Policies in Germany and the United States*, Providence, Berghahn.

1999, 'A Reply to Meilaender: Reconsidering Open Borders', *International Migration Review* 33, 4 (Winter): 1082–97.

2000, *Culture, Citizenship and Community*, Oxford University Press.

Caron, Vicki 1999, *Uneasy Asylum: France and the Jewish Refugee Crisis, 1933–42*, Stanford University Press.

Castles, Stephen 1984, 'Racism and Politics in West Germany', *Race and Class* 25, 3: 37–51.

1986, 'The Guest Worker in Western Europe – An Obituary', *International Migration Review* 20, 4: 761–78.

1990, 'Global Workforce, New Racism and the Declining Nation State', *University of Wollongong Occasional Paper Series*, No. 23, October.

2002, 'The International Politics of Forced Migration' in C. Leys and L. Panitch (eds.), *The Socialist Register 2003*, London, Merlin Press.

Castles, Stephen and Godula Kosack 1985, *Immigrant Workers and the Class Structure in Western Europe*, 2nd edn, Oxford University Press.

Castles, Stephen and Mark Miller 1993, *The Age of Migration*, Basingstoke, Macmillan.

Cels, Johan 1989, 'Responses of European States to *de facto* Refugees' in G. Loescher and L. Monahan (eds.), *Refugees and International Relations*, Oxford University Press.

Chimni, B. S. 1998a, 'The Geopolitics of Refugee Studies: A View from the South', *Journal of Refugee Studies* 11, 4: 350–74.

1998b, 'The Global Refugee Problem in the 21st Century and the Emerging Security Paridigm: A Disturbing Trend' in A. Anghie and G. Sturgess (eds.), *Legal Visions in the 21st Century: Essays in Honour of Judge Christopher Weeramantry*, The Hague, Kluwer.

2002, 'Globalisation, Humanitarianism and Refugee Protection', *Refugee Studies Centre Working Paper*, University of Oxford, February.

Clad, James C. 1994, 'Slowing the Wave', *Foreign Affairs* 95 (Summer): 139–50.

Cohen, Roberta and Francis M. Deng 1998, *Masses in Flight: The Global Crisis of Internal Displacement*, Washington, DC, Brookings Institution.

Colley, Linda 1992, *Britons: Forging the Nation, 1707–1837*, New Haven, Yale University Press.

Collins, Jock 1988, *Migrant Hands in a Distant Land: Australia's Post-War Immigration*, Leichhardt, Pluto.

Collinson, Sarah 1993a, *Beyond Borders: West European Migration Policy Towards the 21st Century*, London, RIIA.

1993b, *Europe and International Migration*, London, Pinter.

(CAAIP) Committee to Advise on Australia's Immigration Policies 1988, *Immigration: A Commitment to Australia*, Canberra, Australian Government Publishing Service.
Constant, Benjamin 1988, *Political Writings*, ed. and trans. Biancamaria Fontana, Cambridge University Press.
Cranston, Maurice 1973, *What Are Human Rights?*, London, The Bodley Head.
Crock, Mary 1998, *Immigration and Refugee Law in Australia*, Annandale, NSW, Federation Press.
Crock, Mary and Ben Saul 2002, *Future Seekers: Refugees and the Law in Australia*, Annandale, NSW, Federation Press.
Crowley, F. K. (ed.) 1973a, *Modern Australian Documents: Volume 1 1901–1939*, Melbourne, Wren.
1973b, *Modern Australian Documents: Volume II 1939–1970*, Melbourne, Wren.
Cruz, Antonio 1991, 'Carrier Sanctions in Four European Community States: Incompatibilities Between International Civil Aviation and Human Rights Obligations', *Journal of Refugee Studies* 4, 1: 63–81.
Dempsey, J. 1992, 'Cracks Behind the Unity', *Financial Times*, 16 November, p. 12.
Dinnerstein, L. 1994, *Antisemitism in America*, Oxford University Press.
Divine, R. A. 1957, *American Immigration Policy, 1924–1952*, New Haven, Yale University Press.
Dominguez, J. 1990, 'Immigration as Foreign Policy in US–Latin American Relations' in R. W. Tucker, C. B. Keely, and L. Wrigley (eds.), *Immigration and US Foreign Policy*, Boulder, Westview.
1992, 'Cooperating with the Enemy? US Immigration Policies Towards Cuba' in C. Mitchell (ed.), *Western Hemisphere Immigration and United States Foreign Policy*, University Park, Penn State University Press.
Dowty, Alan 1989, *Closed Borders: The Contemporary Assault on Freedom of Movement*, New Haven, Yale University Press.
Dummett, A. (ed.) 1986, *Towards a Just Immigration Policy*, London, Cobden Trust.
Dummett, A. 1992, 'The Transnational Migration of People Seen from Within a Natural Law Tradition' in B. Barry and R. Goodin (eds.), *Free Movement: Ethical Issues in the Transnational Migration of People and Money*, Hemel Hempstead, Harvester Wheatsheaf.
Dummett, A. and A. Nicol 1990, *Subjects, Citizens, Aliens and Others: Nationality and Immigration Law*, London, Weidenfeld and Nicolson.
Dummett, Michael 2001, *On Immigration and Refugees*, London, Routledge.
Dunn, John 1969, *The Political Thought of John Locke*, Cambridge University Press.
1990a, *Interpreting Political Responsibility: Essays 1981–1989*, Cambridge, Polity.
1990b (ed.), *The Economic Limits to Modern Politics*, Cambridge University Press.
1992a, *Democracy: The Unfinished Journey*, Oxford University Press.
1992b, 'Property, Justice and the Common Good after Socialism' in J. A. Hall and I. C. Jarvie (eds.), *Transition to Modernity: Essays on Power, Wealth and Belief*, Cambridge University Press.

1993a, 'Crisis of the Nation State?', unpublished paper, Political Studies Conference, King's College, Cambridge, 10 & 11 September.

1993b, 'The Nation State and Human Community: Obligation, Life-Chances and the Boundaries of Society', unpublished lecture, Wendy and Emery Reves Center, College of William and Mary, Williamsburg, March.

1993c, 'The Paradoxes of Racism', *Government and Opposition* 28, 4 (Autumn): 512–25.

1994, 'Trust' in R. E. Goodin and P. Pettit (eds.), *A Companion to Contemporary Political Philosophy*, Oxford, Blackwell.

2001, *The Cunning of Unreason: Making Sense of Politics*, London, HarperCollins.

The Economist 1994, 'Welcome and Stay Out', 14 May, p. 55.

1999, 'Immigration Policy: The Next Masses', 1 May, pp. 26–8.

2002, 29 June, pp. 29–30.

Esser, H. and H. Korte 1985, 'Federal Republic of Germany' in Tomas Hammar (ed.), *European Immigration Policy: A Comparative Study*, Cambridge University Press.

Evans, Gareth and Bruce Grant 1991, *Australia's Foreign Relations in the World of the 1990s*, Carlton, Melbourne University Press.

Feinberg, Joel 1984, *Moral Limits of the Criminal Law: Volume 1: Harm to Others*, New York, Oxford University Press.

Ferris, Elizabeth G. 1987, *The Central American Refugees*, Praegar, New York.

Financial Times 1992, 1 December, London.

1992, 8 December, London.

1994, 2 November, London.

Fishkin, James S. 1982, *The Limits of Obligation*, New Haven, Yale University Press.

Fitzgerald, Keith 1996, *The Face of the Nation: Immigration, the State, and the National Identity*, Stanford University Press.

Fonteyne, J.-P. 1994, 'Refugee Determination in Australia: An Overview', *International Journal of Refugee Law* 6, 2: 255–64.

Fragomen, A. T. 1997, 'The Illegal Immigration Reform and Immigrant Responsibility Act of 1996: An Overview', *International Migration Review* 31 (Summer): 438–60.

Freeman, Gary 1986, 'Migration and the Political Economy of the Welfare State', *Annals AAPSS*, 485 (May): 51–63.

1993, 'From "Populate or Perish" to "Diversify or Decline": Immigration and Australian National Security' in M. Weiner (ed.), *International Migration and Security*, Boulder, Westview.

1994, 'Can Liberal States Control Immigration?' *Annals AAPSS* (July): 17–30.

1995, 'Modes of Immigration Politics in Liberal Democratic States', *International Migration Review* 29, 4: 881–902.

Freeman, Gary and James Jupp 1992, 'Comparing Immigration Policy in Australia and the United States' in Gary Freeman and James Jupp (eds.), *Nations of Immigrants: Australia, the United States and International Migration*, Melbourne, Oxford University Press.

Friedman, M. 1992, 'Impartiality' in L. C. Becker and C. B. Becker (eds.), *Encyclopedia of Ethics, Volume II*, London, St James.

Fullerton, M. 1990, 'Persecution Due to Membership in a Particular Social Group: Jurisprudence in the Federal Republic of Germany', *Georgetown Immigration Law Journal* 4, 3 (Summer): 381–444.

Garnaut, Ross 1994, 'The New Gold Mountain and the Young Green Tree' in D. Grant and G. Seal (eds.), *Australia in the World: Perceptions and Possibilities*, Perth, Black Swan.

Geddes, Andrew 2003, *The Politics of Migration and Immigration in Europe*, London, Sage.

Gellner, Ernest 1983, *Nations and Nationalism*, Oxford, Blackwell.

George, S. 1990, *An Awkward Partner: Britain in the European Community*, Oxford University Press.

George, Susan 2003, 'Globalizing Rights?' in M. J. Gibney (ed.), *Globalizing Rights: The Oxford Amnesty Lectures 1999*, Oxford University Press.

Gibney, Mark 1986, *Strangers or Friends: Principles for a New Aliens Admission Policy*, Westport, Greenwood Press.

Gibney, Matthew J. 1999a, 'Liberal Democratic States and Responsibilities to Refugees', *American Political Science Review* 93, 1: 169–81.

1999b. 'Kosovo and Beyond: Popular and Unpopular Refugees', *Forced Migration Review*, 5 (September), pp. 28–30.

2000a, 'Asylum and the Principle of Proximity', *Ethics, Place and Environment*, 3, 3: 313–17.

2000b, 'Between Control and Humanitarianism: Temporary Protection in Contemporary Europe', *Georgetown Immigration Law Journal* 14, 3 (Spring): 689–707.

2000c, 'Outside the Protection of the Law: The Situation of Irregular Migrants in Europe', *Refugee Studies Centre Working Paper* 6, University of Oxford.

2004, 'The State of Asylum: Democratization, Judicialization and the Evolution of Refugee Policy' in Susan Kneebone (ed.), *The Refugees Convention 50 Years On: Globalization and International Law*, Aldershot, Ashgate.

Gibney, Matthew J. and Randall Hansen 2003, *Asylum Policy in the West: Past Trends, Future Possibilities*, UN University/Wider Discussion Paper, 2003/68, September.

Gibney, Matthew J. and Randall Hansen (eds.) 2004, *Migration and Asylum in the Twentieth Century*, Santa Barbara, ABC Clio.

Glazer, Nathan (ed.) 1985, *Clamor at the Gates: The New American Immigration*, San Francisco, ICS.

Goodin, Robert 1988, 'What Is So Special About Our Fellow Countrymen?' *Ethics* 98 (July): 663–86.

1992, 'If People Were Money . . .' in B. Barry and R. Goodin (eds.), *Free Movement: Ethical Issues in the Transnational Migration of People and Money*, Hemel Hempstead, Harvester Wheatsheaf.

Goodwin-Gill, Guy S. 1983, *The Refugee in International Law*, Oxford, Clarendon.

1996, *The Refugee in International Law*, 2nd edn, Oxford University Press.

1999, 'Refugee Identity and Protection's Fading Prospect' in Frances Nicholson and Patrick Twomey (eds.), *Refugee Rights and Realities: Evolving International Concepts and Regimes*, Cambridge University Press.

Gordenker, Leon 1987, *Refugees in International Politics*, New York, Columbia University Press.

Gordon, L. W. 1996, 'The Origins and Initial Resettlement Patterns of Refugees in the United States' in D. W. Haines (ed.), *Refugees in America in the 1990s: A Reference Handbook*, Westport, Greenwood Press.

Grahl Madsen, Alte 1982, 'Refugees and Refugee Law in a World in Transition', *Michigan Yearbook of International Law*, New York, Clark Boardman.

Grant, Richard 1994, 'Dead Heat', *The Independent Magazine*, 6 August: 34–9.

Grotius, H. 1925, *De Jure Belli Ac Pacis Libri Tres, Book II*, trans. F. W. Kelsey, Washington, Carnegie Institute.

The Guardian, 2002a, 23 May, p. 1.

2002b, 13 June, p. 1.

Habermas, Jürgen 1992, 'Citizenship and National Identity: Some Reflections on the Future of Europe', *Praxis International* 12, 1 (April): 1–19.

Hague, William 2000, *Common Sense on Asylum Seekers*, London, Conservative Party.

Hailbronner, Kay 1989, 'Citizenship and Nationhood in Germany' in William Rogers Brubaker (ed.), *Immigration and the Politics of Citizenship in Europe and North America*, Lanham, University Press of America.

1990, 'The Right to Asylum and the Future of Asylum', *International Journal of Refugee Law* 2, 3: 341–60.

1993, 'The Concept of a Safe Country and Expeditious Asylum Procedures', *International Journal of Refugee Law* 5, 1: 31–65.

Hansen, Randall 2000a, *Citizenship and Immigration in Post-war Britain: The Institutional Origins of a Multicultural Nation*, Oxford University Press.

2000b, 'British Citizenship after Empire: A Defence', *The Political Quarterly* 71, 1: 42–9.

2003, 'Response to Layton-Henry' in Wayne A. Cornelius, P. L. Martin and T. Tsuda (eds.), *Controlling Immigration: A Global Perspective*, Stanford University Press.

Hardy, Luke 1992, 'Running the Gamut: Australia's Refugee Policy' in Paul Keel (ed.), *Ethics and Foreign Policy*, St Leonards, Allen and Unwin.

Harrell-Bond, Barbara 1996, 'The Evolution of Solutions: A History of Refugee Policy', *Oxford International Review* 3 (Summer): 2–9.

Harris, H. L. 1938, *Australia's National Interests and National Policy*, Melbourne University Press.

Harvey, Colin 2000, *Seeking Asylum in the UK: Problems and Prospects*, London, Butterworths.

Hathaway, James C. and Alexander R. Neve 1997, 'Making International Refugee Law Relevant Again: A Proposal for Collectivized and Solution-Oriented Protection', *Harvard Human Rights Journal* 10 (Spring): 115–211.

Hawkins, Freda 1991, *Critical Years in Immigration: Australia and Canada Compared*, Montreal and Kingston, McGill and Queen's University Press.

Held, David 1991, 'Democracy, the Nation-State and the Global System' in David Held (ed.), *Political Theory Today*, Cambridge, Polity.

1998, 'Democracy and Globalization' in D. Archibugi, D. Held and M. Kohler (eds.), *Reimagining Political Community*, Cambridge, Polity.

Helton, Arthur C. 2002, *The Price of Indifference: Refugees and Humanitarian Action in the New Century*, Oxford University Press.
Henderson, David 1994, 'International Migration: Appraising Current Policies', *International Affairs* 70, 1: 93–110.
Hendrickson, David C. 1992, 'Migration in Law and Ethics: A Realist Perspective' in B. Barry and R. Goodin (eds.), *Free Movement: Ethical Issues in the Transnational Migration of People and Money*, Hemel Hempstead, Harvester Wheatsheaf.
Hobbes, Thomas 1968, *Leviathan*, ed. C. B. Macpherson, Harmondsworth, Penguin.
Holman, P. 1996, 'Refugee Resettlement in the United States' in D. W. Haines (ed.), *Refugees in America in the 1990s: A Reference Handbook*, Westport, Greenwood Press.
Immigration and Naturalization Service (INS) 1999, 'Refugees, Asylees, Fiscal Year 1998' at *<www.ins.usdoj.gov/graphics/aboutins/statistics.Ref,Asyl98.text.pdf>*
Holmes, Colin 1988, *John Bull's Island: Immigration and British Society 1871–1971*, Basingstoke, Macmillan.
1991, 'Immigration' in Terry Gourvish and Alan O'Day (eds.), *Britain Since 1945*, Basingstoke, Macmillan.
Holmes, Stephen and Cass R. Sunstein 1999, *The Cost of Rights: Why Liberty Depends on Taxes*, New York, W. W. Norton.
Home Office 1992, *Immigration and Nationality Department Annual Report 1991/1992*, Croydon.
2002, *Safe Haven, Secure Borders: Integration with Diversity in Modern Britain*, London.
Hont, Istvan 1990, 'Free Trade and the Economic Limits to National Politics: Neo-Machiavellian Political Economy Reconsidered' in John Dunn (ed.), *The Economic Limits To Modern Politics*, Cambridge University Press.
Horowitz, D. L. and G. Noriel 1992, *Immigrants in Two Democracies: French and American Experience*, New York University Press.
House of Lords 2002, *Hansard*, 7 February, Column 743.
Hucko, E. M. 1989, *The Democratic Tradition: Four German Constitutions*, Leamington Spa, Berg.
Hudson, James 1984, 'The Ethics of Immigration Restriction', *Social Theory and Practice* 10, 2: 201–39.
1986, 'The Philosophy of Immigration', *The Journal of Libertarian Studies* 8, 1 (Winter): 51–62.
Hugo, Graeme, 2002, 'Australian Immigration Policy: The Significance of September 11', *International Migration Review* 36 (Spring): 37–40.
Hurwitz, Agnès, 2002, 'Responsibility-Sharing Arrangements for the Protection of Refugees, with Particular Reference to Europe and the Determination of Claims for Refugee Status', D.Phil. Thesis. Faculty of Law, University of Oxford.
Huysmans, Jef 1993, 'Migrants as a Security Problem: Dangers of "Securitizing" Societal Issues' in Robert Miles and Dietrich Thränhart (eds.), *Migration and*

European Security: The Dynamics of Inclusion and Exclusion, London, Pinter Publishers.
Hyman, A. 1992, 'Refugees and Citizens: The Case of the Volga Germans', *The World Today* 48, 3 (March): 41–3.
The Independent 1992a, 14 September, London.
1992b, 16 September, London.
1994, 11 November, London.
1995, 26 April, London.
Jackson, R. H. and A. James (eds.) 1993, *States in a Changing World: A Contemporary Analysis*, Oxford, Clarendon.
Johnson, D. H. N. 1980, 'Refugees, Departees, and Illegal Immigrants', *The Sydney Law Review* 9, 1 (January): 11–57.
Jones, T. D. 1995, 'A Human Rights Tragedy: The Cuban and Haitian Refugee Crises Revisited', *Georgetown Immigration Law Journal* 9, 3: 479–523.
Joppke, C. 1999a, 'Asylum and State Sovereignty: A Comparison of the United States, Germany and Britain' in C. Joppke (ed.), *Challenge to the Nation State: Immigration in Western Europe and the United States*, Oxford University Press.
1999b, *Immigration and the Nation State: The United States, Germany, and Great Britain*, Oxford University Press.
JSCMR (Joint Standing Committee on Migration Regulations) 1992, *Australia's Refugee and Humanitarian System: Achieving a Balance Between Protection and Control*, Canberra, Australian Government Publishing Service.
Jupp, James 1991, *Immigration*, Sydney University Press.
1993, 'The Ethnic Lobby and Immigration Policy' in J. Jupp and M. Kabala (eds.), *The Politics of Australian Migration*, Canberra, Australian Government Publishing Service.
2002, *From White Australia to Woomera: The Story of Australian Immigration*, Cambridge University Press.
Kabala, Marie 1993, 'Immigration as Public Policy' in J. Jupp and M. Kabala (eds.), *The Politics of Australian Migration*, Canberra, Australian Government Publishing Service.
Kant, Immanuel 1991, *Political Writings*, 2nd edn, ed. Hans Reiss, trans. H. B. Nisbet, Cambridge University Press.
Katzenstein, P. J. 1987, *Policy and Politics in West Germany: The Growth of a Semisovereign State*, Philadelphia, Temple University Press.
Kay, D. and R. Miles 1992, *Refugees or Migrant Workers? European Volunteer Workers in Britain 1946–1951*, London, Routledge.
Kaye, R. 1992, 'British Refugee Policy and 1992: The Breakdown of a Policy Community', *Journal of Refugee Studies* 5, 1: 47–67.
Kaye, R. and R. Charlton 1990, 'United Kingdom Refugee and Admission Policy and the Politically Active Refugee', *Research Papers in Ethnic Relations No 13*, Coventry, Centre for Research in Ethnic Relations.
Kielmansegg, P. G. 1989, 'West Germany's Constitution – Response to the Past or Design for the Future?' *The World Today* 45, 10 (October).
Kirby, M. W. 1991, 'The Economic Record Since 1945' in Terry Gourvish and Alan O'Day (eds.), *Britain Since 1945*, Basingstoke, Macmillan.

Koser, Khalid, Walsh, M. and R. Black 1998, 'Temporary Protection and the Assisted Return of Refugees from the European Union', *International Journal of Refugee Law* 10, 3: 444–61.

Krasner, Stephen D. 1993, 'Economic Interdependence and Independent Statehood' in R. H. Jackson and A. James (eds.), *States in a Changing World: A Contemporary Analysis*, Oxford, Clarendon.

1999, *Sovereignty: Organized Hypocrisy*, Princeton University Press.

Kymlicka, Will 1989, *Liberalism, Community and Culture*, Oxford, Clarendon.

1993, 'Community' in R. E. Goodin and P. Pettit (eds.), *A Companion to Contemporary Political Philosophy*, Blackwell, Oxford.

1995, *Multicultural Citizenship: A Liberal Theory of Minority Rights*, Oxford University Press.

Lambert, H. 1999, 'Protection Against *Refoulement* from Europe: Human Rights Law Comes to the Rescue', *The International and Comparative Law Quarterly* 48: 515–44.

Lavenex, Sandra 2001, *The Europeanisation of Refugee Policies: Between Human Rights and Internal Security*, Aldershot, Ashgate.

Layton-Henry, Zig 1985, 'Great Britain' in Tomas Hammar (ed.), *European Immigration Policy: A Comparative Study*, Cambridge University Press.

1987, 'The State and New Commonwealth Immigration: 1951–1956', *New Community* 14, 1/2 (Autumn): 64–75.

Leiner, N. 1998, 'Welfare Effects of Immigration in the Presence of Public Goods: A Case for Entrance Fees?' in Cees Gorter (ed.), *Crossing Borders: Regional and Urban Perspectives on International Migration*, Aldershot, Ashgate.

Lichtenburg, Judith 1983, 'Mexican Migration and US Policy: A Guide for the Perplexed' in H. Shue and P. Brown (eds.), *The Border that Joins: Mexican Migrants and US Responsibility*, Totowa, Rowman and Littlefield.

Linklater, Andrew 1990, *Men and Citizens in the Theory of International Relations*, 2nd edn, Basingstoke, Macmillan.

1998, *The Transformation of Political Community*, Cambridge, Polity.

Lobel, J. 1989, 'The Constitution Abroad', *American Journal of International Law* 83, 4 (October): 871–9.

Locke, John 1964, *Two Treatises of Government*, ed. Peter Laslett, Cambridge University Press.

Loescher, Gil 1993, *Beyond Charity: International Cooperation and the Global Refugee Crisis*, New York, Oxford University Press.

2001, *The UNHCR and World Politics: A Perilous Path*, Oxford University Press.

Loescher, Gil and John Scanlan 1985, 'Human Rights, Power Politics, and the International Refugee Regime: The Case of the US Treatment of Caribbean Basin Refugees', *World Order Studies Program Occasional Paper No. 14*, Princeton, Center for International Studies.

1986, *Calculated Kindness: Refugees and America's Half-Open Door 1945 to the Present*, New York, Free Press.

Lundahl, Mats 1992, *Politics or Markets: Essays on Haitian Underdevelopment*, London, Routledge.

Luper-Foy, S. (ed.) 1988, *Problems of International Justice*, Boulder, Westview.

MacIntyre, Alistair 1984, 'Is Patriotism a Virtue?', The Lindley Lecture, Dept. of Philosophy, University of Kansas.
Mallet, Nina 1991, 'Deterring Asylum-Seekers: German and Danish Law on Political Asylum – Part 1', *Immigration and Nationality Law and Practice* 5, 4: 115–24.
Malley, William 2002, 'A Global Refugee Crisis?' in William Malley *et al.* (eds.), *Refugees and the Myth of a Borderless World*, Canberra, ANU.
Martin, D. A. 1982, 'The Refugee Act of 1980: Its Past and Future', *Michigan Yearbook of International Legal Studies 1982*, Ann Arbor, University of Michigan Law School.
1983, 'Due Process and Membership in National Community: Political Asylum and Beyond', *University of Pittsburgh Law Review* 44, 2 (Winter): 165–235.
1991, 'The Refugee Concept: On Definitions, Politics, and the Careful Use of a Scarce Resource' in Howard Adelman (ed.), *Refugee Policy: Canada and the United States*, Toronto, Yorks Lane Press.
1998. 'The Obstacles to Effective Internal Enforcement of the Immigration Law in the United States' in K. Haibronner *et al.* (eds.), *Immigration Controls: The Search for Workable Policies in Germany and the United States*, Oxford, Berghahn.
Martin, P. L. and M. J. Miller 1990, 'Guests or Immigrants? Contradiction and Change in the German Immigration Policy Debate Since the Recruitment Stop', *Migration World* 18, 1: 8–13.
Martin, Susan F. 2001, 'Global Trends and Asylum', UNHCR, Working Paper 41 (April).
Massey, Douglas S. *et al.* 1993, 'Theories of International Migration: A Review and Appraisal', *Population and Development Review* 19, 3 (September): 431–66.
Masud-Piloto, F. R. 1988. *With Open Arms: Cuban Migration to the United States*, Totowa, Rowman and Littlefield.
Matthews, C. 1991, 'The Pawns of Brindisi', *The Independent Magazine*, 23 March: 32–5.
Meissner, D. 1990, 'The Refugee Act of 1980: What Have We Learned?', *Revue Européenne des Migrations Internationales* 6, 1: 129–40.
Meissner, Doris *et al.* 1993, *International Migration Challenges in a New Era*, New York, Trilateral Commission.
Mill, John Stuart 1958, *Considerations on Representative Government*, New York, Bobbs-Merrill.
1989, *On Liberty*, ed. Stefan Collini, Cambridge University Press.
1993, *Utilitarianism, On Liberty, Considerations on Representative Government*, ed. Geraint Williams, Everyman's Library, London, J. M. Dent.
Miller, David 1988, 'The Ethical Significance of Nationality', *Ethics* 98 (July): 647–62.
1995, *On Nationality*, Oxford University Press.
Mitchell, Christopher 1992, 'Conclusion' in Christopher Mitchell (ed.), *Western Hemisphere Migration and US Foreign Policy*, University Park, Pennsylvania State University Press.

Mitchell, W. L. 1962, 'The Cuban Refugee Programme', *Social Security Bulletin*, March, p. 5. Reprinted in C. Cortes, 1980, *Cuban Refugee Programs*, New York, Arno.

Morris, M. 1985, *Immigration: The Beleaguered Bureaucracy*, Washington, DC, Brookings Institution.

Morrison, J. and B. Crosland 2001, 'The Trafficking and Smuggling of Refugees: The End Game in European Asylum Policy?' UNHCR, Working Paper 39, April.

Muir, Edwin 1960, *Collected Poems*, London, Faber and Faber.

Muller, Thomas 1985, 'Economic Effects of Immigration' in Nathan Glazer (ed.), *Clamor at the Gates: The New American Immigration*, San Francisco, ICS.

Münz, Rainier and Ralf Ulrich 1997, 'Changing Patterns of Immigration to Germany, 1945–1995: Ethnic Origins, Demographic Structure, Future Prospects' in K. J. Bade and M. Weiner (eds.), *Migration Past, Migration Future: Germany and the United States*, Oxford, Berghahn.

Nagel, Thomas 1991, *Equality and Partiality*, Oxford University Press.

National Population Council 1991, *Refugee Review*, Canberra, Australian Government Publishing Service.

Neilson, Kai 1988, 'World Government, Security and Global Justice' in S. Luper-Foy (ed.), *Problems of International Justice*, Boulder, Westview.

Newland, Kathleen 1995, 'The Impact of US Refugee Policies on US Foreign Policy: A Case of the Tail Wagging the Dog?' in M. Teitelbaum and M. Weiner (eds.), *Threatened Peoples, Threatened Borders*, New York, Norton.

New York Times 1994, 27 July.

1997, 18 May.

O'Keefe, D. 1992, 'The Free Movement of Persons and the Single Market', *European Law Review* 17, 1: 3–19.

Olson, J. S. and J. E. Olson 1995, *Cuban Americans: From Trauma to Triumph*, New York, Twayne.

O'Neill, Onora 1991, 'Transnational Justice' in David Held (ed.), *Political Theory Today*, Cambridge, Polity.

1992, 'Magic Associations and Imperfect People' in B. Barry and R. Goodin (eds.), *Free Movement: Ethical Issues in the Transnational Migration of People and Money*, Hemel Hempstead, Harvester Wheatsheaf.

Palley, Claire 1991, *The United Kingdom and Human Rights*, London, Stevens and Sons/Sweet and Maxwell.

Parekh, Bhikhu 1986, 'The "New Right" and the Politics of Nationhood' in Gerald Cohen *et al.* (eds.), *The New Right: Image and Reality*, London, The Runnymede Trust.

1994, 'Three Theories of Immigration' in Sarah Spencer (ed.), *Strangers and Citizens: A Positive Approach to Migrants and Refugees*, IPPR, London, Rivers Oram Press.

2000, 'A Britain we All Belong To', *Guardian Unlimited*, 11 October. Accessed at: http://www.guardian.co.uk/Print/0,3858,4074768,00.html

Peach, Ceri 1968, *West Indian Migration to Britain: A Social Geography*, London, Institute of Race Relations.

Perry, Stephen R. 1995, 'Immigration, Justice and Culture' in Warren A. Schwartz (ed.), *Justice in Immigration*, Cambridge University Press.

Perusse, R. I. 1995, *Haitian Democracy Restored: 1991–1995*, Lanham, University Press of America.

Peters, C. A. (ed.) 1948, *The Immigration Problem*, New York, H. W. Wilson.

Plender, Richard 1988, *International Migration Law*, 2nd edn, Dordrecht, Martinus Nijhoff.

Poggi, Giofranco 1990, *The State: Its Nature, Development and Prospects*, Cambridge, Polity.

Price, Charles 1981, 'Immigration Policies and Refugees in Australia', *International Migration Review* 15, 1/2 (Spring/Summer): 99–108.

Pufendorf, Samuel 1991, *On the Duty of Man and Citizen According to Natural Law*, ed. James Tully, trans. M. Silverthorne, Cambridge University Press.

Pybus, C. 1992, 'Dilemmas by the Boatload', *The Australian*, 29 January: 15.

Räthzel, N. 1991, 'Germany: One Race, One Nation?' *Race and Class* 32, 3 (January–March): 31–8.

Rawls, John 1971, *A Theory of Justice*, Oxford University Press.

1996, *Political Liberalism*, New York, Columbia University Press.

Raz, Joseph 1994, *Ethics in the Public Domain: Essays in the Morality of Law and Politics*, Oxford University Press.

Rees, Tom 1982, 'Immigration Policies in the United Kingdom' in Charles Husband (ed.), *Race in Britain: Continuity and Change*, London, Hutchinson.

Reiman, J. 1989, 'Can Nations Have Moral Rights to Territory?' in J. R. Jacobson (ed.), *The Territorial Rights of Nations and Peoples*, Lampeter, Edwin Mellen.

Reimers, David M. 1998. *Unwelcome Strangers: American Identity and the Turn Against Immigration*, New York, Columbia University Press.

Rich V. 1992, 'Refugees: A Burden for Sharing', *The World Today* 48, 7 (July): 114–15.

Roberts, Adam 1998, 'More Refugees, Less Asylum: A Regime in Transformation', *Journal of Refugee Studies* 11, 4: 375–95.

Robertson, Geoffrey 1989, *Freedom, The Individual and the Law*, 6th edn, London, Penguin.

Robinson, W. Courtland 1998, *The Terms of Refuge: The Indochinese Exodus and the International Response*, London, Zed Books.

Rorty, Richard 1999, *Philosophy and Social Hope*, London, Penguin.

Rousseau, J. J. 1990, 'Discourse on Political Economy' in R. D. Masters and C. Kelly (eds.), *The Collected Writings of Rousseau: Volume 3*, Hanover, University Press of New England.

Ruddock, Philip, 1997. 'The Balancing Act: Immigration Decision Making, the Department, Tribunals and Courts', Ministerial Speech, 12 November. Accessed on line at: http://www.minister.immi.gov.au/media/transcripts/transcripts00/speech11.htm

Ryan, Alan 1991a, 'A Society of Nations? In Search of a Rationale for an International Order', *Times Literary Supplement*, 22 March: 5–6.

1991b, 'The British, the Americans, and Rights' in M. J. Lacey and K. Haakonssen (eds.), *A Culture of Rights: The Bill of Rights in Philosophy, Politics and Law – 1791 and 1991*, Cambridge University Press.

Sandel, Michael J. 1982, *Liberalism and the Limits of Justice*, Cambridge University Press.
1996, *Democracy's Discontent: America in Search of a Public Philosophy*, Cambridge, MA, Harvard University Press.
Saunders, J. 1991, 'Introduction' in J. Saunders and L. Freedman (eds.), *Population Change and International Security*, London, Brassey's.
Scanlan, John A. and O. T. Kent 1988, 'The Force of Moral Arguments for a Just Immigration Policy in a Hobbesian Universe: The Contemporary American Example' in Mark Gibney (ed.), *Open Borders? Closed Societies?: The Ethical and Political Issues*, Westport, Greenwood Press.
Schmitt, E. 2001, 'When Asylum Requests Are Overlooked', *The New York Times*, 15 August.
Schrag, P. G. 2000, *A Well-Founded Fear: The Congressional Battle to Save Political Asylum in America*, New York, Routledge.
Schuck, P. H. 1984, 'The Transformation of Immigration Law', *Columbia Law Review* 84, 1: 1–90.
1991, 'The Emerging Consensus on Immigration Law', *Georgetown Immigration Law Journal* 5, 1: 1–33.
1997, 'Refugee Burden-Sharing: A Modest Proposal', *Yale Journal of International Law* 22: 243–97.
1998, 'The Treatment of Aliens in the United States' in P. H. Schuck and R. Münz (eds.), *Paths to Inclusion: The Integration of Migrants into the United States and Germany*, New York, Berghahn.
Scruton, Roger 1990, *The Philosopher on Dover Beach: Essays*, Manchester, Carcanet.
Seidman, Louis Michael 1995, 'Fear and Loathing at the Border' in Warren A. Schwartz (ed.), *Justice in Immigration*, Cambridge University Press.
Shacknove, Andrew 1985, 'Who Is a Refugee?' *Ethics* 95, 2:274–84.
1988, 'American Duties to Refugees' in Mark Gibney (ed.), *Open Borders? Closed Societies?: The Ethical and Political Issues*, Westport, Greenwood Press.
Sherington, Geoffrey 1990, *Australia's Immigrants 1788–1988*, 2nd edn, Sydney University Press.
Sherman, A. J. 1973, *Island Refuge: British Refugees from the Third Reich 1933–1939*, London, Paul Elek.
Shiva, Vandana 2003, 'Food Rights, Free Trade, and Fascism' in M. J. Gibney (ed.), *Globalizing Rights: The Oxford Amnesty Lectures 1999*, Oxford University Press.
Shklar, Judith N. 1991, *American Citizenship: The Quest for Inclusion*, Cambridge, MA, Harvard University Press.
1993, 'Obligation, Loyalty, Exile', *Political Theory* 21, 2 (May): 181–97.
Shue, Henry 1981, 'Exporting Hazards' in P. Brown and H. Shue (eds.), *Boundaries: National Autonomy and its Limits*, Totowa, Rowman and Littlefield.
Sidgwick, Henry 1891, *The Elements of Politics*, London, Macmillan.
Simon, Julian L. 1989, *The Economic Consequences of Immigration*, Oxford, Basil Blackwell.

Simon, R. J. 1996, 'Public Opinion on the Admission of Refugees' in D. W. Haines (ed.), *Refugees in America in the 1990s: A Reference Handbook*, Westport, Greenwood Press.
Singer, Peter 1972, 'Famine, Affluence, and Morality', *Philosophy and Public Affairs* 1 (Spring): 229–43.
1979, *Practical Ethics*, Cambridge University Press.
Singer, Peter and Renata Singer 1988, 'The Ethics of Refugee Policy' in Mark Gibney (ed.), *Open Borders? Closed Societies?: The Ethical and Political Issues*, Westport, Greenwood Press.
Skeldon, Ronald 1990/91, 'Emigration and the Future of Hong Kong', *Pacific Affairs* 63, 4 (Winter): 500–23.
Skinner, Quentin 1989, 'The State' in Terence Ball, James Farr and Russell Hanson (eds.), *Political Innovation and Conceptual Change*, Cambridge University Press.
Smith, Anthony 1979, *Nationalism in Twentieth Century*, New York University Press.
Smith, Rogers M. 1988, 'The "American Creed" and the American Identity: The Limits of Liberal Citizenship in the US', *The Western Political Quarterly* 41, 2 (June): 225–51.
1996. 'The Unfinished Tasks of Liberalism' in Bernard Yack (ed.), *Liberalism Without Illusions: Essays on the Liberal Theory and the Political Vision of Judith N. Shklar*, University of Chicago.
2001, 'Citizenship and the Politics of People Building', *Journal of Citizenship Studies* 5, 1: 73–96.
Smith, T. E. 1981, *Commonwealth Migration: Flows and Policies*, London, Macmillan.
Soguk, N. 1993, 'Western Spaces and Democracy: Resistance and Accommodation in Refugee and Immigrant Movements', Unpublished Paper.
Sontheimer, K. 1988, 'The Federal Republic of Germany 1949: Restoring the Rechtsstaat' in V. Bogdanor (ed.), *Constitutions in Democratic Politics*, Aldershot, Gower.
Soysal, Y. N. 1994, *Limits of Citizenship: Migrants and Postnational Membership in Europe*, University of Chicago Press.
Steiner, Niklaus 2000, *Arguing About Asylum: The Complexity of Refugee Debates in Europe*, London, Macmillan.
Stepick, A. 1992, 'Unintended Consequences: Rejecting Haitian Boat People and Destabilizing Duvalier' in C. Mitchell (ed.), *Western Hemisphere Immigration and United States Foreign Policy*, University Park, Penn State University Press.
Tamir, Yael 1993, *Liberal Nationalism*, Princeton University Press.
Tapinos, G. P. 1983, 'European Migration Patterns: Economic Linkages and Policy Experiences' in M. Kritz (ed.), *US Immigration and Refugee Policy: Global and Domestic Issues*, Lexington, Lexington Books.
Taylor, Charles 1985, *Philosophy and the Human Sciences, Philosophical Papers 2*, Cambridge University Press.
1993, *Reconciling the Solitudes: Essays on Canadian Federalism and Nationalism*, Montreal, McGill-Queen's University Press.

1996, 'Why Democracy Needs Patriotism' in Martha Nussbaum (ed.), *For Love of Country: Debating the Limits of Patriotism*, Boston, Beacon Press.
Teitelbaum, M. S. 1984, 'Political Asylum in Theory and Practice', *The Public Interest* 76 (Summer): 74–86.
Thielemann, Eiko 2003, 'Between Interests and Norms: Explaining Burden-Sharing in the European Union', *Journal of Refugee Studies*, 6, 3 (September): 253–73.
Thränhardt, Dietrich 1999, 'Germany's Immigration Policies and Politics' in Grete Brochmann and Tomas Hammar (eds.), *Mechanisms of Immigration Control: A Comparative Analysis of European Regulation Practices*, Oxford, Berg Publishers.
Todorov, Tzvetan 2003, 'Right to Intervene or Duty to Assist?' in Nicholas Owen (ed.) *Human Rights, Human Wrongs, Oxford Amnesty Lectures 2001*, Oxford University Press.
Treasure, C. 1991, 'Search for a Homeland', *Geographical* 63, 4: 24–7.
Tuck, Richard 1989, *Hobbes*, Oxford University Press.
Turton, David and Peter Marsden 2002, *Taking Refugees for a Ride: The Politics of Refugee Return to Afghanistan*, Kabul, Afghanistan Research and Evaluation Unit (AREU).
Tyler, P. (ed.) 1956, *Immigration and the United States*, New York, H. W. Wilson.
UNHCR 1995, *The State of the World's Refugees 1995: In Search of Solutions*, Oxford University Press.
1997, *The State of the World's Refugees 1997–98: A Humanitarian Agenda*, Oxford University Press.
2000, *The State of the World's Refugees 2000: Fifty Years of Humanitarian Action*, Oxford University Press.
UN Population Division Report 2000, *Replacement Migration: Is it a Solution to Declining and Ageing Populations?* ESA/P/WP.160, Department of Economic and Social Affairs, New York, United Nations Secretariat.
US Committee for Refugees 2001, 'Country Report: United States'. Accessed online at *http://www.refugees.org/world/countryrpt/amer˙carib/us.htm*
2002, *Sea Change: Australia's New Approach to Asylum Seekers*. Accessed online at: *http://www.refugees.org/downloads/Australia.pdf*
US Government 1963, *Public Papers of the Presidents of the United States: Harry S. Truman, January 1 to December 31, 1947*, Washington, US Government Printing Office.
1964, *Public Papers of the Presidents of the United States: Harry S. Truman, January 1 to December 31, 1948*, Washington, US Government Printing Office.
Van Hear, Nicholas 1998, *New Diasporas*, Seattle, University of Washington Press.
Van Selm-Thorburn, Joanne 1997, *Refugee Protection in Europe: Lessons of the Yugoslav Crisis*, The Hague, Kluwer.
de Vattel, E. 1916, *The Law of Nations or the Principles of Natural Law, Volume 3*, trans. C. G. Fenwick, Washington, Carnegie Institute.
Viviani, Nancy 1983, 'Refugees – The End of Splendid Isolation?' in P. J. Boyce and J. R. Angel (eds.), *Independence and Alliance: Australia and World Affairs*, St Leonards, George Allen and Unwin.

1984, *The Long Journey: Vietnamese Migration and Settlement in Australia*, Beaverton, Melbourne University Press.

1988, 'Indochinese Refugees and Australia' in S. Chantavanich and E. B. Reynolds (eds.), *Indochinese Refugees: Asylum and Resettlement*, Bangkok, Institute for Asian Studies, Chulalongkorn University.

Waever, Ole, Barry Buzan, Morten Kelstrup and Pierre Lemaitre 1993, *Identity, Migration and the New Security Agenda in Europe*, London, Pinter Publishers.

Walvin, James 1984, *Passage to Britain: Immigration in British History and Politics*, Harmondsworth, Penguin.

Walzer, Michael 1981, 'Response to Chaney and Lichtenburg' in P. Brown and H. Shue (eds.), *Boundaries: National Autonomy and its Limits*, Totowa, Rowman and Littlefield.

1983, *Spheres of Justice: A Defense of Pluralism and Equality*, Oxford, Martin Robertson.

1995, 'Response to Bader', *Political Theory* 23, 2: 247–9.

Weiner, Myron 1985, 'On International Migration and International Relations', *Population and Development Review* 11, 3 (September): 441–55.

1992, 'International Population Movement: Implications for Foreign Policies and Migration Policies' in D. L. Horowitz and G. Noriel, *Immigrants in Two Democracies: French and American Experience*, New York University Press.

1992/93, 'Security, Stability and International Migration', *International Security* 17, 3 (Winter): 91–126.

Wheeler, Nicholas 2001, *Saving Strangers: Humanitarian Intervention in International Society*, Oxford University Press.

Whelan, Frederick 1988, 'Citizenship and Free Movement: An Open Admission Policy' in Mark Gibney (ed.), *Open Borders? Closed Societies?: The Ethical and Political Issues*, Westport, Greenwood Press.

Widgren, Jonas 1990, 'International Migration and Regional Stability', *International Affairs* 66, 4: 368–81.

Willard, Myra 1967, *History of the White Australia Policy to 1920*, London, Frank Cass.

Williams, Bernard 1985, *Ethics and the Limits of Philosophy*, Cambridge, Harvard University Press.

Wolfe, Alan 1989, *Whose Keeper?: Social Sciences and Moral Obligation*, Berkeley, University of California Press.

Woodward, James 1992, 'Liberalism and Migration' in B. Barry and R. Goodin (eds.), *Free Movement: Ethical Issues in the Transnational Migration of People and Money*, Hemel Hempstead, Harvester Wheatsheaf.

Zolberg, Aristide R. 1994, 'Commentary on Current Refugee Issues', *Journal of International Affairs* 47, 2 (Winter): 341–9.

2001, 'Introduction: Beyond the Crisis' in A. R. Zolberg and P. Benda (eds.), *Global Migrants, Global Refugees: Problems and Solutions*, New York, Berghahn.

Zolberg, Aristide R., A. Suhrke, and S. Aguayo 1989, *Escape from Violence: Conflict and the Refugee Crisis in the Developing World*, Oxford University Press.

Zucker, N. L. and N. F. Zucker 1996, *Desperate Crossings: Seeking Refuge in America*, Armonk, NY, M. E. Sharpe.

Index